Bioinvaders

Copyright © The White Horse Press 2010
First published 2010 by
The White Horse Press, 10 High Street, Knapwell, Cambridge, CB23 4NR, UK

Set in 10 point Times

All rights reserved. Except for the quotation of short passages for the purpose of criticism or review, no part of this book may be reprinted or reproduced or utilised in any form or by any electronic, mechanical or other means, including photocopying or recording, or in any information storage or retrieval system, without permission from the publishers.

British Library Cataloguing in Publication Data
A catalogue record for this book is available from the British Library

ISBN   978-1-874267-55-3 (PB)

Contents

Publisher's Introduction	Sarah Johnson	iv

Strangers in a Strange Land:
The Problem of Exotic Species
                            Mark Woods and Paul Veatch Moriarty   1

Nativism and Nature: Rethinking Biological Invasion
                            Jonah H. Peretti   28

Exotic Species, Naturalisation, and Biological Nativism
                            Ned Hettinger   37

Plant Transfers in Historical Perspective
                            William Beinart and Karen Middleton   68

Weeds, People and Contested Places
                            Neil Clayton   94

Re-writing the History of Australian Tropical Rainforests:
'Alien Invasives' or 'Ancient Indigenes'?
                            Rachel Sanderson   124

Prehistory of Southern African Forestry:
From Vegetable Garden to Tree Plantation
                            Kate B. Showers   144

Rhododendron ponticum in Britain and Ireland:
Social, Economic and Ecological Factors in its Successful Invasion
                            Katharina Dehnen-Schmutz and Mark Williamson   171

Fighting With a Weed: Water Hyacinth
and the State in Colonial Bengal, c. 1910–1947
                            Iftekhar Iqbal   197

'An Enemy of the Rabbit': The Social Context of
Acclimatisation of an Immigrant Killer
                            Philippa K. Wells   221

Motives for Introducing Species:
Palestine's Carp as a Case Study
                            Dan Tamir   248

Publisher's Introduction

Sarah Johnson

KNOWING THE ENEMY: PROBLEMS OF DEFINITION

In a globalised and cosmopolitan world, the mobility of human beings, culture and commodities across continents is taken for granted, and it is a liberal orthodoxy that the resulting 'multiculturalism' is desirable. Similar movements in the biosphere, however, are highly contentious. Discourse about 'alien' species such as mink in Scotland and kudzu in the Southern United States often bespeaks fear and loathing. The present volume seeks to define and explore what is meant by the categories 'exotic', 'alien' (and the corollary 'native'), and 'invasive', suggesting that while there are clear-cut exempla of the 'nefarious' (Peretti, p. 28) and broad agreement that ill-managed introductions are dangerous, both history and philosophical thought raise as many questions as they resolve about the nature and status of such species.

The volume opens with three essays – by Woods and Moriarty, Peretti and Hettinger – that problematise the easy categorisation of species and resist 'catch-all' definitions and solutions. Woods and Moriarty (p. 2) present Noss and Cooperrider's 1994 definition of an exotic as 'the result of direct or indirect, deliberate or accidental introduction of the species by humans' which has 'permitted the species to cross a natural barrier to dispersal', but question and complicate the assumptions that such attempts at single-sentence analysis entail. They offer a list of 'exotic' and 'native' qualities, illustrating the general consensus of views about alien species: they are human-introduced, whether directly or indirectly, intentionally or unintentionally; they exist outside their historical or natural range; they tend to 'damage or degrade the local ecosystem, displacing or eliminating native species'; and they are not integrated with the 'ecological community' (pp. 11–12). Natives, on the other hand, are characterised, broadly, by belonging and benignity.

Woods and Moriarty's definitions function as 'cluster concepts: a given 'exotic' or 'native' species will not possess all these characteristics but it is likely to exhibit some of them, and thus the distinction between natives and exotics admits of degrees. They propose that an invasive species will almost always be non-native, while a non-native species might not be invasive. This distinction is collapsed in Hettinger's 'precising definition of exotics as any species significantly foreign to an ecological assemblage, whether or not the species causes damage, is human introduced, or arrives from some other geographical location' (p.38). Hettinger observes that, 'Unless one accepts an idyllic conception of perfectly-harmonious natural systems, one must admit that native species can wreak havoc in their native ranges' (p.40). Beinart and Middleton, in a paper that deals specifically with plant transfers but illuminates the wider problem of definition, raise questions that reverberate through the essays in this volume:

> Is it possible to make a useful distinction between human agency in plant transfers, and other forms of plant spread? When does an intentional and apparently controlled transfer become an invasion? What is the borderline between useful plants and those seen as weeds? (p.69)

So, 'invasiveness' is established as a fuzzy concept, its vagueness compounded by anomalies: for example, there exist certain North American tamarisks, descended from human introductions, but now evolved into a new species, present nowhere else in the world; it would seem bizarre to assert that these are not in some sense native. As Woods and Moriarty observe, addressing the subject of 'bio-invaders' opens 'a Pandora's box of conceptual and normative quandaries' (p.1) over the ideas of 'native', 'alien', 'invasiveness' and even 'species'.

These quandaries permeate the present volume. Several authors offer examples of clearly 'nefarious' species, including the brown tree snakes that have decimated bird populations on Guam (cited by both Peretti and Woods and Moriarty) and the water hyacinth that has choked the canals of Bangladesh, as described by Iqbal. Such introductions, made thoughtlessly or on an aesthetic or socio-economic whim, have had catastrophic effects on native ecosystems, in the latter case 'choking up the natural arteries of trade, impeding agricultural operations and menacing the health of the people' (Iqbal, p.198). However, even undeniably destructive introduced species have their advocates – Hettinger notes that there are those who consider the Japanese kudzu vines that drape southern telegraph poles to be attractive camouflage, though they are fearsome stranglers of native trees; and Williams and Dehnen Schmutz relate anecdotally that, while conservation biologists unite in condemning naturalised *Rhododendron ponticum*, local communities vociferously defend the shrubs' aesthetic value. Even species that are accepted as 'invasive' are able to win hearts and minds.

Species rarely sit obediently in a single category and, as many of the authors represented here discuss, 'cultural definition allows the same plant to change status in the context of historically dynamic socio-ecological systems' (Beinart and Middleton, p.82, outlining different attitudes to *Opuntia* (prickly pear) in southern Africa and Madagascar). Clayton engages with

Introduction

similar questions in his study of weeds – both as a concept and in the specific context of New Zealand agriculture. From prehistory, the loaded categories of 'weed' and 'useful plant' (Beinart and Middleton, p.69) have structured human responses to flora, but, despite attempts to taxonomise 'weediness', these surely say more about society at a given point in time or space than innate qualities of the plants. Beinart and Middleton address this in their decision to 'include cultivated crops, garden plants, weeds and plant invaders within the same frame of analysis because many plants [...] fit uneasily into any one of these categories' (p.88).

Much of world agriculture relies on 'exotic' species, introductions from elsewhere that we are accustomed to regard as beneficial and would certainly not consider exterminating – wheat in North America, potatoes in Europe, chillies in India and corn in Africa – introductions that have been comprehensively assimilated into each culture's definition of itself. As Beinart and Middleton argue, 'most agricultural development has been dependent on plant transfers' (p.68) and their chapter traces the literature concerning networks of formal (by means of agriculture, forestry, trade and botanical collecting) and informal plant transfers. Showers pursues the case of forestry further, noting in South Africa an irony of the sort that recurs frequently in the study of species introductions: as well as fuelling 'the growing demand for wood products: supports for mines, fuel for steamdriven machinery, timber for railroad construction, and bark for tanning' (p.152), nineteenth century scientists had an improving vision that silviculture of alien species in South Africa would eventually allow the manipulation of the natural climate to make it wetter. However, tree root systems over time had an opposite, dessicatory effect and forestry is now categorised and discouraged as a 'stream flow reduction activity' (p.160).

Fallacious assumptions about the greater good have dogged species introductions since Columbus and Captain Cook brought goats and gardening to their 'New Worlds', and the 'ecological imperialism' thesis of species transfer, posited by Crosby, is well known. However, the picture of species transfer as an instrument of colonialism is only partial: Peretti points out that,

> native people and aboriginal people alter and influence the natural environments they inhabit. The influence of native people on nature makes it difficult to maintain the thesis that European colonialists are the sole reason that native nature is threatened. (p.30)

While Wells reiterates that the numerous and often disastrous species introductions experienced by New Zealand were 'neither accidental nor incidental but were in large part a reflection of a popular and official conceptualisation of the colony as the 'Britain of the South''(p.222), despite its palpable failure to comport itself as such, other power dynamics should be entertained. The essays by Beinart and Middleton and Iqbal critique aspects of Crosby's theory: for example Iqbal argues that, in the wake of Crosby,

> a lot more focus has been placed on the relationship between plant transfer and imperial expansion than on the actual encounter between a secure colonial state and an invasive plant which has already established itself in local ecological systems. (p.197)

His paper redresses the balance by exploring the efforts of the independent East Bengal government to deal with the home-grown invader, water hyacinth. Beinart and Middleton point out flaws in Crosby's assumption that the flow of alien species is asymmetric, based on colonial imposition of species on colonised countries. Noting that, with their love of exotic gardening, European nations are perhaps even net importers of species, they also assert the great importance of informal means of species transfer – individual people's movements with seeds within and between landmasses – which are often overshadowed in the alien species discourse by discussion of socio-political policy (such as establishing botanic gardens or trading and supply posts) and economics (agriculture).

NATURE, NATIVES AND NATION

Reducing the compass somewhat, in the volume's fourth essay Clayton proposes that, whilst weeds have ever been among 'humanity's camp followers'(p.103), New Zealand is a useful case for examining their effects on ecosystems, in that the history of European introductions is both short and well documented. The essay explores the spread of weeds through New Zealand's agricultural systems and methods and ideologies of weed control. The latter reappear in Iqbal's narrative of State efforts to extirpate or to turn to productive use the water hyacinth in Bangladesh, and the stagnating effect of political inability to decide on and pursue an effective management strategy. Wells's essay on late nineteenth century debate surrounding the introduction of mustelids to control (also European-introduced) rabbits in New Zealand pursues similar issues in the realm of fauna (where of course the concerns surrounding extermination tend to be more emotive). That protests against the proposed introduction segued into 'nativist' discourses – some wished to protect 'native' avifauna by resisting the weasels – links Wells's essay to Sanderson's account of changing perceptions of the Australian rainforest based on its degree of 'nativeness'. These cases remind us that the question of invasive species is inextricably tied to socio-political rhetoric. According to Sanderson, nineteenth century ecologists such as Joseph Hooker emphasised the *non*-nativeness of the Australian vegetation in order subtly to undermine any challenge to European alterations and importations: if the vegetation was non-native anyway, changing it could scarcely matter since the autochtnonous vegetation had long been suppressed by succesful Southeast Asian 'invaders':

> Whether this explanation of the rainforests' origin was regarded as scientifically tenable or not, the story itself was seen clearly as a parallel to the European invasion of the continent and the historical processes of colonisation. (p.132)

Redefining the rainforest (which is indeed descended from an Asian biota) as a native, national treasure in later years was arguably less scientifically accurate, but had inescapable rhetorical value. As Peretti suggests, the interconnections of 'Nature, natives, natality, and nation' (p.29) form part of the powerful narrative of 'ecological imperialism', even if, as Beinart and Middleton point out, 'indigenous people do not necessarily favour indigenous plants' (p.83) – colonised peoples have enthusiastically embraced species brought from elsewhere. Several authors represented here interrogate the analogy between human migration, colonisation, establishment and eventual adaptation and the trajectories of other species arrivals. Indeed Woods and Moriarty teasingly suggest that, 'Because *Homo sapiens sapiens* probably originally evolved in Africa, perhaps people today are exotic to all other continents' (p.14). Of course, we are the only species that seeks to define and legislate the purity of other species, and in so doing we reveal much of ourselves. Peretti likens 'hardline biological nativism' (p.33) to Nazism or apartheid, and proposes that 'questioning purist pieties may protect modern environmentalists from reproducing the xenophobic and racist attitudes that have plagued nativist biology in the past' (p.35). Hettinger, though, counters the notion that purism is self-evidently undesirable, arguing that biologists may admire plants in their original ecosystems but wish to avoid their spread. While he accepts that 'nativisms based on irrational fear, hatred, or feelings of superiority are morally objectionable' he argues that by analogy with the 'protection and preservation of indigenous peoples and cultures [being] desirable' and their dilution something to be avoided, 'biological nativism is laudatory because it supports a kind of valuable biodiversity that is increasingly disappearing' (p.58) as the biosphere, like human culture, becomes increasingly homogenised. In a striking analogy, he declares that,

> Keeping a dandelion out of Yellowstone is much like keeping Wal-Mart out of a small New England town or McDonald's out of India. Kudzu in the American South is like T.V. in Nepal, a threat to the diversity of the planet's communities and ways of life. (p.61)

TO 'DERACINATE SUCH SAVAGERY'[1]: HOW TO MANAGE INVADERS

However, what if the dandelion makes its own way to Yellowstone? Alien species management strategies are complicated by several factors. The conundrum Woods and Moriarty pose about the status of nine-banded armadillos in Florida illustrates the potential fluidity of a given species' status, and the conceptual barrier to management that results:

> Nine-banded armadillos native to Texas have been migrating east for some time, and today they have reached north Florida and have begun to mingle and reproduce with the exotic populations descended from the zoos and the circus truck. Prior to the natural migration from Texas, armadillos had been classified as exotic pests in Florida. Should we now accept them as native fauna? (p.1)

Added to this issue of natural mobility is the vexed question of naturalisation and eventual evolution, as with the hybridised and adapted *Rhododendron ponticum* or the new tamarisk species. If even 'native' and 'exotic' are concepts with 'fuzzy boundaries' and 'there is no bright line separating native and exotic species' (Woods and Moriarty, p.13), the exact point at which an exotic becomes naturalised is almost impossible to gauge: battles are waged between those who would remove from Hawaii the feral pigs that decimate the native biota and those who argue that the creatures, introduced 1500 years ago, have the right to remain unpersecuted. Hettinger offers a nuanced account of the notion of naturalisation, considering both ecological adaptation, which it is reasonable to assume might be measured empirically, and which will depend upon the relationship of the introduced organism with the ecological community it has entered; and evaluative adaptation, which is linked to human understanding of the status of a species. This latter process occurs over a long but not necessarily definable period, through what Hettinger calls a 'washing away' (p.55) of human influence – this has not yet occurred, he argued, with either the 1500 year-resident Hawaiian pigs or the two century-resident kudzu; and species may be 'no longer exotic (because they have ecologically naturalised)' but not yet 'natives either (because the human influence on their presence is still significant)' (p.56). Of course ecological adaptation can occur very quickly – an 'exotic fit' species might arrive in an ecosystem already well suited to it – but evaluative naturalisation is generally a slower process.

Woods and Moriarty and Hettinger address many of the paradoxes and problems of managing alien species. The former propose that prevention

---
[1] *Henry V* Act V, Sc. II, 1.47

Introduction xi

of arrivals is a priority and that efforts might then be made to remove less 'embedded' introductions, with any removal projects targeting established species requiring careful thought: 'heavy handed management', such as inhumane exterminations of animals, herbicides that also damage native species or introducing alien pests to control alien invaders, inevitably breeds problems (p.21). In such cases, Woods and Moriarty argue, several value systems will need to be balanced to achieve reasonable management outcomes: 'in many cases involving exotic species hard decisions will have to made that necessitate sacrificing one or more values in order to promote other values' (p.19). Iqbal offers an interesting perspective on the dilemmas of management in his comment that,

> The dilemma of pursuing simultaneous programmes in development and conservation persists today in an even more complex form. For the specific case of the water hyacinth, in Bangladesh as well as in other developing countries, the debate continues whether to completely eradicate the weed or utilise it for profit and development. (p.214)

Another aspect of introduction management requires brief comment – reintroduction. As Hettinger observes, 'when humans return a species to a location where the ecological assemblage is significantly different from that present when the species was last there' (one thinks of the reintroduction of beavers in Scotland), then such a 'restoration' takes on the character of an 'introduction' (p.43). Yet it has been deliberately undertaken as part of an ecosystem management project that in all likelihood objects to any new introductions.

We may be tempted to lambast Enlightenment improvers who sought to 'correct' large ecological systems that they only imperfectly understood and in so doing tipped many a delicate balance, but the modern mobility of plant species in particular (via gardens and agriculture) suggests we have learnt little. Hettinger argues that the aim of conservation today should not necessarily be to prevent all changes in species balance (after all it was not human agency that drove the dinosaurs to extinction):

> National Parks like Yellowstone should not be in the business of trying to prevent nature from changing on its own. Respect for wild nature should lead such parks to minimise human-induced change and typically to let non-anthropogenic changes take place. Natural parks should attempt to preserve natural processes, not some particular status quo in nature. (p.47)

As Peretti notes, some modern conservationists are actually keen to foster 'natural' migrations (he cites the Wildlands Project, p.32), despite the general determination to prevent and undo 'unnatural' ones. It is worth bearing in mind that 'Invasions may occur as the result of climatic and tectonic changes as well as through introduction by humans.' (Vermeiij, cited by Woods and Moriarty, p.6). Sanderson introduces a note of humility in her recognition that human agency is only part of the story of alien 'invasions':

> Vegetation is vibrant with change – with short-term fluctuations, medium-term successions and longer-term evolutionary changes; its constituent taxa are ever able to migrate wherever conditions in some way change to allow it. This dynamism needs to be superimposed over the palaeogeographical picture of slowly sliding continents, upthrusting and downwearing mountains, the rise and fall of land and sea, and the changing picture of world climates. (p.139)

Indeed Hettinger asserts that, 'it is likely that many, perhaps most, of the species in any given ecological assemblage did not first evolve in that assemblage and were originally foreign to it' (p.51): at some point, by some means – human or otherwise – species arrived in every ecological community. Beinart and Middleton do, however, introduce a caveat here, lest we be tempted to abnegate responsibility: 'Human disturbance of environments can unintentionally facilitate the spread of particular species by other natural forces' (p.79).

To return briefly to the most intentional introductions, Tamir, focusing more on causes than impacts, reminds us of the extent to which species transfers and reactions to them are culturally, economically and ideologically determined. He points out that, while alien species often tag along with human migrations, as with the arrival in Palestine of Eastern European immigrants and their prized culinary carp, these cultural elements do not necessarily tell the whole story: species are often introduced from areas whence there has been no or little human migration, as with the arrival in Europe and the Middle East of trout from the north-western United States 'although human immigration from these regions was marginal to non-existent' (p.254). Importations of garden plants, crops and other commodity species are obviously analogous. Tamir's case study of carp introduction in 1930s Palestine investigates economic and ideological motivations for inviting alien species (which might or might not later turn vicious) into countries, concluding that,

> Introductions of exotic species into one's own environment are aimed at improving and ameliorating the human condition. Whether consciously or not, they are accompanied by a certain level of optimism and belief that these deeds are positive and beneficial. (p.263)

He aligns this sanguine approach with the ideology of modernity; today's more pessimistic view of introductions perhaps reflects a broader shift in how we view the world.

Introduction xiii

Post-modern man agonises over invasions, more out of guilt than fear. The writers represented in this volume make compelling cases for the desirability of intervening on a case by case basis – but the process itself remains often out of our hands. Playing God in the age of empire ravaged certain delicate ecosystems, and it were rash to assume that, merely by intending to right wrongs, we have learnt to control every ramification. The best we can attempt is a value-balancing case-by-case approach, and gung-ho extirpations may be no less problematic than gung-ho introductions. Peretti declares that, 'The study of biological invasion needs more effective ways to determine which invader species are ecologically damaging, and which are neutral or beneficial' (p.32). At the other extreme, one logical extension of our notions of purity and protection is that, as 'we desire to control other exotic species [...] we also must control the introduction and impacts of humans' (Woods and Moriarty, p.15), for what is more invasive than ourselves?

Strangers in a Strange Land:
The Problem of Exotic Species

Mark Woods and Paul Veatch Moriarty

INTRODUCTION

Three different lines of armadillos existed in Florida during the Pleistocene Epoch (1.6 million to 10,000 years ago). For reasons unknown, they went extinct. In 1920 several nine-banded armadillos (*Dasypus novemcinctus*) escaped from the Hialeah Zoo; in 1924 several more escaped from a private zoo in Cocoa during a hurricane; and in 1926 several more escaped near Titusville when a circus truck overturned (Carr 1994). Due to high rates of reproduction, a lack of parasites and competitors, and the decimation of predators – panthers, black bears, and bobcats – armadillos now exist everywhere in Florida except for the Everglades and the Keys. Their burrows dry out the roots of orange trees, and they destroy the organisation and productivity of the leaf-mold stratum of hardwood hammock forests, as well as eating and outcompeting native millipedes, centipedes, isopods, snails, mites, spiders, skinks, lizards, salamanders and snakes. In spite of the fact that guns and motorised vehicles kill armadillos by the tens of thousands every year, they continue to thrive. Nine-banded armadillos native to Texas have been migrating east for some time, and today they have reached north Florida and have begun to mingle and reproduce with the exotic populations descended from the zoos and the circus truck. Prior to the natural migration from Texas, armadillos had been classified as exotic pests in Florida. Should we now accept them as native fauna?

This example illustrates the problem of distinguishing native from exotic species. If we hope to create and enact sensible environmental policies for dealing with exotics, we first must answer some important philosophical questions: What exactly makes a species native as opposed to exotic? Are exotic species always bad? Under what circumstances should exotic species be killed, removed, or left alone? Attempting to answer questions such as these opens up a Pandora's box of conceptual and normative quandaries. In this paper, we argue that there are no necessary and sufficient conditions for being native or exotic. The proposition 'This is an exotic species' may be neither clearly true nor clearly false because the distinction between natives and exotics admits of degrees. When we turn to normative considerations, the number of competing values at stake pose serious problems, and the claim that exotics are bad and ought to be removed should not be held as dogma. In the final sections of this paper, we offer suggestions for answering the demarcation and values questions and offer some tentative guidelines for setting policies to deal with exotic species.

WHAT IS AN EXOTIC SPECIES?

There is a general consensus among biologists, ecologists, environmental managers, and other environmental professionals that exotic species can be readily identified, that exotic species are bad because of the deleterious effects they have on people and nature, and that exotic species should be removed or killed whenever possible. Many of these people believe that the problem of exotic species is one of the most serious environmental problems we face today (Soulé 1990; Wilson 1992; Wuerthner 1996; Bright 1998; Devine 1998; Pimentel et al. 1999). Jared Diamond (1989) identifies exotic species as one member of the 'Evil Quartet' – four mechanisms responsible for overall species extinction and the loss of biodiversity.[1] Because of the problems posed by exotic species, some leading biologists have called for the formation of a presidential commission on exotic species in the United States (Schmitz, 1997). Deborah Dyer (1996) argues that federal laws in the United States do not adequately address the role of exotic species, and Steven Wade (1995) has called for an Exotic Species Act. Before we enact such policies, however, we should first attempt to answer the question 'What is an exotic species?' In this section, we distinguish several possible criteria for determining whether a species is native or exotic to a particular area and show some demarcation problems raised by each criterion. While we distinguish between five different criteria, we should note that considerable overlap exists between them.

The Human Introduction Criterion

One answer to the question of what makes a species exotic is that proposed by Reed Noss and Allen Cooperrider (1994, 392): An exotic species is 'the result of direct or indirect, deliberate or accidental introduction of the species by humans, and for which introduction permitted the species to cross a natural barrier to dispersal'. According to this criterion, human activity is the key element in determining whether a species is native or exotic. This criterion appeals to many people who value ecosystems because they are unhumanised (or less humanised) and continue to exist relatively free from human activity (Throop 2000), and this criterion importantly is used to establish management objectives and environmental policy by bureaucracies such as the United States National Park Service and the Society for Restoration Ecology (Hettinger 2001).[2]

One problem that this criterion faces is how to interpret indirect introduction. We have an intuitive idea of what it means for humans to indirectly introduce a species. If, for example, humans allow coyotes to move into an area which they previously did not occupy by killing off the wolves in the area, it looks

STRANGERS IN A STRANGE LAND

as though humans have indirectly introduced the coyotes. Hence, this criterion can be understood as a counterfactual – if not for human activity, this species would not be here. However, given the extent of human impacts on the planet over the past several million years, it looks as though this interpretation would rule out far too many species from the realm of nativity. That is, the 'butterfly effect' would make it so that only those species whose existence in an area predated the existence of human beings on the planet would qualify as native.

For these sorts of reasons, one might want to say that only those species that are directly introduced by humans are exotic. However, there are further problems in understanding how to correctly apply this criterion. Consider the following case. 'Saltcedar' tamarisk (*Tamarix chinensis* and *Tamarix ramossisima*) was introduced to the United States via the nursery trade in the 1820s and 1830s. By 1880 it had escaped from cultivation and had turned up in the desert Southwest of the United States (Rodman 1993).[3] The tamarisk, which was not native to this region, has spread rapidly along river banks where it forms a dense monoculture thicket and tends to deplete water supplies and impoverish wildlife habitat. John Rodman (1993, 149) notes that 'there is no consensus on whether saltcedar (the deciduous, shrubby, incredibly prolific form of tamarisk) should be thought of as one species, several distinguishable species, or a group of highly adaptive, rapidly speciating forms'. If in fact the tamarisk has undergone adaptation and speciation since its introduction into the desert Southwest, then it is unclear whether these new species should be considered native or exotic. According to the human introduction criterion, a species is exotic if it was introduced by humans. Was this new species of tamarisk introduced to North America by humans or not? Its ancestor was introduced by humans, but the species that exists here now is not the same species that was originally introduced. Given that this species exists nowhere else in the world, and never has, it would seem odd to say that it is not native to this region. However, it would not be here now if not for the activity of humans. And it may still belong to a genus which is exotic according to this criterion. This example raises the possibility that an organism could belong to a native species and an exotic genus.

In addition to distinguishing between direct and indirect introduction, one might wish to have a human introduction criterion which distinguished between intentional and unintentional introduction. What if, for example, a burr clings to the leg hair of a person walking through the area and rides its human ferry across to the other side of a mountain range? Is this not the plant's normal mechanism of dispersal? Could it not just as easily have hitchhiked on the leg of a non-human animal? Should we say that just because it happened to catch a ride on a human leg that it is exotic?

In spite of the above problems, the human introduction criterion captures an important component of the way many people think about nature as that which exists independently from human cultures. This criterion picks out a characteristic that can be typical of native species – the origins of their existence in a particular area is independent of people. Frequently people value native species just because of this fact and correspondingly regard exotic species negatively. We discuss this below in relation to the value of naturalness. While we believe that this criterion picks out an important feature of the distinction between natives and exotics (and the corresponding value), we do not believe that this criterion alone can provide a complete account of the distinction. As the tamarisk and armadillo examples show, it will not always be clear how this criterion should be applied. Furthermore, we believe that even in the cases where this criterion can be clearly applied, it provides neither necessary nor sufficient conditions for the distinction between natives and exotics. A species may be exotic to a given area even if it has not been introduced (directly or indirectly, intentionally or unintentionally) by people. Consider the case of the finches on the Galapagos Islands. The fourteen different species of finches found on these islands apparently descended from a single species which arrived in the Galapagos from South America less than one million years ago (Lack 1983). The finches thrived in this environment relatively free from predators and formed new species as they adapted to relatively unfinchlike ecological niches. According to the human introduction criterion, the first finches to arrive in the Galapagos were native; however, these finches that evolved elsewhere were outside of their traditional range, and they were foreigners to the ecological communities on the islands. The next four criteria we discuss appeal to ideas of evolutionary origin, historical range, ecological degradation, and membership within an ecological community.

The Evolutionary Criterion

Perhaps a species ought to be considered native to an area if it originally evolved in that area. The first finches to arrive on the Galapagos Islands originally evolved on the South American mainland and were not adapted to the ecological conditions found in the Galapagos. The finches that exist on these islands today have undergone speciation and have evolved and adapted to the unique conditions of their environments. While the current species of finches seem to be native, following the evolutionary criterion, their ancestors were not. According to the human introduction criterion, both the current species of finches are, and their original ancestors were, native, but this account misses important differences between the original migrants and the subsequently evolved species. The tamarisks in the southwestern United States today may be in a position similar to the finches shortly after their arrival in the Galapagos.

The evolutionary criterion has some advantages over the human introduction criterion in that it captures the intuitive appeal of the idea that a species which has evolved in one area and just recently crossed some natural barrier to dispersal does not seem to be native to the area in which it has just arrived. Like a species introduced by humans, it has not evolved or adapted to 'fit' into this new environment. It may be highly invasive and could even wipe out species that currently exist in this area. The evolutionary criterion captures the idea that a species is native to an area if this is where the species comes from.

However, the evolutionary criterion also faces problems. How, for example, are we to determine the 'area' in which a species evolved? We tend to say that gray wolves (*Canis lupis*) are native to North America, that nine-banded armadillos are native to Central America, and that Florida panthers (*Felis concolor coryi*) are native to Florida. We seem to have a very loose sense of what constitutes an area of origin. Trying to identify the place at which a species came into existence is plagued by the problem of spatial scale. If nine-banded armadillos first came into existence in a particular valley in Central America (if we could ever know such a thing), does this mean that these armadillos are native just to that valley, to a larger landscape, or to the entire region of Central America? Stephen Spurr (1980, 441) shows this spatial scale problem when he proposes that 'all plants and animals are exotic... except at the very point in space where the particular gene combination was constructed'. By defining the area in which a species evolved as a precise point in space, Spurr reduces the idea of nativity to absurdity.

Furthermore, the evolutionary criterion faces the problem that species are not clearly demarcated and well-defined. It is usually not possible to pinpoint the precise time at which one species divides into two. The Mexican gray wolf (*Canis lupus baileyi*) is commonly classified as a subspecies of the North American gray wolf. The Mexican gray wolf is morphologically distinct from its cousins up north. It is generally smaller, its coat looks different, and it is usually more aggressive. The Mexican gray wolf generally does not interbreed with the gray wolves from farther north, but it could in principle produce viable offspring. The German shepherd, on the other hand, is commonly classified as belonging to a separate species from the gray wolf. German shepherds and wolves do not commonly interbreed, but they are capable of producing viable offspring. This all illustrates the point that it is not always clear when two varieties of the same species have become sufficiently separate to be classified as separate species. Given the vagaries of determining when one species becomes two, application of the evolutionary criterion will be inherently difficult.

The Historical Range Criterion

While the science of conservation biology is grounded in modern evolutionary theory, few if any conservation biologists advocate the evolutionary criterion for distinguishing between native and exotic species. Instead, many conservation biologists are committed to a historical (or natural) range criterion: '*Exotic* is the adjective most commonly used by conservation biologists to describe a species living outside of its native range' (Hunter 1996, 215; see also Primack 1998). This criterion is similar to the human introduction criterion in that both involve species moving into areas where they have not previously existed. However, while human agency is all-important for the human introduction criterion, human agency is not necessary for a species to be considered exotic under the historical range criterion. As invasion biologist Geerat Vermeij (1996, 4) says:

> By invasion I mean the geographical expansion of a species into an area not previously occupied by that species. Invasions may occur as the result of climatic and tectonic changes as well as through introduction by humans.

The 'historical range' of a species presumably is identified with the areas in which it has historically been found. According to Walter Westman (1990, 252):

> As the term is used widely in park practice, an 'exotic' species is one that is newly established at a significant distance from its former geographic range. In park practice, the term includes both significant range extensions by species native to another part of the state or region, and introductions of species from distant regions or continents (whether by natural dispersal or human agency).

One difficulty faced by proponents of this criterion is that of locating the historical range of a species in space and time. Field guides to birds, mammals, trees, flowers, etc. typically illustrate the range of a species by shading in a portion of a map. However, this representation of the range is really very crude. Within the shaded area for a particular tree species, for example, there may be a valley where that tree species has never existed. If the tree species were to move into the valley, would it be moving outside of its historical range? The temporal problem may be even more complex than the spatial one. Aspens (*Populus tremuloides*) once extended as far as Southern California and the Baja Peninsula in Mexico. Due to changing climate patterns, the aspens have all but vanished from this region. Two small stands remain – one in the San Bernardino Mountains east of Los Angeles and one on the Baja Peninsula in Mexico. The nearest large groves of aspens are hundreds of miles to the north and separated from these small stands by desert. If humans decided to plant aspens in the nearby San Gabriel Mountains, where aspens apparently existed at some time in the past, would they be planting them within the historical range of aspens?

In addition to these difficulties of applying the historical range criterion, many would claim that this criterion does not provide a complete account of the concepts of nativity and exoticality. This criterion captures the intuition that a species moving into an area where it has not previously existed is a stranger to this area. However, by ignoring any distinction between anthropogenic introduction and natural migration, this criterion fails to capture one of the important values many people associate with native species (Throop 2000). Further, many people are concerned about exotic species because of the harmful environmental impacts of these species – some strangers are worse guests than others. For this reason, some people identify invasive and harmful species as the significant subcategory of non-indigenous species (Scherer 1994; Devine 1998). We shall call this the degradation criterion.

STRANGERS IN A STRANGE LAND

The Degradation Criterion

Robert Devine (1998) uses the terms 'alien', 'non-native', 'exotic', 'introduced', and 'non-indigenous' synonymously. 'These labels', he says, 'apply to any animal, plant, or microbe found outside its natural range' (p. 4). However, he is not particularly concerned with such species unless they degrade the environment and cause harm. He says, 'It's the invasive ones that we have to watch out for, the ones that proliferate out of control, degrade our ecosystems, make us ill, and devour our crops' (p. 5). Devine uses the term 'invasive' to identify these harmful species; he claims that invasive species are almost always non-native, but not all non-native species are invasive. Thus, invasives are a subcategory of non-natives. Donald Scherer (1994) has a similar classification scheme, though he uses the terms differently. Scherer uses 'non-indigenous' to refer to species existing outside of their historical ranges. He reserves the term 'exotic' for that subset of non-indigenous species that harms or degrades the ecosystem or displaces indigenous species. Both Scherer and Devine appeal to the important idea that what is significant about many exotics is that they cause biological and ecological degradation or harm.[4]

A paradigm example of an invasive species which degrades the ecosystem and displaces or wipes out indigenous species is the brown tree snake (*Boiga irregularis*) in Guam. Less than fifty years ago the brown tree snake was accidentally introduced to the island of Guam via cargo ships. This mildly venomous snake easily adapts to many forms of prey and eats, among other things, birds' eggs. The snake has no predators on Guam, so its population has multiplied rapidly. The island of Guam is now infested with these snakes; in the areas of highest density, there are as many as 10,000 snakes per acre. The snakes have decimated Guam's bird population. Thus far, they have wiped out fifteen species of birds, and they are threatening to wipe out the Marianas crow (*Corvus kubaryi*) and the Marianas fruit bat (*Pteropus marianus*) as well (Barela 1993). The brown tree snake's decimation of wildlife on Guam is being referred to by local environmentalists and media as 'The Massacre on Guam'. The snakes are so numerous that residents have reported them coming up through the toilets, chewing through power lines, and allegedly attacking human infants on occasion. The order is out to all Guam residents to kill brown tree snakes on sight, but still their population continues to grow. Officials are currently examining different possibilities for eradicating the snakes such as poison or snake-sniffing dogs, and biologists are trying to develop a disease specific to the brown tree snake which would be introduced into the population. Brown tree snakes have caused similar problems in Australia and have been reported in Hawaii and other Pacific islands where they pose a similar threat.

While the degradation criterion captures an important sense of exoticality – both in terms of what it means to be exotic to an area and in terms of the negative values associated with exotics – this criterion is not trouble-free. Questions remain about what it means for an ecosystem to be harmed or degraded.

One question is whether an ecosystem is the sort of thing that can be harmed at all. Some people such as Harley Cahen (1988) and Dale Jamieson (1995) have argued that ecosystems are incapable of caring about what happens to them and thus lack interests. Only those beings with interests, they argue, are capable of being harmed.

Even if we can meaningfully talk about harming or degrading an ecosystem, it sometimes appears to be the case that an exotic species both harms and benefits a natural ecosystem. Eucalyptus trees were introduced into California from Australia over 125 years ago. The state of California decreed in 1979 to remove all exotic plant species capable of naturalising. While removing all the eucalyptus trees would be a difficult (if not impossible) task, the trees have been a target for removal and control. The eucalyptus trees use large quantities of water and displace other less aggressive species. In some respects, the eucalyptus trees appear to be degrading the Californian ecosystems into which they have been introduced. However, the eucalyptus' impacts on local species may not be all bad. Monarch butterflies (*Danaus plexippus*) are apparently native to California by any of our criteria. Large populations of monarch butterflies have become reliant upon the trees for their annual migrations. According to Westman (1990, 255), eucalyptus trees are 'utilised by a wide range of native species, in some cases preferentially'. In addition to the monarchs, a number of native bird species and one species of salamander are found as frequently, or more frequently, in eucalyptus forests as in native oak woodlands. Hence, eucalyptus trees are apparently beneficial to some species in this ecological community and harmful to others, and the removal of these trees at this time could be both harmful to some native species such as monarch butterflies *and* helpful to other native species.

The Community Membership Criterion

John Rodman (1993) has proposed yet another criterion. He asks us to '[s]uppose that the essence of exoticality is existence outside a community, lack of a membership in a community of mutual dependence and mutual controls' (p. 150). The central idea that Rodman captures is that a species is native to the degree that it is an integrated member or component of an ecological community. This criterion is similar to the degradation criterion in that a species is exotic to the degree that it is not integrated into an ecological community, it violates relationships of dependence and control with other species, and it degrades or harms the ecological community. However, the community membership criterion differs from the degradation criterion because a non-integrated species that causes no degradation or harm to the ecological community is still considered to be exotic under the community membership criterion. The first finches to arrive in the Galapagos Islands were not integrated members of the ecological communities of these islands, and, because of this fact, they would be classified as exotic under the community membership criterion. To the degree that they subsequently caused disruptions to the biological and ecological assemblages and processes present in the Galapagos, the finches became exotic under the degradation criterion. In time the ecological communities of the Galapagos evolved and adapted to the newly evolved species of finches, and the finches became integrated members of these communities. The finches are now native species according to the community membership criterion.

One problem the community membership criterion faces is the ability to spell out what an ecological community is. Although ecologists have used a community model to describe nature since the 1920s (McIntosh 1985; Hagen 1992; Worster 1994; Kingsland 1995), this model today has become questionable. Kristin Shrader-Frechette and Earl McCoy (1993) claim that there has never been consensus among ecologists over what precisely constitutes an ecological community, and Daniel Botkin (1990) claims that most attempts to create mathematical equations that express the notion of an ecological community cannot be empirically verified (see also Kingsland 1995). Beyond theoretical problems of trying to describe what an ecological community is, it can be notoriously difficult to determine which species of any given ecological community are integrated natives (Diamond 1987). Accurate ecological data for any given ecological community seldom go back more than one or several hundred years. Further, paleoecologists remind us that natural communities are consistently shifting and are seldom as stable as we once thought. For example, most plant communities in the eastern United States are relatively short lived – from a paleoecological perspective, having established their current species composition in the past 4,000 to 8,000 years (Graham 1988; Hunter et al. 1988). Viewed from this perspective, ecological communities look more like relatively arbitrary collections of assemblages, and it might be difficult to define native species as species that are integrated well within a community.

Beyond the difficulties involved in determining a particular ecological community, proponents of the community membership criterion also face difficulties in determining what Rodman calls 'mutual dependence and mutual controls'. Rodman (1993, 153) claims that members of an ecological community participate in a form of 'balance in a disturbed world'. This might lead us to see some form of ideal balance of multispecies, ecological communities (or balance of nature) that can be used as a yardstick to distinguish natives from exotics: organisms and species are native to the degree to which they fit into such a balance and exotic to the degree to which they upset or alter such a balance. However, we must reject a simplistic notion of balance because it originates largely from a now-defunct ecological understanding of nature. Disturbance ecologists tell us that natural systems may rarely exist in stable forms of balance and instead are more properly characterised by persistent changes and disturbances (Pickett and White 1985; Botkin 1990). The community membership criterion is problematic because it presupposes a pristine, balanced ecological community composed of native species against which we can compare exotic outsiders, and such communities may be nothing more than fictions (Peretti 1998).

Ned Hettinger (2001) argues that Rodman's community membership criterion requires not merely community membership for nativity but *good* community membership. That is, for a species to be considered native, it must have adapted well into the ecological community. Holmes Rolston (1994, 115) proposes a similar standard when he argues for the removal of feral mustangs in the western United States because these mustangs are not 'good adapted fits on today's landscapes', in spite of the fact that they've been on such landscapes for hundreds of years and now have federal, legal protection via the U.S. Wild and Free Roaming Horses and Burros Act of 1971. In place of this strong version of a community membership criterion as advocated by Rodman and Rolston, Hettinger (2001, 198) argues instead for a weaker version of this criterion:

> In contrast with native species, an exotic species is one that is foreign to an ecosystem in the sense that it has not significantly adapted to the resident species and/or abiotic elements that characterise this system and, perhaps more importantly, the system's resident species have not significantly adapted to it. [On this account] species that are introduced to new geographical locations by humans, or that migrate or expand their ranges without such assistance, may or may not be exotics in these new regions. Species are exotic in new locations only when the species movement is ecological and not merely geographical.

The mere act of geographical movement does not make a species exotic because species that move into a type of ecological assemblage that already exists in the 'home range' of the species would be considered native, according to Hettinger, in spite of the fact that the species now has a new geographical location. Because Hettinger focuses on ecological assemblages rather than on ecological communities, his criterion might get around two of the problems associated with the community membership criterion: the problem of what constitutes an ecological community and the problematic notion of a balance of nature. A version of the community membership criterion might appeal to people who advocate a holistic environmental ethic such as Rolston (1994).

NATIVE AND EXOTIC SPECIES AS CLUSTER CONCEPTS

We have identified five different criteria for classifying a species as exotic. Using case studies, we have illustrated that a species may be classified as exotic using one criterion, but non-exotic using another criterion. The selection of a criterion for classifying a species as exotic will have significant practical consequences when it comes to the establishment of policies for dealing with native and exotic species. Which criterion then should we use? Our suggestion is that there is no 'bright line' which separates native species from exotic species. We believe that none of the five criteria we have identified constitutes either a necessary condition or a sufficient condition for a species being exotic. Rather, we suggest the concepts of 'exotic' and 'native' as applied to species are *cluster concepts*.

As Heather Gert (1995) says, there has been an ongoing debate in philosophy between those who believe that conceptual analysis is a matter of determining the necessary and sufficient conditions for falling under a concept – the so-called classical view – and those who believe that the attempt to do so is generally futile. Critics of the classical view argue that we cannot always give necessary and sufficient conditions because many concepts lack 'sharp borders' and may admit of some degree of vagueness. In response, one might wish to point out that the classical view does not always rule out the possibility of vague concepts (Gert 1995). We might wish to maintain, for example, that there are necessary and sufficient conditions for being a bachelor and that one of the necessary conditions is being an adult. Since adulthood seems to have fuzzy boundaries, one who accepts the classical account might reasonably maintain that the concept 'bachelor' is vague. But perhaps this only pushes the problem back. Unless one can give necessary and sufficient conditions for being an adult, one has not really given necessary and sufficient conditions for being a bachelor. Any analysis which uses concepts that have not been, or cannot be, analysed properly without vagueness is not a complete analysis.

A second reason for criticising the classical view is that according to the classical view, no property can be mentioned in the analysis of a concept unless that property is a necessary condition for falling under the concept. For example, since having four legs is not a necessary condition for being a dog, the property of having-four-legs would not be a part of the analysis of the concept 'dog'. One alternative which has been offered is that of cluster concepts.[5] On this view, an analysis of a concept will include a variety of properties, but it is only required that something possess some subset or cluster of these in order to fall under the concept. Hence, something might be a dog if it possess a sufficiently large subset of the properties associated with the species *Canis domesticus*, although it need not exhibit all of those properties.[6] As applied to extocality, the traits which are characteristic of exotic species are exemplified by each of the five criteria we have identified in this paper. An exotic species typically will exhibit the following traits:

- The species' existence in the area is the result of human introduction at some time. That introduction may be intentional or unintentional, direct or indirect.
- The species originally evolved somewhere else.
- The area is outside of the historical (or natural) range of the species.
- The species tends to damage or degrade the local ecosystem, displacing or eliminating native species.

- The species is not an integrated member of the ecological community. It has not developed significant relationships of mutual dependence and mutual control with other species in this community.

Any one of these traits on its own will not be sufficient to make a species clearly exotic. Consider, for example, the first trait. Are all species whose presence in a particular area is a result of human introduction clearly exotic? We contend that they are not. The Guam rail (*Rallus owstoni*), a flightless bird endemic to Guam, has been virtually wiped out by the brown tree snake. Guam rails are now being bred in captivity and 'reintroduced' to the small nearby island of Rota which has no brown tree snakes. Although Rota is ecologically similar to Guam, rails have never existed on Rota. Is the on Rota an exotic species? Further, is a species which was indirectly introduced to an area by humans in the past always exotic? Consider again the case of the saltcedar tamarisk discussed above. Are the new species, which may have evolved since the tamarisk was introduced, exotic to the southwestern United States? Their presence there now is a direct result of human introduction; however, these new species evolved in the southwestern U.S. and exist nowhere else. Human introduction is not *sufficient* to make a species exotic, though it is a trait which is characteristic of exotic species. The same is true of the other traits that are characteristic of exotic species, although we lack the space here to demonstrate this in each case.

Furthermore, none of the above traits is a *necessary* trait for an exotic species. That is, a species could be exotic while lacking any one of the five traits. Consider again human introduction. Must a species be introduced by humans in order to be exotic? We think not. Consider a species of bird which manages to find its way onto an island where it has not previously existed. This island is not part of the historical range of this species; the species originally evolved somewhere else; it may be quite disruptive to the ecosystem of this island, displacing native species; and it has not yet become an integrated member of the island's ecosystem. It seems reasonable to say that this species is exotic to the island, even though it was not introduced by humans.

When we say that 'exotic' is a cluster concept as it applies to species, what we mean is that there are a number of traits which are typical of exotic species. We have identified five of these traits. None of the traits is either necessary or sufficient for a species to be exotic. The more of these traits a species has, the more likely we are to think of it as exotic. As a contrast to extocality, there are a number of corresponding traits which are characteristic of native species:

- The species' presence in the area is not the result of human introduction.
- The species originally evolved in the area.
- The area is part of the historical range of the species.
- The species does not tend to degrade the ecosystem or displace or eliminate other native species.

- The species has become an integrated member of the ecological community, forming mutual relations of dependence and control with other species.

Once again, none of these traits is, on its own, necessary or sufficient for a species being native. They form a cluster of traits which are characteristic of native species. The more of these traits a species has, the more likely we are to think of it as native.

There are two ways in which nativity and exoticality can be understood either as indeterminate or as admitting of degrees.[7] First, they may be vague in the way that concepts such as 'adult' are vague – having fuzzy boundaries. If we think of a native species in terms of its historical range, for example, the historical range may be vague both geographically and temporally. Secondly, if the categories of 'native' and 'exotic' function as cluster concepts, as we have suggested, then we will often find species which exhibit some, but not all, of the characteristics which are typical of native species. It seems reasonable to say that a species which exhibits more of these traits is 'more native', or at least more clearly native, than one which exhibits fewer of these traits. That is, because there is no bright line separating native and exotic species, a particular species might be more or less native, depending on the presence of traits listed above which are characteristic of native species, and a particular species might be more or less exotic, depending on the presence of traits listed above which are characteristic of exotic species.

People frequently use the terms 'naturalisation' or 'naturalised species' to refer to species which were considered exotic in the past but which are now native. This sense of naturalisation matches up well with the community membership criterion. Hettinger (2001, 209) says that '[a]n exotic species naturalises in an ecological sense when it persists in its new habitat and significantly adapts with the resident species and to the local abiota'. Rather than calling such species 'naturalised', we propose to call such species 'native' and to reserve the term 'naturalised' to refer to species that are on their way to becoming native. That is, we understand naturalisation to represent a grey area between extocality and nativity. To the degree that a formerly exotic species is beginning to exhibit traits that seem more characteristic of native species, that species is now naturalised. At some future point in time naturalised species might come to be considered native. As Walter Westman (1990, 252) notes: 'Today's exotics may be tomorrow's naturalised species... In turn, it is unclear how long a species must be naturalised before it can be considered native'. When the first species of finches arrived in the Galapagos Islands, this species was probably exotic in every sense except that of being introduced by humans. As the finches began to adapt and evolve, and as the ecological communities of the Galapagos began to evolve and adapt in response to the finches, the finches became naturalised. Further adaptation and evolution has led to the nativity of the finches that now exist in the Galapagos.

While we are primarily interested in non-human species such as finches and tamarisks in this paper, we wish to point out that the five different criteria for nativity and extocality also might be applied to humans (*Homo sapiens sapiens*). According to the human introduction criterion, human actions (direct or indirect, intentional or unintentional) make a species exotic. This suggests that we are always exotic in any environment. Rolston (1994) argues that we are a nicheless species strongly separated from non-human nature because of the development of our cultures. Making such a distinction is crucial for people such as Robert Elliot (1997) who value naturalness because it connotes having a non-human origin and causal continuity with other non-human origins. According to the evolutionary criterion, a species is exotic to an area if it did not evolve there. Because *Homo sapiens sapiens* probably originally evolved in Africa, perhaps people today are exotic to all other continents. As indicated by the title of Neil Evernden's (1993) book *The Natural Alien*, we are exotic, and we are exotic according to Evernden because of the development of human technology which takes us out of environments in which we evolved. According to the historical range criterion, a species is exotic if it is outside of its historical range. What is our historical range? Proponents of the historical range criterion might argue that when people first arrive and colonise a new area – such as when people first came to North America at least ten to fifteen thousand years ago – they are exotic if outside their historical range. Further, when people first arrive in a new area, typically they cause ecological and biological harm (Nabhan 1995), thus making people exotic as per the degradation criterion. Because of extensive anthropogenic harms to the environment today, we might still be exotic over much of the Earth. Finally, according to the community membership criterion, a species is exotic to an ecological community if it has not forged mutual relations of dependence and control. Because we typically fail to adapt to ecological communities and establish such relations and instead alter and/or destroy ecological communities to fit our own needs and wants, we are usually exotic following this criterion. And just as non-human exotic species can become naturalised and eventually native, so might people. As per the community membership criterion, we become naturalised to the degree that we restrain our control over ecological communities and instead become 'plain member and citizen' (Leopold 1949, 204) of these communities; this might help make sense of the idea many people have that groups of people such as so-called 'indigenous peoples' who live closer to and more in harmony with non-human ecological communities are more native.[8] Similar to this and as per the degradation criterion, to the degree that we create minimal ecological and biological harm, we become naturalised. As we become established over time in various areas, such areas then become part of our historical range, and we become naturalised following the historical range criterion; e.g., while people might have been exotic in North America ten thousand years ago, perhaps today naturalisation has occurred here. As we continue to evolve as a species, perhaps culturally as well as biologically, we can become naturalised as per the evolutionary criterion in given locations. But if we are always exotic as per the human introduction criterion, naturalisation and nativity will always elude us.[9] In those relatively natural areas where humans would qualify as an exotic species according to most or all of the criteria we have identified, we ought to take active measures to prevent the introduction of humans, as we would with any exotic species. For the same reasons that we desire to control other exotic species – their lack of naturalness, their impact on the biological integrity of the ecosystem, etc. – we also must control the introduction and impacts of humans as an exotic species.

Accounts of nature from invasion biologists – who study how exotics invade, impact, and change native flora and fauna – may be helpful in rounding out our discussion of nativity and extocality as cluster concepts.[10] One of the central tasks for invasion biologists is to develop a theory of community assembly that explains the patterns and processes of how flora and fauna assemble to form given ecological communities (Townsend 1991; Moyle and Light 1996; Vermeij 1996).[11] We begin with an existing community of native species. Following the evolutionary, historical range, community membership, and the human introduction criteria, many of these natives may have at one time been exotics. Three ongoing stages of community assembly may be gleaned. At the first stage of *colonisation*, new exotic organisms that did not previously visit or occupy the existing community arrive. They may arrive via speciation as per natural evolution; arrive via natural means outside of their historical range; be transported directly, indirectly, intentionally, or unintentionally by people; or arrive by some combination of these means. As newly arrived exotics, these organisms are not integrated within the existing community and are exotic as per the community membership criterion. It is quite possible that these organisms are exotic as per the degradation criterion because they are causing harm or degradation to the existing ecological community and/or to native organisms. Those exotic organisms who stay find and follow ecological opportunities. Many exotic organisms might either leave or die due to an inability to find food, establish a habitat, successfully mate, compete with other organisms, etc. Those exotics who stay in a community stay precisely because they become established and persist through either local reproduction or continuous recruitment of new breeding members from outside the community, and these exotics establish viable bridgehead populations (or viable beachhead population colonies in the case of insects (Moller 1996)). At this second stage of *establishment*, exotics are not integrated members of the ecological community (as per the community membership criterion). In the third stage of *integration*, exotics forge ecological links with native species, and an altered ecological community results that has adapted to the exotics.[12]

While we have noted difficulties with each of the five different criteria used to distinguish natives from exotics, each of these criteria still can play a useful role in helping explain the phenomenon of biological invasions as studied by invasion biologists. While some biologists make no distinction between anthropogenic and non-anthropogenic means of invasions, others wish to regard these different means as significant (Vermeij 1996). There may be functional, historical (non-anthropogenic) and evolutionary limits in any natural system (Pickett et al. 1992), and this helps explain what might be attractive about the human introduction criterion. Further, anthropogenic invasions may be more harmful to the ecological community (following the degradation criterion), and it may be harder for organisms that arrive via anthropogenic means to become established within an ecological community (following the community membership criterion). The evolutionary criterion plays an important role in helping explain the process of biological invasion. Invading exotics can be exotic because they have not co-evolved with other species in a particular area. A number of exotic organisms undergo genetic, evolutionary changes following a successful invasion into a new ecological community (Carroll and Dingle 1996), such as the Galapagos finches. Although there are problems in trying to determine the precise historical range of many species, the historical range criterion helps capture the important idea that an organism is exotic because it is a stranger to a new land. Residents – natives – do not invade the homes where they live, and invasion biologists rely upon the notion of a non-resident – exotic – to help explain the process of invasions. The degradation criterion helps capture the idea that an organism is exotic because it is a stranger in a strange land. The organism is new to an area, and, because of the deleterious presence of the organism (or, more probably, groups of organisms), the ecological community has become strange for the worse.[13] The community membership criterion corresponds well with accounts of community assembly from invasion biologists. We can examine the role an organism or species plays within the larger context of an ecological community: exotics are organisms and species whose presence and behaviour fail to conform to historical functions and patterns in a particular ecological community and who are not integrated members of the community.

While each of the five different criteria for distinguishing natives from exotics can help ground invasion biology, we should note that there can be considerable overlap between these five criteria. One hundred and forty-five exotic fishes, invertebrates, fish disease pathogens, plants, and algae currently exist in the North American Great Lakes (Mills et al. 1994).[14] Virtually all of these exotics have been documented as being introduced by humans. None of these exotics have evolved in the Great Lakes. All of these exotics are outside of their historical ranges. Many of these exotics are causing harm to native species and to the ecological communities of the Great Lakes. Few of these exotics are integrated members of these ecological communities. Convergence of all five of the different criteria for distinguishing natives from exotics clearly indicates the presence of exotic species. This leads to important questions concerning what to do about these 145 exotic species in the Great Lakes. Before we can begin to suggest policy guidelines, however, we must first examine the values at stake in matters concerning native versus exotic species.

STRANGERS IN A STRANGE LAND

ARE EXOTICS BAD?

While some scientists and environmental managers who make policy decisions regarding exotic species might wish to avoid talking about values, values are at the heart of such policy decisions. That is, the problem of exotic species, as alluded to in the title of this paper, is a problem precisely because of conflicts of values.

A good example of this is the case of feral pigs in Hawaii. The first humans to arrive in Hawaii – Polynesian settlers sometime between 400 and 800 AD – brought small pigs to a pigless Hawaii. The presence of the pigs, along with other settlement impacts such as farming, led to the extinction of at least thirty-five species of birds (Royte 1995, 26). When Europeans arrived in Hawaii over two hundred years ago, they brought numerous exotic flora and fauna, including large European boars. These flora and fauna have proliferated, and today Hawaii is considered the endangered species capital of the United States. Three quarters of all extinct American plants and birds once lived in Hawaii, and more than a third of the plants and birds currently listed as endangered and threatened in the U.S. are found in Hawaii. According to *National Geographic* magazine,

> The causes of Hawaiian species' decline are numerous and complicated, but if conservation biologists had to name the most significant threat to native rain forest species today, they would, without hesitation, indict the feral pig. (Royte 1995, 14)

The feral pigs in Hawaii today are a breeding combination of the small domestic pigs brought by the Polynesians and the larger European boars. These pigs cause large-scale destruction as they uproot shrubs, gnaw at plants, disturb soils, and spread seeds from harmful alien plants. Efforts to remove the pigs have been hampered by the fact that they often inhabit remote and heavily forested areas. In a well-publicised dispute between the Nature Conservancy and People for the Ethical Treatment of Animals (PETA), PETA has opposed methods such as neck-hold traps used by the Nature Conservancy to kill pigs in Hawaiian forests.

What are the values at stake in this example? Some people such as conservation biologists argue that the pigs threaten the health of the Hawaiian rainforests and native Hawaiian biodiversity. The solution then is to kill and remove the pigs. Other people such as animal activists argue that it is wrong to harm and kill the pigs because they are sentient animals. The solution then is to leave the pigs alone. Still other people such as wilderness advocates might find some of the efforts to remove and kill the pigs problematic because these efforts can be highly invasive and threaten the naturalness of Hawaiian rainforests. And still other people might object to efforts to remove and kill the pigs because these efforts interfere with aesthetic appreciation of and outdoor recreation in the rainforests. The solution to the pig problem becomes less clear.[15]

What is clear from this example is that there are a number of different values at stake that create the problem of exotic species. While we lack the space here for an adequate discussion of these values, we wish to identify five of them. This list is not meant to be exhaustive. First, there is the value of **ecosystem health** (Costanza et al. 1992). Conservation biologists argue that the pigs threaten or harm certain features of the Hawaiian rainforests. Such features include integrity, stability, disturbance regimes, resilience, and other such ecological functions. An analogy is made between human health – something most people find valuable – and the health of an ecosystem.[16] Second, there is the value of **biodiversity** (Noss and Cooperrider 1994). Conservation biologists also argue that the pigs threaten the biodiversity found in Hawaiian rainforests. While the focus typically is on biodiversity at the species level and at the level of sustainable metapopulations (or minimum viable populations), biodiversity also may include genetic and ecosytemic biodiversity (Noss and Cooperrider 1994).[17] Third, there is the value of **naturalness** (Woods, forthcoming). Wilderness advocates argue that the management efforts needed to remove and kill the pigs can be highly intrusive to the naturalness of the Hawaiian rainforests. Some people value this naturalness because it has a non-human origin and causal continuity over time (Elliot 1997). Fourth, there is the value of **animal welfare**. Animal activists argue that it is wrong to harm or kill individual pigs because the pigs are sentient (Singer 1990) and/or because the pigs have basic rights (Regan 1983).[18] Fifth, there are **anthropocentric values of nature** such as economic, aesthetic, and recreation values. Some people who engage in outdoor recreation in Hawaiian rainforests might oppose management efforts to remove or kill the pigs because such efforts interfere with a recreational or aesthetic appreciation of the rainforests; other people might question whether such management efforts are economically efficient. In identifying these values, we do not intend to provide an exhaustive list of all the possible values at stake for each and every case involving exotic species. We have picked out some of the values which we believe are most important, and in doing so we hope to show that policy decisions cannot be reduced to a single value.

As the case of the pigs in Hawaii shows, exotic species typically diminish or destroy some of these values. This is why many people believe that exotic species are bad. But such a blanket condemnation cannot be made against exotics because in many cases exotics also can enhance and even create values. Traditional subsistence farming at the oasis of Ki:towak in the Sonoran Desert can enhance biodiversity by creating habitat for more species of birds (Callicott 1991), and modern monoculture farming in North Dakota creates economically valuable wheat that is exported all over the world. Of course, some environmentalists might wish to oppose both of these farming practices because the naturalness of the Sonoran Desert and the naturalness of the North Dakota prairies are diminished. Such opposition involves a conflict of values, and this precisely is the problem of exotic species.[19]

While we have argued elsewhere (Moriarty and Woods 1997) that there are some cases where a conflict of values can be resolved without a net loss of values, we recognise that in many cases involving exotic species hard decisions will have to made that necessitate sacrificing one or more values in order to promote other values. We wish to point out, however, that in many cases such hard decisions are circumvented simply by ignoring values. Some conservation biologists simply fail to see the value of animal welfare at stake in the Hawaiian rainforests, while some animal activists simply fail to see the values of ecosystem health and biodiversity at stake. In many other cases a decision is made that a species is exotic, it is bad, and therefore it should be removed or killed.[20] We have argued above that it is problematic to define a species as 'exotic' simply by using only one of the five criteria for distinguishing an exotic from a native while ignoring the other four criteria. Similarly, it is also problematic simply to appeal to only one or two values at stake to show why an exotic species is problematic while ignoring other values.[21] When making policy decisions concerning what to do about an exotic species, all the values at stake should be articulated.

ENVIROMENTAL POLICY IN A VALUE PLURALISTIC WORLD

Many policies concerning the elimination of exotics are written and implemented with the assumptions that exotics can be easily identified and that removing them is our sole concern. As Walter Westman (1990, 251–252) notes:

> Current policies for managing exotic plant species in most park reserves in the United States reflect the influence of the report produced by A. Starker Leopold and colleagues (1963) for the National Park Service. The Leopold Committee suggested that the goal for biotic management within the National Park Service be to maintain or recreate biotic associations "as nearly as possible in the condition that prevailed when the area was first visited by white men."

Westman further notes that 'As such language became translated into public policy in federal and state park systems throughout the country, the goals of exotic species management were framed in more absolutist terms' (p. 252). Policy directives generally call for the removal of all exotic species from federal and state park lands. However, given the limited budgets available for management of exotic species, park managers are forced to prioritise, focusing their efforts on only a few species. In the absence of guidelines for prioritising, such decisions are often made on pragmatic grounds such as which species are easiest to control and the estimated economic costs of control, rather than on ecological grounds.

While absolutist policies which use only one criterion for identifying exotic species and call for the removal of all exotic species have the benefit of providing theoretically consistent procedures which might seem easy to follow, they are problematic for a number of reasons. Such policies are overly simplistic in their interpretation of what it means for a species to be native or exotic, and they are impractical without guidelines for determining which species and locations should be given the most attention. Furthermore, such policies can be inconsistent with the ecosystem level goals of environmentalists, conservation biologists, and environmental managers. For example, policies of eradicating exotic species do not always benefit native plants and animals. Removal of exotic plants may simply open the door for invasion by other, more aggressive, exotics. It may also harm native wildlife which utilises the exotic hosts. As Westman (1990) points out, native birds and butterflies utilise the exotic eucalyptus trees in California, and if those trees were removed, it would be decades before a native forest of equivalent stature could develop. Finally, the removal of exotic species may have a number of costs – economic, aesthetic, ethical, and environmental.

The removal of exotic plants is often achieved with the use of herbicides, the environmental impact of which is not always confined to the target species. The removal process may also require heavy machinery, which can also be ecologically damaging. When exotic plants are removed, increased erosion may become a problem until native plants become reestablished. The removal of exotic animals often involves inhumane trapping or poisoning. Furthermore, the removal of exotics often involves the introduction of other exotics, such as predators or diseases, which are intended to eliminate the target species, but which may themselves become invasive exotics.

Rather than seeking policies which give absolute answers about whether a particular exotic species should be removed, we need to develop policies which are sensitive to the genuine complexities of these issues. Policies should recognise that 'native' and 'exotic' are not absolute categories which can be clearly identified. Rather, the concepts of 'native' and 'exotic' should be treated as cluster concepts such that a species may have some, but not all of the characteristics which are generally associated with exotic species. Policy makers should recognise that there are a number of competing values at stake. The ecological impact of a species must be weighed against the ecological impact of removing the species. Likewise, the economic costs brought about by exotic species must be weighed against the economic costs of removal and restoration programmes. The naturalness which is lost due to the spread of anthropogenically introduced exotic species must be weighed against the naturalness which is lost through long-term programmes for controlling exotic species – programmes which may themselves be quite invasive. Then these values must be weighed against each other and against other values such as animal welfare and human recreation.

Rather than developing blanket policies for dealing with the very serious problems posed by exotic species, we should develop policies which allow for the individual evaluation of each species, and we should develop guidelines for prioritising our efforts at controlling exotic species. We should ask questions such as, 'In what sense is this species native?', 'What impacts does it have on ecological and human resources?', 'What would be the costs (economic, ecological, etc.) of controlling or removing this species?', and 'What are the prospects of successfully controlling or removing this species?'

STRANGERS IN A STRANGE LAND

We offer the following tentative guidelines for prioritising efforts to control exotic species.

(1) The first priority should be the prevention of anthropogenic introduction (intentional or unintentional, direct or indirect) of species, especially into relatively natural areas. This is illustrated by the current efforts to prevent brown tree snakes from being introduced to other islands in the Pacific. Species introduced to a new area via humans tend not to be well-integrated members of ecological communities, they denude the naturalness of the area, and, in many cases, these new species may cause damage or degradation to other species and/or to the ecological community. Emphasis should be placed on protecting wild areas that have not been severely impacted by the anthropogenic introduction of exotic species. This will require severely limiting human activities in and access to these areas.

(2) The next priority should be given to the removal of recently introduced species where the prospects for success are high and the costs of removal (economic, ecological, costs to sentient life such as pain and death) are low.

(3) For species which have become well established, we should be cautious about heavy-handed management. Before engaging in a management project of a well-established species, we should ask, 'Is it clearly exotic by all criteria?', 'What impacts does it have on values such as ecosystem health, naturalness, biodiversity, animal welfare, economics, aesthetics, etc.?', and 'For each type of value, would the attempt to eliminate or control the exotic species do more or less to conserve that value than a laissez-faire policy?' We may decide to do nothing about well-established species if the species is so well established that we would be fighting a losing battle or if the species has become sufficiently 'naturalised' and is in the process of becoming native.

A good example that illustrates the problem of heavy-handed management is the attempted control of knapweed, particularly Russian knapweed (*Centuria ripens*) and spotted knapweed (*Centuria noculousia*). The roots of knapweed link themselves with the roots of native grasses via soil fungi, and this allows for knapweed to suck energy from native grasses. The end result is that knapweed flourishes, and native grasses diminish and ultimately die. For many years the solution to this problem has been to kill knapweed by poisoning or burning it. This, however, has failed to halt the spread of knapweed throughout the northern Rockies in spite of massive eradication efforts. Further, pesticides used to poison knapweed also poison native plants, and the constant eradication efforts can diminish the naturalness of the surrounding areas. The latest solution to the problem of knapweed has been to release exotic insects that eat and destroy the seed heads of knapweed (the insects are native to Eurasia – the native home of knapweed – and, as such, are 'native' pests of knapweed). While these insects might destroy 95% of the seeds of each knapweed plant, the remaining 5% of the thousands of seeds from each plant still survive. And these seeds still thrive because knapweed plants respond to the introduced insects by drawing more energy from the native grasses with which the knapweed roots are linked. Further, the exotic insects are now ubiquitous and harm native plants.[22] Fighting knapweed appears to be a losing battle, and, as the use of exotic insects shows, the 'solution' to the problem of knapweed might be no solution at all.

(4) Some of the most difficult cases with which we are faced might be those in which we must try to weigh different types of value against each other – for example, the value of sentient life (pigs, goats, etc.) against the ecological value or biodiversity represented by native plants. The case of the pigs in Hawaii discussed above illustrates this. This issue of killing exotic animals in order to protect native plants is often seen as an issue that divides environmentalists and animal activists. A friend who considers himself an environmentalist once said to us, 'I would have no problem killing a few animals in a situation like that in order to save some native plants'. Another friend who considers himself an animal advocate said, 'I would have no problem sacrificing a few plants in order to save those animals.' We would have a problem killing a few animals (or a few thousand animals as the case may be) in order to protect some native and endangered species of plants. *And* we would have a problem sacrificing the last members of a native and endangered species of plant in order to save a few animals. Multiple values such as biodiversity and animal welfare are all relevant. This means that there might be some genuine moral dilemmas, and on occasion there might be no good solution. We hope to avoid these difficult situations by appealing to (1), (2), and (3) above. However, a number of these cases do arise. In these cases we should avoid oversimplifying by focusing on only one value. By identifying different criteria for distinguishing between natives and exotics and identifying some of the different values at stake, we hope that new policies for managing exotic species can avoid some of the pitfalls of existing policies. However, it would be a mistake to believe that we will find absolute answers to these most difficult policy questions.

In conclusion, we suggest that in order to deal with the wide variety of cases involving exotic species of plants and animals, we must avoid absolutist policies which use only one criterion for determining whether a species is native or exotic. We also must create policies that are sufficiently flexible to acknowledge the multiplicity of values which are at stake. We hope that by recognising this the policies which govern the strangers in strange lands will themselves become less strange.

NOTES

We would like to thank the participants at The Practice of Restoring Native Ecosystems National Conference, sponsored by the National Arbor Day Foundation, where an earlier

STRANGERS IN A STRANGE LAND

version of this paper was presented. We also would like to thank Ned Hettinger for his extensive comments and suggestions. Finally, we wish to thank three anonymous referees and Kathy Darrow for their insightful comments.

[1] Exotic species are the second most destructive member of the evil quartet (following anthropogenic habitat destruction). In the United States, about forty percent of the threatened and endangered species listed on the U.S. Endangered Species Act are at risk primarily because of exotic species (Pimentel et al. 1999).
[2] See Seligsohn-Bennett (1990) for a discussion of some of the problems that have resulted from the National Park Service's reliance on the human introduction criterion in relation to 'exotic' ponies in Assateague National Seashore.
[3] T.W. Robinson, *Introduction, Spread, and Aereal Extent of Saltcedar* (Tamarix) *in the Western United States* (U.S. Geological Survey Professional Paper 491-A) (Washington, D.C.: U.S. Government Printing Office, 1965), cited in Rodman (1993).
[4] Interestingly enough, the degradation criterion raises the possibility that even natives could be classified as 'exotic' because they degrade their native landscapes. The United States National Park Service (1988) has policies for managing native species that cause degradation. We thank Ned Hettinger for pointing this out to us. See Garrot et al. (1993) for a discussion of how overabundance of a species – whether native or exotic – can cause ecological and biological degradation.
[5] See Putnam (1975) and Searle (1958).
[6] Gert (1995) points out that this view need not be seen as a radical departure from the classical view. It may be possible for one to give a classical analysis in terms of necessary and sufficient conditions in which one of the conditions is a long disjunct or a long conjunct. For example, 'X is a dog *iff* $((A\&B\&C)/(A\&B\&D)/(A\&C\&D)...)$'.
[7] B.J. Garrett (1988) points out that we can distinguish between the thesis that an identity statement is *indeterminate* as a result of vagueness and the more radical thesis that an identity relation is one of *degree*. Thus, one might wish to maintain that the claim that a species is native may be of indeterminate truth value while denying that nativity is a matter of degree.
[8] See Callicott (1996) for an interesting discussion of how people can be native and can become naturalised within a human community.
[9] See Jackson (1996) and Snyder (1990) for discussions of how people might become native to a place.
[10] As Holland (1995) argues, it is problematic to derive philosophical accounts of what nature is – in this case in terms of native and exotic species – from scientific accounts. We agree. We discuss invasion biology to show how philosophical accounts of the different criteria for nativity and extocality already are at work within the science of invasion biology.
[11] See also Groves and Burdon (1986), Drake et al. (1989), and Hengeveld (1989).
[12] Westman (1990) discusses how plant species with generalised traits may be already *preadapted* for the final stage of integration when these species first colonise a new area.
[13] According to Bright (1998, 25), about ten percent of the newly introduced exotics in an area will establish breeding populations, and about ten percent of these breeding populations will become highly invasive and cause degradation. This is known as the 'tens rule'.
[14] While Mills et al. (1994) count 139 exotic species in the Great Lakes, five more species recently have been discovered in this region.
[15] See Graber (1995) for a discussion of some of the management problems caused by

competing values such as these.

[16] As mentioned above, some people dispute this analogy and the policy implications that can be drawn it. See the special issue of *Environmental Values* **4** (1995) devoted to philosophical discussions of ecosystem health.

[17] While the new arrival of exotic species in an area might immediately increase species biodiversity in that area, over the long term exotic species tend to lead to decreased biodiversity because they tend to homogenise landscapes (Hettinger 2001). Bright (1998, 17) calls this 'evolution in reverse'.

[18] In addition to arguing against the killing of exotic animals by appealing to sentience or rights, animal activists sometimes also appeal to ecosystem health by arguing that in some cases exotic animals are not harmful to native species because exotics may be replacing native species that have already been extirpated from an area (Clifton 1991). Thus, according to such activists, the health of the ecosystem now depends on these exotic replacements..

[19] According to Pimentel et al. (1999), the economic benefits of exotic species in the United States – estimated to be $800 billion annually – exceed the economic damages caused by exotics species.

[20] Peretti (1998) argues that the 'nativist' trend in conservation biology to regard natives as good and exotics as bad may be rooted in xenophobic and racist attitudes in people. We lack the space here to discuss this. See also Evans (1998). See Pollan (1994) for a discussion of what he calls the unfair stereotyping of exotics.

[21] And in some cases a value singled out is attached to a single defining criterion. An example is this is 'The Nasty Necessity: Eradicating Exotics' where Stanley Temple (1990) argues for killing exotics solely because they threaten biological and ecological diversity.

[22] We thank George Nickas from Wilderness Watch for this knapweed example.

REFERENCES

Barela, Tsgt. Timothy P. 1993. 'Massacre on Guam', *Airman* **37**: 28–31.

Botkin, Daniel B. 1990. *Discordant Harmonies: A New Ecology for the Twenty-first Century*. Oxford: Oxford University Press.

Bright, Chris 1998. *Life Out of Bounds: Bioinvasion in a Borderless World*. New York: W. W. Norton & Company.

Cahen, Harley 1988. 'Against the Moral Considerability of Ecosystems', *Environmental Ethics* **10**: 195–216.

Callicott, J. Baird 1991. 'The Wilderness Idea Revisited: The Sustainable Development Alternative', *The Environmental Professional* **13**: 235–247.

Callicott, J. Baird 1996. 'Do Deconstructive Ecology and Sociobiology Undermine Leopold's Land Ethic?', *Environmental Ethics* **18**: 353–372.

Carr, Archie 1994. *A Naturalist in Florida: A Celebration of Eden*, Marjorie Harris Carr (ed). New Haven: Yale University Press.

Carroll, Scott P., and Hugh Dingle 1996. 'The Biology of Post-Invasion Events', *Biological Conservation* **78**: 207–214.

Clifton, Merritt 1991. 'Feral Animals: Alien Menace?', *The Animals Agenda* **XI**: 16–22.

Costanza, Robert, Bryan G. Norton, and Benjamin D. Haskell (eds) 1992. *Ecosystem Health: New Goals for Environmental Management*. Washington, D.C.: Island Press.

Devine, Robert 1998. *Alien Invasion: America's Battle with Non-Native Animals and Plants*. Washington, D.C.: National Geographic Society.

Diamond, Jared 1987. 'Reflections on goals and the relationship between theory and practice', in William R. Jordan III, Michael E. Gilpin, and John D. Aber (eds) *Restoration Ecology: A synthetic approach to ecological research*. Cambridge: Cambridge University Press.

Diamond, Jared 1989. 'Overview of Recent Extinctions', in David Western and Mary C. Pearl (eds) *Conservation for the Twenty-first Century*. New York: Oxford University Press.

Drake, James E. et al. (eds) 1989. *Biological Invasions: A Global Perspective*. New York: John Wiley.

Dyer, Deborah R. 1996. 'The Role of Exotic Species Within Ecosystem Management', *Environs* **19**: 75–86.

Elliot, Robert 1997. *Faking Nature: the ethics of environmental restoration*. London: Routledge.

Evans, Paul 1998. 'Response to Peretti, "Nativism and Nature"', *Environmental Values* **7**: 198–200.

Evernden, Neil 1993. *The Natural Alien: Humankind and Environment*, 2nd ed. Toronto: University of Toronto Press.

Garrett, B.J. 1988. 'Vagueness and Identity', *Analysis* **48**: 130–4.

Garrott, Robert A., P.J. White, and Callie A. Vanderbilt White 1993. 'Overabundance: An Issue for Conservation Biologists?', *Conservation Biology* **7**: 946–9.

Gert, Heather 1995. 'Alternative Analysis', *The Southern Journal of Philosophy* **33**: 31–7.

Graber, David M. 1995. 'Resolute Biocentrism: The Dilemma of Wilderness in National Parks', in Michael E. Soulé and Gary Lease (eds) *Reinventing Nature? Responses to Postmodern Deconstruction*. Washington, D.C.: Island Press.

Graham, Russell W. 1988. 'The Role of Climatic Change in the Design of Biological Reserves: The Paleoecological Perspective for Conservation Biology', *Conservation Biology* **2**: 391–4.

Groves, Rob H., and Jeremy James Burdon 1986. *The Ecology of Biological Invasions*. Cambridge: Cambridge University Press.

Hagen, Joel B. 1992. *An Entangled Bank: The Origins of Ecosystem Ecology*. New Brunswick: Rutgers University Press.

Hengeveld R. 1989. *Dynamics of Biological Invasions*. New York: Chapman and Hall.

Hettinger, Ned 2001. 'Exotic Species, Naturalisation, and Biological Nativism', *Environmental Values* **10**: 193–224.

Holland, Alan 1995. 'The Use and Abuse of Ecological Concepts in Environmental Ethics', *Biodiversity and Conservation* **4**: 812–826.

Hunter, Malcolm L., Jr. 1996. *Fundamentals of Conservation Biology*. Cambridge, MA: Blackwell.

Hunter, Malcom L., Jr.; George L. Jacobson, Jr.; and Thompson Webb, III 1988. 'Paleoecology and the Course-Filter Approach to Maintaining Biological Diversity', *Conservation Biology* **2**: 375–385.

Jackson, Wes. 1996. *Becoming Native to This Place*. Washington, D.C.: Counterpoint.

Jamieson, Dale 1995. 'Ecosystem Health: Some Preventive Medicine', *Environmental Values* **4**: 333–344.

Kingsland, Sharon E. 1995. *Modeling Nature: Episodes in the History of Population Ecology,* 2nd ed. Chicago: The University of Chicago Press.

Lack, David 1983. *Darwin's Finches*. Cambridge: Cambridge University Press.
Leopold, Aldo 1949. *A Sand County Almanac: And Sketches Here and There*. London: Oxford University Press.
McIntosh, Robert P. 1985. *The Background of Ecology: Concept and Theory*. Cambridge:Cambridge University Press.
Mills, Edward L., Joseph H. Leach, James T. Carlton, and Carol L. Secor 1994. 'Exotic Species and the Integrity of the Great Lakes: Lessons from the past', *BioScience* **44**: 666–676.
Moller, Henrik 1996. 'Lessons for Invasion Biology from Social Insects', *Biological Conservation* **78**: 125–142.
Moriarty, Paul Veatch, and Mark Woods 1997. 'Hunting ≠ Predation', *Environmental Ethics* **19**: 391–404.
Moyle, Peter B., and Theo Light 1996. 'Biological Invasions of Fresh Water: Empirical Rules and Assembly Theory', *Biological Conservation* **78**: 149–161.
Nabhan, Gary Paul 1995. 'Cultural Parallax in Viewing North American Habitats', in Michael E. Soulé and Gary Lease (eds) *Reinventing Nature? Responses to Postmodern Deconstruction*. Washington, D.C.: Island Press.
National Park Service, U.S. Department of the Interior 1988. *Management Policies*.
Noss, Reed F., and Allen Y. Cooperrider 1994. *Saving Nature's Legacy: Protecting and Restoring Biodiversity*. Washington, D.C.: Island Press.
Peretti, Jonah H. 1998. 'Nativism and Nature: Rethinking Biological Invasion', *Environmental Values* **7**: 183–192.
Pickett, S.T.A., and P.S. White (eds) 1985. *The Ecology of Natural Disturbance and Patch Dynamics*. San Diego: Academic Press.
Pickett, S.T.A., V. Thomas Parker, and Peggy L. Fiedler 1992. 'The New Paradigm in Ecology: Implications for Conservation Above the Species Level', in Peggy L. Fiedler and Subodh K. Jain (eds) *Conservation Biology: The Theory and Practice of Nature Conservation Preservation and Management*. New York: Chapman and Hall.
Pimentel, D., L. Lack, R. Zuniga, and D. Morrison 1999. *Environmental and Economic Costs Associated with Non-indigenous Species in the United States*. Presentation at the American Association for the Advancement of Science, Anaheim, CA.
Pollan, Michael 1994. 'Against Nativism', *New York Times Magazine* May 15: 52–5.
Primack, Richard B. 1998. *Essentials of Conservation Biology*, 2nd ed. Sunderland, MA: Sinauer Associates.
Putman, Hillary 1975. 'The Analytic and the Synthetic', *Mind and Language: Philosophical Papers*, Volume 2. New York: Cambridge University Press.
Regan, Tom 1983. *The Case for Animal Rights*. Berkeley: University of California Press.
Rodman, John 1993. 'Restoring Nature: Natives and Exotics', in Jane Bennett and William Chaloupka (eds) *In the Nature of Things: Language, Politics, and the Environment*. Minneapolis: University of Minnesota Press.
Rolston, Holmes, III 1994. *Conserving Natural Value*. New York: Columbia University Press.
Royte, Elizabeth 1995. 'On the Brink: Hawaii's Vanishing Species', *National Geographic* **188** September: 2–37.
Scherer, Donald 1994. 'Between Theory and Practice: Some Thoughts on Motivations Behind Restoration', *Restoration and Management Notes* **11**: 31–4.
Schmitz, Don 1997. 'Call for Exotic Species Task Force', *Science* **275**: 915.
Searle, John 1958. 'Proper Names', *Mind* **67**: 166–173.

Seligsohn-Bennett, Kyla 1990. 'Mismanaging Endangered and 'Exotic' Species in the National Parks', *Environmental Law* **20**: 415–440.

Shrader-Frechette, Kristin S., and Earl D. McCoy 1993. *Method in Ecology: Strategies for Conservation*. Cambridge: Cambridge University Press.

Singer, Peter 1990. *Animal Liberation*, 2nd ed. New York: Avon Books.

Snyder, Gary. 1990. *The Practice of the Wild*. New York: North Point Press.

Soulé, Michael E. 1990. 'The Onslaught of Alien Species, and Other Challenges in the Coming Decades', *Conservation Biology* **4**: 233–9.

Spurr, Stephen H. 1980. 'Wilderness Concepts', *Idaho Law Review* **16**: 439–448.

Temple, Stanley A. 1990. 'The Nasty Necessity: Eradicating Exotics', *Conservation Biology* **4**: 113–5.

Throop, William 2000. 'Eradicating the Aliens: Restoration and Exotic Species', in William Throop (ed) *Environmental Restoration: Ethics, Theory, and Practice*. Amherst, NY: Humanity Books.

Townsend, Colin R. 1991. 'Exotic Species Management and the Need for a Theory of Invasion Biology', *New Zealand Journal of Ecology* **15**: 1–3.

Vermeij, Geerat J. 1996. 'An Agenda for Invasion Biology', *Biological Conservation* **78**: 3–9.

Wade, Steven A. 1995. 'Stemming the Tide: A Plea for New Exotic Species Legislation', *Journal of Land Use & Environmental Law* **10**: 343–370.

Westman, Walter E. 1990. 'Park Management of Exotic Plant Species: Problems and Issues', *Conservation Biology* **4**: 251–260.

Wilson, Edward O. 1992. *The Diversity of Life*. Cambridge, MA: Harvard University Press.

Woods, Mark forthcoming. *Rethinking Wilderness*. Peterborough, Ontario: Broadview Press.

Worster, Donald 1994. *Nature's Economy: A History of Ecological Ideas*, 2nd ed. Cambridge: Cambridge University Press.

Wuerthner, George 1996. 'Alien Invasion', *National Parks* **70**: 32–5.

Nativism and Nature: Rethinking Biological Invasion

Jonah H. Peretti

INTRODUCTION

Environmentalism is a heterogeneous mix of science, politics, ecology and culture. Environmental values are inextricably linked to these diverse influences and vitalise what is perhaps the most exciting movement of our time. This paper begins at the messy interface of conservation biology and environmental ideology, and attempts to illuminate the social and political implications of environmental science. Resisting the temptation to accept science as value-free, this analysis highlights the political and ethical dimensions of conservation biologists' efforts to conserve nature and protect biodiversity. The central contention of this essay is that nativism in the biological sciences raises troubling scientific, political and moral issues that merit discussion and debate on a broad scale.

THE PROBLEM OF BIOLOGICAL INVASION

Ecologists and especially conservation biologists have become keenly aware of the ecological damage that can result when alien species invade new territories (Soulé 1990, Drake et al. 1989, Groves and Burdon 1986, Macdonald et al. 1986, Mooney and Drake 1986). The protection and restoration of native species is one of the major foci of conservationists' attempts to protect biodiversity. Biological nativism pervades the environmental movement. Native plant societies have sprung up across the United States, encouraging the exclusive use of indigenous plants in urban gardens (Pollan 1994). Since 1963, the United States national parks have attempted to follow the Leopold Report's directive to re-create original ecological conditions – including the restoration and protection of native species (Wilson 1992, Chase 1987). The popular press dramatises biological invasions, frightening and entertaining the public with African 'killer' bees, voracious cane toads, and other nefarious species (*Science* 1990, Edwards 1990).

Despite the considerable attention given to the problems of biological invasion, ecologists and wildlife managers have not developed satisfactory methods for dealing with the onslaught of alien species. Eliminating them has proved impossible in the overwhelming majority of cases (Brown 1989, Chase 1987). I will identify some issues and problems that thwart conservationists' attempts to manage biological invasions. These obstacles suggest not only that ecologists and conservationists will have to adapt and update their methods of managing biological invasion, but also that they question the political and ethical supposition implicit in their approach. Current trends in ecological theory (Hengeveld 1989, Fox and Morrow 1981), the increasing spread of alien species (Soulé 1990, Drake 1989), and current debates and ambiguities around defining what is natural (Soulé and Lease 1995, Bennett and Chaloupka 1993, Cronon 1995), all indicate a period of turmoil for ecological science and politics. This turmoil is often focused on the status and definition of alien species. Innovative, cross-disciplinary work on biological invasion is central to the further development of ecological theory and practice.

IDENTIFYING NATURAL, NATIVE SPECIES

The words 'native' and 'natural' are closely linked. The Latin 'nascor' is the original root for several English words including native, natural, nation, and natality (OLD, OED). When ecologists use the word native, the term retains the flavour of the Latin root. Protecting nat-ure is usually equated with protecting nat-ive flora and fauna. This is done in the interests of preserving life (nat-ality), and often occurs within nat-ional parks. Nature, natives, natality, and nation have been important, interconnected concepts for environmentalists and ecologists. The association of native species with what is natural has fuelled conservationists' interest in biological invasion. The task of identifying, protecting, and restoring native species, and the corollary task of identifying and eliminating alien species, has become a major branch of conservation biology.

How do scientists distinguish between the native and the alien, the natural and the artificial? They are usually forced to rely on partial natural history records. In South Africa, for example, there are 984 documented alien species (Well et al. 1986). This figure is misleading, however, because in 104 of these cases, the origin of the alien species is in doubt. That is to say, in more than 10% of these cases, the 'alien' species might actually be a native. If the natural history record is incomplete, there is no reliable ecological or biological method that can distinguish between aliens and natives. Furthermore, it is unclear how long a species needs to be established in a location before it is considered native. Is a species 'naturalised' in 100 years, 1,000 years, or 10,000 years? The distinctions are arbitrary and unscientific. These factors suggests that the study of biological invasion does not rest on a rigorous scientific foundation.

Although most ecologists agree that alien species can have damaging effects, there is little agreement on what constitutes an alien or how aliens can be identified. Ecologists and managers usually focus on aliens that become 'especially prominent in an economic or nuisance sense' (Groves and Burdon 1986). This draws attention to particularly damaging, and usually atypical, invaders (Hengeveld 1989). This bias limits the possibility for a broader understanding of species migration and biological invasion. Attempting to keep nature 'pure,' 'wild,' and alien-free, may be impractical, impossible, or even undesirable.

In the interests of promoting debate, I juxtapose the nativism of conservation biology with the ecological theory that is currently in vogue in that discipline. Paradoxically, many conservation biologists emphasise the importance and pervasiveness of species migration while maintaining a nativist ideology. By exploring this contradiction, I hope to promote dialogue that will encourage environmentalists to develop an ecological framework that includes sensitivity to the cultural, moral, and political dimensions of ecological science.

HUMANS AND NATIVE NATURE

Anthropogenic changes to natural areas further complicate the determination of what is natural and native. The introduction of alien species is usually associated with anthropogenic disturbance and human migration (Heywood 1989). European colonial expansion, for example, distributed flora and fauna at an unprecedented rate (Crosby 1986). The colonial Europeans are often blamed for the degradation of the ecology of the Americas, Africa, and Asia. This attitude is reflected in U.S. National Park Policy. The 1963 Leopold Committee decreed that:

> The goal of managing the National Parks ... should be to preserve, or where necessary to recreate, the ecologic scene as viewed by the first European visitors. As part of this scene, native species of wild animals should be present in maximum variety and reasonable abundance (quoted in Wilson 1992).

It is assumed that Europeans found the Americas in a pristine, natural state. The goal of management is to protect and recreate native nature, before it was altered, invaded, and degraded by European culture and European biota.

This perspective often relies on an idealised and patronising attitude toward Native Americans (Hecht and Cockburn 1990, Chase 1987). Many anthropologists and archaeologists challenge the view that Native Americans lived in perfect harmony with nature. Rather, they assert that Native American hunters were responsible for the extinction of the bulk of the Pleistocene megafauna (Chase 1987). By the time Europeans arrived, most of these native species had already gone extinct. Native Americans also altered their environment in beneficial ways. In Yellowstone, Native Americans set fires that interrupted serial succession. This promoted 'more varied vegetation' and supported 'more diverse wildlife' (ibid.). Native Americans are neither saints nor villains. Like colonial Europeans, native people and aboriginal people alter and influence the natural environments they inhabit.

The influence of native people on nature makes it difficult to maintain the thesis that European colonialists are the sole reason that native nature is threatened. One scientist has remarked that:

> [t]he botanical traveler soon becomes aware that there is scarcely a region in the

NATIVISM AND NATURE

world where the vegetation has not been disturbed to some degree by man's activities, usually leading to the introduction of alien species ... Ellenburg (1979) observes that the reason he traveled to Peru and other tropical countries was to study 'real nature' but after several months of field work he could not fail to discover traces of man's impact there too, even in the Amazonian rain forest area (Heywood 1989).

Humans have existed with nature for tens of thousands of years. If 'real nature' is human-free, it becomes questionable if 'real nature' even exists. People have been moving biota for thousands of years on five continents. This biological mixing has intensified in recent years due to the globalisation of cultures. In this milieu, it becomes extremely difficult to identify the natural, native, or original conditions of an ecosystem. These factors, combined with current trends in ecological theory, have complicated conservation biology's stated task of protecting biodiversity.

POPULATION AND CONSERVATION BIOLOGISTS REJECT THE BALANCE-OF-NATURE PERSPECTIVE

In the 1970s papers began to appear that challenged community and ecosystem balance-of-nature paradigms. This new scholarship asserted that '[c]hange is without any determinable direction and goes on forever, never reaching a point of stability' (Worster 1993). Population biologists and more recently conservation biologists, highlighted data suggesting that 'species move freely on all geographical scales' (Hengeveld 1989). This theory 'posits that the collection of species that exists in a particular place is a matter of historical accident and species-specific, autecological requirements' (Soulé 1990). Specialisation has been shown to occur haphazardly, and in the absence of co-evolution (Fox and Morrow 1981, Knight and Macdonald 1991). Nature is seen as a chaotic, random, and structurally open system. Conservation and population biologists tend to view species migration as natural and normal. Conservation biologists emphasise the importance of biodiversity and have identified free species migration as a central element in preventing species extinctions.

This theoretical shift in certain biological disciplines challenges most of the previous work on biological invasion. Biological invasion has traditionally been conceptualised in terms of 'outside' invaders, that infiltrate 'closed,' 'co-evolved,' and 'interdependent' ecosystems. Aliens are damaging because they disturb the balance of an ecosystem. For traditional ecology, species spend centuries passing through serial succession as they evolve to form highly mutualistic climax communities. A hypothetical example of such mutualism is easy to imagine. A species of bird evolves together with a plant to create an efficient seed dispersal system. An alien bird migrates to this ecosystem and out competes the native bird. The alien bird has not evolved with the native plant so its digestive system does not facilitate the germination of the native plant's seeds. The dispersal system is destroyed and the native plant faces extinction.

Recent conservation biology has de-emphasised these types of stories and tends to focus on counter-examples that foreground the importance of species migration. These theorists suggest that frequent invasions are a natural, normal process. Hengeveld (1989) uses the Holocene tree invasion in Europe as an example. The migration began approximately 13,000 BP (before present) and the trees had spread to over half of Europe by 1000 BP. These rapidly migrating trees significantly altered the biological systems that they encountered. Hengeveld concludes that in 'such ecologically unstable conditions selection can only act against the formation of species-specific co-adaptations'. According to Hengeveld, species evolve in unstable conditions that promote tolerance to biological invasions and changing species compositions.

Does this mean that wildlife managers should let menaces such as feral pig and invasive goat populations skyrocket? Certainly not. No one doubts that there are dramatic examples of alien species doing grave environmental damage to an ecosystem. But if we take recent developments in conservation and population biology seriously, we must call into question whether all invader species should be eliminated or controlled. The study of biological invasion needs more effective ways to determine which invader species are ecologically damaging, and which are neutral or beneficial. Indeed, managers may even attempt to facilitate migration in some cases. As species migration is limited by human development, it becomes increasingly difficult for species to migrate naturally. The Wildlands Project's long term goal of connecting wild areas with wildlife corridors is one example of an emerging style of management (Foreman 1993). I will discuss other approaches that encourage migration and mixing in the conclusion of this paper.

THE DISTURBING HISTORICAL LEGACY OF PURIST BIOLOGICAL NATIVISM

Compelling reasons to challenge biological nativism originate not only from within the biological sciences. Although it is impossible to prove an essential link between particular forms of scientific knowledge and the societal context from which they emerged, the purism of biological nativism has historically been associated with fascist and apartheid cultures and governments. Pre-World War II Germany, for example, saw the rise of a natural gardening movement 'founded on nationalistic and racist ideas' (Pollan 1994). Indeed,

> under National Socialism, the mania for natural gardening and native plants became government policy. A team working under Heinrich Himmler set forth 'Rules of the Design of the Landscape,' which stipulated a 'close-to-nature' style and the exclusive use of native plants (ibid.).

NATIVISM AND NATURE

Garden architect Willy Lange was the first German to popularise the nature garden. 'Lange's concept was a mixture of science-oriented design ideas and nationalistic, *volkish* thinking' (Groening and Wolschke-Bulmahn 1989). During this period, 'the subordination of the garden to the landscape by the use of native shrubs and trees became an ideological doctrine' (Groening and Wolschke-Bulmahn 1992). Strict biological nativism was compatible with the Nazi's anti-cosmopolitanism. Ideologically, politically, and ecologically, the Nazis sought to prevent mixing and to purify categories. They attempted to purify nation and nature, by eliminating people and biota that were supposedly not native.

A more recent and subtle example of this can be found in South Africa in the 1980s. This is where the initial proposal for the Scientific Committee on Problems of the Environment's (SCOPE) invasive species project was proposed. 'South African scientists were instrumental in preparing the project proposal that was put to SCOPE for approval in 1982' (Macdonald et al. 1986). Since the early 1980s, SCOPE has been influential in shaping how biological invasion is studied. South African scientists have had a great deal of influence over the SCOPE project. They have been over-represented at international SCOPE conferences on biological invasion and have published a disproportionate number of articles on the subject (Drake et al. 1989). Why are scientists from South Africa especially concerned with biological invasion? The answer may be similar to the Nazi proclivity for the nature garden. Like Nazism, apartheid thinking is concerned with separating the pure from the impure. Even anti-racist scientists living in an apartheid culture may be influenced by this sort of purist, xenophobic, and racist way of thinking. It is not surprising that SCOPE's hard-line biological nativism has roots in South Africa.

The Nazi nature garden and apartheid South Africa are cautionary historical examples for the would-be nativist zealot. As xenophobic anti-immigration laws such as California's proposition 187 (1994) spread across the United States and Western Europe, environmentalists must be careful not to reinforce a politically conservative nativist agenda. Although environmental purism is not inherently racist, there are compelling arguments that nativist purism is undesirable in all spheres – politically, culturally and ecologically. Nature and society are both complex and damaged systems. To protect biological life and create a better society we must move beyond simplistic, purist responses to ecological and social crises.

THE BEGINNINGS OF 'MIXOECOLOGY' OR 'RECOMBINANT ECOLOGY'

Ecologists are faced with increasingly complex assemblages of native and non-native species. Soulé has predicted that a 'new ecological discipline will develop to deal with the interactions within these new, biogeographically complex assemblages. The field might be called 'recombinant ecology' or 'mixoecology' and it will offer manifold opportunities for research' (Soulé 1990). This field will not begin with the premise that alien species are bad. Instead, it will assume that communities are biogeographically diverse and attempt to determine why some species mix better than others. Completely 'eradicating' alien species is impossible in the majority of cases and bio-control campaigns are always a costly drain on resources. To avoid these problems, mixoecology will not strive to eliminate mixing, but rather to use limited economic resources to help mixed ecosystems thrive. This may require the elimination of certain invasive species, as well as the possible introduction of species into empty niches (ibid.).

Threats to nature should not be underestimated. The environmental crisis often provokes a feeling of hopelessness and a longing to 'turn back the clock.' Although understandable, hopelessness and nostalgia do little to mitigate the continuing degradation of nature. Ecologist James H. Brown provides us with useful advice:

> It has become imperative that [as] ecologists, evolutionary biologists, and biogeographers ... we use our expertise as scientists not for the futile effort to hold back the clock and preserve some romantic idealized version of a pristine natural world, but for a rational attempt to understand the disturbed ecosystems that we have created and to manage them to support both humans and wildlife (Brown 1989).

Brown is not advocating putting human interests before environmental interests. Instead, he is asking us to recognise the complex interactions that humans have with a natural world that is almost universally characterised by anthropogenic disturbance and cosmopolitan species composition. It will require creativity and ingenuity to protect nature in this troubling milieu.

Fortunately, nature often exhibits surprising resiliency. Diverse assemblages often exist in the most unlikely places and include native and alien species. The native korhaan bird in South Africa effectively disperses the seeds of the alien *A. cyclops* in a highly efficient, and ecologically beneficial dispersal system (Knight and Macdonald 1991). The Hutchenson Forest in New Jersey is a biodiverse collection of new and old world species (Botkin 1990). In the San Luis Valley in southern Colorado, Chicano farmers have developed agricultural techniques that produce food for humans and create wetlands and habitat for hundreds of native and non-native species (Pena and Gallegos 1993). These are just a few of the many locations where native and alien species coexist with some degree of harmony. Why do these assemblages work? Investigating this question could potentially lead to the development of new paradigms in ecological theory and wildlife management. Such paradigms could help us understand and manage the damaged, cosmopolitan nature that our global, cosmopolitan society has helped produce.

NATIVISM AND NATURE

CONCLUSION

This paper is meant to provoke the following question: If peaceful coexistence in a multicultural society is a good goal for humans, why not for other species? The idea of purity is central to current debates in environmental science, politics, and values. What sort of nature should environmentalists admire, protect, and value? The way that nature is represented by biologists is of tremendous philosophical importance to environmentalists. Do biologists think nature is 'red in tooth and claw,' or do they describe a harmoniously mutualistic community of species? Do they characterise nature as a system with frequent migration and cosmopolitan species composition, or is nature better described as being composed of closed, co-evolved communities of native species? These questions are germane to more than just the scientific understanding of flora and fauna. They are at the heart of environmentalist conceptions of humans' interactions with each other and the natural world.

It is unclear whether the majority of ecologists will embrace a version of mixoecology. Although there is some movement in that direction, many environmental scientist are committed to the idea of pure, 'native' nature. Both nativist and mixoecologist camps are composed of progressive individuals determined to protect the earth from further degradation. This paper seeks to expand this scientific debate by inviting social scientists and philosophers to critically engage nativist discourse in the biological sciences. Questioning purist pieties may protect modern environmentalists from reproducing the xenophobic and racist attitudes that have plagued nativist biology in the past. It will require a broader and more inclusive debate to establish the scientific, political, and moral implications of nativist biology.

REFERENCES

Bennett, J. and Chaloupka, W. (eds) 1993. *In the Nature of Things: Language, Politics and the Environment*. University of Minnesota Press.
Botkin, D. 1990. *Discordant Harmonies: A New Ecology for the 21st Century*. Oxford: Oxford University Press.
Brown, J. 1989. 'Patterns, modes, and extents of invasion by vertebrates', in J.A. Drake et al. (eds), *Biological Invasions: A Global Perspective*, pp.85-105. New York: John Wiley.
Chase, A. 1987. *Playing God in Yellowstone*. New York: Harcourt Brace and Company.
Cronon, W. (ed.) 1995. *Uncommon Ground: Toward Reinventing Nature*. New York and London: W.W. Norton.
Crosby, A. 1986. *Ecological Imperialism: The Biological Expansion of Europe, 900-1900*. New York: Cambridge University Press.
Drake, J.A., et al. (eds) 1989. *Biological Invasions: A Global Perspective*. New York: John Wiley.

Edwards, P. 1990. 'Way down under, it's revenge of the (yech!) cane toads', *Smithsonian* **21**(7): 139.
Foreman, D. (ed). 1993. *The Wild Earth*. Special issue on the Wildlands Project.
Fox, L.R., and Morrow, P.A. 1981. 'Specialization: species property or local phenomenon?' *Science* **211**(27 February): 887-893.
Groening G. and Wolschke-Bulmahn, J. 1989. 'Changes in the philosophy of garden architecture in the 20th century and their impact upon the social and spatial environment', *Journal of Garden History* **9**(2): 53-70.
Groening G. and Wolschke-Bulmahn, J. 1992. 'The ideology of the nature garden: nationalistic trends in garden design in Germany during the early twentieth century', *Journal of Garden History* **12**(1): 73-80.
Groves, R.H. and Burdon, J.J.. 1986. *The Ecology of Biological Invasions*. Cambridge: Cambridge University Press.
Hecht, S. and Cockburn, A. 1990. *The Fate of the Forest*. New York: Harper Perennial.
Hengeveld, R. 1989. *Dynamics of Biological Invasions*. London and New York: Chapman and Hall.
Heywood, V.H. 1989. 'Patterns, extents and modes of invasion by terrestrial plants', in J.A. Drake et al. (eds), *Biological Invasions: A Global Perspective*, pp.31-51. New York: John Wiley.
Knight, R., and Macdonald, I.A.W. 1991. 'Acacias and Koraans: an artificially assembled seed dispersal system', *S.-Afr. Tydskr. Plantk* **57**(4): 220-225.
Macdonald, I.A.W., Kruger, J.J. and Ferrar, A.A. (eds) 1986. *The Ecology and Management of Biological Invasions in Southern Africa*. Cape Town, Oxford and New York: Oxford University Press.
Mooney, H.A., and Drake, J. (eds) 1986. *Ecology of Biological Invasions of North America and Hawaii*. New York: Springer-Verlag.
The Oxford English Dictionary.
The Oxford Latin Dictionary.
Pena, D. and Gallegos, J. 1993. 'Nature and chicanos in southern Colorado', in R. Bullard (ed.), *Confronting Environmental Racism: Voices from the Grassroots*, pp.141-160. Boston: South End Press.
Pollan, M. 1994. 'Against nativism', *The New York Times Magazine*, May 15: 52-55.
Science 1990. How African are 'Killer' Bees? *Science* **250**(Nov. 2, no. 4981): 628.
Soulé, M.E. 1990. 'The onslaught of alien species, and other challenges in the coming decades', *Conservation Biology* **4**(3): 233-239.
Soulé, M.E. and Lease, G. (eds) 1995. *Reinventing Nature? Responses to Postmodern Deconstruction*. San Francisco: Island Press.
Well, M.J. et al. 1986. 'The history of invasive alien plants in southern africa', in I.A.W. Macdonald, J.J. Kruger and A.A. Ferrar (eds), *The Ecology and Management of Biological Invasions in Southern Africa,* pp.21-36. Cape Town, Oxford and New York: Oxford University Press.
Wilson, A. 1992. *The Culture of Nature*. Cambridge, MA and Oxford: Blackwell.
Worster, D. 1993. 'Organic, economic, and chaotic ecology', in C. Merchant (ed.), *Major Problems in American Environmental History*, pp.465-478. Lexington, Massachusetts and Toronto: D.C. Heath and Company.

Exotic Species, Naturalisation, and Biological Nativism

Ned Hettinger

'Invasive alien species ... homogenise the diversity of creation. ... Weeds – slowly, silently, almost invisibly, but steadily – spread all around us until, literally encircled, we can no longer turn our backs. The invasion is now our problem, our battle, our enemy. ... [We must] act now and act as one [in order to] beat this silent enemy.'
Former U.S. Interior Secretary Bruce Babbitt (1998)

'I just hate them. They are genetically deviant miscreants that have no rightful place on this planet. We all have to be a part of this war on weeds.'
Former Montana Governor Marc Racicot (Associated Press 1999)

'It's hard to imagine a New England roadside without its tawny day lilies and Queen Anne's lace, yet both these species are aliens marked for elimination. ... Could it be these plants have actually improved the New England landscape, adding to its diversity and beauty? Shouldn't there be a statute of limitations on their alien status?'
Harper's editor Michael Pollan (1994)

The presence of exotic species has become one of the major ecological evils that environmentalists are called upon to resist. Environmentally-sensitive people are waging war on flora and fauna judged to be exotic. Nature lovers poison hillsides covered with leafy spurge (*Euphorbia esula*) and shoot mountain goats (*Oreamnos americanus*) from cliffs. What are we to make of such policies and the attitudes that underlie them?

It is well-known that the spread of exotic species has caused – and continues to cause – significant environmental degradation, including extinction of native species and massive human influence on natural systems. What is less clear, however, is how we are to conceptualise exotic species. Consider, for example, the U.S. National Park Service's exotics policy. It requires treating mountain goats migrating south out of the Absoroka Mountains into Yellowstone National Park as exotics to be removed because they are descendants of human-introduced populations. The policy also requires that if mountain goats move into the Park from the west, they be treated as welcome natives because these goats come from a population not established by humans (Wagner 1995: 10). Or consider the wild pigs (*Sus scrofa*) in the Hawaiian rainforest, whose ancestors were brought to Hawaii by Polynesians perhaps 1500 years ago.[1] Are they still an exotic species or have they 'naturalised' despite constituting an ongoing threat to the native biota in this extinction capital of the world? One commentator put his finger on the problem of understanding exotic species when he said, 'The terms "exotic" and "native" ... are ... about as ambiguous as any in our conservation lexicon (except perhaps "natural")' (Noss 1990: 242).

Nor is it clear what justifies a negative evaluation of exotic species. In human affairs, nativist policies favouring native inhabitants over immigrants are morally troubling. Are biological nativists who eschew planting alien species and who eradicate those they encounter unwittingly supporting a xenophobic prejudice that is very much in evidence in many countries' treatment of immigrants? Is the assumption that exotics are bad and damaging an unfair stereotype that ignores the variety of exotic species? Are there good reasons for opposing exotics that are human-introduced or is such opposition mere misanthropy?

This essay sifts through the mix of biological theorising and philosophical evaluation that constitutes this controversy over understanding, evaluating, and responding to exotic species. I propose a precising definition of exotics as any species significantly foreign to an ecological assemblage, whether or not the species causes damage, is human introduced, or arrives from some other geographical location. My hope is to keep separate the distinct strands typically woven into this concept while still capturing most of our fundamental intuitions about exotics. In section I, I critically examine several proposals for distinguishing between native and exotic species and advance an ecological account whereby a species is exotic to the extent that it has not significantly adapted with the local ecological assemblage. In section II, I identify problems with defining exotics as human-introduced species. Section III outlines the argument for why the human introduction of species creates disvalue and traces some consequences of this evaluation for the U.S. Park Service's exotics policy. Section IV critically evaluates the notion that exotics must be or invariably are damaging. In section V, I explore how exotic species become native via the processes of ecological naturalisation and the washing away of human influence on their presence in ecosystems. Finally, in section VI, I argue that the foreignness of exotic species gives us a reason to disvalue them and that such a biological nativism, like certain cultural purisms, is praiseworthy and not xenophobic.

I. WHAT IS AN EXOTIC SPECIES?

Talk of exotics brings to mind species like kudzu (*Pueraria lobata*), a vine introduced to the United States from Japan and China as a porch plant in 1876. Kudzu was promoted as livestock forage and in the 1930s, the U.S. Department of Agriculture paid farmers to plant it for erosion control. Kudzu can grow almost a foot a day and it now chokes out trees in the southeastern U.S., blanketing about 7 million acres (Stewart 2000).[2] Kudzu is paradigmatic of the popular conception of exotics: it was introduced by humans, causes damage, and originates from a distant geographical location. Such exotics exemplify a major premise of the environmental worldview: ignorant human alteration of nature that destroys nature's balance.

Although the exotic species of concern to environmentalists typically are human introduced, damaging, and geographically remote, we should not conceptualise exotics in these ways. The fundamental idea underlying the concept of an exotic species is a species that is alien or foreign. Such a species is foreign in the sense that it has not significantly adapted with the local species and to local abiotic environment. I develop this notion by comparing it with alternative accounts of the exotic/native distinction.

Geographical considerations are typically taken as what distinguishes natives from exotics. Exotic species are seen as species that are away from home; they hail from some other place and are presumptively out of place. In contrast, natives are those who come from the region which is their home. Consider an analogy with human nativity: a native South Carolinian is seen as one who was born and raised in South Carolina. If we translate this idea to species, we get the notion that a native species is one that originated as a species in this particular place; this region is where the species comes from. On this account, exotics are species that originally evolved in some other place. Woods and Moriarty (2001) call this the 'evolutionary criterion'.

Specifying the natives of a region as those that originally evolved there is both too stringent a requirement and perhaps overly broad. Too stringent because, by this criterion, humans would be native only to Africa. But all species move around. Species evolve in one locale, then migrate or expand their range to other places, and thrive for thousands of years perfectly at home in these new regions. Few species in a region would be natives if we accepted this evolutionary origin criterion of native species.[3] To see why this criterion may be overly broad, consider that when a species first evolves, it may be quite alien to the species that are long-time inhabitants of a region. This would be especially likely if its evolution was so rapid that other inhabitants did not have time to adapt. John Rodman (1993: 149) suggests that introduced species of tamarisk (*Tamarix*) in southwestern United States may have evolved into new species. Perhaps these species are sufficiently foreign to the local ecological assemblage that they ought to be considered exotic. If so, we have a species that is exotic in its place of origin (and not native anywhere).

Species are often said to be native to a river, a region, or a continent. Such a geographical use of 'native' can be quite misleading. Imagine someone selling 'native South Carolina trees' along the South Carolina coast. That Carolina hemlock (*Tsuga caroliniana*) is 'native to South Carolina' hides the crucial fact that it has adapted with ecological assemblages found in the Blue Ridge escarpment and not with those found on the coastal plain. A species from the mountains of South Carolina might be more exotic to the sandy soil of the South Carolina coast than a species from the Mexican desert. Although exotics are often characterised as species that cross political or geographical boundaries, I argue that we should think of exotics instead as species that are found in foreign ecological zones.

John Rodman and Holmes Rolston have offered ecological accounts of the native/exotic distinction which should be distinguished from the account I am proposing. Rodman suggests that a native species is one that is a well-integrated member of a self-regulating and balanced community. He says, 'The essence of exoticality is existence outside a community, lack of membership in a community of mutual dependence and mutual controls' (1993: 150). For Rodman, to become native, an immigrant species must join a community, depend on it, and be part of its system of mutual controls.

In a similar vein, Holmes Rolston argues that mustangs (*Equus caballus*) in the American West are not native species in part because they are not 'good adapted fits' there, despite being present for several centuries after escaping from European-introduced domestic populations. Although the U.S. Congress has deemed that they belong on the western range, Rolston points out that 'nature, not Congress, decides what is an integral part of the natural system'. Even though horses were present in North America thousands of years earlier, those horses went extinct naturally, 'presumably no longer fit for an altering landscape'. Rolston argues that 'the western ranges in this hemisphere developed without them', and although the introduced mustangs have survived, they are not 'good adapted fits on today's landscape, where there have been dramatic changes in climate, predation pressure, disease and parasite vectors and so on' (1994: 115). That the mustangs are not good adapted fits is further evidenced by the fact that they overpopulate and contribute to the degradation of their range.

The idea that native species – unlike exotics – have adapted to the local environment is helpful. But both Rodman and Rolston have more in mind than this. For them, a native is not simply one that has adapted with other natives but is one that has adapted *well*. For Rolston, the immigrant must not only 'fit' the ecosystem, that is, be an 'integral part of the natural system', but also be 'a good adapted fit'.

I do not think we should require that natives fit an ecosystem, much less be good fits. There might be 'native misfits' as well as 'exotic fits.' A native South Carolinian, for example, might be a deranged criminal and a drain on the state's social system, while an exotic Yankee from 'up north' may be an model citizen of South Carolina. Consider that the Asian long-horned beetle (*Anoplophora glabripennis*) recently discovered devouring trees in Chicago is also an important threat to trees in its native range (Corn et al. 1999). Barnacles are an example of species that proliferate wildly in their native ranges. The U.S. National Park Service even has management policies to deal with 'native pests' (National Park Service 1988). Unless one accepts an idyllic conception of perfectly-harmonious natural systems, one must admit that native species can wreak havoc in their native ranges.[4]

Similarly, we should not assume that natives are well-integrated into 'balanced' and 'self-regulating communities', as Rodman would have it. Presupposing a tightly integrated and balanced, community conception of natural systems is highly controversial given the recent emphasis in ecology on disequilibrium, instability, disturbance, and heterogeneous patchy landscapes (Hettinger and Throop 1999). Although there may well be many tightly integrated and balanced ecological communities (when described from certain scales and perspectives), numerous natural aggregations of species are not appropriately characterised in this fashion. Rodman's characterisation of natives would rule out the existence of species native to such 'unbalanced' assemblages.

Nevertheless, Rodman's and Rolston's characterisations of native species point us in the right direction. Native species will have significantly adapted with resident species and the local abiotic environment, not in the sense that they necessarily have become good fits or are controlled by others, but in the sense that native species will have 'forged ecological links' (Vermeij 1996: 4) with some other natives. Natives will have 'responded to each other ecologically' and frequently evolutionarily (Vermeij 1996: 5). Natives are established species (i.e., more or less permanent residents) tied to some other residents via predation, parasitism, mutualism, commensalism, and so on. Often native species will have affected the abundance of other native individuals, perhaps altering the frequencies of alleles in the gene pool of native populations and thus exerting selective pressure on other natives. A native species will also likely have adapted to the abiotic features of the local environment.

Let me stress again that by 'adapted' I do not mean 'positively fit in'. A species has adapted when it has changed its behaviour, capacities, or gene frequencies in response to other species or local abiota. Aggressively competing is as much adapting as is establishing symbiotic relationships. By adapted, I also do not mean fit or well-suited to survive in an environment. Species that have historically adapted in my sense may go extinct and species that have never actually adapted to a local assemblage may nonetheless be suited to survive there.

In contrast with native species, an exotic species is one that is foreign to an ecosystem in the sense that it has not significantly adapted to the resident species and/or abiotic elements that characterise this system and, perhaps more importantly, the system's resident species have not significantly adapted to it.[5] On the account defended here, species that are introduced to new geographical locations by humans, or that migrate or expand their ranges without such assistance, may or may not be exotics in these new regions. Species are exotic in new locations only when the species movement is ecological and not merely geographical. That is, if a species moves into a type of ecological assemblage that is already present in its home range(s), then the immigrant species is not exotic (foreign) in this new locale: It will already have adapted with the species and types of abiotic features there. If, on the other hand, the species movement results in its presence in a type of ecological assemblage[6] with which it has not previously adapted, then the species is an exotic in this new location.[7]

For example, when cattle egrets (*Bubulcus ibis*) made their way from Africa to South America, they became exotics because the ecological assemblages they encountered were significantly distinct from those from which they came. When the first finches appeared on the Galapagos Islands, they were exotics because they had not adapted with the local species and to the local environment (Woods and Moriarty 2001). A seed stuck to a log travelling from Japan to Hawaii will likely produce a plant that is exotic in this new location, because that species of plant is unlikely to have adapted with the residents of the habitat it now inhabits. In contrast, when bison (*Bison bison*) expand their range north or west out of Yellowstone National Park into the surrounding grasslands, they are not exotics because they enter a habitat with species with which they have adapted. Similarly, a person who moves from Mississippi to South Carolina is still in her 'native southern range', whereas a person moving from New Jersey to South Carolina is out of her native range, even though the distance travelled is roughly the same. What counts is ecological difference, not geographical distance.

Whether a species is exotic to an assemblage is a matter of degree. The greater the differences between the species, the abiota, and their interrelationships in the old and new habitats, the more exotic an immigrant will be. After passing a certain threshold of difference, we can be quite comfortable with judgements about a species being exotic. For example, Japanese snow monkeys (*Macaca fuscata*) in the thermal areas of Yellowstone National Park would clearly be exotic because little if anything in the Park has ever adapted with any species of monkey. But there will be borderline cases where neither the designation exotic nor nonexotic is clearly appropriate.[8] For example, the mountain goats that are moving into Yellowstone Park from the north would be neither clearly exotic nor nonexotic to the Yellowstone assemblages they join, if the flora, fauna, and abiota in their native habitat is somewhat but not all that similar to those they encounter in Yellowstone.

By requiring that a native species has actually adapted to (some of) the other natives in an ecological assemblage, we allow for the possibility of 'exotic fits'; that is, aliens that arrive in new ecosystems but are well-suited to them. Westman (1990: 254) calls this phenomenon 'preadaptation' and says it is possible because different species can play functionally similar roles. For example, even if Asian snow leopards (*Panthera uncia*) could play the same ecological roles that the restored grey wolves (*Canis lupus*) play in the Yellowstone assemblage, this would not make them native. For elk (*Cervus elaphus*), moose (*Alces alces*), and coyote (*Canis latrans*) (among others) and snow leopards have never actually adapted to each other, and thus the leopards are exotic even if they are well-fit for a top predator niche in the ecosystem.[9] Similarly, even if an Asian immigrant to the U.S. fitted easily into American culture, she would still not be native. In contrast, individuals who grew up overseas in American communities would be relatively native on their arrival into the U.S.

II. EXOTICS AND HUMAN-INTRODUCED SPECIES

Although exotics are often defined as human-introduced species, the examples of cattle egrets moving to South America and the Galapagos' first finches show that exotic species need not be introduced by humans. Nor need human-introduced species be exotics.[10] Species that humans place into an assemblage as part of a restoration project are often not exotics. For example, the restoration of grey wolves to Yellowstone Park is not exotic introduction, even though humans captured wolves from Canada and released them in regions (Wyoming and Montana) hundreds of miles south of their home. Despite the fact that the individual organisms involved were not previously in the recipient assemblages and despite the fact that they were put there by humans, on the account given here, the released wolves are not an exotic species.

It might be argued that the native prey in Yellowstone find the introduced wolves 'foreign' because they as individuals have never encountered such a creature.[11] Yellowstone elk and moose, accustomed to running from coyotes, now find themselves trying to outmanoeuvre a much larger and more powerful canine. But elk and moose as species have adapted with wolves, and so although the individual elk and moose in Yellowstone would not have had experience avoiding wolves, they are members of species that have adapted to the immigrant wolf species. Grey wolves have adapted with the species in this ecological assemblage and thus the restored wolf species is not exotic to Yellowstone.

One might think *of course* human restoration of species does not count as exotic introduction, because restoration implies returning a species to a place it previously resided and that ensures the species is native, not exotic. But not all human-caused return of species should count as native restoration. When humans return a species to a location where the ecological assemblage is significantly different from that present when the species was last there, human 'restoration' should count as exotic introduction, not native restoration.[12] Consider Michael Soulé's (tongue-in-cheek?) suggestion that we think of the 'reintroduction' to North America from Africa of camels and elephants as 'restoration' of 'native taxa' (1990: 235). Camels and elephants roaming North American seems a paradigm case of the presence of exotics, even though their genera once inhabited this landscape. Soulé argues that although they went extinct over ten thousand years ago, this was 'only moments ago in evolutionary time' and 'most of their plant prey survived'. If it were true that the plant prey of these animals are still adapted to them, that would count against seeing these species as exotics. But presumably much else in the present day ecological assemblages in North America would not have adapted to these creatures and thus their 'restoration' should be considered the introduction of significantly exotic species. Similarly, returning dinosaurs to the North American continent (by way of frozen and cloned DNA) would be exotic introduction and not native restoration, because these species would not have adapted with the species present on the continent today.

Those who equate exotics with human-introduced species will have a hard time explaining why human return of species need not count as exotic introduction and accounting for cases (like the above) where it is. For example, the U.S. National Park Service's management guidelines define exotic species as 'a species occurring in a given place as a result of direct or indirect, deliberate or accidental action by humans'. A native species is defined as 'a species that occurs and evolves naturally without human intervention or manipulation'. The guidelines go on to say that, 'Species that move into an area without the direct or indirect aid of humans are considered native. ... Those that invade with human intervention are considered to be exotic' (National Park Service undated: 284). Unfortunately, by these definitions, the restored Yellowstone wolves are exotic species.[13]

Another Park Service document qualifies the definition of exotics to avoid this problem. Exotics, it says, are 'species occurring in a given place as a result of direct or indirect, deliberate or accidental action by humans (not including deliberate reintroductions)'. But what rationale is there for excluding human reintroductions from the category of exotics, if one is defining exotics as human-introduced species?[14] The document goes on to provide a reason that could justify such an exclusion: 'For example, the construction of a fish ladder at a waterfall might enable one or more species to cross that natural barrier to dispersal. ... The exotic species introduced because of such human action would not have evolved with the species native to the place in question and, therefore, would not be a natural component of the ecological system characteristic of that place' (National Park Service, 1988: 4:11). But if the reason that human reintroduction of species are not exotic introductions is that such species have adapted with the local natives, then the human-introduced definition of exotics has been abandoned in favour of the criterion of exotics defended here, namely, species that have not significantly adapted with the local ecological assemblage.[15]

Even human introduction of species to locations they have never previously existed need not count as exotic introduction. As long as the resident species have adapted with the introduced species, the immigrant will not be exotic. Consider a case in which an ecological assemblage moves en masse to a new location, except for one species who is left behind (perhaps a forest edge assemblage is receding and one tree species cannot move fast enough). If humans were to place this straggler species into this assemblage, the species would be significantly adapted with the other species there and hence not exotic on the account defended here. Or consider introducing a fish species into a high mountain lake previously devoid of that species of fish because a waterfall blocks its dispersal pathway. This need not count as exotic introduction, if the life forms in the lake had adapted with that species of fish and if that species had adapted to abiotic conditions like those in the lake.

A controversial endangered-species project involves just such an introduction. There is a proposal to poison all the fish species in Cherry Lake/Upper

EXOTIC SPECIES

Cherry Creek, Montana and then introduce the endangered westslope cutthroat trout (*Oncorhynchus clarki lewisi*). All of the major fish species in this aquatic system were introduced by humans in the early 1900s, including Yellowstone cutthroat trout (*Oncorhynchus clarki bouvieri*) which are native to and endangered in Yellowstone Park waters, fifty miles away. The project is touted as native rather than exotic introduction on the grounds that westslope cutthroats, unlike those slated for poisoning, are 'native to the upper Missouri drainage' (of which Cherry Lake/Creek is a part), even though they have never been in Cherry Lake/Upper Cherry Creek.

On the account of exotics given here, that westslope cutthroats are 'native to' (i.e., found in) that drainage is only relevant if it signals a similarity between the ecological assemblages in different parts of the drainage. The mere geographical fact that this species exists in other parts of the drainage is not relevant. If the insect prey base (and other species) in Cherry Lake/Upper Cherry Creek have significantly adapted with westslope cutthroats, then humans placing that fish there is not exotic introduction. Otherwise westslope cutthroats would be exotics there, despite being present in other areas of the drainage.

III. DISVALUING HUMAN-INTRODUCED EXOTICS AND U.S. PARK SERVICE POLICY

Although exotics need not be human introduced, recently many – likely most – are introduced by humans, including those that are the most exotic in their new habitats. Modern humans regularly transport exotics distances, speeds, and between ecological assemblages that do not frequently occur (or are impossible) with naturally-dispersing exotics.[16] When an exotic species is introduced by humans, whether directly or indirectly, intentionally or nonintentionally, this provides one reason for the negative appraisal commonly levelled at such species. This negative evaluation is justified independently of whether the human-introduced exotic causes damage. Negatively evaluating human-assisted immigrant species – and not those arriving on their own – is a controversial value judgement. It is supported by a number of reasons, briefly outlined below.[17]

Massive human alteration of the earth is ongoing (Vitousek 1997). Perhaps half of the planet's surface is significantly disturbed by humans, and half of that is human dominated (Hannah et al. 1993). Humans are increasingly influencing, altering, and controlling the planet's natural systems. The result is a radical diminution in the sphere of wild nature on earth. An important reason to value natural areas and entities is because they are relatively free of human influence. Such a valuation is essential if nature as independent other is to continue to flourish on this planet. Respect for nature as independent other is a key environmental value, in part because proper human flourishing requires that humans be part of a world not of their own making. It would be tragic were humans to live in a totally human-made world.[18] A positive evaluation of natural areas and entities to the extent that they are wild is a rational and justified response to the increasing human dominance of the earth's natural systems and the resulting rarity of earthen nature significantly uninfluenced by humans.[19]

The presence of human-introduced species diminishes the wildness of natural systems and thus provides a reason for disvaluing exotic species when they are human introduced. For example, Yellowstone Lake has been humanised by the introduction of lake trout (*Salvelinus namaycush*) and the Park is less wild as a result. Even though lake trout have been present in much smaller Park lakes for about a century (Schullery and Varley, 1999), their recent introduction into Yellowstone Lake threatens to significantly increase human influence over Park processes. Lake trout prey on the much smaller Yellowstone cutthroat trout, which in turn are an important food source for other Yellowstone species, including grizzly bears (*Ursus arctos*) and bald eagles (*Haliaeetus leucocephalus*). Rather than feeling in touch with wild natural processes, a knowledgeable angler who catches a lake trout while fishing for cutthroat trout in Yellowstone Lake will be reminded of humans and their ill-advised acts. Removing these lake trout will make Yellowstone a wilder, less human-influenced place, as did closing the garbage dumps to grizzly bears.

Some charge that there is misanthropy behind such a distinction in value between human introduced and naturally-dispersed exotics (Scherer 1994: 185). But valuing humans, even loving humanity, is quite compatible with not wanting humans or their works everywhere, especially in National Parks and wilderness areas.

One of the mandates of U.S. National Parks like Yellowstone is to let nature take its course. Yellowstone's let burn policy, honoured in the breach, is one manifestation of that policy, as was the Park's refusal to let wildlife veterinarians treat bighorn sheep who were falling from cliffs because of partial blindness caused by a native disease (Rolston 1994: 112). As a natural area where human influences should be minimised, the negative evaluation of human-introduced exotics is especially compelling and Yellowstone has a strong reason to remove human-introduced exotics. For closely related reasons, the Park has a strong rationale for welcoming naturally-dispersing aliens. The presence of such exotics is a manifestation of wild nature, a world that made us rather than one we have made. Removing naturally-dispersing exotics would (typically) increase human control and manipulation over natural systems.

The suggestion that the Park let nature take its course and welcome naturally-arriving exotics might be opposed by those who believe National Parks should preserve and restore native species and ecosystems. Insofar as exotic species, including naturally-dispersing exotics, displace native species and replace native ecosystems with new assemblages, they constitute a threat to native species and ecosystems. If the Park's goal is to 'preserve vignettes of primitive America' – to use the often quoted language of the Starker Leopold report (1963) – then the

EXOTIC SPECIES

Park should oppose all exotics, whether human or naturally introduced, for such exotics will likely alter the character of these primitive vignettes.

But National Parks like Yellowstone should not be in the business of trying to prevent nature from changing on its own. Respect for wild nature should lead such parks to minimise human-induced change and typically to let nonanthropogenic changes take place. Natural parks should attempt to preserve natural processes, not some particular status quo in nature. Thus Yellowstone has a strong reason to welcome naturally-dispersing exotics. This rationale fits with the National Parks management guidelines that count naturally-arriving exotics as 'natives' and thus presumably sanctions their arrival (National Park Service, Undated).

There are limits to this welcome, however. If naturally-dispersing exotics cause sufficient damage, they may warrant control. The policy of letting nature take its course is not absolute. Respect for wild natural processes can be outweighed by concern for certain outcomes in nature. For example, the protozoan parasite (*Myxobolus cerebralis*) that causes whirling disease (an affliction that cripples some fish species) is a recent European immigrant to Yellowstone's ecosystems. If this species somehow travelled from Europe into Yellowstone without the aid of humans, the Park would be hard pressed to justify welcoming such a naturally-dispersing exotic. If the parasite threatened to destroy the entire Yellowstone cutthroat population, the Park would have strong reasons not to let nature take its course.[20]

IV. EXOTICS AND DAMAGING SPECIES

Some define exotic species as those that damage the new regions they occupy (Scherer 1994: 185). Indeed, exotics have caused massive amounts of damage, both ecologically and economically. For example, in the late 19th century, a fungus (*Cryphonectria parasitica*) imported on nursery stock from Asia caused the chestnut blight, decimating a tree species that comprised 25 percent of eastern U.S. forests and removing an important faunal food source in the process (Pimentel et al. 1999, citing Campbell). More recently, Zebra mussels (*Dreissena polymorpha*) were found in the U.S. Great Lakes, having arrived from Europe in ship ballast water in the late 1980s. This species has already spread to most of the aquatic ecosystems in the eastern U.S. and is causing an estimated $5 billion in yearly damage by invading and clogging water intake pipes, water filtration, and electric generating plants (Pimentel et al. 1999, citing Khalanski). Exotic diseases such as A.I.D.S. and influenza cause untold human suffering and death and the threat they pose is increasing with rapid transportation and human incursion into new ecosystems.

Pimentel et al. (1999) estimate that there are about 50,000 species of non-U.S. origin in the country, a fifteenth of the estimated total of 750,000 species. (This figure does not include exotic species whose origin is from other regions of the U.S.) Between one quarter and one fifth of the plants found in the country's natural ecosystems are of non-U.S. origin, as are one in ten birds (Pimentel et al. 1999). According to Pimentel et al., the yearly quantifiable damage these species cause is at least $138 billion. Culprits include human, animal, and plant diseases ($41 billion), weeds ($34 billion), European and Asiatic rats ($19 billion), insects that destroy crops and forests ($17 billion), cats ($14 billion), and zebra mussels ($5 billion). Pigeons (*Columba livia*), fire ants (*Solenopsis invicta*), starlings (*Sturnus vulgaris*), and feral pigs cost about $1 billion each (Pimentel et al. 1999).

Exotics have caused the extinction of native species. For example, the brown tree snake (*Boiga irregularis*) accidentally introduced on Guam extirpated more than 75 percent of both native species of lizards and forest birds (Pimentel et al. 1999). Exotic species are frequently mentioned as the second most serious cause of species extinction, just behind human-caused habitat destruction. Approximately 40 percent of threatened or endangered species on the U.S. Endangered Species lists are at risk primarily because of exotic species (Pimentel et al. 1999).

Despite the massive ongoing harm such species cause, we should not identify exotics with damaging species. We have already noted that some native species also cause damage.[21] Furthermore, not all immigrants to new ecosystems are harmful. Most get extirpated before they become established. In defence of planting exotics, Michael Pollan argues that 'the great majority of introduced species can't even survive beyond the garden wall, much less thrive' (1994: 55). Moreover, even if an immigrant species establishes itself as a permanent addition to a new habitat, there should be no assumption that the immigrant is weedy or a pest, that it is 'aggressive', or that its arrival constitutes an 'invasion' (i.e., taking over and causing damage). Although some ecological assemblages are highly susceptible to invasion (e.g., recently disturbed ecosystems), many resist invasion quite successfully. According to the 'tens rule', 10 percent of exotics that are introduced into an area succeed in establishing breeding populations and 10 percent of those will become highly invasive (Bright 1998: 25).[22] Even if only 1 percent of exotics typically cause serious problems, this is of little comfort, for as Bright argues, 'since the global economy is continually showering exotics over the Earth's surface, there is little consolation in the fact that 90 percent of these impacts are 'duds' and only 1 percent of them really detonate. The bombardment is continual, and so are the detonations' (1998: 24).

John Rodman argues that because what exotics do when they arrive 'is replace natives, we may suppose that presence of an exotic is bad per se, and invasive behaviour compounds the original sin' (1993: 141). But the assumption that exotics will displace native species is not obviously true. One invasion biologist posing research questions for the field asks whether 'invaders tend to usurp ecological roles of natives or use resources and new ways of life not previously exploited in the recipient community' (Vermeij 1996: 7). Another claims that plant invaders range from 'species with modest resource usurpation spread across many competitors, resulting in no extirpations, to species whose competitive pressure is focused on one or a few resident species' (Westman 1990: 253).

Exotics can even be beneficial in the new habitats they occupy. Vermeij speaks of the 'potentially crucial role invasions and invaders have played in stimulating evolution' and says that 'in the absence of invasions, communities and species and interactions comprising them may stagnate, especially if the economic base of energy and nutrients remains fixed' (1996: 7). Exotics sometimes provide habitat for native species. A species of *Eucalyptus* tree introduced into California from Australia over 120 years ago benefits Monarch butterflies (*Danaus plexippus*) who rely on them during annual migrations (Woods and Moriarty 2001). Eucalyptus also benefits native birds and salamanders (Westman 1990: 255). There are also examples of exotics benefiting endangered species: grizzly bears consume substantial amounts of nonnative clover in Yellowstone Park (Reinhart, et al. 1999) and, in some locations in the U.S., nutria (*Myocastor coypus*) (a South American relative of the beaver) are a principal food source for the endangered red wolf (*Canis niger*).[23]

Consider species like the wild carrot (Queen Anne's lace) (*Daucus carota*) or day lilies (*Hemerocallis*), both European immigrants to the U.S. Michael Pollan's suggestion that these plants have improved the New England landscape – adding to its diversity and beauty – is not implausible. The common apple tree (*Malus sylvestris*) is an import to the U.S. from Europe and West Asia. It is hard to imagine that these apple trees have not benefited the North American landscape.

It is has even been suggested that exotic species introduced into the U.S. have proven beneficial on balance (Corn et al. 1999: 15). Ninety-eight percent of the food crops and animals produced in the U.S. were foreign to North America, including corn, wheat, rice, soybeans, cattle, poultry, and honey bees (Pimentel et al. 1999). The U.S. economic benefits they convey – $800 billion annually, according to Pimentel et al. (1999) – exceeds the estimates of U.S. economic damages caused by exotic species. Treating such economic calculations as a fair assessment of net value or disvalue of exotic species is highly problematic.[24] Nevertheless, it is important to recognise that despite the many disasters caused by introduced exotics, humans have had success introducing, controlling, and benefiting from some exotic species.

The common assumption that exotics must be – or invariably are – harmful results from either unfair stereotyping or accepting an idyllic, balance-of-nature paradigm of natural systems. Pollan makes the case against such stereotyping powerfully: 'The current attack on alien species usually cites a few notorious examples of imported plants that have behaved badly, such as kudzu, Japanese honeysuckle, multiflora rose and purple loosestrife. These demon species are then used to tar the entire class of aliens with guilt by association' (1994: 55). If natural systems were typically comprised of a delicate balance of species well-integrated into communities of members in adapted fit with each other, then the arrival of an outsider not tuned to the system would lead one to expect ecological disaster or ecosystem degradation of some sort. But such a conception of ecological assemblages is problematic given the recent emphasis in ecology on disequilibrium, disturbance, and fortuitous association of species as the norm for many natural systems. Exotics arriving into these types of systems will not be disrupting any stable balance.[25]

Still, there are good reasons for being suspicious of the disruptive potential of exotic species. Exotics often arrive without the predators, parasites, diseases, or competitors that are likely to limit their proliferation in their native habitat. Local prey, hosts, and competitors of exotics have not had a chance to evolve defensive strategies. Past experience, documented by the familiar exotic-invasion horror stories (some mentioned above), is another reason for suspicion. Nevertheless, as with the connection between human introduction and exotics, one ought not to move from an empirical correlation between the presence of exotics and damaging results to a conceptual connection between exotic species and those that cause damage.

When an exotic species causes serious damage or harm, we have a reason for a negative appraisal of this exotic. When exotics cause harm to human interests, the ground for a negative evaluation of these exotics is fairly straightforward: No one doubts the economic damage zebra mussels have caused in the U.S. Such harm, however, will have to be weighed against benefits the exotic provides. According to Mark Sagoff, zebra mussels are responsible for clearing the organic matter that once choked Lake Erie, which had been given up as dead due to eutrophication (1999: 17).[26] Consider another example: dogs (*Canis lupus familiaris*) were originally introduced to North America by nomads crossing the Bering Strait about 10,000 years ago. Although they have caused significant losses for humans (e.g., feral packs killing livestock and dogs biting people and killing small children), no one would deny the importance of the benefits this one-time exotic species provides.

When exotic species harm or impoverish nonhuman nature, the justification for a negative evaluation is less straightforward. Many worry about whether it makes sense to harm natural systems and they challenge us to provide a principled distinction between harming a natural system and changing it (Throop 2000). (For example, in what sense did the chestnut blight harm or damage eastern U.S. forests as opposed to merely changing them?) But when an exotic species invades a diverse native community and changes it into a virtually uniform stand of a single species vastly diminished in suitability for wildlife habitat or forage (e.g., *Phragmites* in eastern U.S. wetlands, *Melaleuca* in Florida), a negative appraisal on nonanthropocentric grounds seems straightforward. Such an appraisal is also clearly called for when an exotic species, plentiful in its native habitat and present as an alien around the world, causes large numbers of extinctions of other species (e.g., brown tree snakes). The damage to humans and to nonhuman nature that some exotic species have caused is a significant reason to be worried about exotic species.

EXOTIC SPECIES

V. NATURALISATION OF EXOTICS

Species expand their ranges, often moving between types of ecological assemblages. Such migration is a natural phenomenon which enriches ecosystems and drives evolution. As with extinction, humans have taken this natural process and dramatically increased its speed and scale, turning a valuable process into a highly problematic one. When species move into foreign ecological assemblages, they become exotics. Over time, exotic species 'naturalise'[27] and become native. John Rodman claims that 'plants resemble people in that many natives are immigrants that have been in a country long enough to become members and citizens of a community' (1993: 151). Mark Sagoff argues that 'many of the alien species among us have become an integral part of our community and our cuisine – cattle, cotton, corn, and striped bass are surely as American as sunflower seeds, cranberries and Jerusalem artichokes' (1999: 22).

One reason we need a notion of naturalisation is because it is likely that many, perhaps most, of the species in any given ecological assemblage did not first evolve in that assemblage and were originally foreign to it. If exotics never naturalised, then we open ourselves to the peculiar possibility that most of the species in ecosystems are exotics. Although recent and massive human transport of species around the globe has created assemblages where the majority of species are exotics,[28] this is not a plausible way to think about typical ecosystems that are relatively untouched by humans. Thus we need a notion of naturalisation of exotics, or as Michael Pollan (1994: 55) puts it, we need a 'statute of limitations on their alien status'. How should we understand this process of naturalisation by which an exotic becomes native?

Some claim that judgements of naturalisation are subjective and arbitrary. Walter Westman, for example, thinks it takes a 'subjective judgement' to answer the question 'how long must the process of evolutionary accommodation between newcomer and residents last before the species can be considered naturalised or native?' (1990: 252). Echoing Westman, Jonah Peretti says, 'It is unclear how long a species needs to be established in a location before it is considered native. Is a species "naturalised" in 100 years, 1,000 years, or 10,000 years? The distinctions are arbitrary and unscientific' (1998: 185).

I suggest that the process of naturalising and becoming native is neither arbitrary nor purely scientific. On the account proposed here, naturalisation involves philosophical evaluation as well as ecological judgment. To become native, an exotic species must not only naturalise ecologically (i.e., adapt with local species and to the local environment), but it must also naturalise evaluatively. This means that for an exotic to become a native, human influence, if any, in the exotic's presence in an assemblage must have sufficiently washed away for us to judge that species to be a natural member of that assemblage.

Ecological naturalisation

An exotic species naturalises in an ecological sense when it persists in its new habitat and significantly adapts with the resident species and to the local abiota. This is a matter of degree and typically increases over time. Immigrant species will immediately causally interact with elements of the local ecological assemblage, but significant adaptation between the immigrant and residents and between the immigrant and the local abiota takes time and increases over time. Exertion of evolutionary pressure between the immigrant, the residents, and the abiota will also not be immediate.

Determining what is to count as significant adaptation requires context sensitive judgement. Adaptation can continue indefinitely. Whether adaptation is sufficient for ecological naturalisation may depend on the adaptive potential of a particular species/ecosystem complex. If a great deal of adaptation is going to take place (perhaps including co-evolution of the exotic and several resident species), then until this occurs, we likely would not judge the exotic to have ecologically naturalised. On the other hand, if the exotic tends to employ resources and modes of living that were not previously exploited in the recipient habitat, then perhaps not much adaptation need take place before we judge the species to have ecologically naturalised. In highly individualistic and loose assemblages, where few ecological or evolutionary links exist between members and where many species have wide-ranging tolerances to a diversity of abiotic factors (and so are unlikely to have adapted much to local conditions), a newcomer may be no more exotic (that is, unadapted to the local species and abiotic conditions) than are the resident species. Perhaps very little adaptation is sufficient to ecologically naturalise to such an assemblage. Ecological naturalisation can also occur in assemblages where the vast majority of species are human-introduced exotics (e.g., Hawaiian forests, or cities and suburbs where people have eradicated the natives and planted exotics). Over a sufficient time period, a large group of exotics would ecologically naturalise with each other and the surviving natives would also adapt with the new assemblage.

Mark Sagoff has challenged the ecological component of the distinction between exotics and natives and thus the idea that ecological naturalisation is relevant to the distinction.[29] Sagoff argues that the distinction between exotics and natives is purely geographical-historical, with no ecological content or economic implications. For Sagoff, an exotic is simply a species that has come from someplace else (after an arbitrarily determined point in time). Exotics, he suggests, do not differ from natives ecologically, and they will be no more likely to be economically damaging than are natives. Sagoff argues that empirical research by ecologists would not enable them to distinguish the exotic species in an assemblage from those which are not. The only way to tell the difference would be to acquire historical information about the past geographical location of these species.

EXOTIC SPECIES

In response to my suggestion that exotics, unlike natives, will not have significantly adapted with the local assemblages, Sagoff argues that we will always be able to tell plausible, but speculative, 'just so' stories about how the new immigrants to an assemblage have adapted. If an immigrant species establishes itself in a new geographical location, it will undoubtedly have survival skills, such as making or catching its food, avoiding or defending itself against local predators, and so on. Immigrants without such skills will not survive. Such skills (preadaptations) will likely enable us to tell a story about how such species have adapted to the local assemblage (even though they have not).

Sagoff is right that this phenomenon of preadaptation will make it more difficult for ecologists to determine which species are exotics and which are natives. But Sagoff's epistemological conjecture about the difficulty of empirically distinguishing exotics from natives is compatible with my definition of exotics as those that have not significantly adapted with local assemblages. Even if it is true that, absent historical-geographical knowledge, we would have a hard time telling which species have actually adapted with the local assemblage and which – though they can survive there – have not adapted, this does not vitiate the distinction between such species.

Additionally, although Sagoff's epistemological conjecture is intriguing, it is not all that plausible. Invasion biologists – those who study, among other things, the differences between recently-invaded and not recently-invaded assemblages – would likely be able to make reasonable judgements about which species are more likely to be exotic. Numerous considerations would provide reasons for thinking a species is more likely to be exotic (i.e., not significantly adapted with the local assemblage). Consider two: (1) We find that nothing eats a given species and then, a year later, discover that several local species are now eating it; (2) A small number of individuals of a rapidly reproducing species has a genetically-based trait that significantly enhances their fitness in the local environment (perhaps they have a tolerance to a toxic metal in the soil); 5 years later, most of the members of this species have this trait. In general, we could identify an optimal engineering design for a given species that would make it most fit in an assemblage and then use distance of the species from this design as a means to assess the probability and extent of its exoticness.

Westman and Peretti worry about how long an exotic must naturalise before it becomes native. I suggest that the speed of ecological naturalisation will vary depending on the immigrating species and the nature of the local ecological assemblage. Some insects 'quickly adapt to new hosts, even within periods as short as 10 years' (Vermeij 1996: 7) and for plants, 'genetic changes by population level selection can sometimes be found in annual invader species within 25–40 years' (Westman 1990: 254).[30] Species that reproduce more quickly will likely adapt and evolve more quickly and thus will ecologically naturalise more quickly than species with longer generation times.[31]

Evaluative naturalisation

Should ecological naturalisation be all that is required before an exotic species is to be considered native? I think not. Many immigrant species have been in their new habitats long enough to ecologically naturalise (i.e., significantly adapt with local species) and yet we justifiably hesitate to consider them natives. Consider kudzu, perhaps a paradigm case of a nonnative. It has been in the U.S. for 125 years and it is likely to have adapted with local residents and to local abiota to a significant degree in at least some of its habitats. Or consider Holmes Rolston's claim that mustangs on the western range are not natives even though they (and the ecological assemblages with which they interact) have had several hundred years to adapt. Many still consider Hawaiian feral pigs nonnative even after some 1500 years. It is hard to believe that significant ecological naturalisation has not occurred during that time span.[32] The judgements that these species are not yet natives – despite having significantly adapted with resident species and to local abiota – can be explained by treating judgements about naturalisation and the resultant nativity as involving an evaluative component in addition to the ecological one.

Onetime exotic species that are judged to have naturalised and become full-fledged natives are ones that we take to be 'natural' members of their ecological assemblages.[33] For this to be the case, we must judge their presence in these assemblages as not representing significant, ongoing human influence. Human involvement in a species' presence in an assemblage calls into question whether they are natural members of this assemblage. To the extent that an exotic species' presence in ecological assemblages continues to be characterised by ongoing human influence, to that extent we should be unwilling to evaluate the species as having fully naturalised and become native. This is true even if the immigrant species has significantly ecologically naturalised and is thus no longer exotic.

We do not prevent human-introduced exotics from becoming native when we require that they not only significantly adapt but also become natural members of their new assemblages. For exotics can evaluatively naturalise as well as ecologically naturalise. Human influence on natural systems and species 'washes out' over time, like bootprints in the spring snow.[34] Natural processes can once again take control, as when old mining roads erode and vegetation overgrows them. This washing away of human influence over time constitutes evaluative naturalisation and it allows human-introduced exotics that have ecologically naturalised to become full-fledged natives.[35]

A number of factors affect the washing away of human influence and the resultant evaluative naturalisation (Hettinger and Throop 1999: 20–21). First, the greater the human influence, the longer it takes to wash out. Perhaps this is why we are reluctant to think of feral animals as capable of naturalising and becoming natives even over long time-periods. Domestication of animals constitutes significant human influence over them, and so even after several hundred years we might think that feral horses, for example, are still not native (fully

EXOTIC SPECIES

naturalised) on the American range, despite having significantly ecologically naturalised. Withholding the judgement that they have evaluatively naturalised reflects the view that the human influence on those species is of ongoing significance. Consider another example. Human introduction of exotic species that take on keystone roles in ecosystems (or extirpate keystone species) result in greater human influence than does human introduction of nonkeystone exotics. Evaluative naturalisation takes longer when there is more human influence over natural systems to wash away.

Increasing temporal distance from human influence is another factor that contributes to the washing away of such influence. For an exotic species to naturalise ecologically, it must significantly adapt with other natives and the local abiota, and this ensures that it will have some temporal longevity in an assemblage. This longevity may – but need not – be sufficient to ensure evaluative naturalisation. Washout of human influence is a function of a variety of factors, only one of which is temporal distance from that influence. Thus one cannot specify a particular time period in which evaluative naturalisation will occur, other than to say that sufficient temporal distance (e.g., geologic time) can wash away almost any degree or type of human influence. For example, any human influence over landscapes by Pleistocene humans is likely to have long since washed away. To take a fanciful example, suppose that contemporary North American wolves were the descendants of domesticated dogs that Pleistocene peoples brought with them to the continent. Although wolves would thus have been human-introduced exotics, these animals would have long since naturalised both ecologically and evaluatively.

A third factor affecting the washout of human influence is the extent to which a natural system becomes similar to what it would have been absent that influence. If mountain goats would be in Yellowstone Park today except for the fact that human roads and other constructs blocked their migration routes, then even though it is a human-introduced population of goats that is now migrating into the Park, this humanising factor is significantly countered by the washing away of human influence that results from nature returning to a pattern it would have displayed absent that influence. In this case, human action overall would not have influenced the outcome in nature: Mountain goats would be in Yellowstone if humans had not influenced natural systems. In contrast, one reason to think of pigs in Hawaii as not evaluatively naturalised and thus not natives (beyond the fact that they are feral) is that the only realistic way pigs could get to the Hawaiian islands is with human assistance. Thus, it is likely that Hawaiian nature would have remained without pigs virtually forever but for human intervention. Thus it is reasonable to view pigs on Hawaii as representing continuing human influence in this respect.

A fourth factor affecting washout of human influence is the extent to which natural forces have reworked a human-influenced system (independently of whether the result is similar to what it would have been absent human intervention). For example, if humans introduce coyotes into an area with significant wolf presence, human influence on the assemblage resulting from coyote introduction would be lessened quickly because wolves significantly dominate coyotes. When a human-introduced exotic has naturalised in the ecological sense, natural forces have reworked the affects of human action to some degree. Thus ecological naturalisation contributes to evaluative naturalisation in this dimension as well, though again there is no reason to think that it is sufficient for it.

All of these factors play a role in our judgement about whether a human-introduced exotic has evaluatively naturalised and become a natural member of its new assemblage. A human-introduced exotic that has less impact, that has been in the system longer, that changes the system's trajectory less, and that has been more greatly influenced by natural forces is one that will be more likely to have naturalised in the evaluative sense. Once it has done so, and if it has also ecologically naturalised, it warrants the appellation 'native species'.

Some argue that an exotic species naturalises when it ceases to cause damage to its new environment. A species is not native, on this account, until it fits in and becomes a stable, sustainable, and productive member of its new community. Besides mistakenly intimating that exotics must cause damage, this suggestion falsely assumes that native species never do. More generally, this account of naturalisation assumes a problematic and idyllic balance-of-nature paradigm of natural systems. It also ignores the importance of the idea that natives must be natural (i.e., not significantly human-influenced) members of their assemblages. Human-introduced exotics (including genetically-engineered species) could quickly and dramatically increase the stability and productivity of native assemblages, but this should not lead us to consider these species natives. That human-introduced exotics are judged to be beneficial is not an appropriate reason for conceptualising them as native.

Let me summarise the implications of my account of naturalisation for the distinction between exotics and natives. Exotics are species that have not significantly adapted with the local ecological assemblage. Once a species has significantly adapted (ecologically naturalised), it is no longer exotic. But such a species might still not be native. If it was human introduced and if its presence in the assemblage represents significant and ongoing human influence, then it is not a natural member of this assemblage and so is not native. Perhaps kudzu, western mustangs, and Hawaiian pigs are such examples of species that are no longer exotic (because they have ecologically naturalised), but are not yet natives either (because the human influence on their presence is still significant).

Although human introduction is not part of my account of exotics, it is a factor in my account of native species. Are the problems I identified with the human-introduced account of exotics applicable to my account of natives? Although I need not count the restored Yellowstone wolves as exotics (as must the human-introduced account of exotics), it might seem that I cannot say that they are natives either, given the significant human involvement in their return

EXOTIC SPECIES

to Yellowstone. But because this is return of a species that humans had previously eradicated, the restoration of wolves to Yellowstone is, in one important respect, a lessening of human influence over both Yellowstone and the wolf as a species. Yellowstone with wolves is now like it would be had humans never eradicated them. Similarly, by returning the wolf to its former range, humans are, in one respect, lessening their overall impact on wolves. Thus, in these respects, wolves are natural and hence native members of Yellowstone, despite being restored by humans.

VI. XENOPHOBIA, BIODIVERSITY, AND DISVALUING EXOTICS AS EXOTICS

Nativists are those who favour native inhabitants over immigrants and/or want to preserve indigenous cultures. Biological nativists favour native flora and fauna, and they combat the introduction and spread of exotic species in order to preserve native assemblages. For example, I planted a mimosa tree (*Albizzia julibrissin*) in my yard after seeing the tree around the Lowcountry of South Carolina. They have pink, silk-like flowers in the spring and are beautiful in bloom. When I discovered the tree was an import from Iran and China, I regretted planting it. I was annoyed with myself, as I was with my neighbours, for planting species not native to the barrier islands of South Carolina. Planting natives and shunning exotics helps to preserve the unique character of our local environments.

Such an opposition to exotic species has been compared to a xenophobic prejudice toward immigrant peoples. Michael Pollan, for example, suggests that biological nativism embodies a purist ideology that is reminiscent of the ethos of the Nazis who had a native plant movement of their own, purifying the biology of their country as they purified their culture of Jews (1994: 54). In a similar vein, Jonah Peretti argues that 'nativist trends in Conservation Biology have made environmentalists biased against alien species' and he wants to 'protect modern environmentalists from reproducing the xenophobic and racist attitudes that have plagued nativist biology in the past' (1998: 183, 191).

In contrast, David Ehrenfeld thinks that comparing the antagonism toward exotics with real biases such as racial profiling of African-Americans and Hispanics 'deserves ridicule.' He argues that

> The ... analogy, between stereotyping alien species and stigmatising human races is ... far fetched. While pejorative generalisations about human races are demonstrably untrue, it is a simple matter to show that gypsy moths, Kudzu vines, and Argentine ants are destructive precisely because they are alien species in new environments.

After noting some exceptions, Ehrenfeld concludes, 'There are more than enough cases in which exotic species have been extremely harmful to justify using the stereotype' (1999: 11).

Ehrenfeld is on shaky ground if the 'ten's rule' is accurate. If only one in one hundred exotics cause serious problems, then stereotypes about the damaging nature of exotic species may be no more statistically grounded than are some of the morally-obnoxious, racial and sexual stereotypes about humans.

Ehrenfeld's response to the charge of bias is also not available to those who separate the notion of exotic species from the idea of being damaging. When exotics are also distinguished from human-introduced species (as I have done), what justification for a negative evaluation of exotics remains? Those who oppose naturally dispersing, nondamaging exotics seem to be doing so because these species are alien, and negatively evaluating a species simply because it is foreign does suggest a xenophobic attitude and a troubling nativist desire to keep locals pure from foreign contamination.

In human contexts, a policy of favouritism for native inhabitants over immigrants is morally troubling. When it is combined with an ideology of racial purity and a fear of 'biological pollution' from those who are different, it is clearly morally obnoxious. In my home state of South Carolina, a great many people believe that blacks and whites should not marry and have offspring. Many dislike Yankees as well, particularly those like myself who have pretensions of naturalising and becoming native. Given the account of exotic species defended here, opposition to exotics must take seriously the criticism that it is xenophobic and supportive of racial purity.

Biological nativists might respond to this criticism by questioning the assumption that because nativism in human affairs is morally troubling, it must also be troubling in environmental affairs. Many acts that wrong humans do not wrong nonhumans (and vice versa). One reason is that plants and animals cannot have hurt feelings resultant from negative evaluations of them, although both can be disadvantaged by such attitudes. If, however, a nativist attitude is itself prejudicial, discriminatory, and irrational, then its condemnation would not depend on toward whom or what it is aimed. Peretti thinks that 'although environmental purism is not inherently racist, there are compelling arguments that nativist purism is undesirable in all spheres – politically, culturally and ecologically' (1998: 188).

Biological nativists' opposition to exotic species can be defended by distinguishing between types of nativism and purism and the reasons for them. While nativisms based on irrational fear, hatred, or feelings of superiority are morally objectionable, I will argue that some versions of both cultural nativism and biological nativism are rational and even praiseworthy. For example, I believe the protection and preservation of indigenous peoples and cultures is desirable. This may involve favouritism for local peoples and opposition to the dilution of local cultures (a kind of purism), but it is based on an admirable attempt to protect the diversity of human culture. Similarly, biological nativism is laudatory because it supports a kind of valuable biodiversity that is increasingly disappearing.

It might seem strange to oppose exotic species on grounds of biodiversity,

EXOTIC SPECIES

for the presence of alien species seems to enhance a region's biodiversity, not decrease it. Mark Sagoff argues that one cannot object to exotics on grounds of loss of biodiversity because 'in the vast majority of instances, newcomers contribute in the sense that they add to the species richness or diversity of local ecosystems' (1999: 18). But this argument takes too narrow a view of biodiversity. Since the breakup of the supercontinent Pangaea some 180 million years ago, the earth has developed into isolated continents with spectacularly diverse ecological regions. Biological nativists value and want to preserve this diversity of ecological assemblages. This diversity is in jeopardy due to modern humans' wanton mixing of species from around the globe. The objection biological nativists can have to exotic species as exotics – at least in the current context – is that although they immediately add to the species count of the local assemblage and increase biodiversity in that way, the widespread movement of exotic species impoverishes global and regional biodiversity by decreasing the diversity between types of ecological assemblages on the planet. For example, adding a dandelion (*Taraxacum officinale*) to a wilderness area where it previously was absent diminishes the biodiversity of the planet by making this place more like everyplace else. Adding a mimosa tree to Sullivan's Island makes the Lowcountry of South Carolina more like some Asian assemblages. When this is done repeatedly, as humans are now doing and at an ever increasing rate, the trend is toward a globalisation of flora and fauna that threatens to homogenise the world's ecological assemblages into one giant mongrel ecology. Bright calls the spread of exotics 'evolution in reverse' (1998: 17) as the branches of the evolutionary bush are brought back together creating biosimilarity instead of biodiversity.

The loss of biodiversity resultant from the presence of exotics is greatly exacerbated by damaging exotics that invade, extirpate endemic species, or turn diverse native assemblages into near monocultures of themselves. But such causal diminishment in diversity is distinct from the conceptual diminution identified here: the mere presence of massive numbers of exotics in a great number of assemblages diminishes the diversity between ecological assemblages independently of whether they physically replace or diminish natives. Note that opposition to exotics on these conceptual grounds avoids the unfair stereotyping charge that must be addressed by those who oppose exotics because they are likely to cause damage.

It might be objected that presence of exotic species can enhance inter-assemblage biodiversity in certain respects, as well as decreasing it in others, and thus that the spread of exotics may not be a threat to overall biodiversity.[36] For example, the movement of Asian snow leopards into Yellowstone Park would not only increase Yellowstone's species count but it would also make Yellowstone's assemblages differ from those of the Absoroka-Beartooth wilderness to the north in a way they previously did not: Now they diverge in the types of mammals present. While snow leopards in Yellowstone would make

Yellowstone's assemblages more like some Asian assemblages, it would also increase differences between Yellowstone and the wilderness areas to the north.[37]

It is true that the presence of exotics can increase inter-assemblage biodiversity in the way suggested. More generally, species movement into new assemblages need not be a threat to overall biodiversity. In evolutionary history, such movement has frequently enriched ecosystems, brought on speciation, and enhanced global biodiversity. Careful planned and monitored human introduction of exotics into selected assemblages might be able to enhance biodiversity as well. But this is no defence for the blind and large-scale human introduction of exotics that is taking place on the planet today. In today's world, the increase in inter-assemblage diversity due to snow leopards' presence in Yellowstone would not last. Snow leopards would quickly find their way (or be introduced) into the Absoroka-Beartooth wilderness, and the increase in regional biodiversity would be lost. If we focus on individual cases of exotic introduction – without considering the cumulative impact of massive numbers of exotic introductions over time – we may be able to convince ourselves that the presence of exotics is benign (or even beneficial) in terms of biodiversity. But in the context of the current flood of exotics, such a focus is myopic. The logical end point of the ongoing, massive spread of exotics is that ecological assemblages in similar climatic and abiotic regions around the world will be composed of the same species. This is a clear case of biotic impoverishment.

Recent calls to accept the increasing cosmopolitanisation of the planet's biota have come from Peretti (1998), Pollan (1994), and Soulé (1990). Dale Jamieson (1995: 340) suggests that

> It is not implausible to suppose that we may come to see our preference for isolated, indigenous ecosystems as anachronistic; and instead come to favour ecosystems that are more cosmopolitan, in much the same way in which many people now prefer multicultural experiences to those which are provincial. A celebration of alien plants and surprising biological juxtapositions may be more in tune with the postmodern world than attempts to protect native species.

Such calls ignore the great value lost as the ever rising flood of exotics diminishes the diversity between ecological assemblages. In the current context, opposition to exotics as exotics (i.e., as foreign species) is justified in order to preserve inter-assemblage biodiversity.

In addition to this tragic loss in biodiversity, the spread of exotics also helps to undermine an important feature of human community. Globalisation of flora and fauna contributes to the loss of a human sense of place. As Mark Sagoff perceptively argues, native species 'share a long and fascinating natural history with neighbouring human communities... . Many of us feel bound to particular places because of their unique characteristics, especially their flora and fauna. By coming to appreciate, care about, and conserve flora and fauna, we, too, become native to a place' (1999: 22). Using knowledge of – and love for – local native species to help ground a sense of place will no longer make sense in a world where most of these species are cosmopolitan.

Just as the spread of exotic species threatens to homogenise the biosphere and to intensify the loss of a human sense of place, so too economic globalisation and the cosmopolitanisation of humans threaten to impoverish the diversity of the earth's human cultures and to undermine people's senses of community. Keeping a dandelion out of Yellowstone is much like keeping Wal-Mart out of a small New England town or McDonald's out of India. Kudzu in the American South is like T.V. in Nepal, a threat to the diversity of the planet's communities and ways of life.

The cosmopolitanisation of humans is multifaceted and so how we should evaluate it is complex. Humans are already cosmopolitan in a biological sense: our species has proliferated wildly all over the planet, much like an aggressive weed that destroys local biodiversity and homogenises the land. Is human cosmopolitanisation in a social/political sense undesirable as well? A worldly person with wide international sophistication will lack the narrow provincialism that often underlies xenophobia and is thus likely to be more knowledgeable and respectful of cultural and natural diversity. On the other hand, a person who treats the whole world as her home, with no attachments to nation states or particular regions, is less likely to understand, care about, or defend local cultural practices or biotic communities. A cosmopolitan person is also likely to be culturally eclectic, choosing appealing cultural practices from around the world rather than adopting those from home. Such a cosmopolitan way of life is parasitic on other people maintaining local cultural practices.[38] Social/political cosmopolitanisation of humans in these senses is not conducive to the preservation of people's sense of local community and I think it an open question whether, on balance, this cosmopolitanisation contributes to the culturally homogenising forces of economic and biotic globalisation. My southern friend who worries about the effects Yankees are having on South Carolina is not all wrong.

The attempt to preserve differing cultures and small town community life by minimising certain types of foreign influence need be neither racist nor xenophobic, and it can be a praiseworthy attempt to protect valuable cultural diversity. When Jewish parents lobby their children to marry other Jews or when people who live in the southern U.S. send their children to southern colleges, the attempt is to preserve diverse cultural practices with significant value, not to reinforce or perpetuate prejudices, fear, or hatred of those who are different. I am not claiming that morally abhorrent motives are never present in the cultural and biological nativism/purism movements. My point is that they need not be present and that types of both cultural nativism/purism and biological nativism/purism can be morally praiseworthy.

Consider the contrast between the biological nativist's commendable desire for local biotic purity and the racists' contemptible desire for human racial purity. In certain respects their goals seem similar, for just as it would be unfortunate for all ecological assemblages to become the same, so too it would be unfortunate to lose racial differences between people and for humans to instantiate one mongrel species. But marriage between blacks and whites in South Carolina (or worldwide for that matter) poses no real threat to the existence of these differing races and the opposition to miscegenation is typically based on fear, dislike, or perceptions of inferiority of the other race. In contrast, the mass importation of exotics does significantly threaten biodiversity and biological nativists typically do not believe in the superiority of the species native to their lands. The charge that biological nativists are xenophobic ignores their admiration of foreign flora and fauna in their native habitats. Although biological nativists favour native biotic purity, they do so in the name of global biodiversity, the preservation of the spectacular diversity between Earth's ecological assemblages. Ironically, it is those who favour the cosmopolitanisation of plants and animals that support purity of an invidious sort: in that direction lies a world with the same mix of species virtually everywhere.

Opposition to exotics as exotic can thus be both rational and praiseworthy. Being a foreign species is a disvalue when humans are flooding the earth's ecological assemblages with exotics. Given the significant and ongoing homogenisation and cosmopolitanisation of the biosphere by humans, we may justifiably oppose exotic species even if they have arrived under their own power and cause no physical damage.

VII. CONCLUSION

Exotic species are best characterised as species that are foreign to an ecological assemblage in the sense that they have not significantly adapted with the biota and abiota constituting that assemblage. Contrary to frequent characterisations, exotics need not cause damage, be introduced by humans, or be geographically remote. Exotic species become natives when they have ecologically naturalised and when human influence over their presence in ecological assemblages (if any) has washed away. Although the damaging nature and anthropogenic origin of many exotic species provide good reasons for a negative evaluation of such exotics, in today's context, even naturally-dispersing, nondamaging exotics warrant opposition. Biological nativists' antagonism toward exotics need not be xenophobic nor involve unfair stereotyping, and it can be justified as a way of preserving the diversity of ecological assemblages from the homogenising forces of globalisation.[39]

EXOTIC SPECIES

NOTES

[1] The contemporary pigs are a cross between the Polynesian-introduced pigs and more recently-introduced European wild boars. For a useful discussion of this example, see Mark Woods and Paul Moriarty (2001).

[2] Kudzu has its defenders. Mark Sagoff points out that besides providing erosion control and forage, it is a nitrogen-fixing legume that nourishes the soil. Some southern cooks serve fried Kudzu leaves and Kudzu products include fibre purses and condiments. When the vine covers telephone poles and wires, it might be viewed as providing an aesthetic benefit.

[3] Christopher Bright (1998: 21) seems to accept this evolutionary origin criterion of the native/exotic distinction. Exotic species, he says, are organisms that 'take up residence in ecosystems where they did not evolve'. If one defines the spatial scale of ecosystems broadly enough, e.g., the North American 'ecosystem', then most species may well be native to the 'ecosystems' (i.e., continents) they currently inhabit.

[4] There are limits to the damage natives can cause their home ecosystem(s). If natives are too damaging, they would destroy the habitat on which they depend and drive themselves extinct. Those parasites that destroy their hosts (and are unable to jump to other host species) are examples.

[5] When I say that exotics 'have not significantly adapted *with* local species', I am referring to this reciprocal adaptive process.

[6] Although this account of exotic species utilises a notion of types of ecological assemblages, these types should not be seen as rigid or clearly delineated. Species groupings are historically contingent and are not fixed packages that come and go as units (Jablonski 1991). Types of ecological assemblages often grade into each other ('ecotones'), and species mix and match in many different ways. I do assume that few, if any, ecological assemblages are completely transitory. If there are assemblages where species arrive and leave so quickly that no significant adaptation occurs among the residents, my account holds that all species in such assemblages are exotics.

[7] Some suggest that what turns a native species into an exotic is crossing a 'natural barrier to dispersal' (e.g., an ocean, mountain range, and so on). But a human barrier to dispersal could also isolate ecological assemblages sufficiently for a crossing species to be exotic. Although species can be exotic without doing so, crossing a barrier to dispersal certainly increases the likelihood a species will have arrived in an ecological assemblage with which it has not adapted.

[8] I use the exotic/nonexotic contrast here, because some nonexotics (i.e., significantly adapted species) are not yet natives, if their presence represents significant ongoing human influence. See the discussion in section V on evaluative naturalisation.

[9] An immigrant species that has not adapted with the particular species in the new assemblage but that has adapted to closely related species would be less exotic in virtue of having done so.

[10] On my account, although human introduction is not relevant in determining if a species is exotic, it is relevant in determining if a species is native. See the discussion on evaluative naturalisation in Section V.

[11] I thank Marc Bekoff for this objection.

[12] I put 'restoration' in scare quotes because one might plausibly argue that restoration of species only occurs when a species is returned to an ecological assemblage sufficiently similar to one it once inhabited, and not when it is simply returned to an earlier

geographic location.

[13] These definitions also put the Park Service in the unusual position (mentioned above) of claiming that mountain goats moving into Yellowstone from the north are exotics but those that may move in from the west are not.

[14] It is also not clear why only 'deliberate' reintroductions are excluded. If deliberately putting a species back where it once was is not to introduce an exotic, why would inadvertently doing so count as exotic introduction? Furthermore, as was argued above, deliberately returning species long since departed (e.g., the Pleistocene megafauna or dinosaurs) should count as exotic introduction. Thus some deliberately-reintroduced species should not be excluded from the category of exotics.

[15] The Society for Restoration Ecology also defines exotics as human-introduced species. According to the Society, an exotic is 'one that was introduced, either intentionally or unintentionally, by human endeavour into a locality where it previously did not occur' (quoted from Scherer 1994: 185). Besides ruling out naturally-dispersing exotics a priori, this definition would count 'restored' Pleistocene megafauna or dinosaurs as nonexotic.

[16] Consider some human vehicles used by hitch-hiking exotics: Ship ballast water, pallet wood, and aeroplane wheel-wells.

[17] For a fuller discussion of the reasons for disvaluing human influence on nonhuman nature (and for valuing wildness), see Hettinger and Throop (1999).

[18] For a compelling discussion of the horror of a totally humanised, artifactual world, see Lee (1999), especially pp. 194–203. According to Lee, bringing about such a world manifests 'moral blindness to something other than ourselves' (p. 119) and makes us guilty of 'ontological impoverishment'. In such a world 'humankind is then imprisoned within an existential or ontological solipsism of its own making' (p. 194), leading to a 'narcissistic civilisation' able to express wonder and awe only at its own handiwork. Failing to recognise and protect the value of nature as independent other would express 'human collective egomania' (p. 203).

[19] The fact that many people do not seem to value wildness, but instead fear it or profess dislike for things not under human control does not provide a sufficient reason for scepticism about this value. See Hettinger and Throop (1999: 16–17) for a response to scepticism about wildness value based on this fact.

[20] In the Section VI, I provide another reason why the Park Service might resist naturally-dispersing exotics: such exotics can decrease the diversity between ecological assemblages.

[21] Mark Sagoff has made the provocative (and in my view dubious) suggestion that exotics are no more likely to be harmful than are natives.

[22] Daniel Simberloff claims that 15% of the foreign species established in the U.S. have become serious problems (Simberloff 1997). Pimentel et al. (1999) claim that 30 percent of exotic insects that are established in forests have become serious pests.

[23] That an exotic benefits some species, even endangered ones, is compatible with it being harmful overall. Perhaps nutria is a good example. The population of this species is exploding and nutria cause severe damage to marsh vegetation, converting it to open water which destroys habitat for birds and fish (Corn et al 1999: 82). Presumably red wolves would have found something else to eat had nutria not been introduced.

[24] In this comparison, costs are mainly the costs to humans that are relatively easy to quantify. Pimentel et al. (1999) note that 'if we had been able to assign monetary values to species extinctions and losses in biodiversity, ecosystem services, and aesthetics, the costs of destructive non-indigenous species would undoubtedly be several times higher than $138 billion/yr.'

EXOTIC SPECIES

[25] Compare Westman (1990: 257) on the implications of different paradigms in ecology for our understanding of exotics.

[26] Stevens' (2000) discussion of the zebra mussel's role in degrading New York's Hudson river suggests it is highly unlikely that this organism should be seen as providing a net ecological benefit and casts doubt on Sagoff's claim that it alleviates eutrophication.

[27] The term 'naturalise' is frequently used by botanists to refer to species that came from some other region and have formed self-sustaining local populations. The account of naturalisation developed below requires much more than this.

[28] Soulé (1990) claims that Hawaii has 4,600 exotic plants, three times the number of native plants.

[29] See Sagoff (1999). Some of the ideas attributed to Sagoff below come from correspondence with him.

[30] Contrast this with John Rodman's claim that one hundred years 'seems scarcely time enough for a plant species to adapt and become a member of a community' (1993: 143).

[31] Will more tightly-integrated ecological assemblages adapt to exotics more quickly or slowly than looser assemblages? In tightly-integrated assemblages, there are more causal connections among member species and thus more accommodations that will likely take place as a result of a newcomer. This might suggest that ecological naturalisation will take longer. On the other hand, tight causal connections between members may speed up the adaptation process when compared with looser ecological assemblages.

[32] That these pigs have cross bred with more recently-introduced European wild boars strengthens the grounds for continued exoticness.

[33] By 'natural', I here mean the degree to which nonhuman nature is not altered, influenced, or controlled by humans. For a response to the objection that human influence on nonhuman nature is perfectly natural, see Hettinger and Throop (1999: 18–19).

[34] The bootprint analogy is Holmes Rolston's.

[35] When human influence over a natural system has sufficiently washed out of that system, any negative value that attached to the system in virtue of its being human influenced washes away with the humanisation. This is one reason that people do not (and should not) judge lingering effects of pre-Columbian Native Americans on the contemporary North American landscape as decreasing its naturalness or wildness value in the way they do and should judge more recent human influence as a loss of such value. Even if pre-Columbian Native Americans introduced exotic species to the continent, or moved species between ecological assemblage types within the continent, any resultant human influence on the landscape and negative value associated with such influence has significantly washed away and pales in comparison to the human influence on the continent and resultant loss of wildness value caused by recent Euro-American-introduced exotics.

[36] I thank Bill Throop for articulating this objection.

[37] Judging increases or decreases in biodiversity is tricky. When biodiversity between ecological assemblages is at issue, much depends on how one carves up or counts types of ecological assemblages. For a helpful discussion of types of biodiversity, see Rolston (1994: 34–40).

[38] Similarly, the United States as the great melting pot of nationalities from around the world reaps energy and rewards from other cultures that have maintained their identities.

[39] I thank Beverly Diamond, Todd Grantham, Arch McCallum, Shaun Nichols, Mark Sagoff, Bill Throop, Billy Want, and Hugh Wilder for helpful comments. I also thank Mark Woods and Paul Moriarty for kindly sharing an early version of their paper on exotic species.

REFERENCES

Associated Press 1999. 'State's War on Weeds Gets Serious', *Bozeman Daily Chronicle*. October 15: 7.
Babbitt, Bruce 1998. 'Kudzu, Kudzu, Kill! Kill! Kill!', *Harper's Magazine*. July: 17–18.
Bright, Christopher 1998. *Life Out of Bounds: Bioinvasion in a Borderless World*. New York: W. W. Norton & Co.
Corn, M.L., Buck E.H., Rawson J., Fischer E. 1999. *Harmful Non-Native Species: Issues for Congress*. Washington, DC: Congressional Research Service, Library of Congress. Available at http//www.cnie.org/nle/biodv26.html.
Ehrenfeld, David 1999. 'Andalusian Bog Hounds', *Orion*. Autumn: 9–11
Hannah, Lee, Lohse, David, Hutchinson, Charles, Carr, John L., and Lankerani, Ali 1993. 'A Preliminary Inventory of Human Disturbances of World Ecosystems', *Ambio* **23**: 246–50.
Hettinger, Ned and Throop, Bill 1999. 'Refocusing Ecocentrism: De-emphasizing Stability and Defending Wildness', *Environmental Ethics* **21**: 3–21.
Jablonski, David 1991. 'Extinction: A Paleontological Perspective', *Science* **253**: 756.
Jamieson, Dale 1995. 'Ecosystem Health: Some Preventive Medicine', *Environmental Values* **4**: 333–44.
Lee, Keekok 1999. *The Natural and the Artefactual*. Lanham, MD: Lexington Books.
Leopold, A.S., Cain, S.A., Cottam, C.M., Gabrielson, I.N., and Kimball, T.L. 1963. 'Wildlife Management in the National Parks', *Report of U.S. National Park Service Advisory Board on Wildlife Management to Secretary of Interior*. Washington, D.C.
National Park Service, U.S. Department of the Interior 1988. *Management Policies*.
National Park Service, U.S. Department of the Interior Undated. *Natural Resource Management Guidelines*. NPS–77.
Noss, Reed 1990. 'Can We Maintain Our Biological and Ecological Integrity?' *Conservation Biology* **4**: 241–43.
Peretti, Jonah H. 1998. 'Nativism and Nature: Rethinking Biological Invasion', *Environmental Values* **7**: 183–92.
Pimentel, D., Lach, L., Zuniga R., and Morrison D. 1999. *Environmental and Economic Costs Associated with Non-indigenous Species in the United States*. Presentation at American Association for the Advancement of Science, Anaheim, CA, January 1999. For text, see http://www.news.cornell.edu/releasesljan99/species_costs.html.
Pollan, Michael 1994. 'Against Nativism', *New York Times Magazine*. May 15: 52–55.
Reinhart, D., Haroldson, M., Mattson, D., and Gunther, K. 1999. 'The Effect of Exotic Species on Yellowstone's Grizzly Bears.' Paper delivered at the *Yellowstone National Park Conference on Exotic Organisms in Greater Yellowstone: Native Biodiversity under Siege*. Mammoth Hot Springs. October 11–13.
Rodman, John 1993. 'Restoring Nature: Natives and Exotics', in Jane Bennett and William Chaloupka (eds) *In the Nature of Things: Language, Politics, and the Environment*, pp. 139–53. Minneapolis: University of Minnesota Press.
Rolston, Holmes, III 1994. *Conserving Natural Values*. New York: Columbia University Press.
Sagoff, Mark 1999. 'What's Wrong with Exotic Species?' *Report from the Institute for Philosophy and Public Policy* **19** (Fall): 16–23.
Scherer, Donald 1994. 'Between Theory and Practice: Some Thoughts on Motivations Behind Restoration', *Restoration and Management Notes* **12**: 184–88.

Schullery, P. and Varley, J.D. 1999. 'The Yellowstone Genetic Reservoir: Quandaries and Consequences of Exotic Introductions in Yellowstone National Park'. Paper delivered at the *Yellowstone National Park Conference on Exotic Organisms in Greater Yellowstone: Native Biodiversity under Siege*. Mammoth Hot Springs. October 11–13.

Simberloff, D. 1997. 'Impacts of introduced species in the United States'. Published by the U.S. Global Change Research Information Office. October 6. Available at http://www.gcrio.org/CONSEQUENCES/vol2no2/article2.html.

Soulé, Michael 1990. 'The Onslaught of Alien Species, and Other Challenges in the Coming Decades', *Conservation Biology* **4**: 233–39.

Stevens, William 2000. 'Zebra Mussels Star in Hudson's Ecological Melodrama', *New York Times* (April 4): F1.

Stewart, Doug 2000. 'Kudzu: Love it – or Run', *Smithsonian* **31**: 65–70.

Throop, William 2000. 'Eradicating the Aliens', in William Throop (ed) *Environmental Restoration: Ethics, Theory, and Practice*, pp. 179–191. Amherst, NY: Humanity Books.

Vermeij, Geerat 1996. 'An Agenda for Invasion Biology', *Biological Conservation* **7**: 83–89.

Vitousek, Peter 1997. 'Human Domination of Earth's Ecosystems', *Science* **277**: 494–99.

Wagner, Frederic H. et al. 1995. *Wildlife Policies in the U.S. National Parks*. Washington, D.C.: Island Press.

Westman, Walter 1990. 'Park Management of Exotic Species: Problems and Issues', *Conservation Biology* **4**: 251–60.

Woods, Mark and Moriarty, Paul 2001. 'Strangers in a Strange Land: The Problem of Exotic Species', *Environmental Values* **10**: 163–91.

Plant Transfers in Historical Perspective

William Beinart and Karen Middleton

INTRODUCTION

Plants have been central to world history. Human demographic growth over the long term, and the development of complex societies, has often been linked to the domestication of plants and animals. Jared Diamond's recent popular overview places domestication of wild species as a first and necessary stage in the early intensification of agricultural production.[1] Equally important in world history has been the transfer of domesticated plants and animals from their core area to new zones. Such transfers have been fundamental in facilitating major expansions of people, agrarian complexes and empires. Given that domestication of the limited number of key staple crops and vegetables is likely, originally, to have been highly localised, it may be true to say that most agricultural development has been dependent on plant transfers. Even where agricultural systems, such as those in the Middle East, China, the Americas, and pockets of Africa, are still based partly upon plants that were domesticated locally (wheat, rice, maize and millet respectively), the regional spread of these crops requires explanation.

Agrarian complexes in northern Europe, north America and the southern hemisphere, which are now amongst the most productive in the world, resulted from the migration or adoption of a wide range of plant species, totally new to these areas, in relatively recent times. As Alfred Crosby argued in *Ecological Imperialism*,[2] it is difficult to conceptualise European imperialism adequately without an understanding of the plants and animals that facilitated and shaped it.

Difficult historiographical questions arise from such an argument. On the one hand, species transfer during the imperial era was intimately connected with expansive, capitalist, European social formations, and the migrations, markets, technologies and sciences that they spawned. European knowledge about the qualities of plants in turn drew on and systematised local knowledge. On the other, the properties of species themselves, from sugar cane in the tropics to sheep on the great antipodean plains, played a major role in shaping the pattern, scale and success of transfers. The tropical American empires took their shape not simply because of capitalism, sea power and the dismal development of the Atlantic slave trade, but because of the opportunities and constraints inherent in the botanical characteristics of sugar-cane. Settler colonialism in Australia, New Zealand, South Africa, Argentina and Uruguay was profoundly affected by their suitability for domesticated livestock from the northern hemisphere. Certainly the limits of domesticated species were greatly extended by the application of human knowledge and investment. Yet an analysis of such adaptability requires recourse to ecological and scientific, as well as social, approaches.

By reviewing a small range of readings on a vast topic, this paper asks how we might reach generalisations about plant transfers. It illustrates some of the lines that have been explored, and indicates others could be usefully pursued. It draws on a range of recent literature that greatly enriches an understanding of these processes, but is seldom considered together. Although our concern here is with plants rather than animals, we recognise that the transfer of the two, not to mention of insects and germs, were sometimes closely connected. The *Jardin d'essai* in Algiers, for instance, although primarily a horticultural institution, experimented with combinations of insects and their host plants: silkworms and mulberry trees, and cochineal insects and prickly pears.[3]

Our focus is on four interconnected questions. Firstly, how useful is Crosby's idea of botanical or ecological imperialism? Has there been any overarching pattern of plant transfers from one region to another, and, if indeed there has, how might it be explained? Has the asymmetry an ecological basis? Have strong species emerged from a particular zone of the world? Are some regions susceptible to rapid transformations of their indigenous flora? Or are asymmetrical geographic patterns of transfer, if these can be detected, better explained within political economy and cultural frameworks?

Secondly, the historical literature focuses on scientific specialists, notably botanists within Europe, as well as on the institutions for which they worked. By implication as much as direct argument it suggests they had a very significant place in the history of plant transfers. But how should we conceive of their role relative to that of more informal practices and local knowledge? Should we use Diamond's arguments about domestication as an analogy: this was a very diverse process, the result of a multitude of daily practices and experiments, rather than of easily dateable major 'discoveries'.

Thirdly, is it possible to make a useful distinction between human agency in plant transfers, and other forms of plant spread? When does an intentional and apparently controlled transfer become an invasion? What is the borderline between useful plants and those seen as weeds?

And fourth, as a corollary, are there general points to be made about the human acceptance and encouragement of botanical change and plant introductions? Which forces operate towards an acceptance of plant transfers, and which against? And how do African experiences on this front contribute to analysis of asymmetrical models?

Scientists and historians, even those who define themselves as environmental historians, tend to start in different places in order to answer these questions. Scientists are primarily interested in the particular characteristics of plant species and natural habitats that lend themselves to transfer or biological invasion. For most historians, almost the opposite is the case. They tend to see human agency as the major factor, and are less concerned with the opportunities and constraints inherent in particular plants.[4]

It would be wrong to oversimplify. Scientists such as Diamond and Flannery, to whom we refer in this essay, write ambitious, well-informed works that draw on a range of historical sources and take a global view of historical processes. They try systematically to answer questions about the development of human cultures and their interface with the natural environment over the long term. Historians of the environment in their turn are paying increasingly close attention to natural science disciplines and scientific research – at least to research done in the past.[5] At a theoretical level, Edward O. Wilson, among others, advocates a unification of scientific and humanist approaches.[6] Nonetheless, in respect of plant transfers, the historical and scientific literatures still remain to a large extent separate. And in practice, it is difficult to combine the different methodologies and research priorities of science and history.

This overview essay stems from a comparative project on the history of meso-American *opuntia* species (prickly pear or cactus pear) in Madagascar and South Africa. Although we will not focus on *opuntia* here, their spread to our areas of investigation, and to other 'Mediterranean' and semi-arid environments, has shaped many of the questions we ask. *Opuntia* travelled in multiple directions during the imperial era, against the tide of the flows identified by Crosby. Although *opuntia* species were usually transferred deliberately, some also had the capacity to spread rapidly beyond the zones that humans designated for the plant. Although some species were considered useful, providing hedging, fodder for animals and fruit for people, on occasion prickly pear became condemned as a pernicious weed and invader. *Opuntia* trajectories have alerted us to the multi-faceted features of plant transfers, to the interplay of human and non-human agency, and to the difficulty of distinguishing between domesticates, wild plants and weeds.

PLANT FLOWS: CAN GENERALISATIONS BE MADE?

Crosby contends that exported Eurasian species including domesticated and wild plants, as well as animals and germs, not only facilitated settler colonialism, but proved more powerful than those originating in the Americas and Australasia. He distinguishes sharply between the deep history of the interconnected 'old world' continents of Asia, Europe and to a lesser extent Africa, and the isolated 'new world' continents. And he sees a clear flow of plant species from the former to the latter.

A high number of 'old world' plants had naturalised in the Americas; roughly 50 per cent of farmland weeds in the United States, 258 in all, and 60 per cent in Canada were of Eurasian, largely European origin.[7] By contrast, he argues, relatively few American species had established in Europe. Australia and New

Zealand demonstrate a similar pattern and there was a significant overlap between the new weeds of all these zones.

Charles Darwin recognised this asymmetry, and teased an American botanist: 'does it not hurt your Yankee pride ... that we thrash you so confoundedly'; his respondent agreed about the 'intrusive, pretentious, self-asserting foreigners'.[8] Crosby gives vivid examples of self-spreaders that took advantage of Europeanised landscapes and further transformed them. Some were regarded as useful, such as white clover in Mexico, red-stemmed filaree in California, and Kentucky bluegrass in the eastern United States; some were destructive, such as thistle in Argentina. His notion of plant imperialism is extended in a metaphorical sweep: 'the sun never sets on the empire of the dandelion'. He sees the capacity to reproduce rapidly as one factor in the success of European plants; another was the similarity in climate.[9]

If climate was the key factor, then one would expect a more reciprocal exchange. With respect to the idea that European plants may be more powerful colonisers, indirect support can be found in some scientific overviews. Cronk and Fuller, in *Plant Invaders*, also invoke a contrast between 'old' and 'new' worlds, but on a geological time-scale.[10] Much of northern Europe was relatively recently covered by glaciers. Its soils were more freshly exposed and generally richer for plant growth. Permanently glaciated areas were mobile, depending upon long-term climatic changes. They suggest that in order to cope with this 'frost heave', some plants evolved invader and opportunist strategies. Natural selection on this mobile frost frontier favoured plants that reproduced and spread rapidly. While they emphasise these points in relation to the apparent lack of invaders in this cool temperate zone – the endemic plants were 'inherently resistant' – such characteristics may have given flora from Europe an advantage in new environments.

Support for this approach may be drawn from Tim Flannery's environmental history of Australia.[11] He challenges concepts of 'old' and 'new' worlds, not only because they are culturally loaded. Viewing the question from the geological and botanical point of view, Flannery would prefer to invert the terminology. Geologically, the southern hemisphere, and especially Australia, is the older world, not the newer world. Its long exposed soils had become leached, eroded and poor. This was a world characterised by resource poverty. The ancient mammals of Australia tended to be smaller than those elsewhere. Many Australian plant species (and this argument could apply equally to semi-arid South Africa and southern Madagascar) were also geared to scarcity; they were restricted to highly specific areas and did not spread easily.

Cronk and Fuller draw on social as well as ecological explanations for the apparent asymmetries in plant invasions: centuries of intense land use and environmental management in Europe, as well as the lack of 'wild' spaces, may have diminished the chances for alien species to establish. A corollary of this argument, which they do not explore, would be that the decimation of the native

Americans facilitated vegetation change.[12] They also note the converse possibility that warmer zones may be particularly prone to colonisation by exotics. Plants from areas of sharp winter frosts, as well as those from other sub-tropical areas, can prosper in such conditions. By contrast, plants from frost-free areas are very unlikely to survive frequent frost, especially when accompanied by long periods of low temperature. Frost-free islands such as Hawaii, the wetter Canaries and Madeira, have provided particularly hospitable habitats. Some coastal stretches of South Africa and Australia share these characteristics and have also been botanically porous.

These arguments may lend substance to Crosby's impressionistic conclusions. However, we need to be cautious asking how directional flows may be judged. Is the key index the number of species that are transferred, or is it the number that become useful, or naturalised, or invasive? Is it the area covered by exotics, even if they are few in number? Is it the volume of production of different transferred crops? Are quantitative criteria necessarily the best way to approach the issue? Should we rather attempt to identify the scale of social impacts? What are the regions and time periods of relevance?

Even in the period from 1500–1900, plant transfers may have been more evenly balanced than Crosby suggests. Ships sailed both ways and from the earliest phases of European expansion there was a significant washback. Agents of European empires were highly alert to plant potential. Many plant species were deliberately brought back from the tropics and southern temperate zones; accidental transfer was always a possibility. It is possible to point to successful colonisers from 'new' worlds including semi-arid zones with long exposed soils. Eucalypts, highly adapted to the specific conditions of Australia, have flourished elsewhere – both in plantations and as naturalised self-spreaders – including areas where few if any indigenous trees could grow. (Crosby admits to this exception.)[13] Pines from North America are widespread. Prickly pears from apparently unpromising semi-arid American environments have proved to be highly adaptable throughout the Mediterranean, South Asia, the Indian Ocean, and parts of Africa and Australia. In some places they became invasive.

Acquisition of Amerindian crop plants had a dramatic impact on 'old world' economies and social histories, as Crosby later recognised.[14] The picture becomes more complex if Africa is considered part of the 'old world' – and south–south flows are taken into account. Sub-saharan Africa over the last three centuries came to depend largely on New World domesticates. If a wider range of food and useful plants, rather than a few staples, is taken into account, and a global rather than European perspective adopted, then plant flows may look more multi-directional. American plants such as maize, potatoes, cassava/manioc, sweet potatoes, tobacco, bean varieties, peanuts, cocoa, avocado, cinchona, chili, rubber, agave, prosopis, as well as prickly pear are important and widely grown. It is difficult to conceive of species that have had more culinary and social impact than potatoes in Europe.[15] A similar argument could be made about maize in Africa or chilli in India.

A longer timescale may raise further doubts. Over the last few thousand years, there have been other major plant movements within the old world: from the Middle East to much of the rest of the temperate world; from the Mediterranean to northern Europe; and the transfer of rice, sugar cane, citrus and bananas from East Asia. The Arab empires played a key intermediary role here and pushed the cultivation of sugar cane in the Mediterranean to its northern limits.[16] Even if it is analytically useful to consider Eurasia as a single zone for the purposes of disease patterns, it is far less so with respect to plants.

If the time-scale is extended to the present, and gardens, houses and nurseries included, Europe may be a net receiver of plant species. Tomlinson notes with respect to Australia that 'ten per cent of the current flora have been introduced since European settlement, with up to twice that figure in the most densely settled regions in the south-east of the continent'.[17] But Britain houses a higher proportion of non-indigenous plant species – if that is to be the measure of plant flows. A seemingly insatiable desire to acclimatise exotics and to hybridise new cultivars has made British garden flora one of the most varied in the world. In the nineteenth century this enterprise was supported by a large published output, some of it beautifully illustrated, not least by women.[18] A vivid pictorial culture helped to make exotic plants an object of interest and desire, just as botanical drawings had stimulated Tulipomania in Holland.[19] Increasing literacy and print cultures were critical in Europe for the growth of interest in botanical gardens, natural history, and plant transfers. A wide variety of trees were absorbed, then and since, in forests, arboretums, public spaces and on private land. There have been successful invaders such as rhododendron, knotweed and an introduced species of speedwell that challenge the assumption of native British flora presenting a 'closed' habitat which few penetrate.[20]

Williamson, a leading British authority on biological invasions, is sceptical of attempts to generalise about the typical characteristics of plant invaders, or of the environments they invade, or of the environments in which they originate.[21] His review finds little evidence to show that species from particular areas, such as Europe, are more successful self-spreaders than those from North America or the southern hemisphere. He doubts that there is typical profile of a successful invader. Some successful invaders have rather low rates of increase. Their success may have more to do with the changed habitat, or absence of predators. Moreover, plants can to some degree change their biological characteristics or hybridise in new environments: Australian *Acacia longifolia* and *Hakea gibbosa* have been found to produce more seeds in South Africa than in their native habitats.[22]

He is similarly uneasy about arguments that emphasise the role of climate in facilitating biota transfer. He recognises that those plants with a wider domestic range of temperature and climate seem to have more adaptive potential.

But he finds 'plenty of exceptions' to intuitive generalisations about climatic matching and sees it as a 'rather weak indicator or predictor' of successful transfer.[23] There is a potentially huge geographic range into which many plant species can move.

Elton suggested that the more diverse a plant community, the less invasible it is likely to be.[24] Reviewing the old-established literature on island ecologies, Williamson suggests these may be more vulnerable because they are likely to have a smaller number of well-established native species; their isolation has tended to mean a high degree of endemicity and internal speciation but a lower degree of historical reception. Islands, it may be added, were important ports of call on shipping routes in the early European maritime empires and they were also favoured for environmentally destructive plantations. Yet islands may not be exceptional. The Cape, which had one of the most diverse floral kingdoms, has been very hospitable to new cultivars and highly susceptible to invasion, especially by alien shrubs and trees.[25] Continental tropical forests are commonly regarded as resistant to plant invaders, but low levels of plant invaders may, at least in part, be due to history as much as ecology. Williamson insists that all systems are potentially invasible.[26]

Yet Williamson, in an aside, is also open to the idea of asymmetries in plant transfers. Without referring to Crosby's thesis, he agrees that in 'the nineteenth century the pattern of colonisation and trade meant that introductions were predominantly from Europe'.[27] 'Nowadays', he continues, 'the flow of commerce is much more widely spread, and faster, and species travel in all directions'.[28] We have already noted that the flow of plants may not simply follow the flow of power. Moreover, a central weakness of Williamson's approach is that, while he admits the significance of human agency in transfer, he does not then develop a theory or methodology that takes full account of that agency. The explanatory value of his models, dependent as they are on interrelationships between plant characteristics and natural communities, is limited. In ascribing the historical asymmetry to trade and imperialism, Williamson lets an important facet of the phenomena slip beyond the scope of population ecology into the domain of history, and thus unintentionally makes the case for detailed social and economic research in understanding transfers, invasions and their longer term impact.

The idea of global historical asymmetry in biota transfer clearly remains attractive to natural scientists and environmental historians, and warrants further scrutiny by both. It would be interesting to know whether plant species endemic to particular parts of the world, or plant invaders in general, do reproduce more quickly than others, or by a greater variety of strategies. But Crosby's conceptual and geographical map of biota transfer is partial and Williamson's brief lapse into social history unhelpful. Empires undoubtedly facilitated plant transfers on an extraordinary scale, but we need to be very cautious about accepting either a plant power bloc, or an overall asymmetry in movement over the longer term.

PLANT TRANSFERS IN HISTORICAL PERSPECTIVE

What is more evident, however, is the importance of combining botanical, ecological and social factors in analysing plant flows and their outcomes.

HUMAN AGENCY: WHO SPREADS PLANTS AND WHY

It is essential to understand plant properties in explaining their spread and utilisation but not enough to do so. A wide range of texts touches upon human agency in plant transfers. The socio-economic history of particular crops, and the agrarian complexes which grew up around them, have attracted illuminating studies: Salaman on potatoes; Mintz on sugar; Miracle on maize in Africa.[29] Comparative studies of this kind provide some opportunity to tease out the interface between plant properties, particular ecologies, and socio-political contexts. 'Biographies' of plants that became important commodities, such as the tulip and coffee, are multiplying.[30] Allowing coverage of both natural and social history, this genre is linked to popular interest in the history of science. Histories of food and of gardens document the spread of cultivated plants of all kinds.[31] A rapidly expanding literature, both academic and popular, on scientific travellers – including annotated editions of their works – is another fertile source for plant history, even when this is not the major focus.[32] Classifying, identifying, collecting, and transferring plants was often a major motive for imperial scientific expeditions, official and private.

One of the most important strategies in writing about plant history has been to follow western botanists, and institutional developments in the spread of economic plants. Lucile Brockway's *Science and Colonial Expansion*, focused largely on Kew Gardens and its Directors – Joseph Banks, William Hooker and his son Joseph – as they assembled resources and cultivated global connections to facilitate key plant transfers: tea from China to India, cinchona and rubber from Latin America to south-east Asia; sisal from Mexico to East Africa.[33] Botanical knowledge was an integral part of imperial expansion. Skills and institutions were required to identify the most suitable species, acclimatise them in new surroundings and breed them to increase yields. New technology, such as Wardian cases – protective miniature glasshouses that also minimised the need for fresh water – greatly improved plant survival during transit by sea and land.

Brockway is well aware that Kew's eminence was preceded by other botanical gardens, both in Europe, such as Leiden, and overseas; some dated to the seventeenth century. Subsequent authors have developed a finer-grained focus on these. Richard Grove's general argument about the significance of the colonial periphery in the origins of conservationist thinking might be adapted here to botanical innovation; the Dutch East India company gardens at Cape Town 'drawing on a global range of plants, some of them intended specifically for medical or commercial use, represented an accurate analogue of the current state of botanical knowledge and endeavour'.[34] Although he would differ from Grove's stress on the centrality of the periphery in environmental thinking, Richard Drayton concurs that colonial botanical gardens became centres for 'harvesting of specimens and information' in the search for useful or rare plants.[35] The establishment of Kew as a national institution depended greatly upon the requirements of empire for a centre of knowledge, bridging colonial establishments, as well as a particular conjuncture of Royal patronage and scientific development.

Private botanical gardens in Italy – for medical as much as agricultural experimentation – preceded those associated with the Dutch and British empires. Mauro Ambrosoli emphasises the centrality of botanical knowledge, and texts, in the intensification of farming in Europe, and especially in the spread of fodder crops during the late medieval and early modern period.[36] Lucerne, a perennial fodder crop, was a case in point. Gradually extended from Iran and Central Asia, through the Mediterranean littorals, as far as northern Europe, and later into colonial empires, it saved considerably on labour and facilitated more concentrated mixed farming at a time when intensification required animal power.

Ambrosoli's emphasis on knowledge and text differs from Crosby's concern with biological processes of plant spread and displacement. While his stated aim is to explore relations between wild and cultivated plants, and between local and foreign species, he largely neglects the exotic plants that were arriving in Europe from the New World in favour of following the single strand of lucerne.[37] His work is not a mirror image of plant transfers to Europe that can be set against Crosby's tapestry of American transformations.

Grove, Ambrosoli and Drayton all adopt the approach of intellectual historians. Drayton pays close attention to the circuits of patronage and knowledge that underpinned Kew – especially the Whig grandees and landowners, improvers and experimenters on their own estates, were also advocates of imperial progress. After the gardens were transferred from Crown to the state in 1840, he argues 'the informal empire of economic botany which Banks had created' became 'a formal bureaucratic instrument for efficient utilitarian colonial government'.[38] For those seeking discussion of botany, plants, or the impact of plants transfers, however, Drayton's book is limited. We hear more about political elites than about professional botany or the popular natural history craze of the nineteenth century that drove botanical interest.

Forestry, a related European scientific specialism, also fostered species transfer. European species were introduced to colonial outposts from the seventeenth century to provide fuelwood and timber. Islands that served as refuelling points on imperial shipping routes were soon denuded and by the eighteenth century plantations were one response. Australian eucalypts and northern hemisphere pines were identified in the nineteenth century as quick growing species suitable for plantation cultivation in a wide range of settings from Uruguay and California to the Cape and India. Scientific forestry techniques evolved in eighteenth-century Germany and France for local species were reproduced in extra-European contexts such as India, and subsequently facilitated the transfer of a wide variety of exotics into colonial lands.[39] Colonial state forestry departments, followed by private forestry enterprise, helped to transform the vegetation of many of the higher rainfall zones of the British empire.

Michael Osborne argues that France and its empire in the nineteenth century, rather than the empires of Great Britain or Germany, sat at the international epicentre of the acclimatisation movement.[40] The *Société zoologique d'acclimatation*, formed in 1854 to pursue 'the introduction, acclimatisation and domestication of useful or ornamental animal species', extended its activities to the transfer of exotic plants, and over the course of the Second Empire became the most successful of national scientific societies. It was especially active in Algeria, where Auguste Hardy, Director of the *Jardin d'essai* in Algiers, described 'the whole of colonisation [as] a vast deed of acclimatisation'.[41] This garden devoted much of its budget to investigating the transfer of Asian and Latin American plants to North Africa, notably, bamboos, Indochinese sugar cane, avocado, coffee, cocoa, and breadfruit. The aim was to identify tropical colonial products that would complement rather than disrupt the French agricultural economy, and replace the lost Caribbean colony of Saint-Domingue (Haiti).

These authors have opened exciting new areas for research in environmental history, agrarian history and the history of science. Yet historians are often attracted to institutions, and texts that leave a strong documentary trail and explain themselves clearly. While a focus on systematic knowledge, governments and institutional history is interesting in its own terms, these may be the tip of the iceberg in relation to long term patterns of global plant transfers. Companies, settlers and plantation owners, rather than the state or scientists, often took the initiative in institutional development; prior to the late nineteenth century, most British colonial states had shoestring bureaucracies with few specialists. Storey argues that Mauritius became a centre of sugar production in the first half of the nineteenth century not because of British officials and Kew, but because the Franco-Mauritian estate-owning elite took a great interest in plant research and breeding.[42]

Orthodox narratives of 'botany as instrument of plant transfer' are open to challenge. Dean has rewritten the story of the successful development of commercial rubber in Malaysia, shifting the emphasis from Kew and the imperial appropriation and development of plant material from Brazil. He argues that the success of rubber owed much to the existence of a virus that prohibited the parallel development of a competitive plantation economy in the plant's native habitats.[43] Like others, he also notes that private plant collectors collected the best cinchona seed; Kew's attempts were a dismal failure.

In South Africa, the Cape botanical garden from the seventeenth century, von Ludwig's private establishment in the early nineteenth century, and subsequently the Grahamstown and Durban gardens, certainly helped in the spread of exotics. The forestry authority also played a major role in planting exotics.[44]

But many of the key transfers were made outside of institutional contexts. Settlers evolved their own intermediate, non-professional, botanical intelligence and technology that informed their decisions about which exotics were useful and desirable – and how they could be grown in a hostile environment. Prickly pear was taken to the farthest reaches of the eighteenth century frontier in the eastern Cape, where a century later it became an invader; jointed cactus (*Opuntia aurantiaca*), introduced privately as a garden plant, was judged an even worse pest.[45] Settlers in the Western Cape helped to create the 'Mediterranean' floral kingdom, an amalgam of exotics, valued for their perceived beauty and their capacity to acclimatise. This hybrid plant complex is discernible through many similar climatic zones. 'Colonisation by gardening' was a ubiquitous, everyday settler activity.

Informal links were even more central to plant transfers of exotic food species in indigenous African societies.[46] In Madagascar, which became a French colony much later than Algeria, state botanical gardens were a relatively late development, although private botanical gardens existed by the late nineteenth century. At the Jardin de Nampoana, near Fort Dauphin, for instance, trials were undertaken for many plants from tropical and temperate climes, including coffee and fruit trees. But the introduction and spread of key field crops in southern Madagascar – maize, manioc, sweet potatoes, and, from the late eighteenth century, prickly pear – took place much earlier, and went largely unrecorded, referenced only intermittently in European travellers' and traders' reports.[47] The transfer of a typically 'Southeast Asian' culture complex based on rice cultivation to the highlands of Madagascar took place under similar circumstances.

There is a history to every transfer, even if specialists were not involved. Ordinary people travelled with seeds as well as possessions and livestock. American pioneer women took them as part of their baggage in the wagon trains going west.[48] Afrikaner trekboers – often thought to be obsessed by their livestock – were able to establish kitchen gardens and fruit orchards within a few years of settling on the remotest Cape frontiers, wherever they could find an adequate water supply. African travellers, former slaves, sailed home across the Atlantic with cocoa seeds.[49] For both settlers and indigenous people migrating to new areas, survival could depend upon successful transfers.

Amongst the historians of botany, Brockway perhaps evinces the clearest sense of these longer and more informal histories. 'Seeds', she notes, 'have been one of the most precious and easily transported cultural artifacts'.[50] She is particularly aware that what Crosby characterised as the Columbian exchange was so quick, and largely preceded botanical specialisation. As one food historian notes, there were 'imperialist cereals' well before European imperialism.[51] The role of earlier Arabic and Indian trading networks has perhaps been recognised in relation to food crops, particularly sugar.[52]

An exploration of informal forms of knowledge and experimentation is essential in understanding human agency in plant transfers, but not easy. Kreike has revealed the role of rural peasants in spreading the partially domesticated marula tree to non-native districts of Namibia during the twentieth century through the extensive use of oral histories.[53] Recovering plant histories for earlier periods is more difficult, at least for environmental historians using conventional research methods. Archival references to plants are often confused and unreliable.[54] A combination of methodologies may be called for. In a classic piece of detection, aspects of the history of Amerindian maize were pieced together by research in anthropology, cytology, and archaeology, each discipline supplying data the others could not.[55]

The sheer variety of transfers makes it very difficult to evaluate the role of botany and institutionalised science. Plants can be highly mobile, and widespread experimentation makes it difficult to generalise beyond specific case studies. Investigation of the history of botany and of institutionally led plant transfers is less likely to tell us about food and fodder crops or garden plants – at least before the age of commercial nurseries (themselves under-researched). And it is least likely to explain accidental transfers – at least before states and botanists became interested in the suppression of weeds. Science clearly penetrated into previously informal domains during the nineteenth and twentieth centuries. Yet even then, informal and accidental transfers may have predominated on a global scale.

UNINTENTIONAL SPREAD, WEEDS AND INVADERS

Recent historiography may be stronger on formal involvement in plant transfers than on informal human agency. But how do we evaluate both of these processes against a backdrop of unintentional or accidental transfers and plant spreads? Ecological dynamics are clearly central here: seeds and plants can be carried along ocean currents or rivers, by wind, or by animals. Yet human agency can be directly responsible for unintentional transfer. Human disturbance of environments can unintentionally facilitate the spread of particular species by other natural forces. Posing this question suggests a range of problems and literatures. What is the boundary between informal agency and unintentional spread? When does an intentional and apparently controlled introduction become an unplanned, uncontrolled invasion. The literature on biological invasions, as well as commentary on the concept of weeds, is a useful way to explore some of these questions.

Natural forces did not disappear with the rise of recent empires but ecological relationships could be radically reorganised on imperial frontiers. Crosby relates the unintentional spread of exotic plants in neo-Europes to the contemporaneous deliberate introduction of domesticated livestock breeds. The scale of growth of introduced animals is worth emphasising: sheep on the great plains of the southern hemisphere, for example, increased from perhaps a few million in southern Africa alone in 1800, to 250 million in Australia, New Zealand, Argentina, Uruguay and South Africa by around 1930; cattle from even fewer to perhaps 50 million. European burrweed and thistle as well as *opuntia* species were spread by livestock, in that they transported seed and cladodes, ate and deposited seed, and disrupted the indigenous vegetation. It may be the case that alien plant migration was particularly rapid in these regions because of this huge build up of mobile livestock. Once new seed was established, indigenous wildlife could also disperse it.

Cultivation, van Sittert notes, similarly 'cleared the way for the unwanted "dump heap" doppelgangers of humanity's chosen crops to compete for the newly broken earth'.[56] For South Africa, it has been suggested that alien plants were often introduced accidentally with agricultural crop seed, and that bulk sowing of grains favoured the unintentional spread of their fellow-travellers.[57] Khakibos (*Applopappus* sp.), ubiquitous in the post-harvest fields of commercial farmers and African smallholders, probably arrived with grain around the South African war (1899–1902). Gardening could be seen as a subset of cultivation, but often created different conditions. Whereas arable activities probably favoured accidentally introduced seeds that germinated in complementary cycles, gardening may have encouraged plants which tolerate disturbance, and reproduce especially from their root systems.[58] For this reason, van Jaarsveld suggests, Eastern Cape plants have become ubiquitous in pots and gardens globally. Pastoralism, arable farming, and suburban gardening could all privilege different kinds of unintentional introductions. New patterns of fire can also help some species and hinder others; weeds or grasses may themselves become fire hazards.

In considering unintentional transfers, it may be unproductive to focus on the process of initial introduction. Plants that remained confined to a few gardens or die out can offer useful insights into failure; but most transfers become important, historically and ecologically, if they spread. Terms such as 'weed' and 'useful plant' are essential but problematic categories in exploring processes of accidental spread. It is interesting that scientists have unselfconsciously adopted culturally loaded terms such as 'invader' and 'colonisers'. The case of prickly pears highlights the difficulty of distinguishing between these categories and evaluating human and non-human factors in the dynamic of specific plant transfers. In both South Africa and Madagascar, species of *opuntia* were intentionally introduced. In both, a degree of human intervention has been central to the process of selection and propagation. Yet prickly pear species were able to reproduce quickly by both sexual and asexual modes (when the succulent cladodes became detached), and spread to areas where at least some people did not want them. They also displaced indigenous vegetation.

Given these difficulties, how might we generalise about accidental transfers and invasions? The terms used are bewildering for the scientist, and more so for laypersons.[59] It is not simply a case of mastering a scientific vocabulary that differs from everyday use; scientists themselves do not share vocabulary, and therefore we need to be careful to understand the sense in which the particular author uses a term.

Elton's use of the term 'invasion' corresponds closely to popular usage, partly because he focuses on the dramatic explosions.[60] By contrast, Williamson's terminology is more idiosyncratic: 'Biological invasion happens when an organism, any sort of organism, arrives somewhere beyond its previous range.'[61] Williamson's concern here is to highlight the important element of failure, and to make it central to any explanation. He argues that to grasp the dynamics of invasion, we need to see the dramatic phenomena that Elton describes in the context of a fuller range of examples.

Williamson's definition might also cover crops. As Allard notes, 'If abundance and world-wide distribution in many diverse habitats are criteria of success in colonisation, many crop plants can be regarded as notably successful colonisers. Barley, for example, is a dependable species in a vast range of habitats between the limits of cultivation marked by desert on one extreme and tundra on the other extreme'.[62] In some senses, crops have invader qualities because they are bred for strength and adaptability, that is, for qualities that ensure success beyond their natural range. Yet to class them as invaders seems paradoxical since, in contrast to 'true' invaders such as thistle or prickly pear, crops generally remain dependent on human agrarian practices. A commonsense view would prefer to consider crops or plantation species as invaders only when they escape cultivated, managed domains and pioneer their own routes of occupation. Cronk and Fuller would agree: they exclude the human factor *a priori* since they define invasive plants as those that succeed outside their native domain without human assistance.[63] As the case of prickly pear illustrates, that may also be too restrictive a definition.

If scientists disagree about definitions, they tend to agree that 'weeds', 'invaders', 'pests' can be measured in relatively objective ways. Others stress the importance of economic interests and cultural perceptions in determining whether species are defined as useful plants or as weeds. Certainly, attitudes to prickly pear in Madagascar and South Africa varied sharply. Richer white livestock farmers, who wished to protect their pastures from an invader, even if it was useful in some circumstances, agitated for its control. Poorer white tenants and black workers, who ate the fruit, brewed it, made syrup, and used the leaves for fodder and medicine, were beneficiaries of its spread. In 1920s Madagascar, where prickly pear was an important resource for southern Malagasy dryland farmers and herders, the plant became the subject of fierce controversy. Colonial debates went far beyond consideration of its economic value to moral and political issues such as the purpose of French colonialism, and the perfectibility of man.[64]

Historians tend to accept that the definition of a weed is subjective. The term describes plants that are not useful to people, that 'outcompete others on disturbed soil', and are usually, but by no means always, alien to the area in which they are found.[65] This cultural definition allows the same plant to change status in the context of historically dynamic socio-ecological systems. The American domesticate amaranth became a weed elsewhere and rye became a crop.[66] Cultural values may compete with utility; botanical nationalists agitate against undesirable 'aliens' even where these have uses. In some cultural systems, plants occupy more fluid positions between weed and cultivated plants. The gathered self-seeding 'greens' in African arable plots are a case in point. In parts of southern Madagascar, prickly pear is classified simultaneously as both 'cultivated' and 'wild'.[67] African literature suggests that many environments are managed as much by leaving, thinning or lopping indigenous species as by cultivating, and that people adapt to the plants that thrive – for example in collecting firewood.

The very categories 'wild', 'domesticated' and 'cultivated' are problematic: it cannot be assumed that other societies classify the world in ways that correspond to western cultural constructs.[68] In South America, Lévi-Strauss observed fifty years ago, 'there are many intermediate stages between the utilisation of plants in their wild state and their true cultivation', a point subsequently developed by anthropologists, ethnobotanists, and historical ecologists for Amerindian agroforestry practices in various contexts.[69] It is also implicit in Diamond's representation of domestication as a slow, gradual process of selection, largely a matter of happenstance, as hunter-gatherers picked, ate and gradually spread bigger ears of what became grain. In Ecuador, the Huaorani 'view of the environment does not discriminate between what is wild, tame or domesticated but only between what grows slowly and what grows fast'.[70]

A linked question is whether there is any botanical definition or phytological characteristic of weeds. Here Ambrosoli agrees with Crosby that 'there is no botanical difference between cultivated species and weeds, it is man who makes the selection'.[71] But a constructivist position can mask actual biological processes taking place. As Ambrosoli notes, contradicting his earlier assertion, cultivated plants develop distinct phytological characteristics through propagation, experimentation and cross-fertilisation.[72] The passage between weed and cultivated crop may not be through a gateway that is equally open to traffic in both directions in that plant-breeding usually diminishes the plants capacity to compete without careful human attention. Both historians and scientists tend to be inconsistent and if it is important to recognise that terms like 'weeds' are social artefacts, it is equally important to challenge the commonplace observation that there is no difference between weeds and cultivated plants.

Definitions, and their epistemological bases, help to shape theoretical and methodological questions in the study of plant transfer, and call for further interrogation by historians and natural scientists alike. While social anthropologists are well aware of the importance of local categories, these are often ignored or assumed. Ambrosoli (and his translator) gloss vernacular terms freely into Italian and English as 'wild' and 'cultivated', without indicating how the terms or their uses might have differed. 'In the fifteenth century', he writes, 'plants were classified as wild or cultivated, more or less as they are now'.[73] Lucerne is perceived in texts at some periods to be growing wild, when a peasant, more familiar with local ecology and local practices, might have known it to be partly cultivated. Ambrosoli talks of plants being 'rustic', 'growing spontaneously', 'in the wild', without allowing for the complexity of agricultural practices on the peripheries of demarcated fields, or in the interstices of formal agrarian systems.

Definitions also matter, as we have argued, if we are to get further in respect of assessing the directions of plant transfers and invasions: a commonsense view of geographic scale, comparative global spread, and impact on local plants and societies are critical. Such knowledge, as well as cultural constructs, shapes political decisions and remains essential in debates about biodiversity and the control of weeds.

WHEN AND WHY DO PEOPLE ACCEPT PLANT TRANSFERS?

Underlying many of the points raised in this review is the question of when and why people welcome alien plants. We asked, for example, whether the demise of Native American people facilitated botanical transformation; would the pace of change have been different if they had remained demographically preponderant and in control of their land? Yet indigenous people do not necessarily favour indigenous plants. African experiences, which are not addressed in the models of asymmetrical plant flows that we have outlined, can be instructive. This concluding section focuses largely on Africa, and on one aspect of human choice – crop innovation, including prickly pear. We cannot generalise comfortably about the overall implications for plant transfers, but we can discuss some of the dynamics involved.

Crosby, following Boserup, suggests that people are mostly conservative, but are driven to adopt alien plants by practical necessity: for instance, demographic pressure on land.[74] With respect to Africa, some authors who develop an anti-colonial position emphasise the resistance of African peasants to colonial introductions. New cash crops, encouraged or forced upon peasants by governments, were seen to intensify labour demands or result in a loss of land and labour for food crops. Cash crops at times contributed to intense food insecurity and even starvation; in West Africa, the interior savannah regions were more susceptible to such costs than the wetter forest zones.[75] Forced cotton cultivation was resisted in Mozambique for similar reasons.[76] Malnutrition has been linked to the gradual spread of maize and cassava, because these American cultivars displaced the more nutritious African staple crops of sorghum and millet.

Fiona MacKenzie suggests that maize types favoured by the Kenyan agricultural officials were unsuitable for local conditions, and that peasants, particularly women, often preferred their own, older varieties, which were seen as either better adapted or more reliable for seed. Official initiatives were frequently resisted, as part of a broader struggle against colonial environmental and agricultural regulation and intervention. The particular importance of her analysis is its illustration of gender relations as an element in rural responses and strategies.[77] The implication of such arguments is that Africans wanted to cultivate familiar species, or that they did not benefit from innovation.

Some African systems have also experienced extended periods of involution or stasis following phases of rapid innovation. In the Eastern Cape, for example, black South Africans adopted ploughs, ox transport, maize, oats, wheat, beans, pumpkins, and woolled sheep so that, between about 1820 and 1900, their agricultural system changed fundamentally. Crops were marketed through a region-wide trading network. But over the next 80 years, innovation was less common, despite the fact that neighbouring white farmers were growing an increasingly diversified range of crops and fruits. This closing down is difficult to explain but it coincided with the extension of migrant labour, restricted access to markets, and decreasing dependence on domestic food production; the survival of forms of communal tenure could make it difficult to isolate and control land for new crops.

Yet, as noted above, Africans adopted many American species. Over a few centuries, these have become amongst the major food plants of Africa, and are now often seen as indigenous or naturalised. It is barely possible to conceive of African food systems without maize, cassava, chilli, tomato, American beans and groundnuts, not to mention prickly pear and tobacco. Cultivars from the east such as sugar, citrus, mangoes, types of rice, and especially plantain and banana, have also been important. So have, more recently, vegetables such as onions, cabbages and potatoes.

Maize is so widespread, and so widely considered by Africans as an African crop, that it is difficult to see its adoption, and subsequent infiltration to the heart of many production systems, as enforced. The earliest varieties may have been introduced by sixteenth-century Portuguese traders seeking to expand supplies for slave ships, and colonial regimes encouraged its cultivation more recently.[78] But the crop spread not least in the nineteenth century, between the era of slavery and colonial rule. It presented many attractive properties to smallholders: a covered cob which diminishes labour required for guarding against bird predation; high yields, given certain water-soil conditions; amenability to plough agriculture and storage; disease resistance; and clearly an attractive taste.

Cash crops such as coffee and cocoa have been widely adopted and brought considerable wealth. Many authors, following Polly Hill's famous study of rural capitalism amongst Ghanaian cocoa growers, have celebrated such innovation as a critique of colonial stereotypes of African backwardness.[79] Laissez-faire policies adopted by the British in their West African colonies encouraged African entrepreneurship. In East Africa, colonial governments were more restrictive in respect of cash crops up to the Second World War. Subsequently, Kenya has increasingly been seen as a hive of innovation. Price-responsiveness is often cited as a key factor in decision-making in both conventional economic models and in radical analyses of peasant innovation. Prices for primary commodities in general and for cocoa in particular were attractive at the turn of the twentieth century and this helps to explain the rapid spread of cash crops in West Africa at the time.

Price incentives help to explain innovation in key cases, but the relationship is seldom straightforward. Some critical periods of expansion of cash crop planting have taken place when prices were no longer favourable, especially in the inter-war years of the twentieth century. Producers had to sell more in order to pay taxes and debts, or for imported commodities and education. Boserup emphasised demographic pressure and the erosion of old agrarian systems, rather than prices *per se*, as a powerful stimulus to innovation. Globally, a very limited number of rural communities have responded to past peaks in commodity prices by adopting new cultivars. Perhaps most importantly, a vast anthropological and historical literature suggests that 'economic' models are too simple. Africans and Asians often failed to respond to price incentives, because of their constructs of the traditional or sacred, as well as risk-aversion and local understandings of ecological processes.

Berry argues that even in West Africa, where the embracing of new agricultural opportunities and crops has been most sustained, there is a 'very weak link with price responsiveness'.[80] She develops a sophisticated model of agrarian innovation, which contextualises price responsiveness in complex interactions between multiple social, economic, and gender influences, both local and external. The idea of social capital is one means of explaining agricultural innovation: the availability of networks, communities, extended family, subordinate groups, as well as capital and land. While her theoretical route is attractive to anthropologists and historians, there are problems in invoking so generalised a set of relations. What should we understand as a high level of social capital? The survival of strong kin and community networks can also be associated with resistance to innovation. Case studies have linked religious conversion, and individualisation, with crop innovation.[81]

Capital as well as social capital can play a major role in crop transfers. Previous opportunities for accumulation and the honing of entrepreneurial skills and knowledge were clearly important to crop innovation in West Africa. Arhin suggests that social framework of production and the organisational methods developed through Asante experience with the kola and wild rubber trades laid the basis for the successful introduction of cocoa cultivation.[82] But not all accumulation of capital and knowledge necessarily goes into crop innovation. In southern Madagascar, the wild rubber boom did not have the same outcome. Income was invested in cattle or was spent in purchasing imported western trade goods, chiefly cloth, guns, and mirrors. After 1900, colonial poll and cattle taxes became priorities. This same people had embraced prickly pear a century before. In many African contexts, successful cash crop producers have chosen education or non-agricultural enterprises as their key investments. A culturally infused analysis of risk is essential in explaining such choices.

In the case of prickly pear, price had some indirect relevance for South African commercial farmers in that it was used as drought fodder, especially for ostriches during the great feather boom from about 1880 to 1914. Like lucerne in Europe, *opuntia* was implicated in a general intensification of pastoral production in parts of Madagascar and South Africa. However, over the longer term, the plant helped to underpin subsistence as much as an export economy.

Approaches that emphasise factors such as relatively free land and labour, rather than simply external price stimuli, have been used in explaining cash crop exports.[83] They can also be useful, when set in a social context, in discussing innovations related to production for local consumption. Leaves of some varieties of *opuntia* could be eaten directly from the plant. But the singeing of the cladodes for fodder, and especially the preparation of fruit and leaves in home manufactures, was time-consuming. *Opuntia* became a multi-purpose plant in Malagasy and African societies that had little access to manufactured commodities. The properties of such plants themselves were of great significance, representing, in a sense, a new technology that expanded the boundaries of cultivation and settlement.

A key question around plant transfer concerns the relationship between innovation and local knowledge systems. Isakandar and Ellen show how sacred law among the upland Baduy of West Java constrained the process of innovation, by prohibiting most new crops or cultivars. However, Baduy were also committed to the practice of swidden cultivation in an area of depleted forest.[84] After initial resistance they successfully adopted the leguminous tree *Paraserianthes falcataria*, which reduced fallow length and afforded some protection against further depletion of surrounding mature forests. The authors argue that successful, ecologically sound innovation in Baduy was grounded in pre-existing understandings of other nitrogen-fixing plants.

The idea that plant introductions are made with an eye to soil and forest conservation is probably not generalisable, even where people have a long established familiarity with the land. While the 'environmentalism of the poor' is a valuable concept, it is always necessary to specify the conditions under which it is possible.[85] The African adoption of maize and plough agriculture, for example, had widespread ecological impacts. We can also question whether crop innovators are able to predict the long term ecological implications of introductions. *Paraserianthes falcataria* is listed by some authorities as an invasive species, and the widespread promotion of it and other fast-growing leguminous trees in tropical agroforestry has been criticised.[86] Prickly pear undoubtedly competed with, and sometimes displaced, indigenous species, and its spikes, untreated, could harm livestock. A boon for some was a curse for others.

PLANT TRANSFERS IN HISTORICAL PERSPECTIVE

Crop innovation often required unpredictable adaptations of technology and knowledge. Many plant transfers take place in 'frontier' contexts, for example when people migrate into unfamiliar lands. Although these hybrid phenomena pose interesting questions about the interface between cultural templates and plant experimentation, they have been generally less well researched by anthropologists and ethnobotanists, who tend to be more interested in indigenous peoples and their knowledge of native flora.

Taste can also be a factor in plant transfers. One aspect of such cultural decision-making involves food preference and addiction.[87] An understanding of changing western taste is an essential element in some of the most significant plant transfers and African cash crop frontiers – sugar, cocoa, tea, coffee and cannabis. Tobacco and sugar were likewise important in changing African consumption, and a taste preference for maize, in one of its many cooked forms, is often expressed anecdotally. Prickly pear may seem a less obvious candidate for cultural appreciation, yet Africans and Malagasy speak with some appreciation about sweet-fruited *opuntia* varieties, and their place in the landscape.

African people were certainly open to plant introductions and many agrarian systems on the continent are now based on exotics. The extent to which prickly pear became a mainstay for southern Madagascar pastoralists is a case in point. In this context, Africa has probably been no less porous to plant transfers than other parts of the world, despite the relatively successful resistance to settler colonialism, and the lack of major demographic setbacks. It could be argued that plants transferred to Africa facilitated resistance, and demographic increase, by helping to underpin food security. In this case also, the relatively late commoditisation of agrarian systems did not inhibit the absorption of new species.

The history of African agrarian systems further undermines the model of asymmetrical transfers from the 'old' to the 'new' world. It is more difficult to mount an argument about the overall patterns of vegetation change in a vast continent. Clearly there are huge differences between, for example, North Africa and the Western Cape on the one hand, and the Congo forest and Kalahari on the other. European settlers sometimes sought to reproduce familiar landscapes in distant places by introducing European plants.[88] Western Cape settlers evolved a vernacular of kinds, drawing also on local species and producing something akin to a Mediterranean botanical bricolage. (The latter also incorporated Cape plants.) In botany as in culture, colonial societies often created new 'hybrid' forms.[89]

Yet there may be an argument that parts of Africa have escaped radical botanical transformation. Aridity, dense forests, sparse populations, resistance to new crops and high proportions of pastureland may be of significance here. Whether this would make Africa exceptional is less clear. One of the weaknesses of Crosby's overview is his failure to consider North America as a whole. The bulk of the continent's surface area is the tundra, the Canadian shield, the great plains, and the Rockies, none of which have been particularly porous, botanically speaking. His model of ecological imperialism – with respect to plants at least – is most relevant to the eastern seaboard and California. Much of the interior of Australia was also partly protected by its aridity. It may be more useful, analytically speaking, to disaggregate the large geographical blocs of old world and new world, or of continents.

This paper has explored some routes into the history of plant transfers, weaving together perspectives from contrasting disciplines. It does not pretend to present a history, which is a much more complex task. However, we hope that it offers a range of researchable questions. We have deliberately tried to include cultivated crops, garden plants, weeds and plant invaders within the same frame of analysis because many plants – and *opuntia* species in particular – fit uneasily into any one of these categories.

The paper raises questions about the value of the concept of ecological imperialism, in relation to the power of European plant species themselves, and about the longer term asymmetry of plant transfers. We argue that human agency is certainly vital in understanding plant transfers and that the focus should be on informal as much as scientific and institutional agency. But a global history – as well as more particular histories – equally requires some understanding of the properties of plants and hence a more systematic incorporation of scientific literature. It is only through such interconnected research strategies that an understanding of the history of plants such as prickly pear, a widespread exotic with a chequered career, can be achieved.

NOTES

[1] Jared Diamond, *Guns, Germs and Steel: A Short History of Everybody for the Last 13,000 Years* (London: Vintage, 1998).

[2] Alfred W. Crosby, *Ecological Imperialism: The Biological Expansion of Europe 900–1900* (Cambridge: Cambridge University Press, 1986. Revised edn Canto, 1993).

[3] Michael A. Osborne, *Nature, the Exotic, and the Science of French Colonialism* (Bloomington, Indianapolis: Indiana University Press, 1994), 166.

[4] Lucile Brockway, *Science and Colonial Expansion: The Role of the British Royal Botanic Gardens* (New York, London: Academic Press, 1979); Mauro Ambrosoli, *The Wild and the Sown: Botany and Agriculture in Western Europe, 1350–1850* (Cambridge: Cambridge University Press, 1997); Richard Grove, *Green Imperialism: Colonial Expansion, Tropical Island Edens and the Origins of Environmentalism, 1600–1860* (Cambridge: Cambridge University Press, 1995); Richard Drayton, *Nature's Government: Science, Imperial Britain, and the 'Improvement' of the World* (New Haven: Yale University Press, 2000).

[5] See note 4; other recent examples include N. Jardine, J.A. Secord and E.C. Spary (eds), *Cultures of Natural History* (Cambridge: Cambridge University Press, 1996); Stephen J. Pyne, *Vestal Fire: An Environmental History, Told through Fire, of Europe and Europe's Encounter with the World* (Seattle: University of Washington Press, 1997); Tom

Griffiths and Libby Robin (eds), *Ecology and Empire: Environmental History of Settler Societies* (Edinburgh: Keele University Press, 1997); Paul Slack (ed.), *Environments and Historical Change: the Linacre Lectures* (Oxford: Oxford University Press, 1999); John McNeill, *Something New Under the Sun: An Environmental History of the Twentieth Century* (London: Allen Lane, 2000).

[6] Edward O. Wilson, *Consilience: The Unity of Knowledge* (London: Abacus, 1999).

[7] Crosby, *Ecological Imperialism*, 164.

[8] Crosby, *Ecological Imperialism*, 165.

[9] Edgar Anderson noted this in respect of Mediterranean plants in California, in his *Plants, Man and Life* (London: Andrew Melrose, 1954), 19.

[10] Quentin C.B. Cronk and Janice L. Fuller, *Plant Invaders: The Threat to Natural Ecosystems* (Royal Botanic Gardens, Kew and London: Chapman and Hall, 1995).

[11] Tim Flannery, *The Future Eaters* (London: Secker and Warburg, 1996) and 'The Fate of Empire in Low- and High-Energy Ecosystems', in Griffiths and Robin (eds), *Ecology and Empire*.

[12] The idea of a denser indigenous vegetation consequent on Native American depopulation is suggested in Timothy Silver, *A New Face on the Countryside: Indians, Colonists and Slaves in South Atlantic Forests, 1500–1800* (Cambridge: Cambridge University Press, 1990).

[13] Crosby, *Ecological Imperialism*, second edition, xiv.

[14] A.W. Crosby, 'The demographic effect of American crops in Europe', in A.W. Crosby (ed.) *Germs, Seeds, and Animals: Studies in Ecological History* (New York: Armonk, 1994), 148–66.

[15] Radcliffe Salaman, *The History and Social Influence of the Potato* (Cambridge: Cambridge University Press, 1949, revised edn 1985).

[16] Sidney W. Mintz, *Sweetness and Power: The Place of Sugar in Modern History* (New York: Penguin, 1986).

[17] B. R. Tomlinson, 'Empire of the Dandelion: Ecological Imperialism and Economic Expansion, 1860–1914', *Journal of Imperial and Commonwealth History*, 26, 2 (1998), 89.

[18] Lynn Barber, *The Heyday of Natural History, 1820–1870* (London: Jonathan Cape, 1980); W. Blunt, *The Art of Botanical Illustration* (London: Collins, 1950); Jardine, Secord and Spray (eds) *Cultures of Natural History*.

[19] Anna Pavord, *The Tulip* (London: Bloomsbury, 1999).

[20] For 'open' and 'closed' habitats, see Anderson, *Plants, Life and Man*, 127. See also Charles Elton, *The Ecology of Invasions by Animals and Plants* (London: Methuen, 1958, republished 1977).

[21] Mark Williamson, *Biological Invasions* (London: Chapman and Hall, 1996).

[22] Williamson, *Biological Invasions*, 54.

[23] Williamson, *Biological Invasions*, 70.

[24] Elton, *The Ecology of Invasions*.

[25] I.A.W. MacDonald, F.J. Kruger and A.A. Ferrar (eds), *The Ecology and Management of Biological Invasions in Southern Africa* (Cape Town: Oxford University Press, 1986).

[26] Williamson, *Biological Invasions*, 77.

[27] Williamson, *Biological Invasions*, 30; see also F. di Castri, 'History of Biological Invasions with Special Emphasis on the Old World', in J. A. Drake, H. A. Mooney, F. di Castri, R.H. Groves, F.J. Kruger, M. Rejmánek and M. Williamson (eds), *Biological Invasions: A Global Perspective* (Chichester, UK: John Wiley & Sons, 1989), 1–30.

[28] Williamson, *Biological Invasions*, 30

[29] Radcliffe Salaman, *Influence of the Potato*; Mintz, *Sweetness and Power*; Marvin P. Miracle, *Maize in Tropical Africa* (Madison: University of Wisconsin Press, 1966).

[30] Pavord, *The Tulip*; Mark Pendergrast, *Uncommon Grounds: The History of Coffee and How it Transformed our World* (New York: Basic Books, 1999). Mark Kurlansky, *Cod: A Biography of the Fish that Changed the World* (London: Jonathan Cape, 1998) has been one of the most successful of this genre.

[31] Maguelonne Toussaint-Samat, *A History of Food* (Oxford: Blackwell, 1994); S. G. Harrison et al., *The Oxford Book of Food Plants* (London: Peerage Books, 1985); Kenneth F. Kiple and K.C Ornelas (eds), *The Cambridge World History of Food* (Cambridge: Cambridge University Press, 2000).

[32] Mary Lousie Pratt, *Imperial Eyes: Travel Writing and Transculturation* (London: Routledge, 1992); Peter Raby, *Bright Paradise: Victorian Scientific Travellers* (London: Chatto and Windus, 1996).

[33] Brockway, *Science and Colonial Expansion*.

[34] Grove, *Green Imperialism*, 93.

[35] Drayton, *Nature's Government*, 122.

[36] Ambrosoli, *The Wild and the Sown*.

[37] Ambrosoli, *The Wild and the Sown*, 109.

[38] Drayton, *Nature's Government*, 160.

[39] Richard Grove, Vinita Damodoran and Satpal Sangwan (eds), *Nature and the Orient: The Environmental History of South and Southeast Asia* (Delhi: Oxford University Press, 1998).

[40] Osborne, *Science of French Colonialism*.

[41] Auguste Hardy, 'Importance de l'Algérie comme station d'acclimatation', Extrait de *L'Algérie agricole, commerciale, industrielle* (Paris, 1860), 7. Cited 145, n.1.

[42] William Storey, *Science and Power in Colonial Mauritius* (Rochester: University of Rochester Press, 1997).

[43] Warren Dean, *Brazil and the Struggle for Rubber: A Study in Environmental History* (Cambridge: Cambridge University Press, 1987).

[44] G. Shaughnessy, 'A Case Study of Some Woody Plant Introductions to the Cape Town Area', in MacDonald et al., *Biological Invasions in Southern Africa*, 37–43.

[45] W. Beinart, *The Rise of Conservation in South Africa: Settlers, Livestock and the Environment, 1770–1950* (Oxford: Oxford University Press, 2003), chapter 8.

[46] M. Miracle, *Agriculture in the Congo Basin: Tradition and Change in African Rural Economy* (Madison: University of Wisconsin Press, 1966); Jan Vansina, *Paths in the Rainforest* (Madison: University of Wisconsin Press, 1990).

[47] Karen Middleton, 'The Ironies of Plant Transfer', in W. Beinart and J. McGregor (eds), *Social History and African Environments* (Oxford: James Currey, 2003).

[48] Annette Kolodny, *The Land Before Her: Fantasy and Experience of the American Frontiers, 1630–1860* (Chapel Hill: University of North Carolina Press, 1984).

[49] William Gervase Clarence-Smith and François Ruf (eds), *Cocoa Pioneer Fronts since 1800: The Role of Smallholders, Planters and Merchants* (London: Macmillan, 1996).

[50] Brockway, *Science and Colonial Expansion*, 36.

[51] Toussaint-Samat, *A History of Food*, 130.

[52] Mintz, *Sweetness and Power*.

[53] Emmanuel Kreike, 'Hidden Fruits: A Social Ecology of Fruit Trees in Namibia and Angola, 1880s–1990s', in Beinart and McGregor (eds), *Social History and African Environments*.

[54] Miracle, *Maize in Tropical Africa*, 60; Ambrosoli, *The Wild and the Sown*.

[55] Anderson, *Plants, Man and Life*, 99–104.

[56] Lance van Sittert, '"The Seed Blows About in Every Breeze": Noxious Weed Eradication in the Cape Colony, 1860–1909', *Journal of Southern African Studies* 26, 4 (2000), 655–74.

[57] MacDonald et.al., *Biological Invasions in Southern Africa*, 26.

[58] This idea is suggested in Ernst van Jaarsveld, 'Shaped by Suffering', *Veld and Flora: Journal of the Botanical Society of South Africa*, 87, 1 (2001), 16–19, in a brief comparison between eastern and western Cape plants. Pelargonium (geranium), crassula, sansevieria (mother in law's tongue), chlorophytum (spider plants) are cited as cases in point. Sima Eliovson, *South African Wild Flowers for the Garden* (Cape Town: Howard Timmins, 1960).

[59] E. Mayr, 'Introduction', in H.G. Baker and G.L. Stebbins (eds), *The Genetics of Colonizing Species* (New York: Academic Press, 1965).

[60] Elton, *The Ecology of Invasions*, 1, 15, 61.

[61] Williamson, *Biological Invasions*, 1–2, 30.

[62] R.W. Allard, 'Genetic Systems Associated with Colonizing Ability in Predominantly Self-Pollinated Species', in Baker and Stebbins (eds), *The Genetics of Colonizing Species*, 49.

[63] Cronk and Fuller, *Plant Invaders*, 1.

[64] Karen Middleton, 'Who Killed "Malagasy Cactus"? Science, Environment and Colonialism in Southern Madagascar (1924–1930)', *Journal of Southern African Studies*, 25, 2 (1999), 215–48.

[65] Crosby, *Ecological Imperialism*, 149.

[66] For crop–weed complexes see also J.R. Harlan and J. R. and J.M.J. de Wet, 'Some Thoughts about Weeds', *Economic Botany* 19 (1965), 16–24.

[67] Middleton, 'The Ironies of Plant Transfer'.

[68] Elizabeth Croll and David Parkin, 'Cultural Understandings of the Environment', in E. Croll and D. Parkin (eds), *Bush Base, Forest Farm: Culture, Environment and Development* (London: Routledge, 1992).

[69] Claude Lévi-Strauss, 'The Use of Wild Plants in Tropical South America', in J. Steward (ed.), *Handbook of South American Indians*, vol. 6, *Physical Anthropology, Linguistics, and Cultural Geography of South American Indians* (Washington, D.C.: Smithsonian Institution Press, 1950), 465. William Balée, 'The Culture of Amazonian Forests', in

Darrell Posey and Willaim Balée (eds), *Resource Management in Amazonia: Indigenous and Folk Strategies Advances in Economic Botany*, vol. 7 (Bronx: New York Botanical Garden, 1989), 1–21; W. Balée, 'Indigenous Transformation of Amazonian Forests: An Example from Maranhão, Brazil', *L'Homme*, 33 (1993), 231–54; D. Posey, 'Indigenous Management of Tropical Forest Ecosystems: The Case of the Kayapó Indians of the Brazilian Amazon', *Agroforestry Systems*, 3 (1985), 139–58.

[70] Laura Rival, 'Domestication as a Historical and Symbolic Process: Wild Gardens and Cultivated Forests in the Ecuadorian Amazon', in William Balée (ed.), *Advances in Historical Ecology* (New York: Columbia University Press, 1995), 244.

[71] Ambrosoli, *The Wild and the Sown*, 2.

[72] Ambrosoli, *The Wild and the Sown*, 102, 110.

[73] Ambrosoli, *The Wild and the Sown*, 96.

[74] Crosby, *Germs, Seeds*; Ester Boserup, *The Conditions of Agricultural Growth: The Economics of Agrarian Change under Population Pressure* (London: Allen and Unwin, 1965); see also Mary Tiffen, Michael Mortimore and Francis Gichuki, *More People, Less Erosion: Environmental Recovery in Kenya* (Chichester: John Wiley and Sons, 1994).

[75] Michael Watts, *Silent Violence: Food, Famine and Peasantry in Northern Nigeria* (Berkeley: University of California Press, 1983).

[76] Allen Isaacman, *Cotton is the Mother of Poverty: Peasants, Work, and Rural Struggle in Colonial Mozambique 1938–61* (Oxford: James Currey, 1996); Allen Isaacman and Richard Roberts (eds), *Cotton, Colonialism and Social History in Sub-Saharan Africa* (Oxford: James Currey, 1996).

[77] A. Fiona D. MacKenzie, *Land, Ecology, and Resistance in Kenya, 1880–1952* (International Africa Institute: Edinburgh University Press, 1998).

[78] Miracle, *Maize in Tropical Africa*.

[79] Polly Hill, *Studies in Rural Capitalism in West Africa* (Cambridge: Cambridge University Press, 1970); A. Hopkins, *An Economic History of West Africa* (London: Longman, 1973); Robert H. Bates, *Essays on the Political Economy of Rural Africa* (Cambridge: Cambridge University Press, 1983); Michael Mortimore, *Roots in the African Dust: Sustaining the Drylands* (Cambridge: Cambridge University Press, 1998).

[80] Sara Berry, *No Condition is Permanent; The Social Dynamics of Agrarian Change in Subsaharan Africa* (Madison: University of Wisconsin Press, 1993).

[81] David J. Parkin, *Palms, Wine and Witnesses: Public Spirit and Private Gain in an African Farm Community* (London: Chandler, 1972).

[82] Raymond Dumett, 'The Rubber Trade of the Gold Coast and Asante in the Nineteenth Century: African Innovation and Market Responsiveness', *Journal of African History*, 12, 1 (1971), 79–101; Kwame Arhin, 'The Ashanti Rubber Trade with the Gold Coast in the Eighteen-Nineties', *Africa*, 42, 1 (1972), 32–43; Berry, *No Condition is Permanent*.

[83] Hopkins, *History of West Africa*; Clarence-Smith and Ruf (eds), *Cocoa Pioneer Fronts*.

[84] Johan Iskandar and Roy F. Ellen, 'The Contribution of *Paraserianthes (Albizia) falcataria* to Sustainable Swidden Management Practices Among the Baduy of West Java', *Human Ecology*, 28 (2000), 1–17.

[85] Henry Bernstein and Philip Woodhouse, 'Telling Environmental Change Like it Is?', *Journal of Agrarian Change*, 1 (2001), 283–324; Ramachandra Guha and J. Martinez Alier, *Varieties of Environmentalism: Essays North and South* (London: Earthscan, 1997).

[86] Cronk and Fuller, *Plant Invaders*.

[87] M. Douglas, 'Deciphering a meal', *Daedalus* 101 (1972): 61–82; John Brewer and Roy Porter (eds.), *Consumption and the World of Goods* (London: Routledge, 1993). For flowers see Pavord, *The Tulip* and Jack Goody, *The Culture of Flowers* (Cambridge: Cambridge University Press).

[88] J. Rousseau, 'Des colons qui apportent avec eux leur ideologie', in Jacques Barrau and Jacqueline Thomas, (eds.) *Langues et techniques, nature et société*, vol. 2. (Paris: Klincksieck, 1972).

[89] Ann Laura Stoler, 'Rethinking Colonial Categories: European Communities and the Boundaries of Rule', *Comparative Studies in Society and History*, 31 (1989), 134–61; Ann Laura Stoler and Frederick Cooper (eds.), *Tensions of Empire: Colonial Cultures in a Bourgeois World* (Berkeley: University of California Press, 1997).

Weeds, People and Contested Places

Neil Clayton

'In naming a plant a weed, man gives proof of his personal arrogance.'

Jean Rostand [1]

INTRODUCTION

In a relatively young country like New Zealand the opportunity arises to study in some detail the evolution of a new flora, induced by European settlement, and the evolving relationships between that flora and those who induced it.[2] The pioneer New Zealand ecologist, Leonard Cockayne, considered that such studies would be 'of the greatest scientific and economic interest not only with regard to New Zealand botany, pure and applied, but also because they may shed much needed light upon the evolution of floras and vegetation in general'. That the plants introduced into New Zealand and into much of the New World from the Old were 'some of them the most aggressive weeds in Europe', heightened the element of conflict within the relationship.[3]

New Zealand presented a singular advantage for Cockayne and others who looked to ecology to gauge the effects of invasions by alien plants. The invasion of this relatively small, isolated archipelago has been documented more or less continuously, although somewhat haphazardly, from the earliest European contact period.

If the evolution of a country's flora was a proper study for the ecologist, the evolving relationships and conflicts between the weedy flora and those who induced it, is the province of environmental history. But, in order to understand a relationship that, in New Zealand, has developed over a comparatively short period of two centuries, it must first be set within the context of the several millennia during which people and their weeds have contested places.

What is attempted here is firstly a synopsis of a range of history-writings, not necessarily historiographical in content or intent, about a societal conflict between weeds and people. This might in due course inform a fuller study of the conflict as it occurred in nineteenth- and early- to mid-twentieth-century New Zealand.[4] Constructing such a context in this essay may also serve as a point of contiguity for regional studies elsewhere of the weed–people relationship. The second part of the essay considers a selection of writings that illustrate several trends of thought (scientific, academic, legislative) on the subject, expressed both within New Zealand's settler society, and about that society by 'outside' observers. The extent to which those threads running through the New Zealand discourse either reflected or initiated similar trends elsewhere might again inform further and fuller regional studies.

From what follows, it might seem that the historical literature touching on weeds is extensive. Writing about the history of weeds has, however, generally been incidental to some other purpose, usually scientific or geographic, sometimes philosophical or moralistic but only occasionally historical. Those who have approached the history of the people–weeds relationship thus far have done so from disparate points of view, bringing disparate agendas to the discourse and addressing disparate audiences. Only recently, and then largely within North American environmental history-writing, has any attempt been made to draw those threads together; in New Zealand, seemingly, not at all.[5]

In what follows I have adopted Clarence Glacken's approach of taking illustrations from several places and from different periods. With Glacken, I acknowledge that 'this procedure is open to the obvious criticism that isolated illustrations have little value in interpreting the nature of change over such a large area or over so long a period'. But I also share his view that in the absence of any coherent body of knowledge, 'they show that certain attitudes did exist'.[6]

In all other respects I have sought to allow the various sources to speak for themselves, so as to avoid, in Frank Uekoetter's words, the 'value laden approaches that only enable historians to reproduce in history certain normative assumptions that they [themselves] subscribed to from the outset'.[7] The views and positions to which my sources subscribed, rather than my own, are central to Uekoetter's 'organisational approach' to the writing of environmental history.

ORIGINS AND DEVELOPMENT OF THE 'WEED' CONCEPT

'Weeds' and 'weediness' are two ideas that have been constructed and reconstructed across millennia. The flora which have come to be called weeds and we, the species which has called them that, have been contesting places for something like ten thousand years. We know from what the palaeobotanists can tell us of Earth's inter-glacial and post-glacial landscapes, that weeds occupied many of those places long before the contest began. We know too, that the great cultural changes of the Neolithic altered the people–nature relationship as agriculture rippled outwards from the Fertile Crescent.

Somewhere along the way 'weed' emerged as a concept, and became embedded in and expressed through language. Some of the historiographical expressions of the changes in human perceptions of, and responses to, a group of plants with which we have had to contend for places, and the deeper cultural significances of the contest itself, are explored in this essay. Within the literature we can trace the ravelling and unravelling of a set of ideologies from the Neolithic, across the Old World and into the New, and from both places into colonial and post colonial Australasia, particularly New Zealand.[8]

Drawing some of the fragments together gives merely the appearance of a coherent historiography. It also becomes apparent that, however simple the idea of weediness may seem at first sight, it is not. It may seem obvious, for instance, to a mid-western American farmer, that 'weeds' have become so, not from any inherent character, but because they 'take territory and profit from agriculture in some way'.

But if that is all there is to it, why do we still find ourselves considering such questions as, which are weeds, and which are 'not weeds'?[9] Perhaps 'weediness' *is* a category of nature?[10] Or is it a set of cultural constructs, particular to people, place and time, something idiomatic? Or something more? Something, perhaps, to do with an evolving relationship between a range of remarkably successful organisms and one competing species, ourselves?

What, to begin with, has been the understanding of the word itself and of its place in western language and culture? That, it seems, is largely dependent on place and time. Lawrence King, lately of the Biology Department at the State University College of New York, published in 1957 one of the few discussions of some early forms of the weed concept. This, and his 1966 study of weed biology and control factors, considered the history of the term 'weed'.[11] He found that the ancient near-eastern languages (Egyptian, Sumerian and Assyrian) apparently did not have an equivalent, collective term, all plants being considered useful.

On the other hand, as we might have known, the Greeks had a word for it. Theophrastus (c.372-c.287 B.C.) used βοταυη (botáne) as 'noxious herb', and thus 'weed'. And although weed and weeding concepts were used by Roman writers like Pliny, Virgil and Columella, the modern term has no apparent Latin counterpart. Rather, it is to the ninth-century Old English *weod* that King suggested we might look or to proto-German forms of *weyt* (c. 1150) or the later Belgian *weedt* (c. 1576) and Dutch *weet*, each of which refers to the dye-plant woad, omnipresent in Europe, North Africa and Asia.[12]

We are left then with an English term that appears to have arisen from Proto-Germanic derivatives, a singular noun with no evident intrinsic meaning. It is, King speculates, perhaps 'another example of language as accidental usage'.[13] And so to define the term, he says, one is dependent upon purely anthropic considerations. He reduced an extensive collection of these, from various sources, to ten principal characteristics, couched in distinctly antipathetic language.[14]

On the other hand, Sir Edward Salisbury, late Director of the Royal Botanic Gardens, Kew, writing in 1961, contented himself with characterising a weed as 'a plant growing where we do not want it'. He admitted qualifications, but doubted that a more precise definition is practicable:

> In general we may say that a certain aggressiveness is implied that defies easy control, but here again the quality is one that exhibits itself in one environment and not in another.[15]

At the same time, it is part of the essence of our concept of a weed that it does in fact flourish and must be 'kept in its place'.[16] Neither King nor Salisbury, however, addressed what is perhaps *the* most fundamental dimension of the ideology of weeds. The conceptual transitions between such terms as 'casual', 'troublesome', 'pest' and 'noxious' have essentially been triggered by and constructed from human experiences wherever and whenever plants behave in ways inimical to our interests. Salisbury came close to the nub of the relationship when he referred to the toxicity of particular arable and pasture plants. Plants like hard rush, ragwort, hemlock, and darnel have had consequences which have been observed and remarked upon at least since Virgil wrote *The Georgics* and, in some instances, from Neolithic times.[17]

Like King, Salisbury used the results of archaeological research to reconstruct the forms of association between, and colonisation of, the open habitats of both pre- and post-Neolithic Europe and Britain by humans and their plants. But because the possible existence of weed species in Britain prior to human colonisation rests on contradictory evidence some of his conclusions are speculative.[18]

Nevertheless, he has made one point that is particularly pertinent to the environmental historian:

> The capacity of a species to maintain itself without the adventitious aid of the artificial conditions created by man, which usually implies a reduction in competition pressure, is a feature of prime significance.[19]

That, as we shall see, is something with which several prominent nineteenth-century naturalists had difficulty in coming to terms. Salisbury argued that the degree to which weeds owe their efficiency to natural or human agency, at least in remote times, is largely unresolved.[20] That environmental historians ought to give more agency to nature is a matter that has been remarked upon elsewhere and quite recently.[21]

A contemporary of Salisbury, Charles Elton, of the Oxford Botanic Garden Bureau of Animal Population, took a firmer line on the question of agency. Elton noted in his 1958 book, *The Ecology of Invasions by Animals and Plants*, that few alien plants are capable of invading natural closed vegetation ecosystems. The majority tended to live in habitats 'drastically simplified by man', places like arable farmland, waste dumps, roadsides and railway tracks. In post-glacial Britain, plants like sea plantain and scentless mayweed, now regarded as weeds, were widely distributed in an open tundra landscape with low competition pressures. Elton's view was that the maintenance of what he called the 'conservation of variety', now commonly referred to as biodiversity, provided the most effective means of combating ecological instability brought about by accidental or deliberate introductions of alien plants or animals into indigenous habitats.[22]

In his 1986 history of the British countryside Oliver Rackham's attitude to weeds stands in marked contrast to that of King and Salisbury. Weeds are, he says, quite simply 'very specialised plants, intimately linked to farming'. Many could not survive in the wild, being unable to withstand shade and with little power of competition. Rackham sees weeds as part of 'the ordinary landscape ... made by both the natural world and by human activities, interacting with each other over many centuries'. Ordinariness is not, he says, an easy idea to grasp. A couple of centuries ago the countryside stood, as the world of Nature, in contrast to the town. 'The opposite exaggeration now prevails: that the rural landscape, no less than Trafalgar Square, is merely the result of human design and ambition.' The other player in the game, Nature, is hardly mentioned. The concept of countryside as recent artefact prevails.[23]

Rackham considered that any certainty about which are weeds and which are not is comparatively modern. Late-glacial survivors got a new lease of life with the arrival of Neolithic agriculture, with its monocultures and open places. Others, introduced from the Near-Eastern homelands of agriculture, 'attached themselves to farming and found a new function'. Roman introductions like ground elder remained garden plants until recently. Tollund Man, from the Danish Iron Age, ate goosefoot and persicaria in his execution porridge. Seed cleaning and a reduction in crop varieties initiated a modern decline in weeds. That might be welcomed by some, but:

> even here it is arguable that enough is enough. Mediterranean peoples live with weeds, enjoy them, and eat some of them. Weedkillers seem to have killed the wrong weeds ... Weeds are part of the historic flora and should be protected from dying out altogether.[24]

King's, Salisbury's and Rackham's syntheses give us an approximate measure of where and when some plants became the Other, and of where and when humanity, at least in the West, began to conceptualise and articulate weediness. From such starting points it becomes possible to trace a fluctuating Otherness. A reconnaissance of the historical landscape from the medieval to the modern illustrates something of the complexity, confusion and ambivalence that has attached to weed species, and which moved into new worlds with European colonisers and their flora.

WEEDS AND MORALS: FROM MEDIEVAL TO MODERN

In her introduction to her 1995 book, *A Medieval Herbal*, Jenny de Gex makes the point that the early herbals reveal a different universe from our own. Each plant, or its parts, had 'virtues' and 'signatures'. The virtues of the bramble, for instance, were that an infusion of it 'surely healeth' sore ears or eased menstruation. Its leaves healed heartache and its blossoms, wounds. Any part of it 'seethe[d] in wine to the third part' relieved infirmity of the joints.[25] Signature related to some physical characteristic(s) of a plant. The red juice of St. John's wort, for example, 'signified its power to heal wounds'.[26]

WEEDS, PEOPLE AND CONTESTED PLACES

Weeds took on a less roseate hue under Will Shakespeare's pen. Dark forces emanated from Elsinore when Hamlet reflected on his father's death:

> Fie on't! O fie! 'tis an unweeded garden,
> That grows to seed; things rank and gross in nature
> Possess it merely. That it should come to this! [27]

'Darnel hemlock and rank fumitory' or 'hateful docks, rough thistles, kecksies, burrs' speak of social and political turmoil.[28] The pre-Romantic hierarchy of plants, thought to mirror the human condition, is reflected, too, in Shakespearean imagery:

> Out of this nettle, danger, we pluck this flower, safety. [29]

Elizabethan aversion to weeds is reflected in Antony FitzHerbert's *Boke of Husbandrie*, published in 1523. May heralded the 'tyme to wede thy corn'. The sixteenth-century English farmer had to deal with 'divers manner of wedes', like nettles and dodder, which 'doe moche harme'. Thistles, docks and kedlokes (charlock), darnolde (darnel) and gouldes (corn marigold) were bad enough. Dog fenell [sic] (stinking mayweed) 'is the worst weed that is except terre' (hairy vetch).[30]

Such weeds and the hard labour they demanded were a far cry from the land of Virgil's *Georgics*, the land that needed no farming, 'the soil that needed no harrowing' and the Golden Age of Hesiod's *Theogony*.[31] Those Arcadian myths would, however, survive the powerful Judeo-Christian theology of the Garden and the Fall, symbolic of good and evil, punishment and atonement, which abound among the plants and fruits of the Old and New Testaments.

W. E. Shewell-Cooper, Principal of the Missionary Horticultural College at Thaxted, Essex, in the 1950s and 60s, saw the human condition after the Fall, (Genesis 1:4), as a transition from Arcadia, a life without toil, to 'a battle with weeds ... a hard life of sweat and toil'.

Thenceforth, the Other had to be always contended with:

> And on all the hills that shall be digged with the mattock, there shall not come thither the fear of briars and thorns (Isaiah 7:25).

The New Testament parable of the sower carries the same message, couched in the language of grim competition:

> And some [seed] fell among thorns; and the thorns sprang up; and choked them (Matthew 13:7).[32]

The imagery is particularly explicit in the 'Parable of Weeds Explained', (Matthew 13:33):

> The one who sowed the good seed is the Son of Man ... The weeds are the sons of the evil one and the enemy who sows them is the devil ... The Son of Man will send out his angels and they will weed out of his kingdom everything that

causes sin and who do evil. They will throw them into the fiery furnace, where there will be weeping and gnashing of teeth.[33]

Michael Zohary, Professor Emeritus of Botany at the Hebrew University, Jerusalem, explored the relationships between 'biblical man' and his natural environment.[34] Zohary's 1982 work points to a conceptual, if not a textual, consistency across time and translation. Solomon gilded his lily among the brambles (Song of Solomon 2:1–2). Christ's tormentors mockingly crowned him with one or other of the dozen or so spiny species that grow around Jerusalem (John 19:5). The crackling of thorny burnet in a cooking fire 'is the laughter of fools; this also is vanity' (Ecclesiastes 7:6).

Each tree could be recognised by its fruit:

> For figs are not gathered from thorns, nor are grapes picked from a bramble bush. [The good man brings good things out of the good stored up in his heart and the evil man brings evil things] (Luke 6: 44–45).[35]

In the early thirteenth century the cleric Alexander of Neckam developed this theme of governance of the earth by moral rather than biological causes. The degraded state of mankind and the natural world served as a constant and painful intimation of the Fall and all that had been lost. That poisonous plants now exist when once there had been none, and that they brought unease into the world, were continuing reminders of the consequences of humanity's pride and deceit.[36]

Post-Reformation reinterpretations of the biblical place of people in the world expanded on the idea of deterioration in nature after the Fall. The earth had degenerated. Thorns and thistles grew up where once there had been fruits and flowers.[37] Some commentators revisited ideas of order and purpose, and human domination of the 'lesser' creation, one of the central ideas of Judeo-Christian theology. 'Thou hast given him dominion over the works of thy hands; thou hast put all things under his feet' (Psalm 8:6).[38]

Taking his cue from natural theologians like John Ray (1627–1705), the herbalist William Cole, in his *The Art of Simples* (1656), thought that even weeds and poisons had their purpose. It required 'the industry of men to weed them out ... Had he nothing to struggle with, the fire of his spirit would be half extinguished.'[39] The English jurist, Sir Matthew Hale (1609–76) went further. Not only did order and purpose exist in the world, but Man also had a duty to exercise his growing control over nature. Hale believed, from his reading of Genesis, that:

> Man was invested with the power, authority, right, dominion, trust and care ... to preserve the Species of divers Vegetables, to improve them and others, to correct the redundancies of unprofitable Vegetables, to preserve the face of the Earth in beauty, usefulness and fruitfulness.[40]

Hale could also look back to Aristotle and the Stoics for support for the belief that nature existed solely to serve humanity's interests.[41] By his 'superintendent industry' Man could prevent the world becoming 'overgrown with excessive excrescences', a wilderness of trees, weeds, thorns and briars. Thomas Sprat (1635–1713), historian of the Royal Society, advanced Hale's position another step. Deteriorated nature could be improved by art. Environmental improvement could come from plant introductions, by using animals and by 'comparative husbandry'.[42]

So too, the seventeenth-century farmer drew a distinct line between crops and weeds. The latter were 'an obscenity, the vegetable equivalent of vermin'. To a thorough agricultural improver like Walter Blith gorse, ferns, rushes, bracken and broom were 'such filth'. The eighteenth-century agricultural writer William Ellis went so far as to lump marigolds, wild irises, honey suckle and water lilies in with weeds. The late seventeenth-century aesthete Roger North proclaimed that 'weeds have no beauty'.

But in seventeenth-century London, willowherb, foxglove and poppies, the last the bane of wheat growers, were sought by gardeners as decorative plants. A mid-century herbalist, William Gerard, noted that some gardeners were wont to 'feast themselves even with varieties of those things the vulgar call weeds'. He admitted that, 'narrowly observed' there is 'a great deal of prettiness in every one of them'. Country gardens, too, could include scabious, campion and larkspur. Keith Thomas tells us that well-known late eighteenth-century gardeners like William Hanbury 'thought heather very elegant and looked kindly on meadowsweet and even thistles'. The agricultural writer William Marshall considered blackberry flowers were 'beautiful beyond expression'. 'Rude, cultivated' tracts of gorse and broom in the royal gardens at Richmond did not, however, impress the Scottish philosopher and agricultural improver, Henry Home, Lord Kames (1696–1782).[43]

Another group perceived weeds differently too. Herbalists and apothecaries had never doubted the medicinal value of wild plants. William Turner, whose herbal was published in Cologne in 1568, worried that 'precious herbs' were dismissed by the ignorant as 'weeds or grass'. Allied to the herbalists, a growing band of naturalists like Robert Sharrock could see beauty in the great-horsetail of bogs and ditches. 'Botanists', wrote Samuel Pegge in his *Curialia Miscellanea*, penned in 1796 and published in 1818, 'allow nothing to be weeds'.

Both groups took a utilitarian view of the plant world. New discoveries considered to be of medicinal value were recorded and transplanted to 'physic gardens'.[44] There is a tradition that the Swedish naturalist Carolus Linneaus (1707–78) fell on his knees at the sight of English gorse 'the enemy of every improver ... and gave thanks for so beautiful a plant'. (Some would have it that it was in fact Johann Dillenius, Sheridan Professor of Botany at Oxford from 1734.)[45]

Other modes of European thought added to a growing confusion about the people–weeds relationship. In the course of one of his critiques of natural theology, the German poet, dramatist and scientist, Johann von Goethe (1749–1832) used weeds to illustrate both the anthropocentric nature of the relationship and the tenuousness of the teleology invoked by the natural theologians. It came as no surprise, given the nature of human experience, that mankind should see itself living in a purposeful world as an end of the creation. The word 'weed', however, revealed the misconception:

> Why should [man] not call a plant a weed, when from his point of view it really ought not to exist? He will much more readily attribute the existence of thistles hampering his work in the field to the curse of an enraged benevolent spirit, or the malice of a sinister one, than simply regard them as children of universal Nature, cherished as much by her as the wheat he carefully cultivates and values so highly.[46]

INTO THE NEW WORLD

The late eighteenth-century American agricultural writer John Lorain took a similar line, albeit at a more practical level. The effect of American settlers' farming practices on soil fertility concerned him. He recognised the interdependency of species within ecosystems, and particularly the role of the smaller organisms ('animalcules') and decaying vegetable matter in maintaining soil fertility:

> The fertilizing effects of the perfect system of economy is equally clearly seen in our glades, as in our forests, where nature is suffered to pursue her own course ... The same may be said of weeds, notwithstanding slovenly farmers complain still more loudly of the injury done by them. [47]

He doubted the notion that soil impoverishment is the result of some biblical curse. Weeds were not the cause, although perhaps an effect. He saw soil impoverishment as an even greater curse.[48]

The Romantics and their precursors, too, were articulating other thoughts on weediness. William Cowper (1731–1800), in his long poem on rural themes, *The Task,* written towards the end of the eighteenth century, venerated the fern and gorse on an overgrown common. John Clare (1793–1864), the poet–gardener son of an impoverished Peterborough labourer, wrote frequently of the beauty of common agricultural weeds like ragwort, yarrow, rushes, spear thistle and corn poppies. John Louden (1783–1843), Scottish founder and editor of *The Gardener's Magazine*, told his readers that briar, sloe thorn, fern and bramble 'would, if introduced into the picturesque grounds of a residence, have a most enchanting effect'. John Ruskin (1819–1900) thought a flower garden an 'ugly thing' compared to wild nature.[49]

Across the Atlantic, Henry Thoreau (1817–62), thought the wild meadow grasses, into which the Pilgrims had stepped two centuries earlier, were more rank, the forests more extensive and open, the trees larger, and the animal population more diverse. The strawberries, the gooseberries, raspberries and the currants were far larger and more abundant than any he knew.[50] Thoreau, ever the romantic journalist, looked back to the mythical Golden Age.

In the century following the Pilgrims, Rational Europe had busied itself subduing Nature in its front gardens. Unlike Thoreau, French writers like Buffon (1707–88) and Raynal celebrated man's role in transforming the landscape. Raynal believed that the European colonists' capacity to change their environment distinguished them from 'Indians'.[51] The Philadelphia physician and politician, Benjamin Rush (1745–1813), thought cultivation of a new country by 'draining swamps, destroying weeds, burning brush and exhaling the unwholesome or superfluous moisture of the air' helped to render it healthy.[52]

To another contemporary writer, the changes wrought upon the New World landscape were reminiscent of something far greater. Writing to a colleague, the clergyman–physician and agricultural improver Jared Eliot enthused:

> Take a view of a Swamp in its original Estate, full of Bogs, overgrown with Flags, Brakes, poisonous Weeds and Vines ... The baleful Thickets of Brambles, and the dreary Shades of the longer Growth ... [then after it is drained] Behold it now cloathed [sic] with sweet verdant Grass, adorned with the lofty wide spreading well set Indian-Corn; the yellow Barley; ... a wonderful Change this! and all brought about in a short time; a Resemblance to Creation ...[53]

Eliot's correspondent begged to differ. Practical John Bartram (1699–1777), the first American to lay out a botanical garden, had observed that the entanglement of mud and debris, brought down by floods, among the hazels, weeds and vines of the bottomlands, maintained soil fertility in riverside lowlands. Clearing the weeds would prevent the deposition of debris and enhance soil erosion.[54]

Nevertheless, in the New World, as in the Old, the improvers took the moral high ground. Edward Johnson envisioned the transformations from savage to civilised as 'the planting of a garden, not the fall from one; any change in the New England environment was divinely ordained and wholly positive'.[55] That, of necessity, included the introduction of Old World weeds. Divinely ordained or not, two rather less positivist commentators recorded that laws were introduced in Connecticut, Massachusetts and Rhode Island at various times during the eighteenth century, to control barberry, a vector in wheat blast disease.[56]

Weeds were one of humanity's camp followers, a global phenomenon, in both the Old and New Worlds of the American lawyer, politician, philologist and diplomat George Perkins Marsh (1801–82). He found that many of the species he had collected during his travels were equally at home in the wheat fields of Upper Egypt, the gardens of the Bosphorus or the cultivations of New England. Man transplanted them.[57] Nature propagated them. In this instance Marsh granted equal agency to both.[58] In the struggle that often followed, one or the other might flourish. In some districts in China, weeds had been entirely eradicated. Elsewhere, long after the abandonment of some rural cottage, luxuriant weeds were the only sign that man and his buildings had once existed.[59] Using the language of rational analysis, Marsh sought to lay open the processes that bound these organisms together.

He had long been a progressivist, albeit a cautious one.[60] He saw agricultural man as an improver (and, for that matter, an improvement; Marsh saw rural America in 1847 as the outcome and 'first example of the struggle between civilised man and barbarous uncultivated nature'). Natural science would contribute much to improving agricultural practice. There were also benefits to be had from improvements to existing farming techniques, including the 'extirpation of thistles and other weeds, and the destruction of noxious insects'. But things could go too far. Some New England hillsides, stripped of forests, had lost their thin soils to erosion 'in the rage for improvement' and now yielded no crop 'but a harvest of noxious weeds to infest with their seeds the rich arable lands below'.[61]

Marsh marked a paradigm shift in the man–nature discourse and the language that structured it. Man 'modified' nature rather than the reverse. With Marsh the new relationship found expression as dialectic, 'a complication of conflicting or coincident forces, acting through a long series of generations'. Moreover the modifications wrought were given a new moral and political dimension.

'Exploitation', 'destruction', 'deterioration' and 'invasion' began to colour and shape the discussion among Marsh's admirers and disciples, and the subsequent environmental debate, for the better part of a century and a half.[62]

SETTLERS AND SCIENCE: NEW ZEALAND

Since then, in Antipodean colonial and post-colonial literature, two other themes have emerged. Some of the participants turned to the explanatory power of science, in its theoretical and applied forms, to try to understand and in due course to attempt to control the unwanted transformations occasioned by European occupation of new environments and the attempted reconstruction of European landscapes in those environments. At the same time, politics and civic institutions became a forum for expressions of concern about these transformations and a tool against the worst of them. Both occurred in the context of a repetition and, often, a compounding of the North American experience in colonies like Australia and New Zealand.[63]

Tim Flannery, in *The Future Eaters*, his 1995 ecological history of Australasia, examined the fundamental differences between European and Antipodean ecosystems. The rapidly opening spaces and comparatively young, rich, post-glacial soils of Europe favoured floral species which had the various traits of those species we now call weeds – rapid colonisation of bare ground, fast breeding, wide dispersal, domination of an environment and tolerance of close human settlement:

> Mobile, fertile and robust, Europe's life forms were purpose-made to inherit new lands ... [In the European contest] only the most disturbance-loving hardy and tenacious [had] survived.

On the other hand the ancient, poor soils of the relict Gondwanaland, with their low energy flows, selected for a diversity of species which, over aeons of time, had become highly specialised, localised and co-operative rather than competitive. One other critical factor influenced what happened next:

> ... Europeans were blind, and still largely are, to endemism and biodiversity and the importance of these features in an ecosystem. They assumed that all ecosystems worked pretty much like the European ones they coevolved with; with its few tenacious species occupying ranges of hundreds of thousands of kilometres.[64]

Flannery's ecological insight was of course inaccessible to settlers and scientists during the early colonial years. Some of their contemporary responses to weeds and the weediness and the follies resulting from their ignorance have been traced by two post-colonial New Zealand writers. One of them, Gordon Ell, professed to be 'an enthusiast for the outdoors, not a scientist'. The other, Ross Galbreath, came from science to historiography.

Ell's enthusiasm for the profusion of exotic wildflowers-turned-weeds, which have been transplanted into New Zealand from virtually every region of the globe, resembles that of the nineteenth-century Romantics. This multiplicity of both species and origins, Ell wrote in 1983, reflects both 'the sources of our settlers and the seeds and sentiment they brought here'. And he mourns the almost-lost knowledge of their medicinal and culinary properties:

> Now that the chemist shop replaces the herb garden, and the vegetable market the roadside patch, the wildflowers are no longer relevant to our survival.

But in a transplanted society, centred upon a utilitarian and improving agriculture, there was little room for sentiment, so that in a very short time the distinction between wildflower and weed became a fine one. Ell was very clear about the mechanisms and agencies involved in this transformation:

> Brutally, suddenly cleared of its native cover, New Zealand has grown a new skin ... [in a different climatic and ecological regime] Wildflowers have become 'as common as weeds'.

Moreover:

> Their toleration in a country dependent on farming has become unendurable ... In the scientific establishment ... the wildflowers have been a particular concern.

The pursuit of chemical and biological controls for agricultural weeds became an industry in itself. But, Ell argued, there is another side to this realism:

> New Zealand shall never be a "virgin" land again. We have remade it with an amalgam of exotic and native wildlife. While it is worth decrying the loss of native species, there remains the fact that much of New Zealand has developed into another country.[65]

Galbreath, in his 1989 biography of Walter Buller, the nineteenth-century New Zealand naturalist, lawyer and politician, explored some of the contemporary scientific efforts to come to terms with this transformation and the attempts to ameliorate, or at least explain, some aspects of it. In particular, he dealt with a nineteenth-century scientific blind alley. Buller and some of his colleagues were attracted to and placed much faith in displacement theory. In their view native flora and fauna, including people, would be displaced by superior European species. They invoked Darwinism. 'It was simply a matter of survival of the fittest.' As an explanatory proposition it had the support of Darwin, Wallace and Hooker. They, each and together, gave natural laws sole agency. In New Zealand W.T.L. Travers, the nineteenth-century gentleman settler, amateur naturalist and politician was one who firmly advocated the theory.[66]

A contemporary, and remarkable, group of largely self-taught settler-scientist-politicians challenged this view. Influenced by his reading of Marsh, the Canterbury runholder Thomas Potts, among others, put a counter-argument. The transformation of New Zealand resulted not from 'any mysterious law of nature, but ... [is] a consequence of human action'.[67]

From his own observations, another runholder, Herbert Guthrie Smith, was in no doubt about human and other animals' agency. He painstakingly chronicled what he called the obliteration of a virgin landscape in the Hawkes Bay region of the North Island and its replacement, largely by his own hand, with alien plants and animals, among which he placed himself. In his preface to the first edition of *Tutira: The Story of a New Zealand Sheep Station*, published in 1921, Guthrie Smith urged his reader to 'mark, learn, and inwardly to digest the subcutaneous erosion of a countryside, the ancient way of the Maori, the fortunes of pioneer man and beast, the acclimatisation of an alien flora and fauna'.

> In the wake of our sailors, explorers, soldiers, and pioneers, they steal unnoticed, unobserved. The proverbial sun that never sets on the flag, never sets on the chickweed, groundsel, dandelion and veronicas that grow in every British garden and on every British garden-path ... Following the destruction [of the ancient vegetation of the sheep-run] through man's agency by fire and stock, a huge area of virgin soil was, to use a New Zealand political term, "thrown open to selection" ... [and] a host of ancient and eager rivals rushed upon the soil. With the assistance and assent of the stock the ground was seized, not only by indigenous plants, whom we may imagine to have been for centuries eagerly waiting for expansion and jealous of their hungry foe, but by aliens brought from thousands of miles – from Europe, Asia, Australia and America; from, in fact the four quarters of the globe.[68]

WEEDS, PEOPLE AND CONTESTED PLACES

G. M. Thomson, a Dunedin teacher turned professional scientist, also questioned the received wisdom. Thomson considered that the isolated, large islands of New Zealand provided a unique opportunity to explore in some detail the processes and agencies involved in the introduction of a host of exotic species. In a book put together in 1922, towards the end of his life, he said he first approached the subject from the point of view of natural selection but, from the evidence, soon came to the conclusion that other agencies were involved. He attributed the first introduction of European weed species to James Cook, who planted vegetable gardens at Dusky and Queen Charlotte Sounds in 1773. What happened to Cook's garden at Dusky intrigued him:

> In 1791 Vancouver visited Dusky Sound and Lieut. Menzies reported that in the garden (made by Cook eight years previously) there had grown up a dense covering of brushwood and fern, which obliterated all sign of the old clearing ... In view of the struggle between indigenous and introduced plants which exercised the minds of many eminent naturalists, and to which reference is made in the writings of Hooker, Darwin, Wallace and others, the record of [these] further visits to Dusky Sound is interesting.[69]

Thomson went on to trace the history of exotic plant introductions, through garden cultivation by itinerant whalers and sealers and the giving of European garden and agricultural seeds and plants to Maori by missionaries. He remarked on other deliberate and accidental introductions, for example in the seed stores, baggage, bedding, rubbish, ballast and packaging materials of immigrant ships.[70]

He also reviewed provincial and national legislative attempts, from the 1850s onwards, to deal with many introduced animals and plants, which had 'increased at a rate that upset all calculations'. The Noxious Weeds Act of 1900, consolidated in 1908, gave some measure of control including, for the first time, reasonably effective border control. But:

> The early settlers were great law-makers, but also great law breakers, for it is of no avail to make laws which cannot be kept or at least enforced, and in a great many of these restrictive ordinances Nature was too strong for the settlers and beat them very frequently.

Lamenting that, one hundred and fifty years after Cook, 'the country has not yet realised the necessity of a scientific treatment of the whole question of naturalisation', Thomson saw the way ahead lying in two directions:

> ... closer settlement of the land coupled with more intensive cultivation; and better education of all those concerned in the primitive [i.e., primary] industries of the country ... as to the economic waste that ensues whenever undesirable animals and plants are allowed to thrive.[71]

On the educational front, F. W. Hilgendorf aimed his 1926 book, *Weeds of New Zealand and How to Eradicate Them*, at farmers, students 'and that large class of people that has no special interest in weeds' but enquired about things generally. Hilgendorf, professor of agriculture at Canterbury Agricultural College, Lincoln, briefly rehearsed some of the history, origins and habits of weeds. He believed that despite a general fear in the 1850s that 'the country would be completely overrun' by some introduced weeds like Scotch thistle, 'the virulence of the attack' of this and other weeds like foxglove and Californian thistle had, by 1926, passed.[72]

Regarding science, it is clear from what Thomson wrote that in New Zealand understandings were changing quite rapidly, away from a purely organismic 'displacement' approach to a systemic, ecological consideration of plant naturalisations.[73] Among that of others, Thomson used the work of Leonard Cockayne, a pioneer New Zealand ecologist, to illustrate the point. Cockayne, a self-educated naturalist, had in 1919 tartly dismissed displacement in favour of ecological explanations.[74] Although many exotic plants:

> at first sight appear better suited to the soil and climate than are the indigenous species ... this is only the case where draining, cultivation, constant burning of forest, scrub and tussock, and the grazing of a multitude of domestic animals have made absolutely new edaphic [i.e., soil, ground] conditions which approximate those of Europe and there is no wonder the European invader can replace the aboriginal.[75]

In their discourse on the history of the colonial New Zealand flora, Travers, Potts, Thomson and Cockayne were using their science to try to understand the profound changes that they witnessed during their lifetimes. Some, among the rising generation of New Zealand professional scientists were, by the 1920s, considering the application of science, and particularly ecological principles, to weed control.

A short history of the investigation of biological control of weeds in New Zealand by the Cawthron Institute, published in 1970, sheds some light on a shift away from the explanatory towards what the Australian environmental historian Libby Robin has labelled 'government science', a science geared to economic development.[76] The author, D. Millar, became director of the programme in 1928. Public funding in 1926, to investigate insect control of weeds in New Zealand, followed the success of similar programmes elsewhere in the Pacific.[77] Limited though Millar's history is, in that it focuses essentially on the narrow framework of the contemporary research and its outcomes, it provides an insight into the emergence of a distinctly agronomistic outlook and mode of thought, characteristic of New Zealand agricultural science from then onwards. Miller could still conclude in the late 1960s that 'the successful biological control of any weed is futile unless *something useful* [emphasis added] is grown in place of the weed'.[78]

This ideology is also evident in the contributions of Miller and another New Zealand scientist to a 1940 international symposium on the control of weeds.

WEEDS, PEOPLE AND CONTESTED PLACES

Bruce Levy, of the grasslands division of the Plant Research Bureau, Palmerston North, advocated weed prevention by carefully balancing sward composition and density, and stock grazing to reduce weed competition and increase land productivity. 'No major work of control can be permanently effective unless the country is at the same time effectively grazed and farmed.'[79] Miller viewed the reversion of four million acres of former pasture to scrub and second growth indigenous forest, *via* infestation by noxious weeds, as an economic waste. He advocated a cultural solution to the weed problem, dependent on sound pasture and stock management. But, echoing Thomson, he said that 'owing to existing conditions, among which lack of population is prominent, cultural control cannot altogether be depended upon'.[80]

In his 1973 review of the history of noxious weeds legislation in the state of Victoria, Australia, W.T. Parsons, director of the Keith Turnbull research station at Frankstown, came to much the same conclusion as Thomson and Miller about the effectiveness of legislation by itself to control weeds. The fragmented nature of Australian administration within and across state borders constituted part of the problem. Parson promoted an understanding of the ecology of weed species and the use of pasture management to control them. Parsons' comments on fragmentation are pertinent to the New Zealand situation following the relatively recent handing over of weed control to regional councils, and the emerging disparities between their localised policies and methods.[81]

This preoccupation with the application of public science to the control of wild nature and thus the enhancement of productivity has been a persistent theme in the New Zealand literature since World War II, virtually up to the present day. An American, A.H. Clark, who spent almost two years in New Zealand during the early years of World War II, drew attention in 1949 to infestations of North Canterbury tussock grasslands by Nasella tussock, an Argentinian import. No agreement had been reached on effective control methods, but the time-honoured recourse to legislation got under way just before Clark left the country in 1942. This would establish control boards, similar to rabbit boards.[82]

Clark also saw the eradication of gorse as problematic. It could be managed where 'good husbandry' kept hedges under control. But farmers held the opinion, almost universally, that wherever gorse had spread across the wide Canterbury riverbeds, up gullies and over hill slopes, cutting and grubbing infested areas became uneconomic because of the low productivity of most of the land involved.[83] They held out some hope that quick-growing pines might in some locations out-compete gorse for sunlight and water. Success on any large scale required either 'a labour of love' from farmers or government assistance.

Broom posed a lesser problem, because it had not spread to anywhere near the same extent. Blackberry, which covered thousands of acres in the higher-rainfall regions of Nelson and Westland, presented a different story. Clark attributed its spread to birds eating the ripe berries. He wondered whether its introduction might have had something to do with west-country English immigrants' taste for blackberry pie and clotted cream. Biological control of gorse had met with limited success. With blackberry, it was a non-starter. The preferred parasites were 'too catholic in their tastes' to permit release without endangering the wider fruit industry.[84]

In *The Western Invasions of the Pacific and its Continents* (1963), the Australian historical geographer A.G. Price picked up Clark's general theme of dogged transformations for the sake of productivity. But he took cognisance of the price of that transformation, in terms of wildly fluctuating imbalances in the new, manufactured ecosystems. Price considered (wrongly, as has been demonstrated here) that only from around 1907 did 'the New Zealanders ... see the practical results of the invasions'. Although by then New Zealand depended on exotic species for its economic prosperity, in the 1950's the country continued to face problems arising from ongoing disturbances to ecological balances. The control of rabbits, for example, had brought in its wake the rapid spread of introduced sweet briar.[85]

Nevertheless an emphasis on weeds and weediness as the antithesis of productivity and prosperity continued. In a booklet published in 1949 for both popular consumption and educational use, the geographer K. B. Cumberland felt sure that 'Grass, livestock, fertilisers and enlightened farmers ... build the prosperity of New Zealand.' He contrasted pastures which 'are maintained by careful grazing and frequent topdressing with artificial fertilisers' to those:

> where methods and management have been deficient [and] pasture grasses have been largely replaced or crowded out by weeds, second growth and shrubby plants of very great variety.

He did grant nature some beneficial agency. When erosion followed in the wake of forest removal from hill country weeds like gorse, bracken and manuka helped to stabilise sheet erosion and provided a nursery for forest re-growth:

> It is a consolation to know that if and when man withdraws from the higher-rainfall hill country, then nature is willing to assume control again.[86]

Not everyone shared Cumberland's patronising, agronomical point of view. Following a sojourn in New Zealand from 1947 to 1949, the American zoologist, ornithologist and oceanographer R. C. Murphy in 1952 set down his own and earlier perceptions of, and current views about, the relationship between people and nature in New Zealand, from pre-European times to the present.[87] He too, saw the transformation of the indigenous flora and fauna in terms of invasion and, more importantly, ecological disturbance.[88] Noting Darwin's and Hooker's mistaken conclusion that Old World plants possessed some intrinsic competitive superiority, he reiterated Thomson's and Cockayne's positions, observing that:

> European plants were superior only in being dominants in a long-established man-made kind of terrain, to which much of New Zealand in turn was being rapidly converted.[89]

WEEDS, PEOPLE AND CONTESTED PLACES

Clearly taken aback by both the speed and scale of the transformation, and the changes that had occurred to the growth and dispersal patterns ('population explosions') of introduced species, Murphy lamented a lack of space to catalogue the 'shocking effects' upon the indigenous flora and the soil. He agreed with Cumberland on one point. Too much of the land had gone 'down to the sea in slips'.[90] But in the same way that Americans had forgotten that their north eastern states had once been a land of wild turkeys and huge white pines, most New Zealanders were, Murphy thought, largely oblivious to what he regarded as changes for the worse. Much 'manufactured' grassland had reverted to scrub, through the agency of gorse and broom. Academics, educators, a very few politicians, enlightened agriculturalists and sections of the press were aware of the situation. But the lag between what the few knew and what all should know was great.[91]

The generally pessimistic tenor of his remarks was not altogether misplaced. In the June 1960 issue of the *New Zealand Journal of Agriculture*, which marked its fiftieth anniversary, three articles reviewed the history of weeds and attempts to deal with them.[92]

One, by G.R. Moss, a farm advisory officer with the Department of Agriculture, dealt briefly with attempted legislative and biological controls, before moving on to consider cost-effective control measures. Moss concluded that the problem would remain 'until every gorse hedge has been destroyed'.[93]

Another article, by P.R Stephens, alluded to the role of weeds in 'man's struggle to develop agricultural production' from biblical times onwards. Drawing from *Journal* files, the author saw the war years, 1939–45, as a turning point in weed control in New Zealand. Failures with biological and chemical control had up to then frustrated a string of local researchers. The article concluded that the first introduction of selective organic weed sprays in 1946 had revolutionised weed control.[94]

Controversial attempts to introduce central government legislation to deal with noxious weeds, beginning in 1892, were reviewed in the third article, also by Stephens. By 1910 there had been a realisation, Stephens said, that the legislation which had finally been passed in 1900, could not of itself rid the country of noxious weeds. Stephens advocated 'careful and repeated cultivation [as] the radical exterminator'. Like Levy before him, he saw salvation from pasture weeds such as Californian thistle coming in the form of competition from stronger-growing grass species.[95]

An ironic twist to the tale of post-war weed control came within a few years. In the late 1970s Cumberland, by then professor emeritus at Auckland University, put together a televised series, *Landmarks*, on human-induced landscape changes in New Zealand, with an accompanying book. The language of agronomics and the imagery of conflict, crusade and battle pervaded his salvational account of the relationship between people and other introduced species:

> Nature exacts its revenge. Haphazard introduction of alien animals and plants

had unforeseen and often disastrous effects. Man's fleeting hold was threatened as the land lost its fruitfulness or the soil slipped away. Lessons were learned the hard way – and only just in time.

But, and for Cumberland it was a very big 'but', he worried that if weed-killers like 2-4-5-T (the Agent Orange of Vietnam, used on gorse in New Zealand) were withdrawn due to mounting concerns about their effects on people, the implications for farm productivity could be 'profound'.[96]

Two other accounts of problems associated with New Zealand weeds, published in the early 1980s, stand in some contrast to Cumberland's position. A. Rahman attributed the introduction of most arable weeds to seed impurities and farm machinery. He foresaw a greater use of selective weed killers but unlike Cumberland, regarded this as a mere panacea. The outcome would be simply a 'continuing and faster change of the weed flora of arable land'. L. J. Matthews was equally explicit. He noted that there were no endemic weeds of improved pastures in New Zealand.[97] 'Mankind must accept full responsibility for present-day problems.' The agronomistic doctrine that management of grazing animals alone would control pasture weeds had 'over-coloured' thinking to the extent that 'a paucity of knowledge still governs many weed control practices'. It could be demonstrated that weeds were to be found in New Zealand pastures as a direct result of excessive control pressures. He took the position that 'each and every agricultural practice develops its own set of weed problems'. He advocated a better knowledge and application of weed ecology including, in some cases, the complete withdrawal of all control measures.[98]

Writing in 1981, B. E.V. Parham of the botany division of the Department of Scientific and Industrial Research, Lincoln, thought otherwise. In New Zealand, 'no form of land use can be undertaken without adequate provision for their control, however difficult and expensive'.[99] By the end of the 1980s, however, control regardless of cost came under closer scrutiny. R. J. Field, professor, and G.T. Daly, reader of plant science at Lincoln University, Canterbury, separated 'control' into three categories – eradication, prophylaxis and containment. Using an economic and 'cosmetic' threshold model they, like Matthews, took the view that in those cases where numbers fall below a threshold level, determined by a farm-based cost–benefit analysis, then weeds should be tolerated.[100].

CONCLUSION

So, these are some of the ways people have conceptualised and written about their relationships with a specific part of nature, which we in the English-speaking West have come to call weeds. However obscure the etymological roots of our name for a group of plants with which we continue to compete and still seek in some measure to control, it is possible to discern, through the various literatures, the varieties of Otherness in which we have cast them.

WEEDS, PEOPLE AND CONTESTED PLACES

The Neolithic monocultures that transformed the ecosystems of the Near East were the seedbeds of a conceptual transition about the relationship between people and their floral competitors. This transition found expression in, among other places, the tribal stories that became the literature of the Old Testament. Genesis 2 and 3 explained not only the 'how' but also the 'why' of the tribulations experienced by an agricultural society in an unforgiving environment.[101]

Reinforced by Greco-Roman traditions of lost innocence and Arcadian places, the retributive and antipathetic symbolisms of weediness passed into the New Testament. From the Parables, weeds took on a moral as well as a theological Otherness. Both were re-emphasised by the new exegeses of the post Reformation years and flowed into the language and imagery of secular affairs. They coloured not only the literature of Shakespearean England but, as van der Zweep has shown, much of that of middle and western Europe.[102]

In the world of the natural theologians, weeds as part of Nature reflected a purposeful Deity, one, which, moreover, looked kindly upon a self-improving humanity. Weeds became part and parcel of the Halesian imperative to subjugate Nature in the raw, the elimination of their Otherness being held up as a mark of moral rectitude, or at least good husbandry.

In the Enlightened Old and New Worlds, some were not so sure. With weediness, reason seemed often to fly in the face of received wisdom. For some, weeds regained their former utility, retaining something of their moral purposefulness. For others like the apothecaries, morality was subsumed by practicality. For some of the botanists, there never had been Otherness.

And as urban humanity moved away from Nature in the raw, aesthetic and poetical considerations gave weeds yet another hue. Otherness became romanticised. At the same time, the new, positivist science and the newer geography occasioned a quite different rethinking of the nature–humanity relationship, one that came down, increasingly, on the side of Nature. With growing clarity, it came to be seen that weediness is not intrinsic, not a category of nature. Whatever Otherness weeds may possess, it is an outcome of human artifice.

Weeds exercised the minds of the Antipodean settler-scientists, their professional successors and their politicians. In New Zealand the public discourse has been constructed around quite disparate scientific, geographic and historical-geographic positions. Initially it centred on ideas about the role of 'natural laws' *versus* human agency. More recently fairly narrow notions of agricultural productivity within a strictly agronomic context have come up against much wider perceptions and expressions of disquiet, largely articulated by historical geographers, about the directions and practical outcomes of the discourse. A very few, like G. M. Thomson, Leonard Cockayne and Gordon Ell, sought to understand weediness and the success or failure of human responses in historical and cultural as well as scientific terms. They brought new insights into a relationship that had been intuitively understood by people like John Lorain in eighteenth-century America and Thomas Potts in nineteenth-century New

Zealand – that humans and weeds had long been competing for the same places, and that human monocultures had long advantaged the weeds.

Some twentieth-century sciences have, however, been intent not only on understanding the natural world but also on providing measures to subdue or improve it in a way that would have been understood by a sixteenth-century divine like Matthew Hale. The poisoning, however, of both places and people has, in some parts of the Western world, brought the relationship and the age-old competition for open places once again into sharp relief. Gradually, though hardly universally, there seems to be a shift in focus, from controlling the invader by whatever means to managing invaded ecosystems. Recent advocacy for the conservation of biodiversity by changing human behaviours with regard to plant introductions and use, land uses and the management of control measures would have appealed to Leonard Cockayne and his pioneering ecologist colleagues.[103]

With the striking exception of Frieda Knobloch's chapter about weeds in her 1996 book *The Culture of Wilderness*,[104] the discourse surveyed here has by and large been written by men, about men. In New Zealand, as elsewhere in the Western world, women's plants have been largely confined to garden culture. Wider aspects of women's cultures are, for example, tantalisingly hinted at in Ell's wildflowers and garden escapees. What might the historical record yield up to closer scrutiny?

It is a discourse of some breadth, but no great depth. Its existence, particularly in New Zealand, is due largely to disparate authors, other than historians. It is, moreover, an historiography that begs the question, why has the relationship between weeds, people and the places they contest, a contest that has gone on for something like ten millennia, been treated, as it were, only in passing? These and other questions about a remarkable inter-species relationship invite answers from environmental historians interested in a societal contest that shows no signs of abating.

GLOSSARY

Botanical nomenclature tends to vary from author to author and over time. To maintain some consistency with the sources, wherever possible the nomenclature used by authors such as Salisbury (1961) and Rackham (1986) has been replicated below. The particular nomenclature followed by an author is usually stated in her or his Preface or Introduction. In those instances where a botanical name is not given by any author cited, Hilgendorf (6th edition, 1960) has been used.

Barberry	*Berberis vulgaris*
Blackberry	*Rubus fruticosus, R. laciniatus* (Hilgendorf)
Bramble	*Rubus fruticosus*
Briar	*Rosa* spp. In New Zealand, usually *R. eglantaria*
Broom	*Cytisus (Sarothamnus) scoparius*

Californian Thistle	*Cirsium arvense* (Hilg.) Also known as Canadian thistle. Actually a native of Europe.
Campion	*Silene* spp.
Charlock (Wild turnip)	*Sinapis arvensis*
Darnel	*Lolium temulentum*
Dock	*Rumex* spp.
Dodder	*Cuscuta epithymum*
Fennel	*Foeniculum vulgare*
Fern (Bracken)	*Pteridium esculentum*
Foxglove	*Digitalis purpurea* (Hilg.)
Fumitory	*Fumaria officinalis* and *F. muralis*
Golden Thistle	*Scolymus hispanicus*
Goosefoot (Fat Hen)	*Chenopodium album*
Gorse (Furze, Whin)	*Ulex europeus*
Ground Elder	*Aegopodium podagraria*
Groundsel	*Senecio vulgaris*
Hairy Vetch	*Vicia hirsuta*
Hard Rush	*Juncus inflexus*
Heather	*Calluna vulgaris*. See also *Erica* spp.
Hemlock	*Conium maculatum*
Horsetail	*Equisetum arvense*
Meadowsweet	*Filipendula ulmaria*
Manuka	*Leptospermum scoparium*
Nasella Tussock	*Nasella trichotoma* (Hilg.)
Nettle	*Urtica dioica* and *U. urens*
Persicaria (redshank, knot weed, lady's thumb, willow weed)	*Polygonum persicaria*
Poppy	*Papaver rhoeas*
Ragwort	*Senecio jacobaea*
Rush	*Juncus* spp.
Sea plantain	*Plantago maritima*
Scentless mayweed	*Matricaria indora*,
St. John's Wort	*Hypericum perforatum*
Scabious	*Scabiosa columbaria*
Scotch Thistle	*Cirsium lanceolatum* (Hilg.)
Stinking Mayweed	*Anthemis cotula*
Thistles	One or other of *Carduus, Carlina, Centaurea, Cirsium, Onopordon* or *Silybum* spp.
Thorny Burnet	*Sarcopoterium spinosum*
Willow-herb	*Epilobium* spp.
Woad	*Isatis tinctoria*
Yarrow	*Achillea millefolium*

NOTES

This article began in a small way as an Honours research paper. That it appears here is due entirely to the gentle persuasion of my doctoral supervisors, Associate Professors Judy Bennett and Tom Brooking of the History Department, University of Otago. They eventually convinced me it was worth publishing and have subsequently guided and encouraged its various iterations. The initial inspiration came from Professor Tom Isern, North Dakota State University, who observed, in the course of a study visit to New Zealand, that quite a lot is understood about the history of Antipodean faunal invasions but little about the floral.

[1] Cited in W. van der Zweep, 'Golden words and wisdom about weeds – weeds in proverbs, quotations verse and prose', *Biology and Ecology of Weeds*, ed. W. Holzner and M. Numata (The Hague: Junk, 1982), 62. Van der Zweep comments that 'Weed scientists had better consider this a dissonance in their public relations.'

[2] 'Young' is used here in terms of length of European occupation. Geologically New Zealand is old, a remnant of Gondwanaland. As we shall see, that age is reflected in the nature of its indigenous flora.

[3] Leonard Cockayne, *New Zealand Plants and Their Story,* 2nd edition (Wellington: Government Printer, 1919), 145, 146.

[4] I am indebted to Associate Professor Judith Bennett, of the History Department, University of Otago, who drew my attention to Greg Bankoff's paper 'Societies in Conflict: Algae and Humanity in the Philippines', in *Environment and History* 5, 1 (1999): 97–123. I share Bankoff's critical view that among most historians there is 'an implicit assumption that humanity stands at the apex of life on this planet'.

[5] Two ideas which have developed some currency in recent years, biodiversity and ecofeminism, may not appear to have been given their due in this essay. With one or two exceptions they are not strongly reflected in the discourse cited here. An essay such as this, however, is by no means exhaustive. Much may have been overlooked in my reading.

[6] C. J. Glacken, *Traces on the Rhodian Shore, Nature and Culture in Western Thought From Ancient Times to the end of the Eighteenth Century* (Berkley: University Of California, 1967, reprinted 1990), 317.

[7] F. Uekoetter, 'Confronting the pitfalls of Environmental History: An Argument for an Organisational Approach'. *Environment and History* 4 (1998): 31–52.

[8] There is, in addition to the few examples cited here, a large, relatively recent and expanding North American literature touching upon various aspects of the history of the humans–weeds relationship. It is a literature that wants surveying in its own right, beginning perhaps with Alfred Crosby's *Ecological Imperialism: The Biological Expansion of Europe, 900–1900* (Cambridge: Cambridge University Press, 1986).

[9] F. Knobloch, *The Culture of Wilderness, Agriculture as Colonization in the American West* (Chapel Hill: North Carolina University Press, 1996): 114–15. 'Not weeds' is Knobloch's term.

[10] M. Pollan, 'Weeds Are Us', in *Second Nature: A Gardener's Education* (New York: Dell, 1991), 116. One-liners abound in both scholarly and popular accounts of weeds. Emerson's, 'A weed is simply a plant whose virtues we haven't yet discovered', is cited by Pollan.

[11] L.J. King, 'Some early forms of the weed concept', in *Nature*, 179 (1957), 1366; King, *Weeds of the World, Biology and Control* (London and New York: Hill, 1966), 1–6.

[12] For a derivation of the term 'weed' see *The New Shorter Oxford English Dictionary* (Oxford: Clarendon Press,1993), v. 2, 3648. King, *Weeds of the World*, 5, observed that in 1958 A. A. Lawrence of the Dictionary's editorial staff disagreed with this theory. King conceded that a philological approach could yield only a tentative connection between the modern term and the ubiquity of woad which, with very few exceptions, has not itself been generally classed as a weed. He commented that perhaps the botanical evidence was more compelling than the etymological. To conserve space in the text, common names for plants are used throughout. A glossary of botanical names is appended to this essay.
[13] King, *Weeds of the World*, 5.
[14] King, *Weeds of the World*, 8–9.
[15] Sir Edward Salisbury, *Weeds and Aliens* (London: Collins, 1961), 18.
[16] Salisbury, *Weeds and Aliens*, 82–3. Other plants, introduced into environments at or near their climatic tolerances, and which tend to be localised or rare, he classed as 'casual aliens'. An American ecologist Marcel Rejmánek, has separated weeds from 'invaders' and 'colonisers'. These, he says, reflect three different points of view: anthropocentric (weeds being plants growing where they are not wanted), ecological (colonisers appear early in plant successions) and bio-geographical (invaders spread into areas where they are not native). See 'What Makes a Species Invasive?' in *Plant Invasions, General Aspects and Special Problems*, P. Pyaek, K. Prach, M. Rejmánek and M. Wade, eds. (Amsterdam: SPB Academic Publishing, 1995), 3. All three aspects of 'weediness' are considered here.
[17] Salisbury, *Weeds and Aliens*, 30, 33, 206, 228, 274. His discussion of these aspects of weediness is, however, incidental, unsystematic and fragmentary.
[18] That may no longer be the case, but subsequent scholarship on the question, if there is any, has not emerged in the course of this survey.
[19] Salisbury, *Weeds and Aliens*, 24–9.
[20] Salisbury, *Weeds and Aliens*, 23.
[21] D. Worster, to the conference of the American Society for Environmental History, cited by M. Egan <michaele@sfu.ca> in 'The Future of Environmental History', contribution to H – NET List, <H-ASEH@H-NET.MSU.EDU>, 27 April 1999.
[22] C. S Elton, *The Ecology of Invasions by Animals and Plants* (London: Methuen, 1958), 117–18, Ch. 9, *passim*.
[23] O. Rackham, *The History of the Countryside – The Full Fascinating Story of Britain's Landscape* (London: Dent, 1986), xiii, 53.
[24] Rackham, *The History of the Countryside*, 53–4. Edward Hyams, *The Story of England's Flora* (Harmondsworth: Penguin, 1979), *passim*, provides an insight into the exotic origins and the history of the introduction into England of many species which have come to be thought of as indigenous to that country.
[25] 'The Herbarium of Apuleius', 11th century, in J. de Gex, *A Medieval Herbarium* (London: Pavilion Books, 1995), 22.
[26] de Gex, *A Medieval Herbarium*, 16. For a modern treatment of the history of those weeds considered to have curative properties, see P. Jones, *Just Weeds, History, Myths, and Uses* (New York: Prentice Hall, 1991).
[27] *Hamlet*, Act I, Scene ii. All quotations are from B. Hodek, ed., *The Complete Works of Shakespeare* (London: Spring Books, n.d.).
[28] Pollan, *Second Nature*, 118.
[29] *Henry IV, Part 1*, I. iii.
[30] Cited in Salisbury, *Weeds and Aliens*, 32–3, 146–7. Salisbury gives FitzHerbert as John in his text and A. in his index.

[31] Virgil, Eclogue IV, cited in R. Williams, *The Country and the City* (London: Oxford University Press, 1973), Ch. 3 *passim*.

[32] W. E. Shewell-Cooper, *Plants and Fruits of the Bible* (London: Darton, Longman and Todd, 1962), 145–8.

[33] *The New International Version Study Bible* (Michigan: Zondervan, 1984), 1462.

[34] M. Zohary, *Plants of the Bible* (Cambridge: Cambridge University Press, 1982), 9, 12–14, 153. Zohary notes that local renderings (Greek, Latin, Aramaic, Syric and so on) of Biblical weed and plant names, often quite unrelated to the Hebrew or Arabic originals, can be attributed to a lack of knowledge of Hebrew floral terminology among translators, from the Septuagint (third century BC) to the present. The same plant, for example, can in English become briar, bramble, thorn and thistle. Something of the significance of the parable is therefore lost in the looseness of the translation. Rackham, p. 23, has made the same general point in relation to the use of translations from Latin, Old English and Norman French as historical sources. Not only do translators misread their texts, but 'guess at the meanings of unknown technical terms or fail to uphold distinctions of meaning'. The 'weeds' in the Parable of Weeds are, according to Zohary, either darnel or Syrian scabious or both. Both plants were difficult to remove from a wheat crop. Both impart a bitterness to flour, while darnel can also harbour a poisonous fungus. Shakespearean England knew it well. 'Want ye corn for bread? 'tis full of Darnel; do ye like the taste?' *Henry VI*, cited in Salisbury, *Weeds and Aliens*, 33.

[35] Zohary, *Plants of the Bible*, 153–67. Zohary uses the Revised Standard Version, 1973, throughout. Luke 6:45, added here in parenthesis, is from the *NIV Study Bible*. The bramble in Solomon is probably Golden Thistle. Zohary gives that in Luke 6:44 as *Rubus sanguineus*. For the way in which biblical images of weediness have passed into Western folk culture and literature, see van der Zweep in *Biology and ecology of weeds*, *passim*.

[36] A. Neckam, *De naturis rerum*, ed. T. Wright, London, 1963, cited in Glacken, *Traces on the Rhodian Shore*, 206.

[37] Keith Thomas, *Man and the Natural World, Changing Attitudes in England 1500–1800* (London: Allen Lane, 1983), 17.

[38] Glacken, *Traces on the Rhodian Shore*, 57–8, 157, 164–5.

[39] William Cole, *The Art of Simples*, 1656, 93, cited in Thomas, *Man and the Natural World*, 19–20. Cole classified weeds as one of seven different kinds of herbs, along with potherbs, medicinal herbs, corn, pulse, flowers and grass. For a discussion of John Ray, see N.C. Gillespie, 'Natural History, Natural Theology and Social Order: John Ray and the "Newtonian Ideology"', *Journal of the History of Biology*, 20 (1997), 1–49.

[40] Sir Matthew Hale, *The Primitive Organisation of Mankind*, 1667, 369–70, cited in Glacken, *Traces on the Rhodian Shore*, 481.

[41] Thomas, *Man and the Natural World* 1983, 17.

[42] Hale, *The Primitive Organisation of Mankind*, 369–70; Thomas Sprat, *History of the Royal Society*, n.d., 119–121, 386. Both are cited in Glacken, *Traces on the Rhodian Shore*, 480–2. Dr Sprat was Lord Bishop of Rochester.

[43] Thomas, *Man and the Natural World*, 272. The anonymous composer of the traditional Scottish air 'The Broom o' the Cowdenowes' did not altogether share his countryman's view about the 'bonnie, bonnie broom'. See J.M. Diack, *The New Scottish Orpheus*, Glasgow, c.1922, 32–3 for score and lyrics and Silly Wizard, *Live Wizardry, The Best of Silly Wizard in Concert*, Green Linnet Inc, CD3036/37, 1988, track 13, for a recent rendition. I am grateful to Dr Alison Clarke, Hocken Library, University of Otago, for drawing my attention to this musical celebration of one of the 'weedy' flora.

WEEDS, PEOPLE AND CONTESTED PLACES

[44] Each is cited in Thomas, *Man and the Natural World*, 270–2. Blith seems to have been something of a super-improver. He published *The English Improver Improved* in 1649. Sharrock, Archdeacon of Winchester Cathedral, published *The History of the Propagation and Improvement of Vegetables by the Concurrence of Art and Nature* in 1660.

[45] G.W. Francis, *The Little English Flora*, 1839, 111–12, cited in Thomas, *Man and the Natural World*, 272.

[46] J. von Goethe, 'An Attempt to Evolve a General Comparative Theory', in *Goethe's Botanical Writings*, trans. Bertha Mueller, 81–4, cited in Glacken, *Traces on the Rhodian Shore*, 535–6.

[47] J. Lorain, *Nature and Reason Harmonized in the Practice of Husbandry*, Philadelphia, 1825, 27, cited in Glacken, *Traces on the Rhodian Shore*, 693–695.

[48] Lorain, *Nature and Reason Harmonized*, 518, cited in Glacken, *Traces on the Rhodian Shore*, 695–6.

[49] W. Cowper, *The Task*, lines 526–30; J. W. Tibble, ed., *The Poems of John Clare*, 1935; E. T. Cook and A. Wedderburn, *The Works of John Ruskin*, 1903–1912; A.T. Tait, *The Landscape Garden in Scotland*, Edinburgh, 1980. Each is cited in Thomas, *Man and the Natural World*, 272. Thomas observes, in a text note, 272, that 'to the reformer H.S. Salt a garden was merely "a zoo with the cruelty omitted"'.

[50] *The Journal of Henry David Thoreau*, B. Torrey and F. Allen, eds., New York, 1962, cited in W. Cronon, *Changes in the Land – Indians, Colonists and the Ecology of New England* (New York: Hill and Wang) 1983, 1–6.

[51] Raynal, *Histoire Philosophique et Politique des Establissements et du Commerce des Europ ens dans les deux Indes*, cited in Glacken, *Traces on the Rhodian Shore*, 682–3. Glacken comments, 663, that Buffon's ideas about man the improver in many ways anticipated George Perkins Marsh.

[52] B. Rush, 'An Enquiry into the Cause of the Increase of Bilious and Intermitting Fevers in Pennsylvania, with Hints of Preventing Them', *Transaction of the American Philosophical Society*, 2, 25 (1786) 206–12, cited in Glacken, *Traces on the Rhodian Shore*, 688.

[53] J. Eliot, undated letter in his *Essays upon Field Husbandry in New England and Other Papers, 1748–62*, ed. H.J. Carmen and R.G. Ingwell, New York, 1934, 96–7, cited in Glacken, *Traces on the Rhodian Shore*, 692–3.

[54] J. Bartram, in *Essays upon Field Husbandry in New England and Other Papers*, 203–4, cited in Glacken, *Traces on the Rhodian Shore*, 691. Bartram's early interest in things botanical is referred to by Hyams, *The Story of England's Flora*, 101.

[55] E. Johnson, *Johnson's Wonder-Working Providence*, J. Jameson, ed., New York, 1910; B. Rush, *Essays, Literary, Moral and Philosophical*, 2nd edn., Philadelphia, 1806, cited in Cronon, *Changes in the Land*, 1–6.

[56] T. Dwight, *Travels in New England and New York*, B. Solomon, ed., Cambridge Mass., 1969. Dwight, was realist enough to believe that it was 'altogether improbable' that barberry would ever be eradicated. He and Thomas Hutchinson are cited in Cronon, *Changes in the Land*, 155. Cronon does not give a source for Hutchinson. Rackham, *The History of the Countryside*, 42–3, cites moralists who, in the Age of Reason, dismissed the prejudice of farmers against barberry as an example of superstition. He quotes from W. Ellis, *The Timber-Tree Improved*, London, 1744:

> This Tree has an ill Name for attracting Blights to the Corn that grows near it an ignorant malicious Farmer of *Frethesden* about the year 1720 conceived such a Hatred against a large one, that grew in his Neighbour's Ground, that he poured several Pails of scalding Water on its Roots, in the Night-season, at different

Times, 'till he killed it.

[57] 'Man' is used here in the same non-gendered sense as Marsh used the term.

[58] G. P. Marsh, *Man and Nature, or Physical Geography as Modified by Human Action*, ed. D. Lowenthal (Cambridge: Harvard University Press, 1965), 61 and n. 18; 62 and n. 23; 63. This is in some contrast to the central thesis of *Man and Nature*, which eschewed environmental determinism in favour of an examination of man's effect on nature.

[59] Marsh, *Man and Nature*, 61 and n. 19; 65, 66. Rackham, in his discussion of historical methods and evidence, *The History of the Countryside*, 7, also comments on this aspect of the relationship, insofar as weed pollens may be the only remaining indicators of early agriculture. Similarly, some palaeobotanists point to an increase in weeds associated with cultivation, as markers of particular historical episodes. See, for example P. Hunter Blair, *An Introduction to Anglo-Saxon England*, 2nd edition (Cambridge: Cambridge University Press, 1977), 272 and n. 1, in relation to the Roman occupation.

[60] For an earlier expression of his views on civilisation and progress see G. P. Marsh, *Address Delivered Before the Agricultural Society of Rutland County*, 30 September 1847, Published by Request of the Society, Rutland, Vermont, Library of Congress, Washington D. C., S532.M36, 1. Marsh gave this address during his first term in the US Congress.

[61] Marsh, *Address*, 17–18.

[62] 'Marsh, George Perkins', *Britannica Online*, <http://www.eb.com:180/cgi-bin/g?DocF=micro/378/4.html> [Accessed 20 May 1999]; K.A. Olwig, 'Historical geography and the society/nature "problematic": the perspective of J.F. Schouw, G. P. Marsh and E. Reclus' in *Journal of Historical Geography*, 6, 1 (1980), 29–45, esp. 36–9; Marsh, *Man and Nature*, 13,19.

[63] The extent to which European and North American traditions of thought shaped the settler view in New Zealand is one of the questions I explore in my doctoral thesis, 'New Zealanders and their Weeds, 1770–1970', University of Otago, New Zealand, in progress.

[64] T. Flannery, *The Future Eaters* (Chatswood, New South Wales: Reed, 1995) Ch 8, *passim*, and especially 303–306.

[65] G. Ell, *Introduced Wildflowers, New Zealand Weeds* (Auckland: Bush Press, 1983) 12, 14, 15, 21, 24, 25.

[66] For their respective positions on displacement of indigenous by exotic species see G. M. Thomson, *The Naturalisation of Animals and Plants in New Zealand* (London: Cambridge University Press, 1922), 526–7.

[67] R. Galbreath, *Walter Buller –The Reluctant Conservationist* (Wellington: GP Books, 1989, 121–2. For an argument in support of displacement see, for example, T. Kirk, 'Displacement of Species in New Zealand', *Transactions of the New Zealand Institute*, 28 (1895), 1–27 and *New Zealand Parliamentary Debates*, 31 July 1874, 351, c.1; G. Wynn, 'Conservation and Society in Late Nineteenth Century New Zealand', *New Zealand Journal of History*, 11:2 (1977), 124–136, and esp. 133. Wynn has argued that Potts' parliamentary and popular advocacy of policies based on Marsh's arguments had only a small degree of support. It came, he says, essentially from among those immigrants from the middle and upper ranks of British society who interested themselves in post-Darwinian natural history.

[68] H. Guthrie-Smith, *Tutira: The Story of A New Zealand Sheep Station* (Auckland: Random House, 1999), 236. See especially Chapters 26–35. This edition carries a forward by William Cronon, who was instrumental in having what has come to be widely regarded as a classic in the field of environmental history, republished in New Zealand and the United States after it had been out of print for some thirty years.

WEEDS, PEOPLE AND CONTESTED PLACES

[69] Thomson, *The Naturalisation of Animals and Plants in New Zealand*, 16.
[70] Thomson, *The Naturalisation of Animals and Plants in New Zealand*, 17–21, 363.
[71] Thomson, *The Naturalisation of Animals and Plants in New Zealand*, 22–3, 543–4, 552, 554–5
[72] F. W. Hilgendorf, *Weeds of New Zealand and How to Eradicate Them* (Christchurch: Whitcombe and Tombs, 1926), iii, 1–14; 6th edition, 1960, Ch. 7 *passim*. He attributed this supposed loss of vigour over time to toxins secreted into the soil by the weeds themselves. The idea of gradual loss of vigour seems to have been first introduced to New Zealand science by a Swedish naturalist, Dr. Berggren, during a discussion of G. M. Thomson's paper 'On some Naturalised Plants of Otago', presented to the Otago Institute in 1873. See *Proceedings of the Otago Institute*, 6 (1873), 444, 446.
[73] L. Robin, 'Ecology: A Science of Empire', in *Ecology and Empire, Environmental History of the Settler Societies*, T. Griffiths and L. Robin, eds. (Edinburgh: Keele University Press, 1997), 63–75. Robin discusses the origins of ecological science and argues that it is an outcome of the science of settling. To what extent Thomson's own understandings were by 1922 grounded in this relatively new science is not clear. He appears to have had at least an intuitive understanding of the explanatory power of ecosystems, although Marsh seems to have remained a stronger influence.
[74] See *The Dictionary of New Zealand Biography* (Wellington: Auckland University Press, 1990), 3, 109 for an assessment of Cockayne's contribution to New Zealand science. H.H. Allan, director of the Botany Division, Plant Research Bureau of the Department of Scientific and Industrial Research, Wellington, thought it necessary, as late as 1940, to support Thomson's and Cockayne's position on 'the still all too prevalent views as to the relative aggressiveness of the introduced and the indigenous species'. See H.H. Allan, *A Handbook of the Naturalized Flora of New Zealand* (Wellington: Botany Division, DSIR, 1940), 9.
[75] Thomson, *The Naturalisation of Animals and Plants in New Zealand*, 528–34; L. Cockayne, 'Observations concerning Evolution, derived from ecological studies in New Zealand', *Transactions of the New Zealand Institute*, 44 (1911), 32. Cockayne hammered the point home in two later books, *New Zealand Plants and their Story* (Wellington: Government Printer, 1919), Ch. 10 *passim*, and *The Vegetation of New Zealand* (Leipzig: Engelmann, 1928), 355–62. From the heavy emphasis in the text of the latter it would appear Cockayne was by then thoroughly exasperated by any remaining proponents of displacement theory.
[76] Robin, *Ecology and Empire*, 65.
[77] D. Miller, *Biological Control of Weeds in New Zealand, 1927–1948* (Wellington: DSIR, 1970), 5. Miller, formerly the director of the Cawthron Institute and of the entomology division of the New Zealand Department of Scientific and Industrial Research (DSIR), was seconded by that organisation to compile the history from available records.
[78] Miller, *Biological Control of Weeds in New Zealand*, 7.
[79] E. B. Levy, 'Pasture Weeds – Their Ecological Relationship to the Pasture Sward', in *The Control of Weeds, a symposium on the prevention and eradication of weeds on agricultural land by cultural, chemical and biological means*, ed. R. O. Whyte (Aberystwyth: Imperial Bureau of Pastures and Forage Crops, 1940), 144–52.
[80] D. Miller, 'Biological Control of Noxious Weeds of New Zealand', in *The Control of Weeds, a symposium on the prevention and eradication of weeds on agricultural land by cultural, chemical and biological means*, ed. R.O. Whyte (Aberystwyth: Imperial Bureau of Pastures and Forage Crops, 1940), 153–7.

[81] W.T. Parsons, *Noxious Weeds of Victoria* (Melbourne: Inkata Press, 1973), v-20. I thank Dr. Graeme Parmenter, Invermay Agriculture Centre, Dunedin, for providing a copy of Parsons' material on noxious weeds legislation. See also 'Staff Recommending Reports Evaluating Submissions on the Pest Management Strategies for Otago', *Proposed Pest Management Strategy for Otago* (Dunedin: Otago Regional Council, 2000), 2, 34. Environment Southland (another regional council, bordering the Otago region) expressed concern about inconsistencies between weed control programmes for the two regions. The Southland council took the view that pests knew no boundaries.

[82] A. H. Clark, *The Invasion of New Zealand by People, Plants and Animals, South Island* (New Brunswick: Rutgers University Press, 1949), 349, footnote.

[83] This view seems to have been shared by Canterbury high country pastoralists. At Lake Heron Station, according to one of those involved with running the station in 1942, desultory attempts were made to grub out stands of gorse only if there was nothing more compelling to do. A.M. Patterson, Highcliff Road, Dunedin, personal communication, July 1999.

[84] Clark, *The Invasion of New Zealand*, 362–5.

[85] A.G. Price, *The Western Invasions of the Pacific and its Continents, A Study of Moving Frontiers and Changing Landscapes, 1513–1958* (Oxford: Clarendon Press, 1963), 197–201.

[86] K. B. Cumberland, *This is New Zealand, A Pictorial Description* (Christchurch: Whitcombe and Tombs, 1949), 17, 22–3.

[87] R.C. Murphy, 'Man and Nature in New Zealand', *New Zealand Geographer*, 8:1 (1952), 1–14. The article first appeared in the *Proceedings of the American Philosophical Society*, 59:6 (1951), 569–82. I am grateful to Roy Goodman, the society's assistant librarian and curator of printed materials, who supplied background material on Murphy's life and work, including the period he was in New Zealand.

[88] Murphy also thought in terms of ecological climax, rather than continuum, a position that inevitably coloured his conclusions. As well, some of his statements, for instance those about moa extinctions, are contrary to evidence that should have been available to him at the time.

[89] Murphy, 'Man and Nature in New Zealand', 5.

[90] Murphy was referring, 12, to *Down to the Sea in Slips*, a booklet written by A. D. Campbell in 1946 for the New Zealand Soil Conservation and Rivers Control Council. He implies, mistakenly, that Cumberland wrote it.

[91] Murphy, 'Man and Nature in New Zealand', 7–14.

[92] Although there have been frequent articles about weeds in the *Journal* over the years, these appear to be the only three which consider the historical background to the problem.

[93] G.R. Moss, 'Gorse, A Weed Problem on thousands of Acres of Farmland', *New Zealand Journal of Agriculture*, 100, 6 (1960), 561–7.

[94] P.R. Stephens, 'Weed Control', *New Zealand Journal of Agriculture*, 100:6 (1960), 581. One researcher, A.H. Cockayne, Leonard's only son, had in 1913 reiterated his father's view that the ecological mechanism of weed spread must be understood if control measures were to have a chance of success. Nobody in New Zealand seemed to pay much heed.

[95] P.R. Stephens, 'Noxious Weeds', *New Zealand Journal of Agriculture*, 100, 6 (1960), 613, 615.

[96] K. B. Cumberland, *Landmarks* (Reader's Digest: Surry Hills, 1981), 6–7, 178–81, 188–91. Cumberland added emphasis with a rather lurid illustration of a weed-spraying helicopter swooping low across a gorse-covered hillside. Television New Zealand pro-

duced and broadcast the television series of the same name.

[97] This may be compared with the problems Australian farmers faced with endemic weeds. See W. Frost, 'European Farming, Australian Pests: Agricultural Settlement and Environmental Disruption in Australia, 1800–1920', *Environment and History*, 4 (1998), 129–43.

[98] Rahman, A., 'New Zealand', and L.J. Matthews, 'Pasture weeds in New Zealand', in *Biology and Ecology of Weeds*, ed. W. Holzner and N. Numata (The Hague: Junk, 1982), 299–308. Rahman was then a scientist at the Ruakura soil and plant research station, Hamilton. Matthews was with the Plant Protection Service of the FAO in Italy.

[99] B.E.V. Parham, *Common Weeds in New Zealand* (Wellington: Government Printer, 1981), 9–11.

[100] R. J. Field and G.T. Daly, 'Weed Biology and Management' in *Pastures, their Ecology and Management*, ed. R.H.M. Langer (Auckland: Oxford University Press, 1990), 409–447. For the time being, that would appear to be a position somewhat in advance of most Regional Councils which, under current New Zealand legislation, are charged with developing and enforcing weed control policies.

[101] For a discussion of the etiological nature of Genesis, see L. Boadt, *Reading the Old Testament, an Introduction* (New York: Paulist Press, 1984), Ch. 6 *passim*.

[102] See Note 1.

[103] For a discussion of this, see 'An Integrated Approach to the Ecology and Management of Plant Invasions', *Conservation Biology* 9, 4 (1995), 761–70.

[104] See Note 9.

Re-writing the History of Australian Tropical Rainforests: 'Alien Invasives' or 'Ancient Indigenes'?

Rachel Sanderson

INTRODUCTION

During the second half of the twentieth century, there was a significant shift in scientific understanding of the origins and history of Australian rainforests. The notion that these rainforests were 'alien and invasive', relatively recent introductions from nearby New Guinea or south-east Asia – a notion attributed historically to Joseph Hooker – was overturned. In its place, a new vision of rainforest as an ancient and truly Australian environment was outlined and promoted. This re-writing of the biogeographical history of the Australian rainforests was not only significant scientifically; it also resonated with potent questions regarding Australian nationhood and identity which would be more fully articulated as these scientific visions were adopted by the conservation movement during the 1980s. However, this was not the 'revolution' it seems to be. In fact, it involved a contemporary re-writing of not only the aims and substance of Hooker's argument, but also of the more nuanced views of some early twentieth century scientists. At a time when rainforests in northern Australia were under threat, their representation as 'ancient and indigenous', and so central to Australian identity and heritage, was a powerful, and useful conflation of scientific and cultural thought.

J.D. HOOKER AND THE AUSTRALIAN FLORA

In 1860, Joseph (J.D.) Hooker had first outlined the evidence regarding the distribution and affinities of the Australian vegetation in the introduction to his *Flora Tasmaniæ*. He took on this considerable task because he believed that it was not possible to understand the flora of a single region without considering its relationship both to those regions surrounding it and – more particularly – to similar species and formations found elsewhere in the world. Hooker's work was based not only on his peerless access to botanical resources from his base at Kew Gardens, but was compiled after a four-year voyage with the *Erebus* and *Terror,* between 1839 and 1843, which had taken him through the southern waters of Antarctica, New Zealand, and Tasmania. By the mid-nineteenth century, according to Hooker, the flora of Australia was:

justly regarded as the most remarkable that is known, owing to the number of peculiar forms of vegetation which that continent presents. So numerous indeed are the peculiarities of this Flora, that it has been considered as differing fundamentally, or in almost all its attributes, from those of other lands; and speculations have been entertained that its origin is either referable to another period of the world's history from that in which the existing plants of other continents have been produced, or to a separate creative effort from that which contemporaneously peopled the rest of the globe with its existing vegetation; whilst others again have supposed that the climate or some other attribute of Australia has exerted an influence on its vegetation, differing both in kind and degree from that of other climates.[1]

Hooker was well acquainted with the ideas of Charles Darwin, a close personal friend with whom he maintained an extended correspondence since their first meeting in 1843. In 1858 it was Hooker, who along with Charles Lyell, had famously encouraged Darwin to publish an excerpt from his 1844 *Essay* on the mutation of species by natural selection in the *Journal of the Linnean Society*, alongside the manuscript sent by Alfred Russel Wallace who had independently discovered the theory Darwin had been nurturing since his first correspondence with Hooker.[2] It is not surprising, then, that in Hooker's discussion of the origin and relationships of the flora of Australia in the *Flora Tasmaniæ*, which was published shortly after, he incorporated and responded to the ideas of Darwin and Wallace, while remaining sceptical of the theory of evolution. He suggested that:

> The Natural History of Australia seemed ... to be especially suited to test such a theory, on account of the comparative uniformity of its physical features being accompanied with a great variety in its Flora; of the differences in the vegetation of its several parts; and of the peculiarity both of its Fauna and Flora, as compared with those of other countries.[3]

Like Wallace and Darwin, Hooker had been influenced by Lyell's unveiling of the great expanse of geological time and his exposition of the radical, inexorable, world-wide geological changes which had occurred over that time. Following Lyell, Hooker argued that there were 'two classes of agents, both of which may be reasonably supposed to have had a powerful effect in determining the distribution of plants; these are changes of climates, and changes in the relative positions and elevations of land'.[4] Given the immense time scales involved, and the paucity of – and difficulty of interpreting – geological and fossil evidence, as well as the incomplete state of knowledge regarding the existing Australian flora, Hooker concluded that:

> The problem of distribution is an infinitely complicated one ... the mutations of the surface of our planet, which replace continents by oceans, and plains by mountains, may be insignificant measures of time when compared with the du-

ration of some existing genera and perhaps species of plants, for some of these appear to have outlived the slow submersion of continents.[5]

Hooker's counter-intuitive vision of forms of plant life actually outlasting massive geological changes was a precursor to later ideas about the antiquity of elements in the Australian – including Australian rainforest – flora.

Hooker tackled the problem of the origin and affinities of the flora by compiling and statistically analysing lists of the natural orders of plants found in Australia, comparing those which occurred only in Australia with those which also occurred in other countries, and in each case noting where they were found. This method of 'botanical arithmetic' was devised by Alexander von Humboldt, and was particularly dominant in botanical studies during the first half of the nineteenth century.[6] Hooker concluded that the families found in Australia were almost all also found elsewhere, though to varying degrees. He identified Indian floral elements in the north-west, Polynesian and Malayan in the north-east, New Zealand and Antarctic in the south-east, and South African in the south-west. Although Australia contains little alpine country, Hooker found that mountainous areas were home to New Zealand, Andean, Fuegian and European genera and species. In order to explain his findings, Hooker argued that there must have been former land connections between the southern temperate landmasses. He concluded that:

> the peculiarities of the [Australian] Flora, great though they be, are found to be more apparent than real, and to be due to a multitude of specialities affecting the species, and to a certain extent the genera, but not extending to the more important characteristics of the vegetation, which is not fundamentally different from that of other parts of the globe.

Hooker wrote, aptly, of his viewing the vegetation of Australia in a 'double light' – as simultaneously having characteristics peculiar to it, and taking its place in 'the existing Flora of the globe'.[7]

It is noteworthy that Hooker's conclusions, based as they were on available specimens and existing taxonomic work, were not made by means of an aesthetic assessment of the appearance of vegetation – such as would later lead explorer George Elphinstone Dalrymple to describe the North Queensland rainforests as being 'Indian'.[8] They were, however, based on the expectation that natural classifications, derived from observable features of plants, offered an indication of closeness of relationship which could ultimately be traced back to a common origin. The exact mechanisms of that relationship, and the implications of an attempt to express it through a system of classification, had yet to be fully explored.[9]

Hooker noted that the number of species in tropical Australia appeared to be 'extremely small', and stated that although 'many discoveries may yet be anticipated', the work of collectors such as Cunningham, Mueller, McGillivray and others led him to 'doubt whether future explorers will raise the known number of 2,200 tropical flowering species to much above 3,000'.[10] Despite Hooker's assertions that the tropical regions of Australia were relatively well-examined, at the time of publication of his 'Introductory Essay' in 1860 the North Queensland rainforests had barely been penetrated by botanical collectors or botanists. Nonetheless, Hooker's outline of the origins of the Australian flora, and the tropical flora in particular, was subsequently regarded by many botanists as a useful and accurate account of the affinities of particular floral regions in Australia, and was not comprehensively reconsidered until late in the twentieth century.

By outlining his findings on the biogeography of the Australian flora, Hooker intended to highlight the connections between the flora of Australia and the vegetation found in other parts of the world. He was arguing against a view that Australian flora was so strange, so different, that its existence required a novel kind of explanation. His characterisation of the vegetation of north-eastern Australia as 'Polynesian and Malayan' was not posited in opposition to 'autochthonous Australian' found elsewhere on the Australian continent, as later scientists would come to suggest, but rather sat alongside the diverse range of connections he argued existed between different geographical regions within Australia and other landmasses.

POST-HOOKER, PRE-CONTINENTAL DRIFT

In an article on 'The Origin of Australia', presented to the Queensland Royal Society in 1907, geologist and past President of the Society, Sydney Barber Josiah Skertchly, began by stating that:

> We are indebted to Sir J.D. Hooker for the first comprehensive view of the flora of Australia, and the long years that have passed since the masterly essay "On the Flora of Australia" was published in 1859, have not materially altered the views therein set forth.[11]

However, one significant change had occurred: the notion of a 'truly' Australian flora had gained currency. Skertchly noted the marked differences between the 'Australian' or temperate flora, found at its most diverse in the south-west of the continent; and the 'Asiatic' or 'tropical' flora found in the north-east. He noted the statistical difference in species dispersal, suggesting that only 14% of the species listed in Bailey's *Queensland Flora* also occurred in Western Australia. Moreover, he wrote that:

> mere numerical statements convey but an inadequate conception of the difference between the so-called Extra-tropical and the Tropical floras. It is the general facies that is most striking, and I can best illustrate it by a personal reference. I came to Queensland after spending years in the primeval forests of the Far East, and my first introduction to the Australian forests was in the scrub of North Queensland.

> To me it was a revelation and somewhat of a disappointment. I knew, so far as the books and specimens can teach, what the peculiarities of the Australian flora were, but this Atherton scrub, this wild tangle of the Barron Gorge, was not Australian at all. It was pure Asiatic "utan rimabau" – the deep forest – I had left in Borneo. The same tall trees with broad shade-giving leaves, the same climbing "rotan" (*Calamus*), and even the insects, gaudy *Ornithopteras* and royal purple *Eupleas*, met me on every hand. It all looked familiar. Some years afterwards, when I had grown accustomed to this flora, I entered W. Australia for the first time, landing at Albany from S. Africa. What a revelation it was! At last I saw Australia-Vera: at last I was in a new and strange land ...

However, despite giving such emphatic statement of the true 'Australian-ness' of the flora adapted to arid and semi-arid conditions, and the 'Asiatic' or 'Oriental' nature of that found in the tropical regions, Skertchly went on to note that 'The Oriental flora is more Asiatic in general aspect than in number of species actually common to Australia and Asia', which, on his count, were 620 flowering plants and 200 species of ferns co-occurring between the two.[12]

Skertchly argued against the widespread view that the Australian flora and fauna were 'ancient'. He suggested, on the basis of both current distribution of plants and animals, and fossil and geological evidence that in fact they had evolved in relatively recent times in response to changes in climate and sea levels.[13] He painted a vision of the very different 'Australia' that would have been found by a 'Cretaceous Cook', during which time, 'there was no Australian continent at all, but instead, an Archipelago consisting of two main islands, one in the west, the other in the north and east, with a number of smaller islands in between'. The influence of the shallow sea found then in what are now desert areas of inland Australia, which he called the 'Opal Sea' and compared with the Arafura of the present, would have been to moderate the climate to 'temperate to warm-temperate, equable, and the land bathed with plentiful rains'.[14]

Skertchly suggested that there had been a much greater level of uniformity in the Tertiary flora than today, and that allied forms had been found across a wide range of latitudes and climates.[15] This was, he suggested, a flora in which *'the characteristic plants of Australia are but feebly represented'*.[16] Skertchly argued that 'the old universal flora had all the makings of the new flora in it – both the Orientalis and the Vera types – but when the Opal Sea became dry, only certain plants had adaptability enough to battle with the increasing heat and decreasing moisture. The rest died.' He continued:

> But there was a great difference between Australia-Orientalis and Australia-Vera. The former, owing to its mountainous and coastal character suffered less in climate – it has continued to receive fairly, and in parts quite, abundant rain and so a portion of the old flora has been preserved, in spite of its inferior adaptability. This is the Tropical Flora which I prefer to call Oriental. It is as has been said, essentially Asiatic in facies, but the bulk is not specifically identical with the

'ALIEN INVASIVES' OR 'ANCIENT INDIGENES'?

> Asiatic flora – it is merely the tropical part of the Universal flora. This portion of our present flora, then, I look upon as a true survival.[17]

Skertchly identified the 'tropical flora' of the north-east of Australia as a relic of a flora much more widespread during the Tertiary, and perhaps established in the Cretaceous era. He went on to acknowledge the more recent incursion of some 'Asiatic' species as a result of the geographical proximity between northern Australia and New Guinea, but his overall conclusions, based on the taxonomic, fossil and geological evidence, belied his immediate response to the physiognomic similarity between the rainforests of Borneo and those of North Queensland. The tropical flora was not a recent invader, identical with the 'utan rimabau' he had met with in Borneo, but was rather a 'true survival' of the massive climatic and geological changes which had taken place on the Australian continent over tens of millions of years.

Skertchly's reaction to the North Queensland and Western Australian flora reflected the background of many colonial observers. During the nineteenth and early twentieth century, many British or European-born botanists and explorers came to Australia with prior experience of India, or of various parts of South-East Asia. As such, the rainforest of the north-eastern coast was a more familiar – if still exotic – form of vegetation than that classed as 'Australian'. The 'Australian' trees, so well-adapted to arid conditions, with their sparse, hard, narrow, vertically-hanging leaves, their peeling bark and dull colouring, appeared alien and strange. This is in stark contrast to the views of those Australian-born scientists of the later twentieth century, who had largely grown up not only surrounded by the 'Australian' flora and with little experience of or exposure to rainforest, but also at a time in which a pastoral landscape dominated by gum-trees was a central national image – a landscape represented as truly and sentimentally 'Australian'. The public re-positioning of rainforest (which had always been considered to have aesthetically 'Asian' overtones) as an 'Australian' flora, and one perhaps even prior in evolutionary terms to the sclerophyll vegetation, thus presents a complex mix of both scientific argument, based on advances in geology, palaeoecology and botany, and an attempt to expand the historical and aesthetic imaginations – and allegiances – of Australians.[18]

Karel Domin, a botanist from Czech University, Prague, visited Queensland in 1909-10, as he felt there was 'no other part of Australia which would be so interesting from the botanical standpoint'.[19] During the visit he undertook fieldwork in North Queensland. Domin followed Hooker in suggesting that the flora of Australia was composed of three main elements 'represented in a very unequal degree in the flora of the different States'. However like Skertchly, his flora now included the 'true *Australian*' element, alongside the 'so-called *Antarctic* element (named by Hooker)' and the '*Malayan* (including the Papuan)' element. He observed that:

> The forest flora consists of true Australian types; the scrub [rainforest] flora for the greatest part of Malayan and Papuan types. The historic evolution of these elements has been *quite diverse*, and we find always that they never come into a friendly contact. They are of quite different character, and on localities where the conditions are not so decidedly in the favour of one of them, there results a *strong struggle* between them.

Domin stated that 'The wet tropical part of Queensland has altogether a true Malayan-Papuan flora, which shows that there was formerly a land or island connection and an easy way for propagation of this equatorial flora southwards.' He also suggested that:

> it would not be correct to regard Queensland's tropical flora only as a new comer and a recent branch of the regions mentioned above. All we know seems to testify that: –
>
> 1. The tropical "Malayan" flora of Queensland is only a small remainder of a flora spread formerly over large areas, which are now mostly sunken into the sea. Accordingly
>
> 2. The flora does not consist only of the original Malayan types. These made only a base, but it has been transformed in the great number of genera and species, which are known only from the Australian Tropics (endemic in Australia). It seems that the separation took place at a very early epoch, so that the ancestors of the present tropical flora in Australia developed themselves quite independent of the Malayan flora, and originated a large number of new forms. [20]

Like Skertchly, Domin asserted the antiquity and floristic distinctiveness of the so-called 'Malayan' flora, found in the rainforest areas of north-east Queensland – though he attributed this distinctiveness to a long period of isolation from the original, Malayan 'parent stock'. Although Domin, unlike Skertchly, was not a geologist, he also highlighted the significance of geological processes in the shaping and distribution of the flora.

Botanist Desmond (D.A.) Herbert considered the evolutionary history of the Queensland rainforests in his Presidential Address to the Queensland Royal Society, delivered in 1932 on the topic of 'The Relationships of the Queensland Flora'. Herbert began by outlining Hooker's argument, and the methods of statistical analysis on which it was based, stating that:

> An important point brought out by Hooker's analysis was that the families of Australia were almost all also found elsewhere, and though various families reach different degrees of development, many of the largest families here are the largest in the world as a whole.

While accepting that the fossil evidence was scant and difficult to interpret accurately, Herbert suggested that recently discovered leaf impressions found in rocks purportedly dated to the middle Jurassic pointed to the 'ancient nature of

'ALIEN INVASIVES' OR 'ANCIENT INDIGENES'?

angiosperm inhabitation of the continent'. Further, he added that fossil evidence indicated that:

> The eucalyptus and various types now characteristic of both open forest and rain forest were well developed in the early Tertiary. Though the rain forest types are not necessarily tropical, they do indicate warmer conditions than obtain in those localities of the present day.

In consequence of this, Herbert stated that:

> We must commence an enquiry of the relationships of the present flora, therefore, by recognizing that the continent has been inhabited by a diversity of both rain and open forest types since, at least, the early Tertiary, and that their geographical range has, in the past, been profoundly modified by climatic and geological change. In other words, the sifting effect of environment has been operating for a long time, and the mixing of types of various origins, and the elimination of others, has culminated in our present flora.

Herbert went on to consider what might be meant by the 'Malaysian flora', and highlighted the distinction between genera of flowering plants found in the eastern and western regions of Malaysia, and the 'unstable insular area' in which the two types meet and mix, between Wallace's line on the west, and Weber's line on the east.[21] Wallace's line, which runs between Bali and Lombok, and Borneo and Celebes, was identified by A.R. Wallace in 1860 and 'separates two markedly different mammal faunas, solely placental in south-east Asia and predominantly marsupial in Australasia'.[22] Other attempts to define the boundaries between the Oriental and Australasian biotas (of which Weber's line is one) reflect the fact that 'different taxa have managed to penetrate different distances from their continent of origin into the islands of the East Indies'.[23] Herbert suggested that these two lines do not represent 'true biogeographic boundaries', but rather 'approximately define the limits of the two centres of origin and distribution, Sunda Land on the west, and New Guinea in the east'. Herbert argued that the large numbers of endemic genera found in Queensland indicate the 'ancient character' of the palaeotropic element in Australia:

> Eastern Malaysia and Western Malaysia differ considerably from one another, but North Queensland shows a further differentiation from New Guinea, North Australia from North Queensland, and South Queensland from North Queensland. The differences are sufficiently accounted for by the long continued sorting of types by climate without reference to the relative ages of the palaeotropic element in the different areas under consideration ... the Australian palaeotropic element is restricted in range by climate and not by age.[24]

In a paper written almost twenty years later, 'Present Day Distribution and the Geological Past', Herbert addressed some of the same issues, and stated some of his conclusions more forcefully. This paper showed a shift in tone to an explicitly nationalist interpretation of the arguments around the evolutionary history of rainforest. Again he discussed Hooker, this time typifying Hooker's presentation of the origins of Australian flora a little more sharply, as being an account:

> of immigrants pouring in from various directions and pushing out the truly Australian plants, and of a very restricted export from Australia ... the whole "set-up" being rather similar to the human settlement of this Continent. When these so-called invasion elements are subtracted from the flora, we are left with those that are more or less peculiar; they are the autochthonous element and no-one can take them away from us.[25]

After outlining the characteristics of this 'autochthonous element', Herbert used the example of Queensland 'dry scrubs' derived from rain forest types, to show how under pressure of climate, some survivors of a dying flora may provide the base for a new association. He further suggested that it is possible that the 'Australian' vegetation found in sub-humid, semi-arid and desert climates could, in fact, have been derived from a previously extensive mesic vegetation (that is, vegetation adapted to moist conditions). He concluded that it seemed reasonable 'to regard the rain forest types, [and] the beech forests as equally Australian [as sclerophylls]. They are very old members of the flora'. Herbert suggested that both the fossil record and the occurrence of residual rainforest types in places now far distant from the extant forests – such as the *Livistona* (Cabbage Palms) of the MacDonnell Ranges of Central Australia – provide strong evidence that such rainforest vegetation was previously much more extensive than at present. To explain this change in distribution, Herbert adapted the notion of a land-bridge, so enthusiastically utilised by Hooker, and instead suggested that a 'climatic bridge' must, at some time past, have linked areas of the continent which now experience such radically distinct climates, and carry such radically different flora.[26]

The debate surrounding the history of vegetation in Australia has invoked clear (sometimes explicit) metaphorical resonances with concerns about the human history of the continent. In discussions of the origins of the Australian rainforests, broader questions of race, identity and belonging have been raised. Rainforest was regarded as 'invader', and its presence was the result of its success in the struggle for survival against the autochthonous vegetation. Whether this explanation of the rainforests' origin was regarded as scientifically tenable or not, the story itself was seen clearly as a parallel to the European invasion of the continent and the historical processes of colonisation. However, the suggested Asian lineage of Australia's rainforests highlighted Australia's proximity to south-east Asia, and connected this invasion narrative with concerns over the security of Northern Australia, and long-held fears amongst many white Australians of a possible future re-invasion of 'their' lands. A closer examination of Herbert's account suggests that the debate about rainforests' origins could

'ALIEN INVASIVES' OR 'ANCIENT INDIGENES'?

also carry a more complicated and nuanced message. Herbert argued against the notion that the separation of the Oriental and Australasian biotas represented a true biogeographic boundary, and highlighted the fluidity, interpenetration and interrelationship which existed between these supposedly separate 'elements'. As such, Herbert implied that any essentialist understanding of biogeographic identity, any exclusive focus on separation and competition as fundamental to the history of the region, was necessarily false. Further, Herbert suggested that even if the rainforest had originated from outside Australia, given the passing of time, it could eventually be legitimately considered as 'Australian'.

Hooker, Skertchly, Domin, Herbert, and others who discussed the origin and distribution of Australian vegetation prior to the 1960s were attempting to grapple with an often scant and confusing array of evidence. Each responded to the problem of where the various floral elements of Australia had originated from and why they were now found where they were. Answers made reference to changes in climate and landform over geological time, to the rise and fall of mountain ranges and sea levels. Their examination of the rainforest flora of Australia showed that, although it did not appear distinctively 'Australian', in taxonomic terms much of it was not simply identical to that found to the north in Malaysia, or nearby in New Guinea. However, the closeness of Northern Australia to south-east Asia and New Guinea – which had been connected by a land-bridge to north-eastern Australia during the Pleistocene glaciation – and the fact that recent floral arrivals were found on northern shores, further complicated the issue. Explanations were based on an analysis of the patterns of distribution observed in both present and fossil flora, and on a belief in 'the steady state of the earth's crust, its continents and archipelagos in supposedly fixed position'.[27] As such, an important focus was placed on the processes by which plants might have arrived in Australia from elsewhere.

DRIFTING CONTINENTS

By the early 1970s, the acceptance of the idea of continental drift revolutionised scientific understanding of the history of the earth and of life; and necessitated a radical rethinking of the origins and history of the Australian flora. This resulted in a re-appraisal of the way scientists – not only geologists, but also zoologists, botanists, biogeographers, and others – talk and think about the past. As geologist David Johnson states:

> It is important to realise that while we say something happened in Canada or South Africa, that is just because that is where the rocks lie today. In the Archaean these fragments were not assembled as they are today. The crust of the Earth has been moving since it first formed. The atlases and geography we know today are only true for now. In the past the landmasses were totally different shapes.[28]

Writing in the late 1980s, ecologist Richard Schodde reflected on the lack of resonance between the way biogeographers in the 1980s were talking about biological history, and the significance of this changed vision of the Australian continent.

> Pick up any modern text and you will see bird geographers and reptile geographers talking about Antarctic dispersal routes into Australia via Gondwana and Indo-Malayan dispersal routes in via Indonesia. Even current phytogeographic treatises talk about Australia receiving its first stocks of angiosperms by northwest land bridges from Laurasia in the Cretaceous. The point I want to make here, and I can't stress it enough, is that whatever biotic elements Australia received before its break from Antarctica in the early Tertiary it inherited from Gondwana. If angiosperms did come into the region from the north in the Cretaceous, they came to Gondwana, and perhaps even the Australian-sector of Gondwana; but not to Australia as such. This point needs absorbing in Australian biogeographic thinking.[29]

To the extent that ecologists, biogeographers and other scientists utilise historical narratives, the theory of continental drift raises some significant historiographical questions: How is it possible to write an historical account which reflects not only the flow of time, but also the movement of the ground on which events were played out? What does such a history mean when its reference to place is set adrift? And at what point is it no longer a history of 'Australia'? The difficulty of separating ecological history from Australian history seems to have been more than a question of geological and terminological accuracy. The rich layers of meaning that biogeography derived from its metaphorical resonance with Australia's human past, seemed to have been abruptly sundered.

RE-WRITING THE HISTORY OF THE AUSTRALIAN TROPICAL RAINFORESTS

In the 1959 paper with which he had begun his ecological career, Len Webb had described the tropical rainforests of Australia as 'a predominantly Indo-Malaysian flora' and used the contrast between it and 'the autochthonous flora characterised by sclerophylls' as a basic division within his classificatory system.[30] Twenty years later, around the time of his retirement from CSIRO, Webb wrote, in a chapter he co-authored with Geoff Tracey,

> The rainforest habitats preserve a remarkable wealth of endemic and, in some areas, primitive biota, as well as exhibiting strong affinities at the generic level with surrounding countries that were continuous with the Australian land mass in Gondwanic time. Although the processes of evolution and community development responsible for the patterns of Australian rainforests are being unravelled only now, evidence already forthcoming indicates a need for revision of traditional

concepts in Australian phytogeography that previously regarded the floristic elements of the northern rainforests as alien and invasive.[31]

Webb and Tracey pointed to three recent events which had provided the opportunity for a new consideration and understanding of that question. Firstly, the intensive ecological surveys of rainforests which had been undertaken in Eastern Australia during the 1960s and 70s, and the use of 'modern numerical and analytical techniques enabling the processing of large data sets to give a comprehensive floristic typology and habitat correlations'. Secondly, the palynological studies which 'furnish an exceptional chronicle of tropical vegetation during the last 80,000 to 100,000 years of the late Quaternary period'. And finally, the 'new and now firmly established evidence for continental drift and an ancient Gondwanaland flora'.[32]

In an interview, recorded for the National Library of Australia, Geoff Tracey recalled that it was during field work for the Australian Phytochemical Survey, which he commenced in 1949, that he and Len Webb began to be puzzled by distribution patterns of species, genera and families of rainforest plants. The patterns they observed did not accord with what Tracey regarded as the accepted notion of rainforest species as recent arrivals, unrelated to the truly 'Australian' flora. As they searched for a particular alkaloid in a genus, related species would be found across a range of environments: in wetter rainforests, dry eucalyptus woodlands, and bottle tree scrubs. On the other hand, there were a number of genera and species – including some endemic angiosperms with primitive morphological traits – which 'didn't ever leave the wet rainforest'.[33] As they continued to collect data and apply a range of methods of analysis, their findings continued to support their sense that what they were examining were not scattered invasive elements, but rather an 'archipelago of refugia', the distribution and composition of which reflected processes of climatic and edaphic sifting over – in some cases – many millennia.[34] Webb and Tracey concluded, as Herbert had before them, that the rainforests were restricted by climate and not by age. They argued that, although the rainforests did contain some newer arrivals, they were in fact largely relict populations of a previously-dominant form of vegetation. As Geoff Tracey put it, 'when this theory of plate tectonics was actually acceptable, the whole thing fell into place ...'[35]

Webb and Tracey eventually decided to publish their conclusions in the new edition of a European volume, *Ecological Biogeography of Australia*, which was to be released in 1981. The 1959 edition, *Biogeography and Ecology in Australia*, had been 640 pages long, and had barely mentioned Australian rainforests. The new edition offered a clear indication of the extent to which knowledge of the Australian environment had increased between the 1960s and 1980s: it was over 2,500 pages long, and comprised three volumes. Len Webb was invited to contribute a chapter, and he and Geoff Tracey thought a prominent European publication was an ideal place to muster the evidence, and outline their interpretation of the origins and evolutionary history of Australian rainforests. According to Tracey, 'you could publish scientific articles in Australian literature, but no scientist worth his salt anywhere else in the world would ever read them.'[36]

In 'Australian rainforests: patterns and change', Webb and Tracey attempted to apply their ecological understanding of the ways in which rainforest environments respond to disturbance in the observable short-term to the longer, middle-late Pleistocene record of vegetation history provided by Peter Kershaw's analysis of palynological evidence from crater lakes on the Atherton Tablelands, and the new model of geological history provided by the theory of continental drift.[37]

They distinguished between two forms of change which occur in all vegetation communities. The first were progressive successional processes in which change is initiated by disturbance, but rainforest communities return to a predictable 'terminal community', similar in structure and species composition to the community which existed prior to the disturbance. The second encompassed longer-term changes through which communities evolve unpredictably, and which involve adaptation, migration, extinction and speciation. Webb and Tracey recognised that the distinction between the two types of change is not always clear, and that the 'extent and duration of disturbance ... the ecological stability [of the original community]; and the area and location of the disturbed community in relation to other communities' all determine the new patterns of community development which result from change.[38]

Webb and Tracey divided the rainforests of Australia into 3 floristic regions: the cool forests of the south-east (A), the warm and moist forests of the north-east (B), and the warm, drier forests of the north and sub-coastal regions (C). Their floristic region B corresponds with the wet tropical rainforest region of north-east Queensland. They argued that floristic regions A and C do not represent 'transitions' or 'attenuations' of the tropical rainforest along a gradient of decreasingly favourable temperature or rainfall, as has sometimes been suggested, but rather the three regions:

> approximate 'core areas' somewhere near where ancient widespread floras from Gondwanaland crystallized under different climatic-edaphic-topographic conditions, accompanied by the interplay of seed and pollen dispersal systems. Ecological differentiation and geographical isolation would have favored independent lines of evolution. [39]

They further divided each of these regions into overlapping 'phytosociological or vegetation provinces', characterised by a range of indicator species, and closely correlated to particular climatic regimes.[40] They interpreted the distribution of some genera and species across provinces as implying 'a long and complex history of climatic-edaphic-topographic sifting often accompanied by fire'. On the other hand, the occurrence of many species as endemics in particular floristic regions was regarded as demonstrating 'a long history of segregation to permit species differentiation'.[41] They concluded that:

biogeographical subdivision often comes to rest on the distribution of relict and narrowly endemic species at a level that corresponds to refuge areas and areas of minor isolation. The subdivision also reveals groups of relatively small and widely separated patches of rainforest with strikingly similar botanical composition. Vegetation classification therefore raises problems of origin and adaptation and of community dynamics on different time scales in habitats of different size and distribution.[42]

Webb and Tracey identified a range of types and probable locations of refugia which would have sheltered wet rainforest communities during periods of climatic stress, particularly from the impact of increased fires associated with drier conditions – these included the summits and gullies on the upper slopes of cloudy wet mountains, very wet lowlands, deep moist gorges of coastal lowlands, and the fringing areas alongside permanently flowing rivers.[43] Webb and Tracey argued that such sites have acted as nuclei for the subsequent re-expansion of rainforest areas which, as the palynological work of Peter Kershaw on the Atherton Tablelands demonstrated, has occurred repeatedly when an unfavourable climate has shifted to one more suited to support the growth of rainforest vegetation.[44] Webb and Tracey suggested that in tropical north-eastern Australia such refugia had allowed 'narrow endemics including primitive angiosperms … to survive in a kind of Noah's Ark situation…' They noted that:

> despite the greater concentration of primitive genera and species in south-east Asia, there is a far greater concentration of primitive families in Australasia. This suggests that the refugia now centered in this region are of great antiquity, extending to the Cretaceous or earlier when many primitive angiosperms originated … and Gondwanaland was still entire.[45]

While the extent and nature of endemism provided one plank to their argument, they also undertook an analysis of the distribution throughout the world of non-endemic rainforest genera found in Australia, and concluded that the floristic affinities of such genera:

> with other tropical countries are consistent with derivation from a Gondwanaland flora for which the land mass that is now Australia also provided a substrate. It seems no longer valid to label taxa also found in India and Indomalesia as 'invasive elements'. It also seems unnecessary to accentuate the role of long-distance seed dispersal throughout this part of the southern hemisphere, although dispersal over moderate distances may have occurred.[46]

Finally, Webb and Tracey concluded that 'the traditional concept that two invasive floristic elements – one from south-east Asia to the north, and the other from Antarctica to the south – form the core of Australian rainforest vegetation is no longer tenable'.[47] They characterised the contemporary patterns of Australian rainforest vegetation as a series of 'chequered layers', of which the base is the 'floristic matrix inherited jointly with other countries from Gondwanic times'. Upon this base has been overlain 'a shadowy mosaic woven from the phylogenetic development of communities in prehistorical and geological times', which remain as fragmentary relicts across a number of locations, such as in the 'ever-moist summits and gorges of the north-east'. The upper and most recent layer they identified as:

> the product of natural disturbances (and most recently white man) in historical times. It is often starkly variegated, ranging from low herbaceous pioneers to advanced secondary growth and broken-canopied forests disrupted by cyclones, as the result of ontogenetic development and recent succession.[48]

During the course of their field work, Webb and Tracey had witnessed the consequences of such 'natural disturbances' time and time again. While they struggled to untangle the ancient history of the rainforests, a more immediate transformation of these forests was occurring before their eyes. Poet and activist, Judith Wright, was a close friend of Len Webb, and she recalled how he returned to Brisbane from field trips 'imbued with the tragedy' of the destruction which was being wreaked, as:

> the rainforest continued to be felled and burned, and plants and animals unknown, or almost unknown, to science, and never to be replaced, went up in smoke. Progress was the cry and progress we got, no matter how destructive and planless.[49]

As Webb and Tracey traced the long evolutionary history of Australian rainforests, they were also brought to confront directly the dramatic recent transformations which had accompanied European settlement and the ongoing clearing of rainforest. The changing history of the rainforests no longer held as a metaphor for the European colonisation of the Australian continent, as had earlier been suggested by D.A. Herbert; it was its stark outcome.

During the course of his long friendship with Wright, Webb shared with her the sense he had developed of the forest. In 1983, the year in which a local council bulldozed a haphazard and controversial road through some of the last remaining lowland rainforest north of the Daintree River, Wright sent him a poem, 'Rainforest'. The poem emerged from their discussions over a number of years, and expressed their belief that 'the forest, like the world generally, could be properly understood only by those who had experienced and shared in its life'.[50] She wrote:

> We with our quick dividing eyes
> measure, distinguish, and are gone.
> The forest burns, the tree-frog dies,
> Yet one is all and all are one.[51]

From the early 1980s fervent lobbying began for the legal protection of the North Queensland rainforests. Conservationists drew strongly (though at times loosely) on the work of Webb and Tracey, highlighting that:

> Refugia, areas where rainforest has existed continuously for some 200 million years, have been identified in this region. Primitive plant families, amongst the first flowering plants to evolve on earth, have surviving representatives. Botanists regard the area as a living museum.[52]

The construction of what became known as the Daintree road was the catalyst by which the North Queensland rainforest emerged into national consciousness in Australia. Although protests did not prevent the road from being built, concern for the future of the rainforest was strong, and the campaign for its protection continued after the road's completion. While the beauty and recreational values of the rainforest provided impetus for the campaign, it was the sense of its antiquity and growing significance to science that clinched the arguments. On 5 June 1987, a month before the federal election, the Australian Government nominated the Wet Tropics for World Heritage listing.[53]

CONCLUSION

Scientific understanding of the evolutionary history of the Australian vegetation on the geological time scale has been shaped by two revolutions: the first, in biological thought, was ushered in by Darwin and Wallace in the mid-nineteenth century; the second, in geological thought, was introduced by Wegener at the beginning of the twentieth century, and then gradually confirmed by force of evidence. Both of these revolutions highlighted the ubiquity of change in the natural world: not only are species mutable and historical entities, but the continental landmasses, which give shape to the world such species inhabit, have also changed dramatically over geological time. In the words of botanist Jeremy (J.M.B.) Smith:

> Vegetation is vibrant with change – with short-term fluctuations, medium-term successions and longer-term evolutionary changes; its constituent taxa are ever able to migrate wherever conditions in some way change to allow it. This dynamism needs to be superimposed over the palaeogeographical picture of slowly sliding continents, upthrusting and downwearing mountains, the rise and fall of land and sea, and the changing picture of world climates. The resultant pattern of kaleidoscopic complexity is simplified in appearance only by the paucity of the fossil data...[54]

While an examination of previous writings on the biogeography of Australian rainforest shows that Webb and Tracey's writing of the history of Australian rainforests as 'ancient and indigenous' was not the unambiguous revolution that it was represented as being, they were nonetheless the first scientists to have based their conclusions on detailed, extensive botanical fieldwork in the rainforests of

North Queensland, and knowledge of the mechanism of continental drift. Their fieldwork inspired them to apply in detail the ecological principles of change they had uncovered to the longer-term evolution of rainforest communities.

Webb and Tracey presented the rainforests as a complex, ancient, and ever-changing Australian environment in which current distribution in space could be investigated to reveal 'antiquity and innovation in time'.[55] The mixing of historical and spatial imagery in their depiction of the patterns of rainforest vegetation is striking: it reveals their understanding that, in the context of geological, evolutionary and historical change, it is the rainforests themselves which offer a thread of continuity. However, Webb and Tracey's investigation of the long evolutionary history of the rainforests, undertaken as it was on the basis of detailed fieldwork, also brought them face to face with the rapid, dramatic and ongoing changes caused by European colonisation and large-scale clearing of rainforest areas. This encounter would lead Len Webb, in particular, to become a leading advocate for their conservation.

Since the 1980s, increasingly detailed palaeoecological evidence has enabled researchers to trace, to finer levels of spatio-temporal resolution, the history of tropical rainforests in Australia. This evidence has led scientists to focus on the interrelationship between rainforests and people: in particular, the role of Aboriginal burning in maintaining rainforest boundaries, and the processing and consumption by Aboriginal people of a diverse range of noxious rainforest plants. Scientists are increasingly finding that rainforests are far from the ancient, stable, unchanging environment some conservationists have presented them as. Rainforests are dynamic systems that have changed in species composition, geographical location and extent, in response both to human activities over thousands of years, and to climatic change over millions. As the past of the forests comes into clearer focus, their future remains in question. How the rapid shift in climate that many scientists claim is already underway will impact on the limited areas of tropical rainforest remaining in Australia is an open question.[56]

NOTES

[1] J.D. Hooker, *The Botany of the Antarctic Voyage of H.M. Discovery Ships Erebus and Terror, In the Years 1839–1843, Under the Command of Captain Sir James Clark Ross, K.T., R.N., F.R.S. & L.S., etc.* Part III. *Flora Tasmaniæ*, Vol. I. Dicotyledones (London: Lovell Reeve, 1860), xxvii.

[2] Charles Darwin, 'On the tendency of species to form varieties, and on the perpetuation of varieties and species by natural means of selection', *Journal of the Linnean Society of London (Zoology)* 3 (1858): 45–62. It was Darwin's reading of Wallace's article, on which Wallace had sought his opinion, which provoked him at last to publicly present his own theory. For further details see J.L. Brooks, *Just before the Origin: Alfred Russel Wallace's Theory of Evolution* (New York: Columbia University Press, 1984).

[3] Hooker, *Flora Tasmaniae*, ii–iii.

⁴ Ibid., xvi–xvii. On Lyell, see Janet Browne, *The Secular Ark: Studies in the History of Biogeography* (New Haven: Yale University Press, 1983), 102–7.

⁵ Hooker, *Flora Tasmaniae*, xxii.

⁶ Browne, *The Secular Ark*, 59.

⁷ Hooker, *Flora Tasmaniæ*, xxvii.

⁸ George Elphinstone Dalrymple, *Narrative and Reports of the Queensland North-East Coast Expedition, 1873* (Brisbane: Government Printer, 1874), 30.

⁹ Hooker, *Flora Tasmaniæ*, iv, xii. David L. Hull, *Science as a Process: an Evolutionary Account of the Social and Conceptual Development of Science* (Chicago: University of Chicago Press, 1988), 102.

¹⁰ Hooker, *Flora Tasmaniæ*, xl. None of the explorers listed had collected extensively in North Queensland rainforest areas – Mueller at this stage had not yet settled Dallachy into his role in Cardwell. A century later, botanist Nancy T. Burbidge, in 'The Phytogeography of the Australian Region', a work which closely followed Hooker's approach, wrote of the North-East Queensland region: 'Unfortunately there is no detailed account of the flora of the area and this analysis has had to be based on scattered records in taxonomic and more general botanical papers...' Nancy T. Burbidge, 'The Phytogeography of the Australian Region', *Australian Journal of Botany* 8 (1959): 134.

¹¹ Sydney B.J. Skertchly, 'The Origin of Australia', *Proceedings of the Royal Society of Queensland* 21 (1908): 66.

¹² *Ibid.*, 67–8.

¹³ This is in contrast to the views of Hooker, who argued that the peculiarities of the Australian flora led to the conclusion that it was 'a very ancient one'. Hooker, *Flora Tasmaniæ*, cii. Skertchly in part was opposing the notion that evolutionary processes are by necessity gradual, and believed that the fossil record suggested that at some times, and under some conditions such as changes in climate, the process of speciation was much more rapid and diverse than Hooker suggested. Skertchly, 'The Origin of Australia', 81.

¹⁴ *Ibid.*, 57–8.

¹⁵ This idea of a uniform flora at an earlier period of life's history stretches back to the work of Brongniart and de Candolle in the early nineteenth century, and was widely debated during the mid-nineteenth century. It is discussed by Browne, *The Secular Ark*, 94–102.

¹⁶ Skertchly, 'The Origin of Australia', 69–70.

¹⁷ *Ibid*, 77.

¹⁸ Those who came with prior experience of the tropics include Skertchly, who spent time in Borneo E.N. Marks, 'Skertchly, Sydney Barber Josiah (1850–1926)', *Australian Dictionary of Biography*, Volume 11 (Melbourne: Melbourne University Press, 1988), 621–2. Explorer George Elphinstone Dalrymple and botanist John Dallachy both came to Australia after managing coffee plantations in Ceylon – C. G. Austin, Clem Lack, 'Dalrymple, George Augustus Frederick Elphinstone (1826–1876)', *Australian Dictionary of Biography*, Volume 4 (Melbourne: Melbourne University Press, 1972), 9-10; Alan Gross, 'Dallachy, John (1808?–1871)', *Australian Dictionary of Biography*, Volume 4 (Melbourne: Melbourne University Press, 1972), 6. For details on environmental symbols of nationhood, see Thomas Dunlap, *Nature and the English Diaspora: Environment and*

History in the United States, Canada, Australia and New Zealand (Cambridge: Cambridge University Press, 1999), 100–102.

[19] Karel Domin, 'Queensland's Plant Associations: Some Problems of Queensland's Botanogeography' *Proceedings of the Royal Society of Queensland* 23 (1910): 58. See also A.D. Chapman, 'Domin and Danes in Java and Australia, 1909–1910', in P.S. Short (ed.), *History of Systematic Botany in Australia: Proceedings of a Symposium held at the University of Melbourne, 25–27 May 1988* (Melbourne: Australian Systematic Botany Society Inc., 1990), 159–63.

[20] Chapman, 'Domin and Danes in Java and Australia', 72.

[21] D.A. Herbert, 'Presidential Address: The Relationships of the Queensland Flora', *Proceedings of the Royal Society of Queensland* 40 (1928): 10–12.

[22] J.M.B. Smith, 'An Introduction to the History of Australasian Vegetation', in J.M.B. Smith (ed.), *A History of Australasian Vegetation* (Sydney: McGraw-Hill Book Company, 1982), 12.

[23] J.H. Brown and A.C. Gibson, *Biogeography* (St Louis: The C.V. Mosby Company, 1983), 234.

[24] Herbert, 'The Relationships of the Queensland Flora', 12, 14–15.

[25] D.A. Herbert, 'Present Day Distribution and the Geological Past', *Victorian Naturalist* (April 1950): 228–9.

[26] *Ibid.*, 230.

[27] R. Schodde, 'Origins, Radiations and Sifting in the Australasian Biota – Changing Concepts from New Data and Old' (Nancy T. Burbidge Memorial Lecture, 1989), *Australian Systematic Botany Society Newsletter* 60 (September 1989): 3.

[28] D. Johnson, *The Geology of Australia* (Cambridge: Cambridge University Press, 2004), 73.

[29] Schodde, 'Origins, Radiations and Sifting of the Australasian Biota', 5.

[30] L.J. Webb, 'A Physiognomic Classification of Australian Rain Forests', *Journal of Ecology* 47 (1959): 551–2, doi: 10.2307/2257290.

[31] L.J. Webb and J.G. Tracey, 'The Rainforests of Northern Australia', in R.H. Groves (ed.), *Australian Vegetation* (Cambridge: Cambridge University Press, 1981), 67.

[32] L.J. Webb and J.G. Tracey, 'Australian Rainforests: Patterns and Change', in A. Keast (ed.), *Ecological Biogeography of Australia*, vol. 1 (The Hague: W. Junk, 1981), 607–8.

[33] Interview with Geoff Tracey, National Library of Australia (hereafter NLA) TRC 2845/46: 3.1.9. As Adam points out, 'Referring to living taxa as primitive does not necessarily imply that they are ancestral, but rather that they possess a larger number of primitive traits than other taxa.' P. Adam, *Australian Rainforests* (Oxford, Clarendon Press: 1992), 158.

[34] Webb and Tracey, 'Australian Rainforests: Patterns and Change', 609. Edaphic sifting refers to the influence of soil type on vegetation formations.

[35] Interview with Geoff Tracey, NLA TRC 2845/46: 3.1.10. However, while continental drift had the status of geological orthodoxy by the early 1970s, it took botanists – many of whom responded to these developments with 'outright rejection' – a little longer to accept the new theories than it did geologists. J.M.B. Smith, 'An Introduction to the History of Australasian Vegetation', 2. For a more recent and detailed overview of Aus-

tralia's rainforest past, see R.J. Morley, *Origin and Evolution of Tropical Rain Forests* (Chichester: John Wiley and Sons, 2000), 225–35.

[36] A. Keast, R.L. Crocker, C.S. Christian (eds.), *Biogeography and Ecology in Australia* (The Hague: W. Junk, 1959). Interview with Geoff Tracey, NLA TRC 2845/46: 2.1.6–7.

[37] A.P Kershaw, 'A Late Pleistocene and Holocene Pollen Diagram from Lynch's Crater, North-Eastern Queensland, Australia', *New Phytologist* 77 (1976): 469–98, doi: 10.1111/j.1469-8137.1976.tb01534.x.

[38] Webb and Tracey, 'Australian rainforests: patterns and change', 628.

[39] Ibid., 637–8.

[40] Ibid., 642–5.

[41] Ibid., 649, 651.

[42] Ibid., 654.

[43] Ibid., 654–61.

[44] Ibid., 663.

[45] Ibid., 661.

[46] They concentrated their analysis on genera as knowledge of species distribution for the region continued to be inadequate, and many species remained unnamed and some undescribed. Webb and Tracey, 'Australian Rainforests: Patterns and Change', 668–669.

[47] Ibid., 672.

[48] Ibid., 676.

[49] Judith Wright, *The Coral Battleground* (West Melbourne: Thomas Nelson, 1977), 3–4.

[50] Veronica Brady, *South of My Days: A Biography of Judith Wright* (Sydney: Angus & Robertson, 1998), 429.

[51] J. Wright, 'Rainforest', *Collected Poems 1942–1985* (Sydney: Angus & Robertson, 1998), 412.

[52] R. Hill and M. Graham, 'Greater Daintree National Park' in J.G. Moseley and J. Messer (eds.), *Fighting for Wilderness. Papers from the Australian Conservation Foundation's Third National Wilderness Conference, 1983* (Sydney: Fontana/ACF, 1984), 9.

[53] See Rainforest Conservation Society of Queensland, *Tropical Rainforests of North Queensland: Their Conservation Significance* (Canberra: Australian Government Publishing Service, 1986), on the basis of which the Australian Heritage Commission recommended World Heritage Listing.

[54] J.M.B Smith, 'An Introduction to the History of the Australasian Vegetation', 27.

[55] Webb and Tracey 'Australian Rainforests: Patterns and Change', 676.

[36] On Aboriginal use of rainforest plants see R. Cosgrove et al., 'The Archaeology of Australia's Tropical Rainforests', *Palaeogeography, Palaeoclimatology, Palaeoecology*, 251,1 (2007): 150–73, doi: 10.1016/j.palaeo.2007.02.023. On rainforests and fire, see D.M.J.S. Bowman, *Australian Rainforests: Islands of Green in a Land of Fire* (Cambridge: Cambridge University Press, 2000). For a detailed analysis of human impacts on tropical rainforest over the past 700 years and a discussion of the implications of climate change see Simon G. Haberle, et al., 'The Impact of European Occupation on Terrestrial and Aquatic Ecosystem Dynamics in an Australian Tropical Rain Forest', *Journal of Ecology* 94,5 (2006): 987–1002, doi: 10.1111/j.1365-2745.2006.01140.x.

Prehistory of Southern African Forestry: From Vegetable Garden to Tree Plantation

Kate B. Showers

INTRODUCTION

In southern African history, it is important to separate the forests from the trees. While forest history has been told from the perspective of Scientific Forestry, forest regulation and government bureaucracies, the history of trees has largely been neglected. South Africa's forest history relates not to the management of indigenous vegetation, but rather to the massive planting of alien tree species. Trees' use and propagation pre-dated the idea of forestry and covered more land than indigenous forests. While closed-canopy forests existed in some places along the coast of Cape Colony (modern South Africa's Western and Eastern Cape Provinces) and that of Natal Colony (modern South Africa's Zulu Natal Province), most of southern Africa's coast and interior were predominantly grassland or herbaceous species ecosystems. Trees grew only in sheltered locations that were relatively enriched with water – their use and protection by indigenous people is beyond the scope of this paper.

The first Europeans to settle in southern Africa – Dutch East India Company representatives – arrived at modern Cape Town in 1652 with notions of tree production and propagation materials for domestically important trees from northern hemisphere humid temperate landscapes. While chopping down indigenous trees growing in the larger landscape for construction and other domestic needs, they planted alien species in domestic spaces for fruit, fuel and shade. As the European population increased, the amount of land claimed expanded, and the area planted to trees increased. Dutch East India Company rule at Cape Town was replaced by Dutch government structures, which were, in turn, replaced by the British Cape Colony government. The Colony of Natal, established later, was initially ruled as an extension of Cape Colony, then received its own (British) colonial government. The subject of this paper is the arrival and spread of alien tree genera and species in southern Africa (modern South Africa, Lesotho and Botswana), with primary emphasis on their arrival points – the Cape and Natal Colonies.

When the concept of forestry arrived with British rule in 1806, it was concerned with formalising the regulation of indigenous tree use and the designation and protection of forest land.[1] In parallel (and understudied), alien species continued to arrive and travel inland with settlers. This tree planting was formally supported

145
PRE-HISTORY OF SOUTHERN AFRICAN FORESTRY

and encouraged by government botanical gardens, and informally by missionary networks. Trees were first planted as a crop for domestic self-sufficiency, then on farms for marketable products, and finally in large plantations to supply industrial needs.[2] This paper will trace the history of trees as southern African crops, rather than forests, concentrating on the importation, propagation and distribution of alien species in the seventeenth–nineteenth centuries. Attention will be given to the specific histories of the dominant imports: fruit trees, acacia (wattle), pine and eucalyptus. Finally, the paper will comment upon the mid-nineteenth-century desiccationist justification for tree planting in light of late twentieth-century campaigns for alien species removal for water conservation.

TREE CUTTING AND TREE PLANTING

Southern Africa's Cape Colony, on the Atlantic Ocean, has Mediterranean moisture regimes on the coast and semi-arid to arid interior regimes inland. Grasses and shrubs – not trees – were the dominant indigenous vegetation. The dry sub-humid upland regions of the Natal Colony, although moister than most of the Cape Colony, were still predominantly grassland ecosystems. Trees only grew in sheltered locations with relatively wetter soils, such as hillsides or mountain 'kloofs' (ravines).[3] In these colonies, forests were not cleared to create agricultural landscapes[4] – isolated patches of trees were harvested to meet settler needs. Wood use habits developed in temperate forested land prevailed among European settlers, despite the scarcity of trees.

The Cape's first settlers were representatives of the Dutch East India Company (*Vereenigde Oost-indische Compagnie*, or VOC). Sent under the leadership of Jan van Riebeeck in 1652, their mandate was supplying fresh water and food to company ships travelling in the spice trade between the Netherlands and Dutch East Indies (modern Indonesia). By 1657 the original VOC plans for minimal settlement had proven inadequate; grants were given to nine men to farm inland from Cape Town settlement along the Liesbeek River,[5] and Leendert Conelisson was granted the right to fell trees. Fifty years later the census listed 1,779 settlers,[6] all of whom needed fuel and wood for construction. According to Jan van Riebeeck's journals, the forest patches on Table Mountain were the first to be cut. By 1660 forests close to the original Cape Town settlement had been cleared, and by 1679 there was little accessible timber within 300 kilometress.[7] The resulting timber shortage was barely offset by imported wood in 1699.[8] This pattern of use exceeding reproduction was replicated as European settlement expanded eastward and northward from Cape Town. Although locally important, more significant long-term environmental consequences resulted from the introduction of trees to a largely treeless landscape.

European tree planting predates both the well-documented desiccation discourse and its need for remediation, and the arrival of Scientific Forestry.[9]

Because the role of fruit and vegetables in maintaining sailors' health was well understood, one of Jan van Riebeeck's first official acts was to create a company garden from seed and planting stock he had brought with him from the Netherlands. Accordingly, R.H. Compton[10] claimed that 'the history of Europeans in South Africa began with a garden'. Van Riebeeck's journals in the 1650s document variety trials of a range of fruit tree species and grape vine varieties,[11] but intensive tree planting did not begin until the arrival of the Huguenot refugees in 1687/88.[12] After being allocated poor soils in the Drakenstein area, they requested, and were granted, better land in the Berg River Valley northeast of Cape Town.[13] The first farm in the valley was allocated to Heinrich Müller from Basel, Switzerland in 1692; two years later nine French Huguenot families were granted adjacent farmland by Governor Simon van der Stel. The French refugees planted fruit trees and grape vines on their farms and developed a trade first in fruit and then in wine with the growing port of Cape Town.[14] By 1713 the region was known as *'de france hoek' (Fransche Hoek)*, which became modern Franschhoek in 1805.[15] During the eighteenth century fruit trees spread to the interior with missionaries and Protestant settlement.[16] In 1792, when missionaries reached Baviaan's Kloof (modern Genadendal[17]), the site of Moravian Brother Georg Schmidt's 1737–1744 attempt to convert the Khoi, all that remained was a very large pear tree.[18]

Non-fruit trees continued to arrive and spread as a separate settler economy developed. Reports from the 1550s had described the Cape as having limited woodland, and thus being unable to supply European wood requirements for construction and fuel. Van Riebeeck's ship, therefore, had a cargo of Norwegian and Swedish planks and beams as well as seed of alder (*Alnus glutinosa*).[19] In contrast to the successful fruit orchards, almost a decade of failed attempts at propagation preceded success, when Alnus seeds were imported in soil containing the nitrogen-fixing bacteria essential for their survival. Van Riebeeck also introduced Norway spruce (*Picea abies*), Scots pine (*Pinus sylvestris*), ash (*Franxinus excelsior*) and oak (*Quercus robur*).[20] Both VOC and Netherlands government (the United Provinces, Lords XVII) urged Cape officials to plant trees to prevent or reduce timber shortages.[21] Commander, then Governor Simon van der Stel (1679–1699) claimed to have planted 28,987 oak, 459 alder and 81 ash trees by 1694, as well as having a policy of compulsory tree planting by colonists. His son, Willern Adriaan, who succeeded him, was responsible for planting 30,000 oaks in the Company's plantation and sending 20,000 inland to Stellenbosch and Drakenstein, as well as experimenting with Norway spruce, Scots pine, lime trees, black poplar and elm[22]. But there was no bureaucracy for enforcing either tree protection or planting.[23] Two species of pine, *Pinus pinaster* (maritime pine, native of the Mediterranean basin) and *Pinus pinea* (stone pine, native to Iberian peninsula/southern Europe) reached the Cape in the late seventeenth century. Possibly introduced by the Huguenots, they were not mentioned in the 1914 report by François Valentijn, the Dutch East India

PRE-HISTORY OF SOUTHERN AFRICAN FORESTRY

Company's church minister and botanist.[24,25] *Pinus sylvestris* (Scots pine, the only pine native to Britain) was also reported in Cape Peninsula gardens at this time. During the 154 years of Dutch rule, fruit, fuel and ornamental trees were introduced from Europe and Australia for planting in corporate gardens and municipal and domestic spaces. Van Riebeeck and subsequent Dutch administrators sought to regulate cutting indigenous trees in an attempt to manage wood and fuel supplies, but did not have mechanisms for enforcement.[26] The elaboration of forestry concepts, institutionalisation of the idea of alien tree importation, and the promotion of tree planting in this largely grassland ecosystem developed under British rule.

PIONEERING TREES

The first half of the nineteenth century was dominated by European exploration – and increasing domination – of Africa's southern tip. The British took control of the region around Cape Town from the Dutch in 1806, creating the Cape [of Good Hope] Colony. European settlement expanded to the east of Cape Town along the coast and inland as Dutch settlers fled British rule. They travelled across landscapes covered with mimosa trees and shrubs like oak, aloe, cacti and many kinds of *Euphorbia*.[27,28] Settler farms with limited water supplies could only support small vegetable gardens and wheat fields for self-sufficiency, but towns such as Graaf-Reinet, situated on river banks, had irrigated tree-lined streets and fruit-filled gardens.[29]

With an increasing settler population, demand for wood products grew, exceeding local supplies. By 1810 pine boards and beams were being imported from the United States of America[30]. Although pines had first taken root in the seventeenth century, it was not until 1825–1830 that the first commercial plantation of *P. pinaster* was established at Genandendal.[31] A representative of the *Eucalyptus* genus, *E. Globulus* (Blue Gum), which became widespread later in the century, arrived at the Cape in 1828.[32]

Trees moved further inland from the Atlantic Coast with missionaries ahead of European settlement. Three French Paris Evangelical Mission Society (Protestant) missionaries travelled for three months in 1833 – first by boat from Cape Town to Port Elizabeth, and then inland by ox-drawn wagon and horse to a blank spot on their map bought in Paris labelled 'sandy' and 'desert plains'.[33] Like van Riebeeck before them, they carried into an unknown landscape seeds and planting stock for vegetables, grape vines and fruit trees, including orange, fig, apple, stone fruits, pomegranate and almond, as well as pines and acacias.[34] What they found was the mountainous Kingdom of Lesotho (British Protectorate of Basutoland from 1868–1966), a landscape both colder and wetter than that at the coast. This grassland's sparse trees grew along river banks, in ravines, and in sheltered and wetter spots on lower mountain slopes. Within 30 years most of these trees had been harvested 'for the glory of God' to build mission stations.[35] Introductions such as orange, pomegranate and almond ultimately failed, but apples and the stone fruits – particularly peach – succeeded, and were rapidly adopted by the local inhabitants, the Basotho[36].

Tree planting reached southern Africa's warm, dry subhumid eastern Indian Ocean coast (Natal Colony) later than the colder and drier Atlantic coast (Cape Colony). Although a place called *Tevia Natalis* (later Port Natal) had served as a refreshment station for Portuguese ships sailing the Indian Ocean since 1497, and the Dutch had attempted to establish settlements there in 1688 and 1721, Port Natal (modern Durban) only became a European settlement point after the British obtained a concession from Shaka, Chief of the Zulus, in 1824.[37] Large-scale settlement in the interior began when Dutch settlers (*voortrekkers*) escaping British rule crossed the mountains from the Cape Colony between 1835–1837. The Free Dutch Republic was proclaimed in 1840 (with modern Pietermaritzburg its capital), but it was annexed as a district or province of the Cape Colony three years later.[38] By 1846 'gums' and acacias were reportedly growing in the town of Howick.[39] Between 1848 and 1850, 35 immigrant ships with passengers largely of British origin arrived at Port Natal; in 1848 'native locations' were defined, and substantial European land acquisition began.[40] As in the Cape Colony, alien trees followed settlers.

SEPARATING FORESTS FROM TREES

The seventeenth- and eighteenth-century Dutch rulers at the Cape were aware of European environmental degradation debates related to tree cutting, and eventually established 'highly restrictive land-use regulations and early forms of conservation and forest laws'.[41] They considered agriculture to be potentially destructive of both soils and forests, but they did not link forests and trees to rainfall or climate change, as had the French and the English.[42] With British rule in 1806 came a government bureaucracy that included a Superintendent of Government Lands and Woods.[43] By the middle of the century Rangers and Conservators were to ensure the Superintendent's mandate to protect indigenous trees, but their duties were broadly defined in terms of preventing 'needless destruction' of existing trees and issuing licenses for their harvest. Tropp[44] records growing official concern about, and attempts to control, the activities of independent woodcutters in the true, closed-canopy forest – near Knysna, along the Cape Colony coast between the towns of George and Port Elizabeth (modern Transkei, Eastern Cape Province). As late as the mid-nineteenth century there was no mention in reports filed by Cape Rangers and Conservators of the need for, or activities to accomplish, reclamation and reforestation of overexploited areas.[45] The similar lack of conservation of the trees in Natal's indigenous forests was mentioned in an 1883 report of the Virginia Planter's Association.[46]

PRE-HISTORY OF SOUTHERN AFRICAN FORESTRY

Forests were separated from trees in the Cape Colony when the government placed responsibilities for *forest protection* under the Superintendent of Lands and Woods while the work of *tree propagation and increase* rested with the botanic gardens. This process was codified in 1858 when the Colonial Botanist, rather than Superintendent of Lands and Woods, was responsible for the identification of new tree species with utilitarian potential. The separation was furthered when, with the achievement of the status of Responsible Government in 1872, the Cape Colony created the Commission of Crown Lands and Public Works with responsibilities not only for forests, but also for roads, bridges, harbour works, jetties, public buildings, lighthouses, railway works, telegraphs and public stores.[47] Forests were, thus, bureaucratically grouped with infrastructure development rather than the natural world, and understood as public resources to be managed by the state for public benefit. Initially they were to serve as a source of fuel wood and, later, to supply timber for public works.[48]

This separation of forest from trees reduced the status of forestry and limited official function. John Croumbie Brown's proposal for the establishment of a school of forestry similar to those in Europe was officially rejected in 1877 by the Cape government.[49] Nevertheless, a Forest Department was created in 1881.[50] The Cape Forester in 1882 borrowed the English concept of 'forest land', as distinct from a 'forest'. But rather than referring to reserved hunting ground, in the Cape Colony 'forest land' referred to those places lacking trees where their growth would be useful to prevent erosion, such as 'denuded mountain slopes' and steep slopes.[51] Thus the official area of forest in this grassland ecosystem had increased – but not the number of trees in need of protection. It is not surprising that the Conservator of Forests reportedly had little idea of his duties in 1883 beyond supervising woodcutting.[52] Although the Cape Colony Forestry Act of 1888 demarcated forests,[53] within three years the post of Superintendent of Woods and Forests had been abolished, and Conservators were made directly responsible to the Commissioner on Lands and Public Works. Formalised efforts to introduce, propagate and distribute alien trees were not a function of the Superintendent of Lands and Woods under British rule. Rather, they remained a function of a garden, the newly proclaimed Botanic Garden.

TREES FROM GARDENS

Empires (Spanish, Dutch, French and British) were built on the harvest and sale of plant parts (roots, tubers, leaves, seeds, nuts, timber) for spices, perfumes, medicinal drugs, oils and dyes, as well as wood. The search for, and propagation of, economically useful plants was a major component of colonial exploration and colonisation. Knowledge of plants evolved from natural science to botany, and moved from the domain of medical doctors to botanists. In the seventeenth and eighteenth centuries botanists and their gardens flourished as empires developed territories. What is now called 'bioprospecting' was encouraged by exchanges of plant materials between individual explorers and botanical gardens and through networks of botanic gardens. By the end of the eighteenth century, Europeans had founded sixteen hundred botanical gardens.[54]

In Cape Colony the post of Colonial Botanist was created in 1858 to 'determine the Cape Colony's economic resources and its future for the growth of exotic trees, as well as perfecting the knowledge of South African flora'.[55] When former missionary John Croumbie Brown was appointed to hold this post in 1863, he brought with him desiccationism and a belief that millions of trees of any kind needed to be planted in order to change the South African climate.[56] Because of the general apathy towards tree planting, Brown argued that 'arboriculture was an enterprise of the future' that should be promoted by 'distributing seeds and seedlings of indigenous, Australian and European trees to civil commissioners, agricultural societies and the public'.[57] He further thought that indigenous trees should be studied for their suitability as crops, possibly as fuel supplies for railways and steam powered engines, and that revenues from sales could finance tree plantations.[58] However, the state should take care not to compete with private enterprise.

By the end of the 1850s, Cape Town's Botanic Garden[59] was well respected and understood to be a major advertiser for, and encourager of, tree introductions and tree planting, as well as a cheap and reliable source of seed and seedlings.[60] The Cape Town Botanic Garden issued a fruit tree catalogue in 1864.[61] Although the post of Cape Botanist was terminated in 1866, ending both Brown's job and support for Cape Town's botanical garden,[62] government-run botanical gardens flourished elsewhere in the Colony during the 1870s. Gardens established at Graham's Town (modern Grahamstown) and Graaf-Reinet were active in promoting tree planting by providing seeds and seedlings locally and to 'Frontier Districts'.[63]

A botanical garden was established at Durban in 1851, six years after the Colony of Natal's government was formalised as a distinct entity under a Lieutenant-Governor (1845), and two years before municipal structures were created in both Durban and Pietermaritzburg (1853).[64] It began making exchanges with botanical gardens in the Cape as well as India and Australia. Tree seeds and seedlings were introduced by, and distributed from, this garden. Interest in planting trees, however, was largely confined to the upland interior areas dominated by grasslands, rather than the tree-covered coastal lowlands. In Natal, the Durban Botanic Garden advocated for a branch garden to be established in the upland town of Pietermaritzburg 'for the acclimatization of European fruit and other trees suited to the climate there'.[65] The Acclimatization Society of Pietermaritzburg, which cooperated with the Botanic Garden in Durban, carried out trials of new species and varieties to assess suitability for the cooler and less humid inland and upland areas during the 1860s. Seeds and seedlings were provided for free or at low cost to planters.[66] The Acclimatization Society became the Pietermaritzburg Botanic Garden in 1874, to serve as a research station that tested the viability of growing large trees such as magnolias, camphors, and swamp cypress. These two gardens together were subsequently referred to as the Natal Botanic Gardens.

During the 1860s the Graham's Town Botanic Garden (Eastern Cape) donated between 100 and 150 trees to 'those barren towns whose municipalities have not the opportunity or advantage of raising timber trees'.[67] The increasing number of visitors to the Durban Botanic Garden came for 'study, or instruction and recreation'.[68] Curators of the gardens actively sought new plants to introduce from Europe, other regions of southern Africa and other British colonies, promoting them to residents.[69] More species of eucalyptus and acacia reached the Durban garden in 1867.[70] In 1864 *Acacia mearnsii* (Black Wattle) was introduced to Natal for firewood.[71] On one of his many trips to Pietermaritzburg, Roman Catholic missionary Father Lebihan acquired some to take back to Lesotho for the newly established Roman Catholic mission established in a foothills valley (modern Roma).[72] Cold, snowy winters made the cultivation of fuel trees essential in Lesotho.

Both the Cape and Natal Colonies expanded in the 1870s, and their botanical gardens were instrumental in promoting tree planting and supplying both propagation materials and instruction. The Graham's Town garden provided 1800 trees for free to 'Public Institutions in Frontier districts' and to individuals.[73] Half the seeds and seedlings received from Europe in 1837 were conifers.[74] The Durban Botanic Garden continued to supply inland planters with 'any seeds on hand useful for timber, firewood or ornament', including four species of eucalyptus and thirteen of acacia. A range of fruit trees had also been successfully introduced, including varieties of apple, cherry, pear, plum, and apricot.[75] Acacia species central to the creation of Natal's wattle bark industry were received by the Durban Botanic Garden in the 1870s.

The problems noted earlier that farmers encountered when attempting to grow trees from seed in the Cape Colony were addressed by the Natal Botanic Gardens in the 1880s. The Curator suggested that someone be hired for the 'special purposes of raising from seed and potting out' trees of the 'most approved varieties for plantations'.[76] When the botanist at the Pietermaritzburg garden proposed formal testing of exotic species that had been introduced (such as acacia and eucalyptus) for their value as timber in 1891, the Conservator of forests supported the proposal.[77]

Despite the availability of trees at botanical gardens, there was a widespread belief that trees did not grow well, especially in the Cape Colony. Reasons cited for not planting trees included the difficulty of raising them from seed, the retardation of root penetration by dense clays close to soil surfaces, the stunting effects of drought, the potential of wind to uproot or snap tree trunks, and the destructiveness of both goats and fire.[78] Increasing tree cultivation beyond planting by 'tree enthusiasts' would require promotion.

Tree planting was encouraged through mechanisms such as subsidies and competitions. The Cape Government's Act No. 4 of 1876 provided towns with matching funds to plant trees along streets and on the grounds of official buildings. Rewards were also given to individuals who successfully cultivated trees.[79] The Natal Colony's Native Affairs Department proposed rewards to any African 'who can show 500 healthy trees of 12 month growth'[80] in 1890. During the first decade of the twentieth century, the Transvaal government contributed funds to municipal and roadside tree planting.[81] The Cape government led the way in stimulating interest through competitions. In 1895 the Cape of Good Hope government announced prizes for the planting of 'forest' trees to be awarded in 1901.[82] Colonial government promotion of tree planting was not restricted to the Cape and Natal Colonies' governments. Anticipating the annexation of the Protectorate of Bechuanaland (modern Botswana) to the north, Cape legislation encouraging tree planting there was passed in 1895.[83] In British Basutoland, on the Cape Colony's northeastern border, the Cape Governor's Agent, Col. Griffiths, similarly instituted prizes for tree cultivation.[84] It was civil society that led government in organising tree planting competitions for settlers in Natal. The Maritzburg Agricultural Society cooperated with the Maritzburg[85] Botanic Society to launch tree planting competitions in 1895.[86]

COMMERCIAL TREES

Despite the existence of official proclamations and promotions, actual tree planting was stimulated not by official concerns about inducing climate change, but by the growing demand for wood products: supports for mines, fuel for steam-driven machinery, timber for railroad construction, and bark for tanning. There had been great difficulty in propagating indigenous species suitable for timber,[87] and demand for wood soon eclipsed supplies possible from limited indigenous forest patches and groves. Fast, strong and straight-growing alien species were seen as the solution – but planted as a crop. Initially, mass tree production was a government endeavour because it was thought to be uneconomic for individual farmers.[88,89] State intervention was soon abandoned and trees became a commercial crop planted on farms.

Nonetheless, the forestry establishment insisted that mass tree growing was a forestry activity because it employed 'silviculture', which had a 'technical meaning', and asserted that 'the supposed connection between Agriculture and Forestry is a popular error confined to persons who are ignorant of the latter. The two have little in common. Most of their principles differ, and all of their practices are widely divergent'.[90] Forester E. Hutchins' derisive statement that Agriculture departments – 'in America and the British Colonies are usually loose collections of experts with advisory functions which no doubt have a value, especially in young countries'[91] actually characterised what was required for the introduction and successful establishment of trees on private – or public – land in the Cape Colony. Little knowledge existed about tree cultivation in southern Africa, and the suitability of alien species was unknown. There was, therefore, a need for identification and testing of alien species for suitability in the wide range of climate and soils in the different colonies. The botanical gardens, with their mandates for plant exploration and introduction, networks of regional and intercontinental exchange of plant materials and information about cultivation and use, not the Forest Department, were best suited to this work.

Around the world, the latter half of the nineteenth century saw the internationalisation of the French and German concepts of Scientific Forestry and tree management through silviculture. This was accompanied by the creation of government departments of forests and forestry and the expansion of forest regulation and legislation.[92] These events coincided, in South Africa, with the European discovery of diamonds in the northern Cape Colony (1867), the declaration of the Transvaal's Witwatersrand as a gold mining area (1886), and the attendant development of mining and industrial centres and crop-based economies linked by railways. There was a need for energy and construction materials as rural and urban infrastructure and production expanded. South Africa's relatively treeless landscape presented a major problem. Indigenous forests were soon unable to supply fuel for steam-powered machinery (from sugar cane refineries to railway engines), props for mine shafts, sleepers (ties) for railroad tracks, and boards and beams for bridges and buildings. Imported wood was increasingly expensive, and the properties of the existing introduced alien species were unknown.

As a wood shortage became obvious,[93] landowners with mature trees on their property saw opportunities for sales, and offered samples to the Cape government for testing.[94] Merchant companies began to invest in forestry, sawmills and forest products.[95] In neighbouring Basutoland, British Magistrate Emille Rolland imagined that the production of trees would be a way to increase the territory's wealth.[96] John Croumbie Brown's proposed aboriculture was in its infancy. The fundamental role of botanic gardens and waning interventions of governments in tree cultivation can be seen in the overlapping histories of fruit and non-fruit trees (the genera *Eucalyptus* and *Acacia*) in the context of a growing demand for fuel, construction and the emergence of four commercial uses of tree products (fruits for export, poles for mine shafts, beams for railway sleepers, and bark for tanning leather). The cultivation of trees proliferated. Fruit production expanded from subsistence to commercial scales, and eucalyptus and acacia became cash crops.

Tracing –and writing about – these tree histories can be linguistically complicated. While botanists were concerned about species and varietal differences, the planting public (official and unofficial) knew trees largely by common names or their function (fruit tree, timber tree, forest tree). Common names could be as confusing for planters, officials and botanists as they are for historians centuries later. Fruit trees were known by the type of fruit (peach, apple, orange), rather than the variety, which would have indicated such traits as seasonality, environmental requirements, disease susceptibility and yield.

Both the genera *Eucalyptus* and *Acacia* have large numbers of species, some similar in appearance, and some with similar function, all of which had been given common names. In the following discussion, the names provided in different documents will be retained, even if contradictions or confusion arise. Not only will original nomenclature allow the paper to remain true to its sources, but it will also exemplify the confusion that persisted – and persists – about species identities, as well as the complexities facing historical researchers in tracing tree movements.

a. Fruit trees

As discussed above, fruit trees arrived with settlers in the seventeenth century, and botanical gardens provided seeds and seedlings, as well as catalogues, for promotion. The expanding frontier was represented in the kinds of trees supplied by botanical gardens. While the Cape Town garden reported minimal interest from the public in fruit tree planting materials in 1871,[97] the Graham's Town garden was having difficulty in meeting demand, as they were supplying not only 'all parts of the Province', but also the diamond fields near Kimberly. A major constraint was skilled labour.[98] The garden was expanded in 1873 to accommodate increased fruit tree production[99]. That year, in addition to meeting requests for 'forest and ornamental' trees, the garden supplied 'about 500 grafted orange and naartje trees, most of them in a bearing state, not less than 1,000 apple trees, and about 2,500 peaches, apricots, plums, pears &c'.[100] There was no botanical garden in Basutoland; missionaries continued to fulfil a tree distribution role. Missionary Maeder reportedly handed out 400 fruit trees as well as poplar and willow in 1877.[101] The rush to produce and distribute trees resulted in varietal identities becoming confused, if not lost completely. At the end of 1870s the curator at the Graaf-Reinet gardens requested fresh planting materials from Europe because the 'fruit trees of the Colony [are] so mixed up that no one can depend on supplying trees true to their names'.[102]

Fruit trees became associated with Transvaal railway lines in the 1890s, when their cultivation around worker's cottages and train stations was seen as a way to enhance the quality of workers' lives as well as the appearance of railway stations.[103] With the advent of railways, Natal fruit growers, who already had markets for dried and processed fruits, began to find markets for fresh fruit. A single mature orange tree was worth two pounds in 1893, and profits were beginning to be found from growing pineapples and bananas. Fruit marketers exerted pressure to ensure refrigeration on steam ships for exports to Britain.[104]

Cape farmers paid minimal attention to the quality of the fruit they produced, other than grapes for wine. So poor was the condition of the Cape Colony's

PRE-HISTORY OF SOUTHERN AFRICAN FORESTRY

fruit trees that the Department of Agriculture had to ask the Curator of the Cape Government Herbarium to prepare a 'Manual of Orchard-Culture'.[105] It was the botanical gardens that promoted fruit tree growing and conducted variety trials, and it was botanical gardens that supplied the planting materials. When advice was required for farmers, it was the botanical garden, and not the Departments of Agriculture or Forests that was expected to provide it. But then, fruit trees are not annual row crops, and scientific forestry did not consider orchards to be forests.

b. Eucalyptus ('Gum')

The arrival and spread of the genus *Eucalyptus* is only sketchily documented and, thus, less easily traced than fruit trees. The name Blue Gum was originally associated with *E. globulus*, but eventually 'gum' became the generic common name for any eucalyptus tree. There is a record of the species *E. globulus* (Blue Gum) reaching the Cape Colony in 1828, of 'gums' growing near the town of Howick, in Natal in 1846,[106] and of eucalyptus seeds having been sent to missionary H.M. Dyke in Lesotho by Sir George Grey, Governor of Cape Colony in 1858.[107] But the beginning of large-scale spread of eucalyptus trees – particularly *E. globulus* – was in the 1860s. Cape Botanist John Croumbie Brown noted having seen 'blue gums' growing at farmsteads 'with greater or less luxuriance' in 1863, which 'had not been the case when I made the tour of the Colony in 1847'.[108]

The sudden proliferation of eucalyptus could have been the result of the international spread of this species as a drainage device and malaria control. In 1856 Dr. Ferdinand von Mueller, the Government Botanist for Victoria and Director of the Melbourne Botanic Garden introduced a M. Ramel from France to the properties of *E. Globulus* ('blue gum' of Tasmania), and provided him with seed. Further supplies of seed sent to Paris in 1856, 1857 and 1860 were distributed throughout southern Europe, North Africa and other parts of the world 'for its power of destroying miasmatic influence of marshy districts',[109] thus earning *E. globulus* the name 'fever destroying tree'. In the era before either the existence of the germ theory or knowledge of mosquito's ability to transmit disease were known, debate existed as to whether the tree's power rose from its drainage capacity or its 'camphoraceous, stimulating odor'. Eucalypts were widely believed to be able to take up ten times their weight in water, so that 'masses of such trees' had 'enormous suction-power'. 'Where thickly planted in marshy places 'the subsoil is drained in a little while as though by extensive piping'.[110] This property was used in the Cape Colony where, a few years after planting, the 'climatic condition' of the 'unhealthy parts of the Colony' had changed.[111] Even after the mosquito connection was well understood, eucalyptus were recommended by Transvaal Forester Charles C. Legat to control malaria around the Komatiepoort railway station because the trees would provide cooling filtered shade while preventing thick vegetation underneath in which mosquitoes could live.[112] Witt[113] also mentions the use of this genus to dry land in South Africa.

Botanical gardens in both the Cape and Natal colonies provided seed and seedlings to individuals and organisations throughout the 1860s and 1870s.[114] The British representative in Basutoland, Col. Griffiths, urged Basotho to plant *E. globulus* when offering tree planting prizes in 1876.[115] That year the Durban Botanic Garden 'supplied 600 trees in pots to the Durban Corporation, 3,000 Blue Gums, 800 others and 700 parcels of seeds to subscribers and other applicants', and three years later reportedly distributed 3,900 '*E. globulus* and others' plus 2,100 other shrubs and trees.[116] Some species of eucalyptus spread inland to the drier and colder Orange Free State (modern Free State Province of South Africa); by 1889 the town of Cloclolan had more than 40 species.[117]

The quality of eucalyptus wood was unknown at first. In 1860 James McGibbon of the Cape Town Botanic Garden requested that four 'Blue Gums – *Eucalyptus diversifolia*' measuring 'at the thick end about 6 feet in circumference, in length 12–20 feet' be accepted for testing 'by experiment' to determine their suitability for use in construction and manufacturing;[118] alien species remained untested in Natal as late as 1891. Because of prejudice against locally grown wood, timber and sawn boards were imported by both the Cape and Natal Colonies.[119] Despite official and commercial lack of interest, in the 1880s Eucalyptus was being grown on farms throughout the Cape and Natal Colonies, and Natal farmers used it as the primary source of wood for 'everything for which timber is applicable'. Eucalyptus was considered to be superior to pine 'in tenacity for holding bolts'.[120] Although 'manufactured wood' and wood for furniture was still imported for commercial use a decade later, 'colonial wood' had begun to be used for railway sleepers.[121]

With the expansion of the railway within and between colonies, the demand for railway sleepers increased dramatically. The mature eucalyptus on many farms seemed a ready supply. But, in 1891, when locally grown timber was cut for sleepers, it was found to be inferior to that being imported from the Baltic region. The imports had been treated with creosote, and there were no creosoting facilities in the Cape or Natal Colonies.[122] This did not stop speculation that the estimated 10,000 mature Eucalyptus on farms in Natal could supply a local railway sleeper industry.[123]

Mines, rather than the railways, emerged as the major market for eucalyptus, and stimulated increased planting in the twentieth century.[124] Mine shafts need supports. At first mining companies cleared their land and used indigenous wood to make props. When this was depleted, the Cape government provided timber from its plantations at Kluitjeskraal. These forests were able to supply the needs of the relatively surficial diamond diggings from 1897.[125] In contrast, the rapidly expanding and deep shafts of the Transvaal Republic's Witwatersrand gold mines required more wood than the mine land could provide, and the Transvaal government had no forests to exploit. To secure their own supplies, mine companies began to plant trees. The first company-owned plantation was established near Braamfontein, on the Witwatersrand, in the 1880s.[126] As the mines expanded, mine-owned plantations spread from the Transvaal, where tree-growing was marginal, to Natal, and the straight, strong, rapidly growing eucalyptus was the tree of choice. Large-scale tree plantations were firmly established as a matter of private enterprise rather than government service, and the gold mining industry became known as the 'tree-growing sector'.[127]

Despite the fact that most species of Eucalyptus could not be grown in Natal's many ecosystems,[128] the genera of eucalyptus and acacias dominated tree plantations in that colony. In the late nineteenth century four private tree nurseries reportedly supplied between 200,000 and 300,000 trees a year, mostly eucalyptus and wattle.[129]

c. Acacia ('Wattle')

The genus *Acacia* has many species which can cluster around similar traits that have ended up with the same common name – but there are also different common names for the same species. Imported with the trees from Australia were common names, many of which contained the word 'wattle'.[130] *Acacia dealbata* was referred to as either Silver Wattle or Mimosa, and *A. decurrens* could be Green Wattle or Black Wattle. *A. mollissima* was also called Black Wattle, as was *A. mearnsii*. According to the Royal Botanic Garden at Kew, *Acacia mearnsii de Wild*, *A. decurrens var Mullis* and *A. mollissima* are synonyms.[131,132] In Afrikaans Black Wattle is *Swartwattel* and in Zulu it is *Uwatela*. Just as 'gums' came to denote any *Eucalyptus*, 'wattle' was used for any species of *Acacia*.

Acacia mearnsii was introduced into Natal from Australia for firewood in 1864,[133] and unspecified species of acacia were among the seeds sent by the Durban Botanic Garden to upland settlers for timber, firewood and ornament in 1871.[134] Its value as a source of wood was investigated in 1889 when acacia samples were sent to London for evaluation, and to two Natal firms as samples for making planks and ox yokes. While there was no reply from London, the manufactured products were exhibited at the Maritzburg Agriculture Show in 1890. By 1892, a 'substantial amount' of acacia wood was used to construct farm implements such as wheel barrows and wagons, but none was sold as boards or beams, and railway sleeper production continued to be constrained by lack of creosoting facilities.[135] Africans requesting seed to produce wood for 'building' and 'other uses' in 1894 were sent packets of black and silver wattle.[136] So common was tree planting that when a tree planting scheme was proposed for Africans in 1908, it was thought that there was no need of instruction because they had learned these skills while working on white farms.[137]

The importance of acacia trees changed in 1888 when the tanning properties of wattle bark were recognised. Some varieties of acacias have significant levels of tannins in their bark which can be used in tanning hides. According to Durban

Botanic Garden reports, *Acacia decurrens T.* and *A. mollissima* arrived from their native Australia in 1875 and 1879, respectively.[138] The first experiments in a Natal tannery were in Dec. 1884 when Mr. Hallon at Lyle's tannery bought samples of a mixture of *A. mollissima* and *A. dealbata* bark from Geo. Sutton – a mixture Mr. Hallon had used in Australia. After further trials in 1885 and 1886, he concluded that *A. dealbata* was inferior, and subsequently wanted only *A. mollissima*. The hides that he tanned, as well as bark samples, were exhibited at an Agricultural show in Maritzburg; bundles were also sent to London for display at the Colonial and Indian Exhibition in 1886.[139] Considerable interest in the production of black wattle bark was created in Natal – but not to supply the local tanning industry. Because the regional leather market was small, production would be for export to Britain. The price paid in Natal for Black Wattle bark (called 'Mimosa bark' in London) rose as the international trade developed, stimulating large-scale plantings of *A. mollissima*.[140]

Sutton's pamphlet 'Wattle bark: A Paying Industry' was published in 1888 as a handbook for growers when commercial interest began. Four years later, when it was reprinted, his conclusion stated that 'the growing of wattle trees for the sake of their bark is now an ordinary business risk'.[141] Requests for Sutton's publication and information about the wattle bark industry reached Natal forest officials from the Cape Colony in 1894, and from the Orange Free State in 1898.[142] The importance of acacias to Natal farmers – and of the botanical gardens to the wattle industry – is revealed in the financial report of the Maritzburg Botanic Society in 1895: wattle and wood sales accounted for three quarters of the garden's sales.[143] In 1902 there were 34,574 acres of wattle in Natal (European settlers) and 1,1075 acres in Zululand (land allocated to the Africans); few other genera had been planted on such a large scale.[144]

TREE PLANTING AND CLIMATE CHANGE

If the narrative about the relationship between trees and climate did not reach the Cape of Good Hope with the London Missionary Society preacher Robert Moffat in 1830, he was its first promoter.[145] These ideas were institutionalised when fellow missionary John Croumbie Brown was appointed as the second Colonial Botanist by the British Cape of Good Hope government in 1863.[146]

It was the missionary community, rather than foresters, who substantially shaped opinion about the significance of trees and urged their large-scale planting to produce climate change. The attitude and influence of the London Missionary Society's Robert Moffat have been discussed elsewhere in detail,[147] as has been the incorporation into government policy of climate concerns with the appointment of fellow missionary John Croumbie Brown as Cape Colonial Botanist. Observations of drought in the early 1820s and late 1840s were fused with beliefs about a god of retribution who used environmental destruction to punish deviants. The dry (and damned) landscape could and should be revived by planting trees to increase rainfall.[148]

Despite forests having a bureaucratic presence in the form of a department, trees were to be planted by individuals and civic organisations to induce climate change and improve aesthetics. Desiccationist concerns remained, and underlay the promotion of tree planting throughout the nineteenth century. For example, the Orange River on the hot and dry northern border of the Cape Colony was identified as being in need of tree planting to 'cool and moisten the winds'.[149] A report to the Virginia Planter's Association in Natal expressed fears that climate could not be changed through voluntary measures because of popular lack of interest in tree planting, so compulsion would be required.[150]

The late nineteenth century commercial and industrial demand for tree products obviated the need for tree planting campaigns. Tree cultivation spread from 'tree enthusiasts' to commercial interests, and was embraced by the forestry establishment in the twentieth century.[151] However, as trees spread, they came to be seen as a detraction, rather than enhancement, of the landscape.

The great success of the wattle industry was perceived as a threat by non-wattle farmers. In 1899 the Farmer's Club of Natal requested that government 'bring forward a measure restricting the formation of new wattle plantations within a certain distance of the boundaries of farms as the effect is to debar a considerable area of adjoining arable ground from cultivation'. Their concern was with the drying out of soil in fields adjacent to tree plantations. Although the motion was passed unanimously by club members, it was rejected by agricultural officials on the grounds that 'every land owner has ... the right to use his land as he sees fit'.[152] Similar complaints about the effects of acacia plantations on neighbouring agricultural land were echoed by land owners near eucalyptus plantations.[153]

The nineteenth century farmers' observations of a changed hydrology – drier soils and reduced (or eliminated) stream flow – have been confirmed by twentieth century hydrology research. By 1935 criticism of afforestation policy was so serious that the South African government asked that the British Empire Forestry Conference (to be held in South Africa that year) 'report on the effects of forests on climate, water conservation and erosion with special reference to South Africa'. The result was a recommendation, among other things, for scientific study of the effects of tree planting on water supplies in South Africa and internationally.[154] The South African Forestry Department responded by establishing five hydrological research stations, three of which (Jonkershoek, Cathedral Peak, Mokobulaan) were catchment-scale and had as their main purpose determining the effects of afforestation on water supplies.[155] South African forester Christiaan Lodewyk Wicht,[156] a pioneer in forest hydrological research, was responsible for setting up the Jonkershoek station. During the mid-twentieth century evidence from these and international research stations (particularly from the United States of America) showed that forests transpired more water than other forms of vegetation.[157] Jonkershoek and Cathedral Peak were the first experiments to show the effects of replacing natural scrub and grassland with tree plantations on stream flow.[158] This idea was not easily accepted, nor widely known. In 1967 J.S. Whitmore presented a paper to the South African Association for the Advancement of Science in which he stated 'we must accept the fact that forests, whether natural or planted, do use more water than either natural grass veld or fynbos', and that 'a small extra water usage may lead to quite considerable reduction in run-off to feed streams and rivers.[159]

The fact of alien tree planting changing South Africa's hydrologies, if not climate regimes, was finally addressed in the late twentieth century. Forestry was classed as a 'stream flow reduction activity' (SFRA) because a large number of introduced tree genera and species had been demonstrated to dry soil bodies, reducing or eliminating springs and wetlands, as well as stream flow.[160] Mass tree plantings were regulated and limited by permitting, while municipalities and districts made plans for mass alien tree removal campaigns and programs.[161] Tree plantations were the only form of land use in twenty-first-century South Africa to have received a classification originally designed to regulate water-consuming industrial practices. Massive tree planting – particularly in the twentieth century[162] – had, indeed, changed South African climates near and in the ground. However, rather than achieving nineteenth century dreams of wetter regimes for plant roots, alien trees were identified as being major contributors to landscape desiccation.

CONCLUSIONS

The Dutch East India Company can be credited with introducing the idea of tree planting as well as alien tree species to southern Africa. Trees had a utilitarian, rather than romantic or decorative significance. Although government policies were predicated on the belief that afforestation would induce a wetter climate, most trees were planted to provide food, fuel, timber and bark. Tree planting was undertaken in domestic and privately owned spaces akin to gardening and farming, rather than in the larger landscape to provide forest cover. South Africa's tree management ancestry is, thus, horticultural. When scientific forestry arrived, it affected bureaucracies more than the landscape or social order. Individual trees moved with missionaries as they pioneered the landscape looking for souls in need of salvation and civilisation, and with settlers to provide windbreaks, shade, wood, sustenance and aesthetics. Despite official rhetoric, the introduction, evaluation and promotion of exotic tree planting fell not to departments of forestry or agriculture, but to the descendents of the Dutch East India Company garden – the botanical gardens of Cape and Natal Colonies. The act of planting trees was left to individuals. It was 'tree enthusiasts' – on their farms, in municipalities, and on mission stations – who initially planted trees in southern Africa.

As nineteenth century European ideas of forestry were marginalised in southern Africa, trees became more central to the economy. The introduction of alien tree species and their planting increased largely beyond the confines and conceptions of a forest. Tree planting became industrialised as trees became plantation crops, proliferating in the locations best suited to tree growth – Natal. These plantations became South Africa's forest industry. But trees were also widely planted in municipalities and on non-corporate private land in other colonies and territories. They came to be valued by Southern African residents for their aesthetic as well as utilitarian functions. Residents of Lesotho, for example, embraced peach trees as a national symbol, and the citizens of Pretoria, South Africa the Brazilian jacaranda tree as part of their city's identity. By the end of the twentieth century, the concerns of the mid-nineteenth century missionaries and tree promoters had been realised. The hydrology of large areas of South Africa had, indeed, been changed by tree planting. But the opposite of the nineteenth century desires had been achieved: stream flow was reduced or eliminated, and the landscape was drier than it had been before trees were planted. A late twentieth-century water conservation measure called for national plans to remove alien tree species from the landscape. 'Denudation' of the landscape should be implemented to save it!

NOTES

The research was supported by grant from the Leverhulme Trust, UK.

[1] Forest land was defined as land on which trees could or should be grown, as well as land covered with indigenous vegetation classified as trees. See discussion below for detail.

[2] These plantations expanded and became the modern South African Forest industry, discussion of which is beyond the scope of this paper.

[3] Western Cape Archives and Records Service, Cape Town AGR 748, ref F 2058E, Hutchins, 'Conservator of Forests, Western Conservancy, Cape Town to Under-Secretary for Agriculture, 16 February 1897'.

[4] Michael Williams, *Deforesting the Earth: From Pre-history to Global Crisis*. (Chicago: University of Chicago Press, 2003) describes the relationship between the spread of Christianity and deforestation for settlement and agricultural production in medieval Europe, and Richard Grove, *Green Imperialism: Colonial Expansion, Tropical Island Edens and the Origins of Environmentalism 1600–1860* (Cambridge: Cambridge University Press, 1995) discusses the systematic deforestation of tropical islands associated with the development of agricultural plantations that supported colonial expansion (British in particular).

[5] Mary Gunn, L.E. Codd and L.E.W. Codd, *Botanical Exploration of Southern Africa: An Illustrated History* (Boca Raton: CRC Press, 1981).

[6] Mia C. Karsten, *The Old Company's Garden at the Cape and its Superintendents* (Cape Town: Maskew Miller Ltd., 1951).

[7] Karsten, *The Old Company's Garden at the Cape*.

[8] For details of tree cutting, see Mikael Grut, 'Notes on the history of forestry in the Western Cape 1652–1872', *South African Forestry Journal* **100** (March 1977): 32–37 and Grove, *Green Imperialism*, 133–145.

[9] Richard Grove, 'Scottish Missionaries, evangelical discourses and the origins of conservation thinking in southern Africa 1820–1900', *Journal of Southern African Studies* **15** (1989): 163–187; Georgina H. Endfield and David J. Nash, 'Drought, desiccation and discourse: missionary correspondence and nineteenth-century climate change in central southern Africa', *The Geographical Journal* **168** no. 1 (2002): 33–47.

[10] Compton, R.H., 'Forward'. In Mia C. Karsten, *The Old Company's Garden*): ix.

[11] Karsten, *The Old Company's Garden*.

[12] After the revocation of the Edict of Nantes, many Protestants fled Roman Catholic France for the Protestant Netherlands. The Dutch East India Company, aware of Huguenot renown in viticulture and winemaking, recruited 176 'to enrich the settlement at the Cape', A. Wilmot, *The Story of the Expansion of Southern Africa* (London: T. Fisher Unwin, 1894). See pp. 42–44 for detail.

[13] Originally this valley was referred to as Oliphantshoek (the place of elephants) because it was home to wild animals such as elephants, hippos and rhinoceros, as well as the hunter-gatherer San and Khoi people (pejoratively referred to as 'Bushmen' and 'Hottentots').

[14] In the mid-nineteenth century, South African wines were 'held in bad repute' in London: one of Cape Botanist John Croumbie Brown's first tasks was to address the problem of the quality of Cape wines (National Library of South Africa, Cape Town, John Croumbie Brown Collection, MSC5.2(2): Vines:MSS(2), John Croumbie Brown, 'Vines' (undated)). When the railway connected Franschhoek to Cape Town in 1904, large scale international trade in fruit and wine became possible.

[15] Gertenbach, Marianne, 'Round and About Franschhoek. Hugenot Memorial Museum' (Franschhoek: Franschhoek Conservation Trust, undated).

[16] Eugene Casalis, *My life in Basutoland: A story of Missionary Enterprise*, Africana Collecteana vol. XXXVIII, 1899. (Facsimilie Reprint, Cape Town: C. Struik (Pty), Ltd., 1971).

[17] Baviann's Kloof (Ravine of the Baboons) was the first mission station in the Cape of Good Hope region. It was renamed Genadendal in 1806, and became the largest settlement in Cape Colony after Cape Town (Genadendal Mission Museum, undated. http://museums.org.za/genadendal).

[18] Casalis, *My life in Basutoland*; Genadendal Mission Museum.

[19] Grut, 'Notes on the history of forestry'; Grove, *Green Imperialism*.

[20] Grut, 'Notes on the history of forestry'.

[21] Grut, 'Notes on the history of forestry'; Grove, *Green Imperialism*.

[22] Names given in source material are repeated without assigning scientific names, since common names can refer to more than one species, or even to trees of different genera.

[23] Grut, 'Notes on the history of forestry'.

[24] François Valentijn was sent to the East Indies by the V.O.C as Minister of the Church in 1685 at the age of 19. During his 20 years in the region, he kept extensive journals, produced maps, and wrote books (Thomas Suárez, *Early Mapping of South East Asia*

(Singapore: Periplus, 1999)). He visited the Cape of Good Hope five times (1685, 1695, 1705, 1714), and described it in the fifth and last part of his *Beschrijvinje van Oud ern Nieuw Oost-Indien*, published in Amsterdam in 1726 (Gunn et al., *Botanical exploration of Southern Africa*).

[25] R.J. Poynton, *Report of the South African Regional Commission for the Conservation and Utilization of the Soil (SARCCUS) on Tree Planting in Southern Africa, vol. 2. The Eucalypts*. (Pretoria: Department of Forestry, 1979).

[26] Grove, 'Scottish missionaries'; see Grove, *Green Imperialism*: 133–145 for detail.

[27] Largest plant family, 300 general, 7,500 species, of which 870 regarded as succulents (International Euphorbia Society, undated. http://www.euphorbia-international.org).

[28] Casalis, *My life in Basutoland*.

[29] Casalis, *My life in Basutoland*.

[30] Western Cape Archives and Records Service, Cape Town. CO 3877, ref 240, Christopher Goldsbury, 'Petition of Christopher Goldsbury, American Brigate Maria for permission to sell boards and beams, Cape Town, Cape of Good Hope, 9th April 1810'.

[31] R.J. Poynton, *Report of the South African Regional Commission for the Conservation and Utilization of the Soil (SARCCUS) on Tree Planting in Southern Africa, vol. 1. The Pines*. (Pretoria: Department of Forestry, undated).

[32] Poynton, *Tree Planting in Southern Africa, vol. 2. The Eucalypts*.

[33] Casalis, *My life in Basutoland*.

[34] M. Gosselin, 'Extracts of a letter, 16 January 1837'. Station de Morija. *Journal des Missions Évangéliques*. (Paris: Société Missions Évangéliques, 1837); Elizabeth A. Eldredge, 'An economic history of Lesotho in the nineteenth century'. Unpublished PhD thesis. Madison: University of Wisconsin – Madison, 1986).

[35] See R.C. Germond, Chronicles of Basutoland (Morija: Morija Press, 1967) for missionary letters. See Kate B. Showers, 'Soil erosion in the Kingdom of Lesotho: origins and colonial response, 1830–1955'. *Journal of Southern African Studies* **15**,2 (1989): 263–286, 1989; Kate B. Showers *Imperial Gullies: Soil Erosion and Conservation in Lesotho* (Athens: Ohio University Press, 2005); Kate B. Showers, 'From forestry to soil conservation: British tree management in Lesotho's grassland ecosystem', *Conservation and Society* **4**,1 (2006): 1–35 for discussion of missionary tree planting in Lesotho (colonial Basutoland).

[36] Eldredge, 'An economic history of Lesotho'; Kate B. Showers, 'Crop or forest? Missionaries, Basotho and government tree planting', in Reginald Kline-Cole and David Kane (eds.), *Making and Remaking Africa: Travel, Environment, and Local Knowledge in a Continent of Movement* (London: Pluto Press; forthcoming).

[37] *Natal Official Handbook, Colonial and Indian Exhibition, 1886*. (London: William Clowes & Sons, Ltd., 1886).

[38] *Natal Official Handbook*.

[39] Harald Witt, 'The emergence of privately grown industrial tree plantations', in Stephen Dovers, Ruth Edgecombe and Bill Guest (eds.), *South Africa's Environmental History: Cases and Comparisons* (Athens: Ohio University Press, 2002): 90–111.

[40] *Natal Official Handbook*.

[41] Grove, 'Scottish missionaries', 165.

[42] Grove, 'Scottish missionaries'.

[43] J.C. Visagie, 'Introduction. A historical administrative development', in *Inventory to the Archives of the Conservator of Forests, Eastern Conservancy, King William's Town, 1882-1918. 1/43*:1-4 (Cape Town: Western Cape Archives and Records Service, 1965).

[44] Jacob Tropp, 'Displaced people, replaced narratives: forest conflicts and historical perspectives in the Tsolo District, Transkei', *Journal of Southern African Studies* **29** (2003): 207-33.

[45] Visagie, 'Introduction'.

[46] Pietermaritzburg Archives Repository. SGO III/1/50, ref. 646/83, A. Wilkinson, 'From Convenor of Committee. Enclosure with letter from Chairman, Victorian Planter's Association, Loutham, Blackbour to Major Hime R.E., Acting Colonial Secretary, Maritzburg, February 20, 1883'.

[47] Western Cape Archives and Records Service, Cape Town, I/68. ISBN 0 7970 0155 5, M. George, 'Introduction', *Inventory of the Archives of the Secretary for Public Works 1872-1911*.

[48] Western Cape Archives and Records Service, Cape Town: AGR48, ref f1110, Knysna Timber Depot, 'Control of Seasoning and Creosoting Timber, etc. To the Under-Secretary for Agriculture, 4 July 1895'.

[49] Western Cape Archives and Records Service, Cape Town. GH 23/24, ref 74:60, H.M.E. Frere, 'Governor, Graham's Town to Earl of Carnarvon, September 2, 1877'.

[50] First on the continent of Africa. For detailed discussion of Cape Colony Forestry see Karen Brown, 'Trees, forests and communities: some historiographical approaches to environmental history on Africa', *Area* **35**,4 (2003): 343-356.

[51] Pietermaritzburg Archives Repository. CSO 1181, ref 935/1888, Report of the Superintendent of Woods and Forests for the Year 1882 (Translation). Cape of Good Hope. Ministerial Department of Crown Lands and Public Works. 1882 (Cape Town: W.A. Richards & Sons, 1882).

[52] Visagie, 'Introduction'.

[53] Karen Brown, 'Trees, forests and communities'.

[54] Londa Schiebinger, *Plants and Empire: Colonial Bioprospecting in the Atlantic World* (Cambridge MA: Harvard University Press, 2004). For review of the development of the field of botany, bioprospecting, and the relationships between plants, botanical gardens and empires and pertinent literature see 'Introduction', p. 1-12.

[55] John Croumbie Brown, 'Report of the Colonial Botanist for the Year 1863. Cape of Good Hope. Annual Report, 15th January 1864' (Cape Town: Saul Soloman & Co., 1864)

[56] Brown, J.C., 'On the conservation and extension of the forests as a means of counteracting disastrous consequences following the destruction of bush and herbage by fire'. Enclosure No. 1. Annual Report. Report of the Colonial Botanist for the Year 1863. Cape of Good Hope. (Cape Town: Saul Solomon and Co., 1863); Grove, 'Scottish missionaries'; Endfield and Nash, 'Drought, desiccation and discourse'.

[57] John Croumbie Brown, 'Report of the Colonial Botanist for the Year 1865. 15th January 1866. Cape of Good Hope' (Cape Town: Saul Solomon & Co., 1966); John Croumbie Brown, 'Letter to Dr. Mueller, Government Botanist and Director, Melbourne Botanical Gardens, relative to Shrubs and Trees used here for Fences, Avenues and Burying Grounds. Wynburg, 14th January 1866'. Annexure 12, p. 108-109. Report of the Colonial Botanist for the Year 1865. Cape of Good Hope. (Cape Town: Saul Solomon & Co., 1866).

[58] J.C. Brown, 'On the conservation and extension of the forests'.

[59] The 17th-century term 'botanic' has been mostly superseded by 'botanical'; it is retained in the official names of older institutions.

[60] J.C. Brown, 'On the Cape Botanic Garden'. Enclosure No. 111: 37–44. Annual Report. Report of the Colonial Botanist for the Year 1863. Cape of Good Hope (Cape Town: Saul Solomon & Co., 1863); John Croumbie Brown, 'Circular to residents of colony regarding relative irrigation facilities. 1 June 1866. Appended to report: Memoire on hydrology of South Africa. Abstract of memoir on Irrigation'.

[61] National Library of South Africa, Cape Town: John Croumbie Brown Collection. MSC5, 3(5): J.M.McGibbon, 'Catalogue', James McGibbon, 'Catalogue. Fruit-bearing trees & plants in the collection of the Botanic Garden, Cape Town'. (Cape Town: Saul Solomon & Co., 1864).

[62] National Library of South Africa, John Croumbie Brown Collection, MSC5, 112(2): Forestry (gen)., John Croumbie Brown, 'Memoire'; John Croumbie Brown, Report of the Colonial Botanist for the Year 1866. Cape of Good Hope. (Cape Town: Saul Solomon & Co., 1866).

[63] C.H.Huntley, 'Report of the Committee of the Botanic Garden, Graham's Town, for Nine Months of the Year 1872'. (Cape of Good Hope: Government Printer, 1873); C.H. Huntley, 'Report of the Committee of the Botanic Garden, Graham's Town for the Year 1871'. (Cape of Good Hope: Government Printer, 1872); 'Report on the Graaf-Reinet Botanic Garden for the period ending 30th April 1874'. Cape of Good Hope, Graaf-Reinet, 30 April 1874. (Cape Town: Government Printer, 1874).

[64] *Natal Official Handbook* 1886; Witt, 'The emergence of privately grown industrial tree plantations'

[65] Killie Campbell Africana Library, University of KwaZulu-Natal, Durban. Memorandum Book 1865–1871. Durban Botanic Society, Book 1. KCM 43065, John Sanderson, 'Report of the Natal Botanic gardens for the last six months of 1867 14th January 1868. Reports on the Natal Botanic Gardens for the years 1866 and 1867'; Killie Campbell Africana Library, University of KwaZulu-Natal, Durban. Memorandum Book 1865–1871. Durban Botanic Society, Book 1. KCM 43065, M.J. 'To the Committee of the Natal Botanic Gardens. Reports on the Natal Botanic Gardens, for the Years 1866 and 1867'.

[66] Killie Campbell Africana Library, University of KwaZulu-Natal, Durban. Memorandum Book 1865–1871. Durban Botanic Society, Book 1. KCM 43065, M.J. M.J. McKen, 'Curator to the Committee of the Natal Botanic gardens. Government Notice No. 191, 1872'.

[67] R.G. Stone, 'Report of the Committee of the Botanic Garden, Graham's Town, for the year 1865'. (Cape Town: Government Printer, 1866).

[68] Killie Campbell Africana Library, University of KwaZulu-Natal, Durban. Memorandum Book 1865–1871. Durban Botanic Society, Book 1. KCM 43065, M.J.McKen, 'Report of the Natal Botanic Gardens for the first six months of 1867. July 1, 1867. Reports on the Natal Botanic Gardens for the years 1866 and 1867'.

[69] McKen, 'Report of the Natal Botanic Gardens for the first six months of 1867'.

[70] McKen, 'Report of the Natal Botanic Gardens for the first six months of 1867'.

[71] Morija Museum and Archives, Morija, Lesotho, Sumitra Talukdar, 'The spread of Australian species and their displacement of the indigenous flora of Lesotho'. Presented at XIII International Botanical Congress, Sydney, Australia, August 1891. Reprint, 'Letter

from Vicaire Apostolique, 3 May 1866', *Missions de la Congrégation des Missionnaires Oblate de Marie Immaculée*, 6:214.

[72] Y. Beaudoin, *Blessed Joseph Gerrard O.M.I., Apostate to the Basotho (1831–1914)*. (Rome: General Postulation O.M.I.).

[73] C.H. Huntley, 'Report of the Committee of the Botanic Garden, Graham's Town, for the Year 1871'. (Cape of Good Hope: Government Printer, 1872).

[74] Huntley, 'Report of the Committee of the Botanic Garden, Graham's Town, for Nine Months of the Year 1872'.

[75] Killie Campbell Africana Library, University of KwaZulu-Natal, Durban. Memorandum Book 1865–1871. Durban Botanic Society, Book 1. KCM 43065, M.J. McKen, 'Curator to the Committee of the Natal Botanic gardens'. Government Notice No. 191, 1872.

[76] Killie Campbell African Library, University of KwaZulu-Natal, Durban. Paper Cuttings. Natal Herbarium, 1882 –. Durban Botanic Society, Book 4. KCM 43068, L. Acutt, 'Report on Tree Planting'. Minutes. Natal Botanic Gardens Committee Meeting 11 April 1883.

[77] Pietermaritzburg Archive Repository. CSO 1298, ref 2979/1891, F. Schoepflin, 'Conservator of Forests to Surveyor General, 1891.

[78] J. C. Brown, 'On the conservation and extension of the forests': 5–17.

[79] National Archives, Pretoria FOR 177, ref A310, J. Storr Lister, 'Practical Hints on Tree Planting in the Cape Colony', Forest Department (Cape Town: W.A. Richards & Sons., 1884).

[80] Pietermaritzburg Archives Repository. SNA I/1/135, ref 1890/1514, A.C.Shepstone, 'Secretary, Native Affairs to Supervisor of Locations, Inanda, Pietermaritzburg, 2nd September 1890, ref SNA 1031/90'.

[81] National Archives, Pretoria PWD vol387,ref RB907/05, Assistant Engineer, 'From Assistant Engineer, Roads and Bridges, Northern Transvaal, Public Works Department, Pretoria to Chief Engineer, Roads and Bridges, 3rd May 1905'; National Archives, Pretoria. AGT vol 29, ref 1335/06, Department of Agriculture, 'Grants in Aid of Tree Planting'.

[82] Western Cape Archives and Records Service, Cape Town. AGR 747, ref 1998, 'Regulations for Tree Planting Competition'. Order of Speaker 1895, Cape of Good Hope; Western Cape Archives and Records Service, Cape Town: AMPT PUBS CCP1/2/1/94, ref G62, E. Hutchins, 1894, 'Reports on the Subject of the Encouragement of An Extensive System of Tree Planting. I. Report of the Conservator of Forests, Western Conservancy, 18th October 1894'.

[83] Western Cape Archives and Records Service, Cape Town. AGR 741, ref F 1998, Assembly 24/7/95, 1895.

[84] J.M. Mohapeloa, *Tentative British Imperialism in Lesotho, 1884–1910. A Study in Basotho-Colonial Office Interaction and South Africa's Influence in it*. (Moirja: Morija Museum and Archives, 2002).

[85] Maritzburg and Pietermaritzburg are the same place; as with trees, the name used in the source will be retained in this text.

[86] Killie Campbell Africana Library, University of KwaZulu-Natal, Durban, Paper Cuttings. Natal Herbarium. Durban Botanical Society, 1896, Book 5. RCM 43069, 'Report of the Council for 1895 Annual Meeting. Maritzburg Botanic Society, 1896'; Witt, 'The emergence of privately grown industrial tree plantations'.

[87] Brown, J.C., 'On the conservation and extension of the forests'.

[88] Western Cape Archives and Records Service, Cape Town: AGR 748, ref F2701, E. Hutchins, 'Conservator of Forests, Western Conservancy, Cape Town to Under Secretary for Agriculture, 8th March 1897'.

[89] The first state-sponsored tree plantations in the Cape Colony were established near Cape Town in the 1870s to provide easily accessible wood for fuel and sleepers (K. Brown, 'Trees, forests and communities'). In Natal, state plantations appeared at the end of the 19th century (Witt, 'The emergence of privately grown industrial tree plantations').

[90] Hutchins, 'Conservator of Forests, Western Conservancy, Cape Town to Under Secretary for Agriculture, 8th March 1897'.

[91] Hutchins, 'Conservator of Forests, Western Conservancy, Cape Town to Under Secretary for Agriculture, 8th March 1897'.

[92] Brown, K., 'Trees, forests and communities'.

[93] Witt, 'The emergence of privately grown industrial tree plantations', claims that the phrase 'timber famine', which became common in the twentieth century, reached Natal in 1902 when forester T.R. Sim arrived from his post as Curator, King William's Town, Cape Colony Forest Department.

[94] Western Cape Archives and Records Service, Cape Town: CO 4116, ref 34, James McGibbon, 'Botanic Garden. Letter, 5th April 1860'.

[95] Brown, K., 'Trees, forests and communities'.

[96] Mohapeloa, *Tentative British Imperialism in Lesotho*.

[97] James McGibbon, 'Report of the Commissioners of the Botanic Garden, Cape Town, for the Year 1871'. Cape of Good Hope. 1872. (Cape Town: Government Printer, 1872).

[98] C.H. 1873. Chairman. 'Report of the Botanical Gardens, Graham's Town, for Nine months of the year 1872'. (Cape of Good Hope: Government Printer, 1873).

[99] Huntley, 'Report of the Botanical Gardens, Graham's Town, for Nine months of the year 1872'.

[100] C.H. Huntley, 'Report of the Committee of the Botanic Gardens, Graham's Town, for the year 1873'. (Cape of Good Hope. Government Printer: 1874).

[101] Eldredge, 'An economic history of Lesotho'.

[102] William Tuck, 'Report on the Graaf-Reinet Botanic Gardens for the Year 1878. Cape of Good Hope. Graaf-Reinet, 15 March 1879' (Cape Town: Government Printer 1879).

[103] Western Cape Archives and Records Service, Cape Town. AGR 228, ref 2096, 'From general Manager of Railways, 23 October 1894, Cape Town to Under Secretary of Agriculture. No g15914'.

[104] Rhodes House, Oxford University, Natal. Agriculture. 621.14r.19(3), Arthurs E. Cave (compiler), *The Book of Natal Industries 1893*, 1st edition (Durban: T.L.Cullingworth).

[105] F.C.S. MacOwan, 'Report of the Government Botanist and Curator of the Cape Government Herbarium for the year 1895'. Cape of Good Hope. Department of Agriculture. (Cape Town: W.R. Richards & Sons, 1896).

[106] Poynton, *Tree Planting in Southern Africa, vol. 2. The Eucalypts*; Witt, 'The emergence of privately grown industrial tree plantations'.

[107] Talukdar, 'The spread of Australian species'.

[108] Brown, J.C., 'On the conservation and extension of the forests'.

[109] Killie Campbell Africana Library, University of KwaZulu-Natal, Durban. Paper Cuttings. Natal Herbarium 1882–. Durban Botanic Society Book 4. KCM 43068, Professor Bentley, 'On the character, properties and use of the Eucalyptus globulus (The 'Blue Gum' of Tasmania) and other species of Eucalyptus'. Lecture to the Royal Botanic Society of London, March 14th 1874.

[110] Bentley, 'On the character, properties and use of the Eucalyptus globulus'.

[111] Bentley, 'On the character, properties and use of the Eucalyptus globulus'.

[112] National Archives, Pretoria. RRC 30, ref 33/05, Charles C. Legat, 'Conservator of Forests, Transvaal Department of Agriculture, 27 April 1905 to Director of Agriculture, Department of Agriculture, Pretoria.

[113] Witt, 'The emergence of privately grown industrial tree plantations'.

[114] Brown, J.C., 'Letter to Dr. Mueller'; H.Hudson, F. TeWater, C.Murray, Harry Bolus, 'Report on the Graaf-Reinet Botanic Garden, for the period ending 30th April 1874'. Cape of Good Hope. Graaf-Reinet. (Cape Town: Government Printer, 1874); Killie Campbell African Library, University of KwaZulu-Natal, Durban. Paper Cuttings. Natal Herbarium, 1882 –, Durban Botanic Society, Book 4. KCM 43068, William Keit, 'Curator's Report for 1875'. Natal Botanic Gardens. Government Notice No. 132, 1876; Killie Campbell African Library, University of KwaZulu-Natal, Durban. Paper Cuttings. Natal Herbarium, 1882 –. Durban Botanic Society, Book -4. KCM 43068, William Keit, 'Curator's Report. Natal Botanic Gardens. January 1st, 1878'.

[115] Mohapeloa, *Tentative British Imperialism in Lesotho*.

[116] Killie Campbell African Library, University of KwaZulu-Natal, Durban. Paper Cuttings. Natal Herbarium, 1882 –. Durban Botanic Society, Book 4. KCM 43068, William Keit, 'Curator's Report for 1875'. Natal Botanic Gardens. Government Notice No. 132, 1876; Killie Campbell African Library, University of KwaZulu-Natal, Durban. Paper Cuttings. Natal Herbarium, 1882 –. Durban Botanic Society, Book -4. KCM 43068, William Keit, Curator's Report. Natal Botanic Gardens. Janurary 1st, 1878.

[117] Poynton, *'Tree Planting in Southern Africa, vol. 2. The Eucalypts'*.

[118] Western Cape Archives and Records Service, Cape Town: CO 4116, ref 34, James Mc Gibbon, 'Botanic Garden. Letter, 5th April 1860'.

[119] Pietermaritzburg Archives Repository CSO 1298 ref 2972/1891, E.W. Hannaford, 'Secretary, Pietermaritzburg Botanic Society to Colonial Secretary, Natal, 5th June 1891; Pietermaritzburg Archives Repository CSO 1298 ref 2979/1891, F.Schoepflin, 'Conservator of Forests to Surveyor General, 1891'.

[120] Pietermaritzburg Archives Repository. CSO 1180, ref 694/1888, Dr. Sutherland, 'To Colonial Secretary, Natal, 13 Feb 1888'.

[121] Cave, *Book of Natal Industries*.

[122] Sutton, *Wattle Bark*.

[123] Pietermaritzburg Archives Repository. CSO 1180, ref 694/1888, D. Sutherland, 'To Colonial Secretary, Natal, 13 Feb 1888'.

[124] See Witt, 'The emergence of privately grown industrial tree plantations', for detail.

[125] Witt, 'The emergence of privately grown industrial tree plantations'.

[126] Witt, 'The emergence of privately grown industrial tree plantations'.

[127] Witt, 'The emergence of privately grown industrial tree plantations'.

128 See Witt, 'The emergence of privately grown industrial tree plantations', for discussion.
129 Witt, 'The emergence of privately grown industrial tree plantations'.
130 According to J.H. Maiden, curator of Technological Museum, Sydney, and quoted by Geo M. Sutton in 'Wattle Bark: A Paying Industry' (Pietermaritzburg: P. Davis & Sons, 1892:2), the name wattle is derived from the Anglo-Saxon *watel*, 'a hurdle covering, the verb is *watelen, to watel*, to twist together, strengthen with hurdles'. The common practice in Australia in the early days was to erect temporary structures of small trees, of Acacias as well as others. Here in Natal, the same thing was done, but there being no Acacias suitable other indigenous saplings were used. The name 'wattle and daub' for a house or hut made of hurdles and covered with mud is well known in Natal. Mr. Maiden says 'The Rev. Dr. Wools, however, assures me that the earliest application of the word wattle was not to an Acacia, but to *Calliconia serratifolia*, a small tree belonging to the *Saxifragae*, and which is generally found near watercourses. It was probably abundant along the course of the streams which flowed into Sydney Cove; and in the earliest records of 'daub and wattle' structures, the tough saplings of this species were alluded to. In Natal we had the word, but not the Acacias, and I think it is only fair to conclude that the reason why the word "wattle" became confined in everyday use in Australia to certain of the Acacia tribe is on account of their habit of seeding so freely, and growing thickly with straight stems, rendering them more easily available for wattling than many species. In Natal no one species of tree predominates to the extent Acacias do in Australia.'
131 Sutton, 'Wattle Bark', citing Maidern, stated that '*Acacia mollisima* is a synonym of *A. Decurrens*, var *mollissima*. It was called black wattle by the older New South Wales colonists. This name was used in Victoria and Tasmania, but called green wattle in New South Wales now.'
132 Royal Botanic Society. 2004. *Flora Zambesiaca*, Taxon detail *Acacia mearnsii*. http://apps.kew.org/efloras/namedetail.do?flora=f2&taxon=2107&n .
133 Talukdar, 'The spread of Australian species'.
134 McKen, 'Curator to the Committee of the Natal Botanic gardens'.
135 Sutton, *Wattle Bark*.
136 Western Cape Archives and Records Service, Cape Town . AGR 212, ref F 1626, W. Power, 'Resident Magistrate, Mount Ayliff, 8 January 1894. Supply of Silver Wattle and Black Wattle Seed. No. 9 GD/94. To Conservator of Forests, Umtata'; Western Cape Archives and Records Service, Cape Town. AGR 207, ref 1563, 'Office of the Secretary for Native Affairs. 1894. To Under Secretary for Agriculture, 11 May 1894'.
137 Pietermaritzburg Archives Repository. SNA I/1/395, ref 1908/966, Charles Hayter, 'Supervisor, Swartkop to Under-Secretary of Native Affairs, 27/3/08'.
138 Keit, 'Curator's Report for 1875'.
139 Sutton, *Wattle Bark*.
140 Sutton, *Wattle Bark*.
141 Sutton, *Wattle Bark*: 43
142 Pietermaritzburg Archives Repository. CSO 1578, ref 1898/6571, D.W. Dienaar, 'Government Secretary, Bloemfontein, 1 September 1898 to Colonial Secretary, Pietermaritzburg' and responses on Minute Paper.1.9.98. Letter to Gov. Sec. 12.9.98.
Western Cape Archives and Records Service, Cape Town. AGR 219, ref 1798, Farmers' Association in Great Brak River, Paarl. 1891. 'Requests to government'.

[143] Report of the Council 1895.

[144] Witt, 'The emergence of privately grown industrial tree plantations'.

[145] Grove, 'Scottish missionaries'; Endfield and Nash, 'Drought, desiccation and discourse'.

[146] Grove, 'Scottish missionaries'

[147] Grove, 'Scottish missionaries'; Endfield and Nash, 'Drought, desiccation and discourse'

[148] Grove, 'Scottish missionaries'.

[149] 'Report of the Superintendent of Woods and Forests for the Year 1882'.

[150] Wilkinson, 'From Convenor of Committee'.

[151] Discussion of the development of South Africa's forest industry is beyond the scope of this paper. Its is of interest, perhaps, to note that the Food and Agriculture Organization of the United Nations (FAO) expanded its definition of forest in 2000 by 'adopt[ing] a threshold of 10% minimum crown cover. The definition includes both natural forest and forest plantations'. 'Executive Summary', *Global Forest Resources Assessment 2001, Main Report*. Rome: FAO, 2001. This definition justifies South Africa's claim to having extensive forests and a forest service, rather than large-scale tree crop production and an advice system for growers.

[152] Pietermaritzburg Archives Repository. CSO 1635, ref 1899/3317, 'Farmers Club of Mid-Illovo, 14th January 1899'.

[153] Witt, 'The emergence of privately grown industrial tree plantations'.

[154] C.L. Wicht, 'Forest hydrology research in the South African Republic', in William E. Sopper and Howard W. Lull, *Forest Hydrology* (Oxford: Pergamon Press), 75–84.

[155] U.W. Nänni, U.W, 'Trees, water and perspective', *South African Forestry Journal* **75** (1970): 9–17.

[156] C.L. Wicht (1908–1978) was Research officer, Department of Forestry (1934–1950), rising to Chief of Forest Research (1947–1950); Forestry Professor, University of Stellenbosch (1950–1973) and, after retirement, consultant to the Forestry Department. Obituary, Dr. C.L. Wicht, *South African Forestry Journal* **106** (September 1978): 1.

[157] Nänni, 'Trees, water and perspective'; C.L. Wicht, 'Timber and water', *South African Forestry Journal* **85** (June 1973): 3–11.

[158] U.W. Nänni, 'The effect of afforestation in streamflow at Cathedral Peak: Report No. 1', *South African Forestry Journal* **74** (1970): 6–12.

[159] Ackerman, D.P., 'Some new directions in forestry policy', *South African Forestry Journal* **68** (1969): 1–4.

[160] Eucalyptus and pine.

[161] Ilse Steyl, 'Strategic Environmental Assessment for streamflow reduction activities in South Africa', undated. Available at: http://www-dwaf.pwv.gov.za/sfra/Articles/Oxford_paper.pdf ; J.M. Bosch and J.D. Hewlett 'A review of catchment experiments to determine the effect of vegetation changes on water yield and evapotranspiration', *Journal of Hydrology* **55**(1982): 3–22.

[162] As documented by Witt, 'The emergence of privately grown industrial tree plantations'.

Rhododendron ponticum in Britain and Ireland: Social, Economic and Ecological Factors in its Successful Invasion

Katharina Dehnen-Schmutz and Mark Williamson

1. INTRODUCTION

There has been a 'rising tide' both of invasions and of books about invasions, building on the well known works of Elton, Williamson and various international programmes.[1] With this, there has been a rising interest in risk analysis with a view to predicting troublesome invaders.[2] But, while it is often possible to explain invasions, 'explanation is not prediction'.[3] There is also a growing awareness of the importance of human effects on biological invasions after the introduction stage, making it more and more evident that invasive species are an interdisciplinary problem requiring a combination of insights from biological and social-economic science and history.[4]

One of the key variables explaining biological invasions seems to be propagule pressure, which comes from the number of introductions and the number of propagules in each introduction. With increasing propagule pressure there is an increasing probability of species establishing.[5] Propagule pressure depends generally on human activity and so is a socio-economic and historical variable. Williamson noted that propagule pressure and previous success were the most useful factors in explaining invasions and were historical rather than biological.[6] Even so, there is rather little research that tries to relate invasion processes to underlying socio-economic factors. For plants, deliberate introduction for horticulture is the main pathway for aliens in many countries (see Groves for Australia, Mack and Erneberg for the USA, and Kühn and Klotz for Germany).[7] Socio-economic factors, like gardening fashions or the structure of the horticultural market, affect the extent to which a species is distributed and planted and so influence the pattern and extent of propagule pressure.

Time lags between the introduction of many species, their naturalisation and the occurrence of recognised damage make it necessary to take into account historical processes that may have favoured their invasion success. For example, many of the species problematic in Britain today are introductions from the eighteenth/nineteenth centuries, the 'Age of the exotic specimen'.[8] *Fallopia japonica, Heracleum mantegazzianum* and *Impatiens glandulifera* were all introduced as ornamentals in the first half of the nineteenth century. Furthermore, of 348 plants listed as garden escapes 97 per cent were introduced before 1900.[9] Their use and promotion soon after their introduction into a new area may be the key to understanding their invasion processes and their distribution today. Although the way a plant is perceived does not influence the invasion process directly, it is the underlying rationale for planting it and controlling it. Differing views on how to value and classify the impact of invasive species are common even within groups of different scholars and have implications for policy.[10] Plants introduced as ornamentals are especially the subject of different views in society as they may be regarded particularly favourably. This may change for ornamentals that become invasive resulting in parts of society seeing the species as a pest and others still valuing it as an ornamental. This change from 'prize-winners to pariahs' has been documented for *Fallopia japonica* in Britain and *Prunus serotina* in central Europe.[11]

In this paper, we consider *Rhododendron ponticum* in Britain and Ireland so as to analyse the interplay of social, economic and ecological factors in its invasion process. *R. ponticum* has been present in Britain for more than 240 years and is today the most damaging alien plant in semi-natural habitats, with high control and restoration costs.[12] These populations are genetically, ecologically and generally morphologically distinct from other populations.[13] Their main ancestor is the population of *R. ponticum* from the southernmost tip of Spain and their minor ancestors are *R. catawbiense* and *R. maximum* from the Appalachian mountains in USA and other *Rhododendron* spp. The Black Sea populations of *R. ponticum*, which are mainly in Turkey, including Pontus, but also in Bulgaria, Georgia and the Russian Caucasus, seem not to have been involved.[14] The Iberian populations are relic and vulnerable, even endangered.[15] How and why did this scarce, not fully hardy (by English standards) plant become a troublesome problem?

Ecologists have attributed its success as an invasive species mainly to its biological-ecological characteristics: the species produces great quantities of small wind-dispersed seeds, it is shade tolerant and out-competes other plants through its dense canopy.[16] The establishment of seedlings seem to be the critical stage in the life cycle of *R. ponticum* as it depends on the presence of damp and partly shady sites with seedlings likely not to survive any droughts.[17] Fallen logs or tree stumps, newly colonised by moss, were identified as the most favourable habitat type for seedling establishment in woodlands.[18] The possession of ericaceous mycorrhizas enables *R. ponticum* to colonise and perform well on sites low in nutrients.[19] The leaves contain andromedo-toxin which is highly toxic if ingested and causes grazing animals to avoid the plant.[20] The impacts of the species are seen as negative because it overgrows and out-competes native plant communities, in particular woodland and heathland on acid soils. The control of the species is difficult as it is able to resprout readily when it is cut back and re-colonises cleared areas quickly if any seed-sources are left. Similarly, fire will destroy seedlings and shoots but re-sprouting will occur from underground buds.[21] However, many of these characteristics describe the genus Rhododendron in general and are not in particular specific for *R. ponticum*. For example, in the southern Appalachian mountains *R. maximum* is causing similar problems, but has not ever been recorded even as a casual in Britain.[22]

In view of the four or five hundred Rhododendron species and many cultivars and hybrids grown as ornamentals in Britain it is remarkable that *R. luteum* is the only other widely naturalised rhododendron in Britain (but has not to our knowledge yet become a conservation problem), and only five other species have been seen growing as casual (temporary) plants.[23] In this paper, we therefore focus on the human mediated factors in the invasion process of *R. ponticum* which may distinguish this species from all the other Rhododendrons used as ornamentals in Britain. We trace its history from an expensive, not fully hardy plant, through selection and hybridisation for hardiness to mass planting and to the recognition of the damage it does to forests and moorlands. We hope that these considerations will bear on other cases and may even be a step towards reliable prediction.

2. METHODS

Our analysis of the historical reasons for planting the species is mainly based on the gardening literature of the nineteenth and early twentieth centuries. Magazines like *Gardeners' Chronicle*, *Gardener's Magazine* and *The Garden* provide, especially in the small contributions of local correspondents, an insight into the importance and handling of the species. Data on the prices paid for the species were obtained from nursery catalogues which also gave recommendations for use and on the habitats regarded as suitable. As there are only a few nursery catalogues preserved from before 1840, which at that time seldom included prices, we have unfortunately only been able to get four prices for this period.[24] Further price information for later years came from commercial advertisements in those gardening magazines. We always used the lowest price for which a plant was available, regardless of the size of the plant or the volume of sales. Historical prices were converted to 2002 pounds, using the online calculator provided by Economic History Services.[25] The calculator uses a retail price index and allows a value in pounds sterling for any year from 1264 to 2002 to be adjusted for inflation and restated at its 2002 equivalent.

First records of *R. ponticum* in the wild were obtained by writing to all 142 vice-county recorders of the Botanical Society of the British Isles (BSBI) who keep records on plants and their locations within their vice-county. (Vice-counties are the approximately equal area sub-divisions of the historical counties devised by H.C. Watson, a friend of Darwin, in 1852).[26] We received 83 answers (a 58 per cent rate of return) and 50 provided the date of the first record in their vice-county.

We also had data on the first occurrence of *R. ponticum* from two surveys run in 1985 and 2002.[27] Both surveys asked managers of nature reserves, private estates and forests to give the date of the first self-sown *R. ponticum* on their sites. In both cases we used the original completed questionnaire forms; the data have not been published. There were 74 responses from the 1985 survey, 88 from 2002. Several respondents in both surveys said their answer was an estimate and also gave the date *R. ponticum* was first planted. The vice-county of sites in both surveys was used for comparison with the BSBI survey.

FIGURE 1. *Rhododendron Ponticum* from *Curtis's Botanical Magazine*, 1803.

3. RESULTS AND DISCUSSION

3.1. Introduction of R. ponticum *in Britain and Ireland*

1763 is usually given as the date of introduction of *R. ponticum* to England. The earliest mention of the species in Britain is in Hill's 1768 list of species cultivated then at Kew.[28] It was William Aiton in 1789 who gave 1763 as the date of introduction and describes the 'Purple Rhododendron' as a native of 'Levant and Gibraltar'.[29] Unlike his entries for other species, he says nothing of who introduced the plant nor is that information in the second edition of *Hortus Kewensis* by his son William Townsend Aiton.[30] So we do not know the source of Loudon's report from 1838, referring to *Hortus Kewensis*, that it was introduced in 1763 by Conrad Loddiges 'who sold the first plant to the Marquess of Rockingham, a noble encourager of botany and gardening'.[31] In 1803, Curtis gave the first detailed description of the plant with an excellent drawing (Figure 1). Although he is unsure whether the plants grown in England originated from Gibraltar or the Black Sea area, he says they resembled precisely the description of the Iberian variety.[32]

For Ireland, Loudon describes a plant in Dublin '60 years planted' which in 1834 was 16 ft high, implying that *R. ponticum* was introduced into Ireland shortly after its introduction to England.[33] Rhododendrons of large size were also described from Derrycunihy Wood, Killarney by Hall & Hall in 1843.[34]

3.2 Biological characteristics

3.2.1 Hardiness

R. ponticum was described by Curtis as 'a hardy evergreen, but apt to be injured by late frosts'. He also says that the species was brought to the London markets in great numbers 'to ornament our houses in the Spring' probably implying that the plants were kept inside houses.[35] His description of a *R. ponticum* flower producing nectar also refers to a plant kept inside: 'standing in a very light airy bow-window facing the North'. There is no further reference to this practice later. Nowadays such a plant would be called 'not fully hardy'.

Throughout the nineteenth century there were years with severe frosts when *R. ponticum* was badly damaged. 1859 saw debilitating autumn frosts which were seen as a good test of hardiness, much discussed in the press of 1860.[36] Another exceptionally cold winter in 1894/1895 seemed to have had similar effect in parts of the country and resulted in a call to nurserymen 'to get us substitutes for this tender ponticum, which is wrongly used to such a vast extent. They might propagate catawbiense and other hardy forms to take the place of the tender ponticum ... Ponticum, as we have seen, is not hardy on its own ... '.[37] We have not noted any further reports of appreciable frost damage. By the twentieth century, late frosts could affect the flowers or autumn frosts the tips as reported for Somerley Park, Ringwood in 1952 but there seem to have been no serious dieback of plants, even in very severe winters such as 1963.[38]

It would seem that the stock has been changed by both natural and artificial selection and by hybridisation so that it has become better adapted to the climate in Britain.[39] Evidence for this comes from the gardening literature. In 1899, Gertrude Jekyll described her rhododendrons planted nine years before and stressed the details by which she could still recognise the original parents *R. ponticum* and *R. catawbiense:* 'these, being two of the hardiest kinds, were the ones first chosen by hybridisers, and to these kinds we owe nearly all of the large numbers of beautiful garden Rhododendrons now in cultivation'.[40] Osborn reported in 1933 that *R. ponticum* 'has been very largely used in breeding the hardy race of large-leaved rhododendrons and it is unsurpassed as a stock for grafting'.[41] Breeding practices were designed to select hardier rhododendron varieties. In his history of rhododendrons in British gardens Elliott describes the 1820s–1850s as the period which was marked by experiments in hardiness where there were systematic programmes for testing hardiness for instance by planting seedlings in the open.[42]

Indirect evidence for the selection of more hardy plants comes from the fact that *R. catawbiense,* which was usually offered as the hardy alternative to *R. ponticum,* was less frequently included in twentieth-century catalogues than in the nineteenth-century ones. A reason for this might be that it was no longer necessary to offer a hardy alternative because the hardiness of *R. ponticum* had improved.

A genetic analysis of *R. ponticum* material from many places in Scotland, England, Wales and Ireland found much hybridisation with several species of *Rhododendron* and that plants with evidence of introgression from *R. catawbiense* were significantly more abundant in Britain's coldest winter region, eastern Scotland, than elsewhere.[43] Altogether there seems little doubt that *R. ponticum* became hardier through selection and hybridisation and that this process went on for much of the nineteenth century.

3.2.2 Ease of propagation

Curtis gives the earliest advice: 'May be propagated by layers ... , but can be easily raised by seeds'.[44] Loudon gives detailed instructions on propagation by cuttings and layers, 'a common mode with sorts which do not seed freely', but points out 'by far the most general method practised in gardens is by seeds. These are produced in abundance in this country'.[45] Although he does not name *R. ponticum,* we can safely assume that he includes it here because he gives this general information on the propagation of rhododendrons in the paragraph where he describes *R. ponticum.* He also depicts its seeds.

From an ecological point of view, the first description of self-sown plants is of particular interest as it is an essential stage on the way to full naturalisation.[46] The first hint was given in 1829 in an article in the *Gardener's Magazine*, where self sown rhododendrons are described, although no particular species is named.[47] The first reference to *R. ponticum* appears in the *Gardeners' Chronicle* in 1841 where Philip Frost, Dropmore, says: 'In the woods here we have by a little attention, thousands of self-sown seedling *Rhododendron ponticum*'.[48] Joseph Hooker in his famous description of the rhododendron species of the Sikkim-Himalaya in 1849 includes a footnote on *R. ponticum* and its self-sowing ability in Britain.[49] He quotes letters: from Embley near Romsey, Hants, Miss Nightingale reports 'the *Ponticum* and var. *roseum* seed themselves to a great extent' and from Penllergare, Glamorgan, Dillwyn Llewllyn writes: 'the seedlings of the common *Rhododendron Ponticum*, ... appear in thousands throughout our woods'. In both places the landowners confirm that *R. ponticum* is still present today.

Setting viable seed and so being easy to propagate allowed extensive plantings, as the landowners could propagate and spread the plants themselves. In 1841, Philip Frost said: 'It is very easy to fill woods with them, by sowing the seeds broad-cast ... . A man and boy can collect enough [seeds] to sow acres in a few hours'.[50] More importantly, ease of propagation made *R. ponticum* an ideal product for the nursery industry that could be offered in large quantities at low prices.

3.3 Reasons for planting

The extensive planting of *R. ponticum*, particularly in the nineteenth century, is seen as one of the major reasons for the success of the species in the British Isles. We consider five aspects.

3.3.1 Gardening fashions
Changing gardening fashions in the nineteenth century suited *R. ponticum* perfectly. In the eighteenth century, the taste for formal gardens changed to a more naturalistic style to include the surrounding landscape. The nineteenth century saw the enrichment of these landscape gardens by adding more colour, which was provided by an increasing number of newly introduced exotic species. In addition, there was great enthusiasm for introduced species in general and rhododendron species in particular. In 1870, William Robinson published the first edition of his influential book *The Wild Garden* which promoted 'the placing of perfectly hardy exotic plants under conditions where they will thrive without further care'.[51] Woodland gardens created in the nineteenth century and the beginning of the twentieth century offered ideal conditions for rhododendron collections and they gradually became the dominant species in those gardens.[52]

3.3.2 Prices
As early as 1783 *R. ponticum* was on offer commercially in the nursery catalogue of Gordon, Dermer and Thomson, Mile End, London, but the catalogue did not give a price for the plant. The first priced entries in nursery catalogues appeared in 1793 in those from John and Grosvenor Perfect, Pontefract, Yorkshire and

John and George Telford in Tanner-Row, York. Both offered 'Rhododendron the Purple or Ponticum' for the price of 7 shillings and 6 pence. The only other rhododendron species on offer in their catalogues was *R. maximum*, at 15s. twice as expensive. The ease of propagation soon made it possible to offer the plant at very low prices. *R. ponticum* was sold per dozen, per hundred and per thousand. In 1833, in F. Mackie's Norwich nursery catalogue, *R. ponticum* is again the

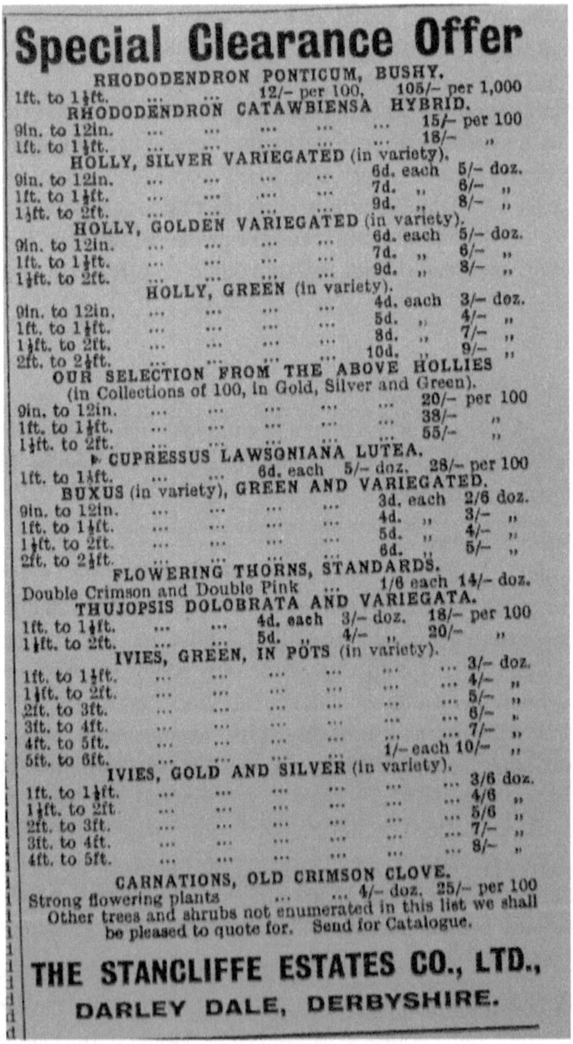

FIGURE 2. Advertisement in *The Garden*, 1912, offering *Rhododendron ponticum* at 105/- per 1000

cheapest of the 14 species on offer and together with *R. ferrugineum* the only one sold per dozen.[53] By 1838 the prices given by Loudon are per hundred and continue to appear like that throughout the nineteenth century in nearly all the catalogues analysed.[54] The only other rhododendron species offered in such quantities was *R. catawbiense*. Together they were often offered apart from the other rhododendrons in special categories like 'Rhododendrons at low prices' or 'Cheap Rhododendrons, for general planting'. For instance, in 1868 Charles Noble's nurseries, a specialised supplier of rhododendron species and hybrids, introduced this category for the first time offering *R. catawbiense* and including *R. ponticum* only two years later. Apart from the nursery trade, estates were trading the plant among themselves using the natural supply of their woodlands thus allowing for even lower prices.[55]

After the Second World War the interest in *R. ponticum* as an ornamental, apart from its use as grafting stock, decreased rapidly. The Sunningdale Nurseries, the successor of Charles Noble's nursery, no longer offered the plant per hundred, the price increased, and by 1955 that catalogue did not include *R. ponticum* (or *R. catawbiense*) at all. The species was also not on offer in the 1953 catalogue of the Knapp Hill Nursery. However, both nurseries later included it in their catalogues again, separately from other rhododendrons, as hedge plants. Today, *R. ponticum* is still available from a few nurseries; the 'Plant-Finder' lists 12 nurseries in the 2003/2004 edition.[56] It is offered as 'good for naturalising' or 'infilling and for woodland planting'.[57] During the whole period *R. ponticum*, sometimes together with *R. catawbiense*, was always the cheapest Rhododendron on offer.

The changes in the market in *R. ponticum* are shown quantitatively in Figure 3 from the first documented prices, 1793, to today by expressing the prices in the catalogues as 2002 pounds. The first pair of prices for *R. ponticum* of 7s. 6d. corresponds to £25.60 in 2002. This was the highest in all the catalogues analysed. There is a gap of 27 years until the next price available, 1820, when it had fallen by nearly 90 per cent to £2.76. The steady decline of the price continues to the 1870s from where it starts to go up again. From 1838 to about 1919 the price remains under £1 in nearly all catalogues, with the lowest at 20s. (one pound) per 1000 plants (£0.07 per plant in 2002 pounds) in 1886, reported for a trade between estates.[58] The rise in the second half of the twentieth century is probably caused by decreasing demand and lower competition among nurseries. Most nurseries now no longer sold the plant with a quantity discount, but Exbury Garden Ltd. was still offering it per hundred. The three rather low prices in the 1970/80s (Figure 3) came from that nursery.

As the marked down-and-up trend in Figure 3 might correspond to a general trend for gardening plants, we got similar data for other ornamentals (Figure 4). In rhododendrons there are few species or hybrids as continuously on sale as *R. ponticum*. We chose *R.* x *nobleanum,* one of the oldest hybrids (*R. arboreum* x *caucasicum*) created in 1835 and still on sale today.[59] This species represents

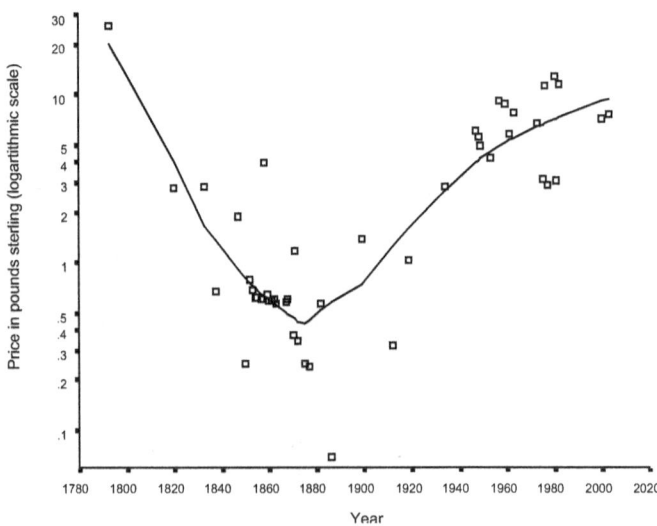

FIGURE 3. Price for one *R. ponticum* plant from 1793 to today. The prices are in 2002 pounds. The line of best fit is from a Lowess regression with a span of 0.5 (3 iterations).

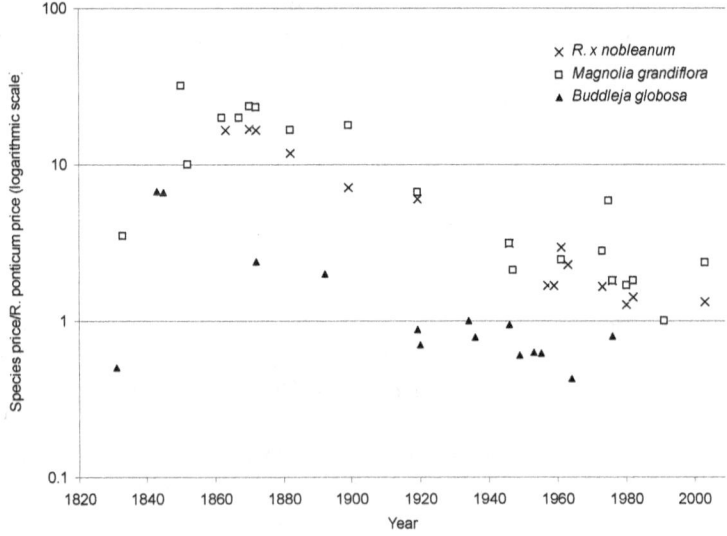

FIGURE 4. The ratio of the price of other ornamental garden plants to the price of *R. ponticum* calculated for every year for which price information for both species was available. Note the logarithmic ordinate.

the large group of hybrid rhododendrons dominating rhododendron catalogues. We also used price data on two other ornamental flowering woody species that have been on sale over the same period: *Magnolia grandiflora*, an evergreen Magnolia species from North America introduced in 1734, and the deciduous *Buddleja globosa* from South America introduced in 1774. In Figure 4 the price for these three is expressed as the ratio, on a logarithmic scale, of the *R. ponticum* price in a particular year. This shows that *R. ponticum* was relatively cheap during the second half of the nineteenth century; e.g. in 1863, the price of one *R. x nobleanum* was that of 16 *R. ponticum* plants whereas today it is only 1.3 plants.

3.3.3 Game cover
Shooting game in England increased in popularity from the beginning of the nineteenth century.[60] In 1866, the Government removed the duty on imported timber resulting in falling timber prices which made the management of woodlands for hunting for sport more attractive.[61] In these woodlands, the primary goal was to create a suitable environment to keep high densities of game animals and the production of timber was only second: 'As the new methods of shooting were widely adopted so the woodlands came to be regarded simply as pheasant coverts in the management of which the keeper took precedence over the forester. It was now the head keeper who decided which areas should be felled and which should be retained and the quality of the crop or the replacement of deteriorating stands by young plantations which could provide timber for the future, was not considered.'[62] Improvements in guns and ammunition made it possible to shoot more accurately, at a faster rate and a longer range, resulting in a high demand for game birds, particularly pheasants *Phasianus colchicus*.[63] Woodlands started to be managed intensively for high pheasant densities and partly this was by providing cover for the birds by planting shrubs.[64] Loudon describes such use of *R. ponticum*: 'In Britain, it is planted as an ornamental shrub, not only in open situations, but, on a large scale, in woods, to serve as undergrowth, and as a shelter for the game'.[65] Nursery catalogues and magazines describe the advantages which *R. ponticum* was believed to have for game cover. These were its ease of culture in almost any lime free soil and even in shady situations under dense canopies, its hardiness and immunity against game bite and rabbits and its low price.[66] The flowers in early summer and the evergreen underwood were seen as additional aesthetic benefits.

Its benefits as game shelter were questioned early. The main concern raised was that the bushes were 'such a tangled mass of branches that it is anything but pleasant quarters for game'.[67] The proponents argued: 'the mere fact of his lordship having killed 1367 pheasants, 500 hares, besides rabbits, in one day, in covers abounding in Rhododendrons, is evidence that Rhododendrons are not disliked by pheasants and hares'.[68] *R. ponticum* was sold widely for game cover up to the start of the twentieth century. The last mention we have found in a nursery catalogue was in the 1936 edition of Sunningdale Nurseries.

3.3.4 Grafting stock

From the 1830s onwards newly introduced rhododendron species and hybrid rhododendrons were grafted on stocks of *R. ponticum*.[69] The supply came from the estates as well as nurseries: '... they grow and increase very rapidly, hundreds of thousands of seedlings being sold to nurserymen, who buy them principally for grafting purposes'.[70] Bean writes 'hundreds of thousands of young plants are used every year as stocks'.[71] *R. ponticum* was the most common grafting stock far into the twentieth century, and it is still used today by a few nurseries.[72] However, the species was not the ideal grafting stock: 'For when planted out and left unwatched the stock frequently sends up sucker-growth, and it then becomes only a matter of time before the finer bred and less assertive scion is overwhelmed'.[73] Bean assumed that the occurrence of *R. ponticum* in many gardens resulted from its use as grafting stock.[74] It could overwhelm what it was supposed to nurture: 'We know an area of about ten acres of *R. ponticum* where a bulldozer would be necessary to clear a path: yet we remember our father and grandfather respectively, telling us that in the early eighties this used to be a thin and pleasant woodland, with glades lined with what was then an excellent collection of new hybrid rhododendrons. Today not one remains, but mounds of *R. ponticum* ... And that is no solitary case'[75]. With *R. ponticum* today it is not possible to tell if they result from planting the plant itself or from its use as grafting stock.

3.3.5 Perception

The literature on *R. ponticum* in the nineteenth century is dominated by technical advice on the use of the plant and how to propagate and plant it, but there are scarcely any enthusiastic descriptions of the plant itself. This may be because it became very common soon after its introduction and from the 1850s many newly introduced rhododendron species and hybrids attracted more attention. Probably one of the last enthusiastic descriptions of *R. ponticum* was published in 1910/11: 'We have no shrub to equal it ... [it] is, when in flower, the most effective of all Rhododendrons. There is a softness in the shade of purple, an elegance in the form and pose of its flower-heads, which are not easily equalled'.[76]

After the Second World War the gardening literature ignored the species or only mentioned its use as grafting stock. This lack of interest is shown by its not being offered by the nursery industry for some years (see the section on prices, above).

3.4 The growth of the conservation problem

3.4.1 Spread

Curtis says *R. ponticum* is 'extremely common'.[77] Loudon implies that by 1838 *R. ponticum* has been distributed over all Britain: '... it has since spread through the country with such an extraordinary degree of rapidity; that there is now scarcely a shrubbery or pleasure-ground in Britain without it ...'[78]

Unfortunately, there are very few data with both the date and site of the original planting and when it started to spread to unintended habitats. This is partly because botanical recording ignored the species for a long time, as an ornamental. For the same reason, herbarium specimens are of no help.[79] This recording problem is shown by comparing our survey of the Vice County recorders of the Botanical Society of the British Isles (BSBI) with the 1985/2002 surveys (Figure 5); they are not in agreement on the timing of the spread. The timings of the 1985 and 2002 surveys are not significantly different but the BSBI timings are significantly later (t tests, $p < 0.001$). For instance, of 27 Vice Counties included in both the BSBI and 1985/2002 surveys, by 1900 *R. ponticum* was present in 16 but had been recorded in just three. The 2002 survey also provides some information on whether the sites were affected because *R. ponticum* had been planted or if it had invaded from outside. For 67 sites respondents gave information on the source of infestation. For sites known to be affected before 1900 planting was seen as the main reason for the establishment in 80 per cent of the cases, whereas at sites affected later the source of infestation was more likely to be spontaneous with increasing time.[80]

Why was recording delayed? One reason was certainly the lack of awareness of the naturalisation of ornamental plants in general. In many cases it was not recorded before the 1950s or later (see the section on perception below). That was partly because it was spreading faster and more conspicuously by

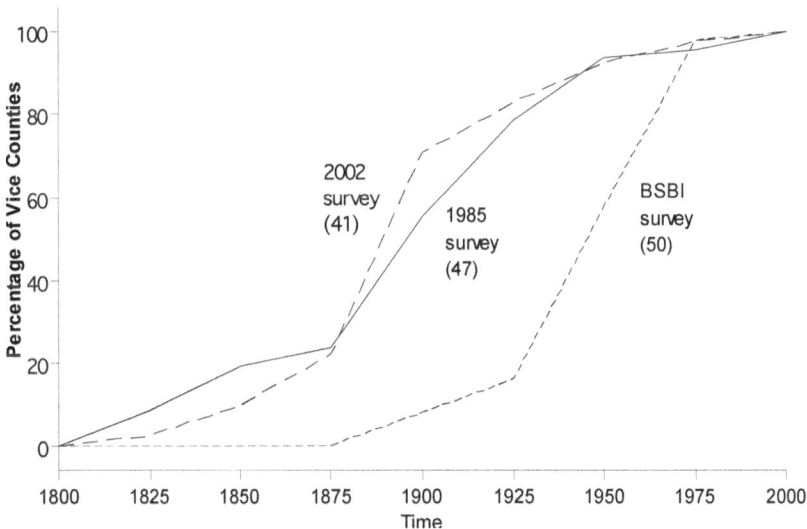

FIGURE 5. Cumulative records of *R. ponticum* in Vice Counties from the 1987 and 2002 surveys of land managers and the 2003 survey of recorders of the Botanical Society of the British Isles. The results are percentages of the total number of Vice Counties surveyed (Number of Vice Counties included in brackets).

then. During and after the Second World War many of the great rhododendron gardens suffered, becoming neglected and overgrown. One of the major problems in their renovation was the need to cut back *R. ponticum*.[81] Less intensive management of gardens and woodlands may have favoured the spread of *R. ponticum*. Other reasons for an increased rate of spread then, discussed in the literature, are land use changes, particularly overgrazing and the sudden decline of rabbits, which fed on seedlings, following the outbreak of myxomatosis in 1954.[82] Aerial photographs from the 1950/60s to 1970/80s show the increase in the Snowdonia National Park and on the Norfolk coast.[83]

Perring and Walters, in the first British hectad atlas, show *R. ponticum* in 993 out of 3614 10-km^2 grid cells.[84] In the second plant atlas *R. ponticum* is present in 2238 out of 3844 grid cells, implying that it more than doubled its distribution in 40 years.[85] But the 1962 Atlas did not give the full distribution at that time and so doubling is an overestimate. Perring and Walters say 'The maps of a few conspicuous aliens ... are inadequate because some recorders ignored them.'[86] So the species is one of those not used by Williamson *et al.*.[87] But that there has been a considerable spread is not in doubt.

3.4.2 Recognition of the problems

There was criticism of the massive plantings of *R. ponticum* in the nineteenth century. In 1872, Salmoniceps said: 'We are threatened with the marring of some of our best home landscapes by the ill-judged planting of the common Rhododendron ponticum'.[88] There seems to be no description of the problems caused by the vigorous growth of the plant before early in the twentieth century: 'It must be said, indeed, that in spite of its great beauty the Pontic rhododendron needs occasionally the curb of a strong hand. I know more than one demesne in the south of England which is overrun with the shrub to such an extent as to have become monotonous.'[89]

The Stapleford Wood Working Plan (see Acknowledgements) dated 1930 shows the problems in woodland in Lincolnshire. The description of the different compartments contains several entries like 'Rhododendrons bad' or 'impossible to remove culls without cutting rhododendrons' and the first evidence on control actions in an handwritten comment added later ('cleared of rhodos in winter 1935'). In addition, problems were caused by visitors coming during flowering time to the wood making it necessary to have constant patrols by the police and private woodland staff. There were also notes on the 'costly operation' essential to maintain rides free of *R. ponticum*, the negative effect on shooting rights and an increased risk of fire caused by the numerous visitors. This was not an isolated case and the Forestry Commission started trials on best control management for *R. ponticum* in 1949.[90]

Botanists and ecologists started to notice the plant and its impact during the twentieth century. The species was 'occasionally planted among indigenous vegetation' in the *Alien Flora of Britain* from 1905 but unlike other species in that flora, naturalisation was not mentioned.[91] This may well reflect the perception of most ornamental plants at that time and the underlying assumption that they had to have been planted wherever they occurred. So it is not surprising that by 1953 *R. ponticum* was included in only one (Sussex) out of 12 county floras and there with the somewhat apologetic remark 'though not usually recorded in county floras, the Rhododendron is ... completely naturalised'.[92] For an ecologist today, maybe equally surprisingly, Benson and Blackwell in 1926 described in detail the succession of vegetation on a clear felled area in Surrey including the occurrence of *R ponticum* seedlings and plants but they did not even mention that it is non-native.[93]

The first description of the ecological impact of *R. ponticum* on native vegetation comes from the Killarney oakwoods in SW Ireland. An international team of experts, the 'International Phytogeographical Excursion', visited the woods in August 1911. They acknowledged the 'luxuriance' of *R. ponticum*, and noted that 'it is not native, but ... evidently feels quite at home here', though did not say anything about its impact on native vegetation.[94] Not until 1939 did Turner and Watt publish a detailed phytosociological account of the oakwoods including a description of the naturalisation and competitiveness of *R. ponticum* which replaced *Ilex aquifolium* and had 'changed [the woodland] markedly in appearance.'[95] Later, Warburg described it as a 'menace' for native vegetation and complained about the insufficient data on its occurrences and spread.[96] In 1958, Elton drew the attention of a wider audience to the problems.[97] Today the problems caused by *R. ponticum*, especially in its impacts on native biodiversity and forestry are widely accepted among ecologists, foresters and conservationists.[98]

The British and Irish lines are also a problem in New Zealand, where they have been found free living since 1958, and may be becoming so in Belgium, the Netherlands and parts of Germany.[99] In logged riparian forest in the southern Appalachian mountains, *R. maximum* may have to be managed to ensure adequate regeneration of trees other than hemlock, *Tsuga canadensis* while in Turkey both *R. ponticum* and *R. flavum* (usually called *R. luteum*) suppress regeneration of the native beech *Fagus orientalis*, again particularly after logging though in neither case does the problem seem nearly as severe as in Britain and Ireland.[100]

3.4.3 The pest species
The growing awareness of the problems caused by *R. ponticum* produced increasing control effort by forestry, nature conservation and private landowners. The first publicly documented control work was undertaken by the Forestry Commission in the 1930s (and see the Stapleford Plan above). Systematic trials on best eradication techniques started in 1949.[101] Private landowners in Scotland started control in 1950 (Argyll Estates, personal communication) and nature conservationists in the 1960s (Scottish Natural Heritage, Royal Society for the Protection of Birds, Dorset Wildlife Trust, all personal communications). Systematic eradication trials in nature conservation were carried out in the early 1970s in the Coedydd Maentwrog and Coed Camlyn National Nature Reserves

in Wales.[102] In 1981 the first work camps for volunteers took place in the Killarney National Park in Ireland and they have continued since then every year.[103] Rhododendron control and eradication work has since become one of the major activities of work camps and working holidays in the British Isles attracting an international spectrum of participants every year, raising awareness of the species in the general public. A journalist taking part in one of these working holidays was titled a 'National hero'.[104]

Attitudes towards *R. ponticum* have changed considerably in Britain over the past 200 years. Starting from probably just an item for a botanical collector, through a period of enthusiastic planting, to a growing awareness of problematic impacts *R. ponticum* is today one of the most disliked non-native plants in Britain. Figure 6 summarises the changing perception of the species as reflected in the topics of publications relating to the species.

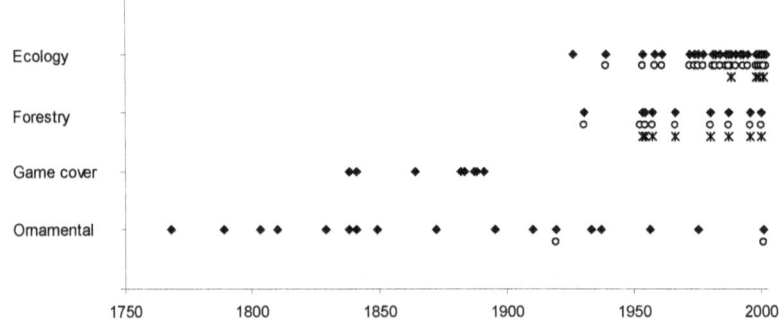

FIGURE 6. Publication of articles related to *R. ponticum* by thematic categories and date. Each black diamond represents at least one publication in a year. Open circles represent years with articles including descriptions of problems caused by the species whereas the star symbol indicates years with publications related to control methods.

Public opinion has a wide spectrum from a hated weed to a countryside attraction especially when flowering. One extreme is Campbell-Culver: ' ... it gradually revealed its true character – that of a killer, a smotherer, a choker-to-death of native woodland species and no plant for polite society. In its search for new victims it also spread along railway embankments, where its only merit is that one can sometimes see the wide variation of colour, from wishy-washy mauve to wishy-washy pink.'[105] The other extreme is the violence reported when *R. ponticum* control work was undertaken on farmland near Huddersfield in Yorkshire. An 'action group' supported by the local press tried to stop the machines and threw stones at the drivers (Elizabeth Elliott, personal communication 2002). Residents expressed their appreciation of *R. ponticum* in a letter to the editor of the local newspaper: the estate owners 'may class rhododendrons as an invasive weed but the floral display was spectacular. Millions travel miles to see such displays in parks all over the UK. Garden centres don't advertise them as weeds'.[106] Also, the two local MPs were 'calling for a change in the law to prevent landowners ploughing up popular beauty spots'.[107]

Nevertheless, professionals regard *R. ponticum* as one of the most harmful introduced plants in Britain. In one audit there are 627 species of vascular plant alien to Scotland listed but only two of them, *Heracleum mantegazzianum* and *R. ponticum*, are said to have an impact of high present significance while another audit includes only six out of 680 flowering plant species as aliens in England 'with demonstrated negative environmental effects', one of them *R. ponticum*.[108] Harmful aliens are a small minority of all aliens but the harm they can do can be great.

4. CONCLUSIONS

Rhododendron ponticum in Britain and Ireland went from an expensive, not fully hardy, plant to a widely planted woodland shrub to a pest of many woodlands and moorlands almost entirely because of human action. It was selected and hybridised for hardiness. Its spread and increase was from propagation by nurseries and estates. It was distributed over distances far greater than its seeds could travel naturally. It was brought directly to habitats offering the most suitable conditions for its survival. Without all this the plant might perhaps still exist in the British Isles today just as specimens in botanical and horticultural collections like thousands of other introduced plants. The biological characteristics of the plant, especially its ease of propagation, matched both the needs for a successful product in the horticultural market and for a successful biological invader.

Rhododendron ponticum shows clearly that British and Irish botanists and ecologists used not to be aware of the naturalisation of ornamental plants. Whereas non-native plants unintentionally introduced with wool in the nineteenth and the early twentieth centuries were precisely recorded in local floras, the same botanists did not include far commoner species like *R. ponticum* in their lists. This lack of data makes it difficult to reconstruct accurately the geographical spread of alien plants originally introduced as ornamentals.

The changing perception of the plant by the general public did not result in a consensus on how to deal with the species. *R. ponticum* in Britain today may still be planted in gardens and woodlands by some people whereas in neighbouring places others try to get rid of it.

Our results offer some insights into factors that promote the establishment and spread of plants introduced for horticultural reasons. It seems that economic and market factors largely determine whether a species with the right potential to become problematic does so. We show elsewhere for a random sample of more than 500 ornamental species that the frequency with which these species appear in the market in the nineteenth century and today are good explanatory variables distinguishing species which escape from gardens from those species which do not.[109] Today, the distribution of ornamental plants by the horticultural trade is much more effective and operating globally. There are more than 73,000 species and cultivars on sale in Britain and the spread of non-native plants from gardens is seen as one of the major causes of changes in the UK flora.[110] It took more than 150 years to recognise that *R. ponticum* was a problem species and even more time to realise its ecological impact.

NOTES

We are very grateful to all the BSBI Vice County recorders who participated in the survey. We particularly thank the BSBI's volunteer officer, the late Pete Selby, who helped to distribute the questionnaire and Irene Weston and Paul Barwick who made the 'Stapleford Wood Working Plan' available. Elizabeth Elliott provided us with information and newspaper articles about the *R. ponticum* control work on her estate in Yorkshire. Jenny Wong and Pat Denne made it possible for us to use the data of the 1985 *R. ponticum* survey. Liz Gilbert of the Royal Horticultural Society's Lindley Library has been very helpful in finding the appropriate nursery catalogues. Charles Perrings and two anonymous referees made valuable comments on the manuscript. KDS had been supported by a fellowship of the Deutsche Forschungsgemeinschaft and a Leverhulme Trust grant to the University of York.

[1] Simberloff 2004; Elton 1958; Williamson 1996; Mooney et al. 2005.
[2] Andersen et al. 2004.
[3] Pyšek et al. 2004; Williamson 1999; Ruiz and Carlton 2003.
[4] Mooney et al. 2005; Beinart and Middleton 2004, Perrings et al. 2000; McNeely 2001.
[5] Lockwood et al. 2005; Williamson 1996,1999.
[6] Williamson 1999.
[7] Groves 1998; Mack and Erneberg 2002; Kühn and Klotz 2002.
[8] Elliott 1996.
[9] Clement and Foster 1994; Ryves et al. 1996.
[10] Beinart and Middleton 2004; Perrins et al. 1992; Perrings et al. 2005.
[11] Bailey and Conolly 2000; Starfinger et al. 2003.
[12] Dehnen-Schmutz et al. 2004; Williamson 2002.
[13] Milne and Abbott 2000; Erfmeier and Bruelheide 2004, 2005.
[14] Cain 1944; Erfmeier and Bruelheide 2004; Milne and Abbott 2000.
[15] Mejías et al. 2002.
[16] Cross 1975; Shaw 1984.
[17] Cross 1975.
[18] Stephenson et al. 2006.

[19] Rotherham and Read 1988.
[20] Cross 1975.
[21] Ibid.
[22] Baker and Van Lear 1998; Vandermast and Van Lear 2002; Clinton and Vose 1996; Clement and Foster 1995.
[23] Clement and Foster 1995; Preston, Pearman and Dines 2002.
[24] Harvey 1972.
[25] McCusker 2003.
[26] Dandy 1969.
[27] Denne 1987; Dehnen-Schmutz et al. 2004.
[28] Hill 1768.
[29] Aiton 1789.
[30] Aiton 1810.
[31] Loudon 1838
[32] Curtis 1803.
[33] Loudon 1838
[34] Cited in Cross 1975.
[35] Curtis 1803.
[36] Elliott 1996
[37] Field 1895.
[38] Brown 1953.
[39] Shaw 1984
[40] Jekyll 1899.
[41] Osborn 1933
[42] Elliott 1996; Waston 1910/11.
[43] Milne and Abbott 2000.
[44] Curtis 1803
[45] Loudon 1838
[46] *Sensu* Richardson et al. 2000.
[47] Rinz 1829.
[48] Frost 1841.
[49] Hooker 1849.
[50] Frost 1841
[51] Robinson 1895.
[52] Elliott 1996.
[53] Harvey 1972
[54] Loudon 1838.
[55] 'J.S.W.' 1886.
[56] Royal Horticultural Society 2003.
[57] Goscote Nurseries Ltd 2003; Weasdale Nurseries Ltd. 2003.
[58] 'J.S.W.' 1886.

[59] Mills 1979.
[60] James 1981.
[61] Dunlop 1997.
[62] James 1981.
[63] Ibid.
[64] Robertson 1992.
[65] Loudon 1838.
[66] Wythes 1891; Webster 1883; Goldring 1888.
[67] Webster 1883
[68] Craw 1864.
[69] Elliott 1996.
[70] Anonymous 1887.
[71] Bean 1919.
[72] Cox 1998.
[73] Bean 1919.
[74] Ibid.
[75] Cox and Cox 1956.
[76] Waston 1910/11.
[77] Curtis 1803.
[78] Loudon 1838.
[79] C. Preston in Usher 1986.
[80] Dehnen-Schmutz et al. 2004.
[81] Elliott 1996.
[82] Cross 1981; Shaw 1984; Fuller and Boorman 1977.
[83] Shaw 1984; Fuller and Boorman 1977; Thomson et al. 1993.
[84] Perring and Walters 1962.
[85] Preston, Pearman and Dines 2002.
[86] Perring and Walters 1962.
[87] Williamson et al. 2003.
[88] Salmoniceps 1872.
[89] Bean 1919.
[90] Holmes 1957.
[91] Dunn 1905.
[92] Warburg 1953.
[93] Benson and Blackwell 1926.
[94] Rübel 1912.
[95] Turner and Watt 1939.
[96] Warburg 1953.
[97] Elton 1958.
[98] Compton et al. 2002; Cross 1975, 2002; Shaw 1984; Usher 1986; Manchester and Bullock 2000; Simons 1988; Tabbush and Williamson 1987.

[99] Williams et al. 2000; Erfmeier and Bruelheide 2004.
[100] Eşen and Zedaker 2004; Vandermast and Van Lear 2002.
[101] Holmes 1957.
[102] Jones 1974.
[103] Barron 2000.
[104] *The Guardian* 'Labour of love' 03.11.2001.
[105] Campbell-Culver 2001.
[106] *Huddersfield District Chronicle* 'Whitley Park', 18.04.1997
[107] *Yorkshire Post* 'Secret weapon in park battle', 15.04.1997.
[108] Welch et al. 2000; Hill et al. 2005.
[109] Dehnen-Schmutz et al. in press.
[110] Royal Horticultural Society 2004; Preston, Telfer et al. 2002.

REFERENCES

Aiton, W. 1789. *Hortus Kewensis or, a Catalogue of the Plants Cultivated in the Royal Botanic Garden at Kew*. London: George Nicol.

Aiton, W.T. 1810. *Hortus Kewensis or, a Catalogue of the Plants Cultivated in the Royal Botanic Garden at Kew*. 2nd edition. London: Longman & Co.

Andersen, M.C., Adams, H., Hope, B., and Powell, M. 2004. 'Risk assessments for invasive species'. *Risk Analysis* 24: 787–93.

Anonymous. 1887. 'Rhododendrons versus laurels'. *The Garden*: 427.

Bailey, J.P., and Conolly, A.P. 2000. 'Prize-winners to pariahs: A history of Japanese Knotweed *s. l.* (Polygonaceae) in the British Isles'. *Watsonia* 23: 93–110.

Baker, T.T., and Van Lear, D.H. 1998. 'Relations between density of rhododendron thickets and diversity of riparian forests'. *Forest Ecology and Management* 109: 21–32.

Barron, C. 2000. *Groundwork Rhododendron Clearance in Killarney National Park 1981-2000, a Report after 20 Years*. Unpublished report for Duchas (Killarney National Park).

Bean, W.J. 1919. *Trees and Shrubs Hardy in the British Isles*. 2nd edition. London: Murray.

Beinart, W., and Middleton, K. 2004. 'Plant transfers in historical perspective: a review article'. *Environment and History* 10: 3–29.

Benson, M., and Blackwell, E. 1926. 'Observations on a lumbered area in Surrey from 1917 to 1925'. *Journal of Ecology* 14: 120–37.

Brown, J.M.B. 1953. 'The Rhododendron problem in the woodlands of southern England'. *Quarterly Journal of Forestry* 47: 239–53.

Cain, S.A. 1944. *Foundations of Plant Geography*. New York: Harper & Brothers.

Campbell-Culver, M. 2001. *The Origin of Plants: The People and Plants that have Shaped Britain's Garden History Since the Year 1000*. London: Headline.

Clement, E.J., and Foster, M.C. 1994. *Alien Plants of the British Isles*. London: Botanical Society of the British Isles.

Clinton, B.D., and Vose, J.M. 1996. 'Effects of *Rhododendron maximum* L. on *Acer rubrum* L. seedling establishment'. *Castanea* 61: 38–45.

Compton, S.G., Key, R.S., and Key, R.J.D. 2002. 'Conserving our little Galapagos: Lundy, Lundy Cabbage and its beetles'. *British Wildlife* 13: 184–90.

Cox, E.H.M., and Cox, P.A. 1956. *Modern Rhododendrons*. London: Nelson & Sons.

Cox, K. 1998. *Rhododendrons and Azaleas*. London: Hamlyn.

Craw, W. 1864. 'Rhododendrons as cover for game'. *The Gardeners' Chronicle and Agricultural Gazette*: 54.

Cross, J.R. 1975. 'Biological Flora of the British Isles: Rhododendron ponticum L.' *Journal of Ecology* 63: 345–64.

Cross, J.R. 1981. 'The establishment of Rhododendron ponticum in the Killarney Oakwoods, S.W. Ireland'. *Journal of Ecology* 69: 807–24.

Cross, J.R. 2002. 'The invasion and control of *Rhododendron ponticum* L. in native Irish vegetation'. In: *Biologische Invasionen. Herausforderung zum Handeln?* ed. I. Kowarik and U. Starfinger. Berlin: Technical University of Berlin.

Curtis, W. 1803. 'Rhododendron ponticum'. *Botanical Magazine* 16: 650.

Dandy, J.E. 1969. *Watsonian Vice-Counties of Great Britain*. London: The Ray Society.

Dehnen-Schmutz, K., Perrings, C., and Williamson, M. 2004. 'Controlling *Rhododendron ponticum* in the British Isles: an economic analysis.' *Journal of Environmental Management* 70: 323–32.

Dehnen-Schmutz, K., Touza, J., Perrings, C., and Williamson, M. in press. 'The horticultural trade and ornamental plant invasions in Britain'. *Conservation Biology*.

Denne, M.P. 1987. 'Introduction to the national R. ponticum survey'. In: *The Spread of Rhododendron ponticum: A National Problem. Report of a Conference*. ed. R. H. Gritten. Plas Tan-y-Bwlch, North Wales: Snowdonia National Park.

Dunlop, B.M.S. 1997. 'The woods of Strathspey in the nineteenth and twentieth centuries'. In: *Scottish Woodland History*. ed. T. C. Smout. Edinburgh: Scottish Cultural Press.

Dunn, S. 1905. *Alien Flora of Britain*. London: West, Newmann & Co.

Elliott, B. 1996. 'Rhododendrons in British gardens: a short history'. In: *The Rhododendron Story: 200 years of Plant Hunting and Garden Cultivation*. ed. C. Postan. London: The Royal Horticultural Society.

Elton, C.S. 1958. *The Ecology of Invasions by Animal and Plants*. London: Methuen.

Erfmeier, A., and Bruelheide, H. 2004. 'Comparison of native and invasive *Rhododendron ponticum* populations: Growth, reproduction and morphology under field conditions'. *Flora* 199: 120–33.

Erfmeier A., and Bruelheide H. 2005. 'Invasive and native *Rhododendron ponticum* populations: is there evidence for genotypic differences in germination and growth?' *Ecography* 28: 417–28.

Esen, D., and Zedaker, S.M. 2004. 'Control of rhododendron (*Rhododendron ponticum* and *R. flavum*) in the eastern beech (Fagus orientalis) forests of Turkey'. *New Forests* 27: 66–79.

Field. 1895. 'The pontic rhododendron and the frost'. *The Garden*: 270–1.

Frost, P. 1841. 'Rhododendrons'. *The Gardeners' Chronicle*: 85.

Fuller, R.M., and Boorman, L.A. 1977. 'The spread and development of *Rhododendron ponticum* L. on dunes at Winterton, Norfolk, in comparison with invasion by *Hippophae rhanmnoides* L. at Saltfleetby, Lincolnshire'. *Biological Conservation* 12: 83–94.

Goldring, W. 1888. 'Rhododendrons for covert'. *The Garden*: 280.

Goscote Nurseries Ltd. 2003. Rhododendron category index. Online edition. Cossington. http://www.goscote.co.uk/goscote/rhodos/html/rhodos.htm

Groves, R.H. 1998. 'Recent incursions of weeds to Australia 1971–1995'. *CRC for Weed Management Systems Technical Series No.* 3: 1–74.

Harvey, J.H. 1972. *Early Gardening Catalogues*. London: Phillimore.

Hill, J. 1768. *Hortus Kewensis. Sistens. Herbas Exoticas, Indigenasque rariores, In Area Botanica, Hortorum Augustissimae Principisse Cambriae Dotissea, apud Kew, in Comitatu Surreiano, cultas; Methodo florali nova dispositas*. Londini.

Hill M., Baker, R., Broad, G., Chandler, P.J., Copp, G.H., Ellis, J., Jones, D., Hoyland, C., Laing, I., Longshaw, M., Moore, N., Parrott, D., Pearman, D., Preston, C., Smith, R.M. and Waters, R. 2005. *Audit of Non-Native Species in England*. Peterborough: English Nature.

Holmes, G.D. 1957. 'Experiments on the chemical control of Rhododendron ponticum'. *Forestry Commission: Forest Record* 34: 1–7.

Hooker, J.D. 1849. *The Rhododendrons of the Sikkim-Himalaya*. London: Reeve, Benham & Reeve.

'J.S.W.' 1886. 'Self-sown Rhododendrons'. *The Garden*: 571.

James, N.D.G. 1981. *A History of English Forestry*. Oxford: Basil Blackwell.

Jekyll, G. 1899. *Wood and Garden*. London: Longmans, Green and Co.

Jones, W.I. 1974. A rhododendron eradication trial. Information Paper No 1, Nature Conservancy Council, UK.

Kühn, I., and Klotz, S. 2002. 'Floristischer Status und gebietsfremde Arten'. *Schriftenreihe Vegetationskunde* 38: 47–56.

Lockwood, J.L., Cassey, P., and Blackburn, T. 2005. 'The role of propagule pressure in explaining species invasions'. *Trends in Ecology & Evolution* 20: 223–8.

Loudon, J.C. 1838. *Arboretum et fruticetum Britanicum*. London: Longman.

Mack, R.N. and Erneberg, M. 2002. 'The United States naturalized flora: largely the product of deliberate introductions', *Annals of the Missouri Botanical Garden* 89: 176–89.

Manchester, S.J. and Bullock, J.M. 2000. 'The impact of non-native species on UK biodiversity and the effectiveness of control'. *Journal of Applied Ecology* 37: 845–64.

McCusker, J.J. 2003. Comparing the Purchasing Power of Money in Great Britain from 1264 to 2002. Economic History Services. http://www.eh.net/hmit/ppowerbp/

McNeely, J.A., editor. 2001. *The Great Reshuffling. Human Dimensions of Invasive Alien Species*. Gland: IUCN.

Mejías, J.A., Arroyo, J., and Ojeda, F. 2002. 'Reproductive ecology of *Rhododendron ponticum* (Ericaceae) in relict Mediterranean populations'. *Botanical Journal of the Linnean Society* 140: 297–311.

Mills, L.P. 1979. 'Rhododendrons: the early history of their introduction and cultivation in Britain'. *Rhododendron and Camelia Group Journal* 1979–80: 6–20.

Milne, R.I., and Abbott, R.J. 2000. 'Origin and evolution of invasive naturalized material of Rhododendron ponticum L. in the British Isles'. *Molecular Ecology* 9: 541–56.

Mooney, H.A., Mack, R.N., McNeely, J.A., Neville, L.E., Schei, P.J., and Waage, J.K., editors. 2005. *Invasive Alien Species: A New Synthesis*. Washington: Island Press.

Osborn, A. 1933. *Shrubs and Trees for the Garden*. London: Ward, Loch & Co.

Perring, F.H., and Walters, S.M. 1962. *Atlas of the British Flora*. London: Thomas Nelson and Sons.

Perrings, C., Dehnen-Schmutz, K., Touza, J., and Williamson, M. 2005. 'How to manage biological invasions under globalization'. *Trends in Ecology & Evolution* 20: 212–15.

Perrings, C., Williamson, M., and Dalmazzone, S., editors. 2000. *The Economics of Biological Invasions*. Cheltenham: Edward Elgar.

Perrins, J., Williamson, M., and Fitter, A. 1992. 'A survey of differing views of weed classification: implications for regulation of introductions'. *Biological Conservation* 60: 47–56.

Preston, C.D., Pearman, D.A., and Dines, T.D. 2002. *New Atlas of the British and Irish Flora*. Oxford: Oxford University Press.

Preston, C.D., Telfer, M.G., Arnold, H.R., Carey, P.D., Cooper, J.M., Dines, T.D., Hill, M.O., Pearman, D.A., Roy, D.B., and Smart, S.M. 2002. The changing flora of the UK. DEFRA, London. www.defra.gov.uk/wildlife-countryside/ewd/flora/FlorainUK.pdf

Pyšek, P., Richardson, D.M., and Williamson, M. 2004. 'Predicting and explaining plant invasions through analysis of source area floras: some critical considerations'. *Diversity and Distributions* 10: 179–87.

Richardson, D.M., Pyšek, P., Rejmanek, M., Barbour, M.G., Panetta, F.D., and West, C.J. 2000. 'Naturalization and invasion of alien plants: concepts and definitions'. *Diversity and Distributions* 6: 93–107.

Rinz, J. 1829. 'Remark on various gardens about London, and in other parts of England, visited in April and May 1829'. *Gardener's Magazine*: 382.

Robertson, P.A. 1992. 'Woodland management for pheasants'. *Forestry Commission Bulletin* 106: 1–18.

Robinson, W. 1895. *The Wild Garden*. 5th edition. London: Murray.

Rotherham, I. D., and Read, D.J. 1988. 'Aspects of the ecology of Rhododendron ponticum with reference to its competitive and invasive properties'. *Aspects of Applied Biology* 16: 327–35.

Royal Horticultural Society, editor. 2003. *Plant Finder 2003-2004*. London: Dorling Kindersley.

Royal Horticultural Society, editor. 2004. *Plant Finder 2004-2005*. London: Dorling Kindersley.

Rübel, E. A. 1912. 'The international phytogeographical excursion in the British Isles. V. The Killarney Woods'. *New Phytologist* 11: 54–7.

Ruiz, G.M., and Carlton, J.T. 2003. 'Invasive vectors: a conceptual framework for management'. In: *Invasive Species: Vectors and Management Strategies*. ed. G.M. Ruiz and J.T. Carlton. Washington: Island Press.

Ryves, T.B., Clement, E.J., and Foster, M.C. 1996. *Alien Grasses of the British Isles*. London: Botanical Society of the British Isles.

Salmoniceps. 1872. 'The Rhododendron mania'. *The Garden*: 377.

Shaw, M.W. 1984. 'Rhododendron ponticum: Ecological reasons for the success of an alien species in Britain and features that may assist in its control'. *Aspects of Applied Biology* 5: 231–42.

Simberloff, D. 2004. 'A rising tide of species and literature: A review of some recent books on biological invasions'. *Bioscience* 54: 247–54.

Simons, P. 1988. 'The day of the rhododendron'. *New Scientist*: 50–55.

Starfinger, U., Kowarik, I., Rode, M., and Schepker, H. 2003. 'From desirable ornamental plant to pest to accepted addition to the flora? The perception of an alien tree species through the centuries'. *Biological Invasions* 5: 323–35.

Stephenson, C.M., MacKenzie, M.L., Edwards, C., and Travis, J.M.J. 2006. 'Modelling establishment probabilities of an exotic plant, *Rhododendron ponticum*, invading a heterogeneous, woodland landscape using logistic regression with spatial autocorrelation'. *Ecological Modelling* 193: 747–58.

Tabbush, P.M., and Williamson, D.R. 1987. 'Rhododendron ponticum as a Forest Weed'. *Forestry Commission Bulletin* 73: 1–7.

Thomson, A.G., Radford, G.L., Norris, D.A., and Good, J.E.G. 1993. 'Factors affecting the distribution and spread of Rhododendron in North Wales'. *Journal of Environmental Management* 39: 199–212.

Turner, J.S., and Watt, A.S. 1939. 'The oakwoods (Quercetum sessiliflorae) of Killarney, Ireland'. *Journal of Ecology* 27: 202–33.

Usher, M.B. 1986. 'Invasibility and wildlife conservation: invasive species on nature reserves'. *Philosophical Transactions of the Royal Society of London B: Biological Sciences* 314: 695–710.

Vandermast, D.B., and Van Lear, D.H. 2002. 'Riparian vegetation in the southern Appalachian mountains (USA) following chestnut blight'. *Forest Ecology and Management* 155: 97–106.

Warburg, E.F. 1953. 'A changing flora as shown in the status of our trees and shrubs'. In: *The changing flora of Britain. Conference Report*. ed. J. E. Lousley. Oxford: Botanical Society of the British Isles.

Waston, W. 1910/11. *Rhododendrons & Azaleas*. London: J.C. & E.C. Jack.

Weasdale Nurseries Ltd. 2003. Nursery catalogue. Online edition. Kirkby Stephen, Cumbria. www.weasdale.com

Webster, A.D. 1883. 'Game coverts'. *The Gardeners' Chronicle*: 792.

Welch, D., Carss, D.N., Gornall, J., Manchester, S.J., Marquiss, M., Preston, C.D., Telfer, M.G., Arnold, H., and Holbrook, J. 2000. *An Audit of Alien Species in Scotland*. Edinburgh.

Williams, P.A., Nicol, E., and Newfield, M. 2000. *Assessing the Risk to Indigenous New Zealand Biota from New Exotic Plant Taxa and Genetic Material*. Wellington, New Zealand: Department of Conservation.

Williamson, M. 1996. *Biological Invasions*. London: Chapman & Hall.

Williamson, M. 1999. 'Invasions'. *Ecography* 22: 5–12.

Williamson, M. 2002. 'Alien plants in the British Isles'. In: *Biological Invasions. Economic and Environmental Costs of Alien Plant, Animal, and Microbe Species*. ed. D. Pimentel. Boca Raton, Florida, USA: CRC Press.

Williamson, M., Preston, C., and Telfer, M. 2003. 'On the rates of spread of alien plants in Britain.' In: *Plant Invasions: Ecological Threats and Management Solutions*. ed. L. E. Child, J. H. Brock, G. Brundu, K. Prach, P. Pyšek, P. M. Wade, and M. Williamson. Leiden: Backhuys.

Wythes, G. 1891. 'The common Rhododendron in woods and drives'. *The Garden*: 424.

Fighting With a Weed: Water Hyacinth and the State in Colonial Bengal, c. 1910–1947

Iftekhar Iqbal

The expanding field of modern India's environmental history has so far given rise to two broad categories of investigations. One relates to colonial policies and their ecological implications, particularly regarding the uses, destruction and conservation of the forest, which has drawn the attention of the majority of environmental historians.[1] Although water regimes of India have received relatively less attention, a number of important works have dealt with the political, economic and ecological implications of irrigation and dams.[2] Another spectrum of debates, informed by a broader postcolonial critique, focuses on the ranges and patterns of the state's coercion into the ecological regimes in different regions of India and corresponding resistance from below.[3] Within both categories of investigations, the colonial state is perceived to play a key role in mediating the relationship between ecology and the public sphere; and, not surprisingly, studies in these areas are mostly conducted from the perspective of state-formation and development processes in both colonial and postcolonial times. Far less focus has been paid to the environmental issues that are outside the realm of grand policies and which are informed neither by the direct 'autonomous' power of the state or its stubborn opponents, but by a host of contending forces within and beyond the state. The state perhaps remains a central player, but its position is never settled in the complex relationship between ecology and economic and social forces.

The story of the water hyacinth, which at the height of its global reach in the early twentieth century was present across four continents, provides insights into the way in which the colonial state in India found itself in its encounter with a biologically alien waterweed.[4] Such a study is necessary in the broader field of environmental history because, following Alfred Crosby's seminal work on biological exchange, a lot more focus has been placed on the relationship between plant transfer and imperial expansion than on the actual encounter between a secure colonial state and an invasive plant which has already established itself in a local ecological system. In this context, this paper, with its focus on East Bengal which approximates to present day Bangladesh, examines four sets of issues: the impact of the water hyacinth on agriculture and health; ambivalent position of the state regarding the destruction or scientific exploitation of the water hyacinth; the government's predicaments in its quest for legislations to contain the weed; and the complications and failures of legislative means of fighting the weed. In examining these issues, the paper focuses on how different bureaucracies and different realms of science as well as private commercial interests imagine, construct and represent the problem of species invasion in a colonial context. In such a context, a wealth of competing players are at work, contradicting one another, struggling over bureaucratic power and funding, and attempting to further and extend their administrative reach. The hyacinth becomes caught up in these machinations in interesting ways, though it is never tamed by the state. This paper attempts to capture these complex and fluid scenarios that centred on an alien aquatic weed in late colonial India.

THE GROWTH OF THE WATER HYACINTH AND THE BENGAL DELTA

The water hyacinth was introduced in East Bengal by George Morgan, a Scottish migrant and jute merchant of Narayanganj, an industrial district in Dhaka, sometime around the turn of the twentieth century. Morgan was impressed by the beauty of the flowers and leaves of the plant and brought it on his way back from Australia.[5] Another narrative relates that the hyacinth was brought to Calcutta Botanic Garden from Brazil in the 1890s and at a later date some ladies, being attracted by its flower, collected and transplanted these weeds to their gardens in Dhaka.[6] Some believe that the weed made its way to the Delta through the river Brahmaputra from Assam upstream.[7] The rapid spread of this weed in Bengal at the outset of the First World War has also been credited to the Germans, who wanted to weaken the British by 'killing their Indian subjects', hence it became known as the *German pana* or German weed.[8] As implied later in this article, a transnational company might also have introduced this plant intentionally.[9]

In 1914, the Narayanganj Chamber of Commerce considered the menace of the weed as one of 'sufficient importance' to bring it before the government's attention. By 1920, it was acknowledged by both government and non-government agencies that the water hyacinth had been 'choking up the natural arteries of trade, impeding agricultural operations and menacing the health of the people' in most parts of East Bengal.[10] In the 1920s, while a Bengali journalist compared the weed with malaria epidemics, which were a formidable cause of mortality in contemporary Bengal, a colonial official considered the weed the most pressing problem after the anti-colonial terrorist movement.[11] A conservative estimate revealed that in 1936 the hyacinth covered an area of over four thousand square miles.[12] The weed was mostly prevalent in the active Delta of East Bengal, which comprised an area of about 35,000 square miles – implying that the hyacinth covered a ninth of the total deltaic plain. If the lands covered by homesteads, office buildings, temples and mosques are excluded and only water-bodies and agricultural lands adjacent to them are considered, the coverage would have been proportionately higher.[13]

FIGHTING WITH A WEED

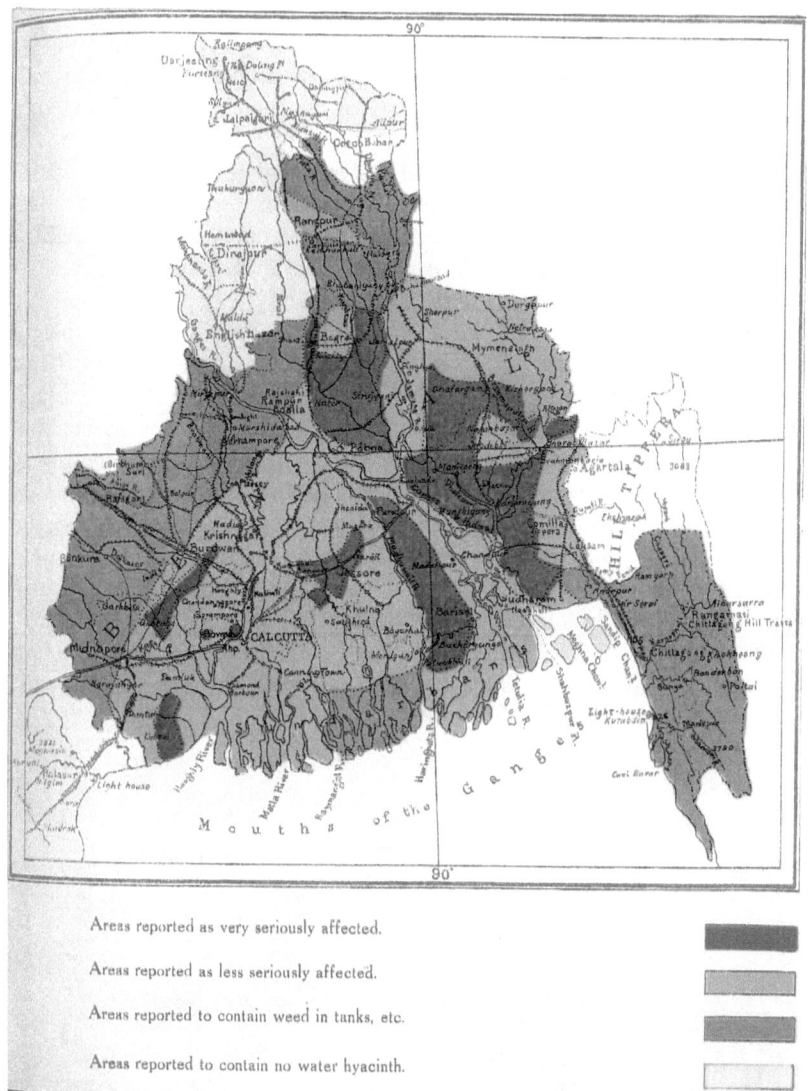

FIGURE 1. A map of Bengal showing areas affected by water hyacinth.
Source: Kenneth McLean, 'Water Hyacinth. A Serious Problem in Bengal',
Agricultural Journal of India XVII (1922).

As the spread of the water hyacinth was left largely unchallenged, the devastation it caused to crops and cultivation processes remained unchecked. In the district of Mymensingh, it was reported that the cultivators gave up producing any crop over an area of a hundred square miles, owing to the extensive damage caused by the water hyacinth year by year. In Khulna *beel* (marshy low land) areas, paddy cultivation was rendered difficult, and low-lying paddy suffered damage from the encroachment of the plant.[14] The people of Nasirnagar subdistrict of Comilla District petitioned the Government alleging that crops of a very large tract of their area had been destroyed since 1915 by flooding and the water hyacinth.[15] A large quantity of paddy grown in the Arial *beel* of Munshiganj of Dhaka District was reported to have been destroyed by the weed.[16] The hyacinth from the Kumar river destroyed paddy and jute plants across an area of more than 174 square miles each year. It was also alleged that inland navigation and the cultivation of paddy of *aman* variety and jute became difficult due to the pervasive presence of the water hyacinth. It was reported in 1926 that 15 to 20 per cent of the *aman* paddy were being damaged 'year after year'.[17] The mover of the Bengal Water Hyacinth Bill (1933) reported that some time ago the annual damage done by the water hyacinth in Bengal was estimated at about six crore rupees (1 crore = 10 millions) and at the time of his speaking it was 'very much more'.[18] This was not an exaggeration since the water hyacinth was particularly damaging for *beel* (marsh) paddy which grew in abundance in the Delta.[19] In a region which mostly comprised deltaic low lands, being uniquely fit for a range of rice species, the chronic challenge from the water hyacinth contributed to what has recently been termed as an 'economic depression'.[20]

The problem with the weed became complicated because of an insufficient flow of water in the region. Where embankments, both protective and railway,

FIGURE 2. Villagers fighting water hyacinth sometime in the early twentieth century.
Source: *A Short Survey of the Work Achievements and Needs of the Bengal Agricultural Department, 1906–1936* (Government of Bengal, 1937).

were erected and only few outlays were given, currents of water were blocked or reduced. In places where canal mouths or smaller streams were blocked by pillars and plates of locks and sluice gates, siltation took place and the water hyacinth found congenial home to stay and multiply in such places. Ditches alongside railways and roads under district authorities were also thought to be places of 'infection'.[21] During the months of *Falgun* and *Chaitra* (roughly in spring) poor cultivators used to destroy all the hyacinths which grew or accumulated on their land; but the hyacinths which grew and accumulated on the *khas* (private) lands of the landlords and of the Government remained intact, and that with the arrival of the rainy season the weed 'grew far and wide and destroyed the crops of the poor cultivators'.[22] In 1946, it was estimated that crops and fish worth at least 10 million rupees were being destroyed by the hyacinth every year.[23]

In the field of public health, the water hyacinth was accused of causing influenza and other water-related diseases.[24] In response to the suggestion that the hyacinth contributed to cholera, C.A. Bentley, the Sanitary Commissioner of Bengal, thought that the hyacinth could not have contributed to the spread of cholera unless its presence encouraged the pollution of water with human excrement, which he doubted. Bentley thought that the only possible indirect way in which it could cause cholera would be by shading polluted water from the action of the sun and, therefore, interfering with the natural process of purification, which took place in a few days in the case of water exposed to sunlight and air. But Bentley thought it to be 'purely hypothetical' and though he admitted that the weed was a 'great nuisance' which needed to be dealt with, he failed to condemn it on sanitary grounds.[25] As far as the relationship between the water hyacinth and malaria was concerned, Bentley noted that water thickly covered with hyacinth rarely showed any evidence of the presence of any anopheles mosquito larvae.[26] However, a report by S.N. Sur, a field-level Public Health official in the Malaria Research Unit in Bengal, contradicted Bentley's assumptions. He observed that the prevailing malarial condition was mainly due to the stagnation of water hosting the water hyacinth which favoured the growth of mosquito larvae by 'reducing the temperature of the water as well as giving shelter against their natural enemies'.[27] In addition to having considerable negative impact on the health, the water hyacinth seemed to have affected public nutrition that was obtained through the consumption of fish. By thriving in the *pukurs* (tanks or ponds) of the countryside during the rainy seasons, it not only polluted drinking water but posed a danger to the culture of fish. This was considered one of the reasons why the production of fish in Bengal rapidly diminished.[28] Along with human health, the health of cattle, which provided the backbone of agriculture in Bengal, appeared to have been affected as they ate the water hyacinth. J. Donovon, a district magistrate in Bakarganj, noted that he had never seen more miserable cattle than those of East Bengal. He learnt from the veterinary officer of the district that due to little or no grazing, the cows were suffering indigestion as a result of eating the water hyacinth.[29] The link

FIGURE 3. Navigation of a load of jute through water hyacinth.

between the water hyacinth and decline in agricultural production and health was graphically described by a local witness in these words:

> The inroads of savage army, through the frontiers, the incursions of a Timurlane, carrying fire and sword into the country, were nothing compared to the inroads of those tiny plants, floating down the East Bengal rivers ... creeks, canals and small rivulets had been clogged and choking up ... even costly careful clearance, twice a year, was not able to arrest its growth ... during flood tides, these plants get into fields and within a few days, by first multiplication, cover them entirely to the destruction of rice and other crops rooted on the earth ... Eastern Bengal, the granary of the Province and hitherto the healthiest portion of it, is being rendered desolate by the bringing of malaria by this plant ...[30]

The official perception of the speedy growth of the weed was that deltaic East Bengal provided a congenial physical environment for it. In an attempt to examine the capacity of the weed to grow in different environments, its seeds were tested in a government laboratory in 1920 for germination on dampened blotting paper, in water, in mud, and in damp soil. The seeds were kept under observation for one month during February and the tests were made both under ordinary atmospheric conditions and in the incubator at a temperature of 86°F. The hyacinth germinated in 'all conditions' and it appeared to be 'perfectly formed and healthy'. As the weed was able to germinate in different environment, so was it able to spread itself by virtue of its bladder-like leaf stalk and sail-like leaves, since the former enabled it to float and the latter, with the help of wind, enabled it to travel into new areas. An observation team made up of officials and local people found in their experiment in the Turag river in Dhaka that the

FIGURE 4. Canal choked with water hyacinth. Source: Kenneth McLean, 'Water Hyacinth. A Serious Problem in Bengal', *Agricultural Journal of India* XVII (1922).

weed could travel at the rate of three miles per hour. Apparently, a single root of the hyacinth could cover an area of more than six hundred square yards in a few months' time. In fact, it was observed in a government report that if there were any case of death of the water hyacinth, it appeared to be due to its being overgrown and submerged by its progeny. Nothing except severe frost could weaken and destroy the weed, and frost was exactly what was wanting in this tropical delta.[31] Such official representation of the 'extraordinary biological strength' of the water hyacinth did not come as a surprise since this was one of the ways to cloak the government's vulnerability in containing the weed effectively.

Though the above discussion indicates the range of predicaments to which East Bengal was exposed because of the water hyacinth, it would perhaps never be known to what extent the water hyacinth was responsible for bringing about the decline in agriculture. This was particularly because officially the weed was either perceived as a harmless nuisance or a potentially profitable plant, rather than a contributing factor to declining agrarian production. Probably on these grounds no comprehensive effort was made to monitor the statistics of the growth and impact of the weed. It is easy to investigate, for instance, the amount of rice or jute production from well preserved government statistics, but it is not so easy to gain an accurate picture on the impact of the weed, even though it had already become a public issue in the 1910s. Fortunately, however, it is possible to obtain information regarding various efforts to combat the weed in the records relating to government policies and actions and relevant responses from the wider public sphere. We will now turn to these issues.

ERADICATION OR UTILISATION?

From the very beginning of its fight against the water hyacinth, the Government of Bengal had to cope with the dilemma of whether the weed should be completely eradicated or be fruitfully utilised. The first working proposal towards utilisation came in 1914 when a Government Fibre Expert, Robert Finlow, suggested that the weed should be dragged out of the rivers and put into heaps for subsequently using it as manure. However, the government was not sure at that time how far that was an economical proposition and it seemed convinced that 'little impression would there be on the weed unless a river or *khal* (canal) was cleared thoroughly and the weed removed entirely'.[32] The Government of India also observed that the hyacinth grew so fast that once it got a start it was almost impossible to stop it and in this connection the government advised that whatever chance there might be of eradicating the weed lay in prompt action, and that when it made its first appearance in a locality it should be dealt with immediately. 'In view of the danger both to material prosperity and to general health which the spread of the plant would cause', the Government of India invited everyone, officials and non-officials alike, to co-operate in eradicating the pest.[33]

In spite of the desire of the government to destroy the hyacinth outright, the Fibre Expert retained his plan of utilisation and he, along with Kenneth McLean, Deputy Director of Agriculture, East Bengal, came forward with proposals for making financial gain for the Government by commercial utilisation of the weed. After conducting experiments in the Dhaka Agricultural Farm in 1916, they suggested that apart from high potash content, the water hyacinth was at least as rich as farm-yard manure in respect of both nitrogen and phosphoric acid. In a more specific analysis, the experts-cum-bureaucrats found that the nitrogen content of the dry material was as high as 2.24 per cent; in the damp state (containing 67.8 per cent of water) it was only 0.72 per cent. Of the 850 *maunds* (about 30 tons) of fresh green plants that were brought for experiment, about 499 *maunds* were heaped and allowed to rot, while the remainder was spread out to dry and afterwards burnt. The experts observed that owing to the high water content the rotting process involved a considerable loss of nutrients. It was found that 'by drying and burning the plant the ash obtained from 300 *maunds* of green plant gave a larger quantity of potash than was obtained from 1000 *maunds* of similar plants after rotting'. The experts noted that the rotting process involved a loss of about 70 per cent of the available potash, and 60 per cent of nitrogen. In other words, the key finding of the research was that burning water hyacinth to ash was much better than rotting it in terms of nutrient value. The experts also observed that since the fresh plant contained about 95 per cent water it could not be transported economically over any distance. The rotted plant containing about 60 per cent of water was comparable with cow-dung and it was likely that the use of the rotted material would be confined to the immediate neighbourhood of its production. But, according to these experts, the dried material was only about one twentieth of the weight of the green plant, and was thus in a much more convenient form for transport than either the green plant or the rotted material.

Such was the spirit of commerce that the water hyacinth began to be represented as something which must be reared in earnest let alone be destroyed. The experts reminded rural people that it was 'unwise to mix earth with the ash' and advised 'not to make ash in the rainy season, but to do in the dry weather after the middle of *kartik* [around Autumn]' so that the plant could be 'dried for burning without fear of rain'. It was further advised that the plant should be collected from the water before it dried up in the winter; otherwise, a lot of earth would 'stick to the roots and make the ash much less valuable'.[34]

Incidentally, a multi-national company, Messers Shaw and Wallace & Co., showed great interest in hyacinth-ash at about the same time.[35] The company offered Government of Bengal Rs.4 per full unit of potash free on rail or on board to Kolkata. The company suggested that if the ash reached them in good condition and was not adulterated, they were ready to pay between Rs. 84 and Rs. 112 per ton. Referring to the ground reality of World War One which restricted global access to potash, the company urged the Government of Bengal to 'make it known among the agriculturists and those who can promote the scheme' and it hoped to hear from the government how the matter was received by them, and later on what progress was being made.[36] The Shaw Wallace Company, however, was not satisfied by the quality of the hyacinth supplied in the early phases of the transaction. In 1918, the Company directors informed the Government of India that in future they would not buy ash containing less than 15 per cent of potash, which was worth less than Rs. 2.4 per *maund* after reaching Kolkata. In this context, the Government of India advised the people: 'Do not collect any and every hyacinth that you can get hold of: but carefully select the plant. Tall, well grown plant gives rich ash and this will only be found in water so deep that its roots cannot touch the bottom such as is found in water-ways. Short leaf stalks with bulbs on them indicate hyacinth which gives poor ash and this latter plant should never be collected for making ash for sale'.[37]

While the Government of India appeared to be informed by the demand from Shaw and Wallace in favouring the cultivation of the water hyacinth, the Government of Bengal intervened strongly at this juncture as it understood the danger of sustaining a policy of selective utilisation of the weed. It reiterated the idea of complete destruction and felt that although there was a possibility of using the hyacinth as fodder, fuel, fertiliser, ash or sale for the extraction of potash, the slow pace of experiments meant these alternatives remained unattained and were not worth waiting for, since the agriculture of Bengal as a whole was in danger. Accordingly, the Governor of Bengal emphasised that the danger from its growth was such that prompt extermination seemed to be 'the first consideration and that the question of its utilisation ... must give place to that of its complete extinction'. He suggested that it was the duty of the local bodies (District Boards, Local Boards, Union Committees and the Municipalities) to eradicate the pest by all means in their power 'whether or not arrangements could be made to use the plant profitably'.[38]

It was about this time when the seven-member Water Hyacinth Committee was appointed by the Government of Bengal with Sir Jagadish Chandra Bose, a renowned Bengali botanist, as President. The Committee held seven meetings between 16 August 1921 and 8 August 1922 before publishing its report. The Committee observed that the districts of East Bengal, except Chittagong and the Chittagong Hill Tracts, were 'all badly infested'. Considering the extraordinary rapidity at which it had been spreading in places the report termed it a 'public menace'.[39] The Committee, however, seemed to be afflicted by the ongoing dilemma of whether to destroy or utilise the weed, which was reflected in their two main recommendations: firstly, it suggested the undertaking of a scientific investigation 'first into the life history of the plant and its mode of propagation, and later on into the practical methods for its check, and the economic utilisation of the hyacinth in various ways so that the cost of operations may, to a certain extent, be recovered'. For this purpose, it was recommended that a plant physiologist, a subordinate officer of the Agricultural Department and an agricultural chemist be appointed for three years. As a whole, it seemed that the Committee took the water hyacinth mainly as an object of scientific experiment for an indefinite period of time and to recover the cost thereof from the commercial utilisation of the same.

It was no wonder that scientific research tended to concentrate more on inventing methods of fruitful utilisation of the weed than on finding ways to challenge its growth. By the time the debates about scientific means of dealing with the weed – for instance, whether the growth of the water hyacinth took place through the seeds or stem – faded in the 1920s, H.K. Sen, Ghose Professor of Applied Chemistry in the University of Calcutta, had started experimenting on the utilisation of the same. Around 1930, Sen claimed that, as with maize-stalks (Mazolith) and waste chips of wood which served a functional use in America, forming solid blocks of materials out of the hyacinth might actually similarly prove productive. Sen envisioned that before the air-dried weed was brought to the plant for converting into manufactured products, over 150 genuine agriculturists and peasants could find work for every 100 *maund*-a-day plant. At a later stage of fabrication at each such factory, 50 young men could find employment. Considering that about 4269 square miles were covered with the water hyacinth, quite a large industry might be established. According to Sen, it was possible to remove the plant to different areas from time to time and the rate of Rs. 1.8 per *maund* should be sufficiently attractive for the cultivator, with his present low wages. He also suggested that alcohol could be made out of this weed.[40]

Meanwhile, B.K. Banerjee, a contemporary commentator, identified available methods of eradication of the hyacinth, namely 'biological', 'mechanical', and 'chemical or thermal'. Banerjee did not favour the biological method on the ground that it had not been possible for biologists anywhere in the world to discover either a fungus or suitable bacterium or an animal or a plant which could destroy or at least contain the water hyacinth. With respect to mechanical method, Banerjee calculated that a labourer could destroy the weed covering an area of 800 to 1000 square feet per day, the daily wage being between six to eight *annas* [1 anna equals one-sixteenth of a rupee]. Thus, to clear an area of about 800 to 1000 square feet from the water hyacinth, the minimum cost would have been between six to eight *annas*. Banerjee also noted that the mechanical solution might lead to coercing the labouring class into clearance activities, depriving them of their daily earning from their own agricultural work. In comparison to the first two options, Banerjee found the chemical or thermal method more satisfactory on economic grounds as effectiveness. He referred to one Subimal Bose who had invented a 'spraying solution' that killed not only floating vegetative parts of the weed but also the stem which remained beneath the surface of water. According to Banerjee, Bose's spraying solution was about two *annas* per gallon—possibly less, if large scale production were arranged. Since one gallon was 'sufficient to destroy completely the weeds covering an area of 300 to 350 square feet', the cost of clearing of 900 square feet came to be about six *annas* only. Keeping all these factors in mind, Banerjee found the spraying solution a 'most satisfactory way of grappling with the problem of eradication'.[41]

In spite of several attempts, informed either by honest intention to deal with the weed or by a desire to make profit out of it, there was neither a breakthrough in scientific means of destruction nor in industrial or other forms of utilisation of the water hyacinth by the middle of the 1930s. In the face of the claims that several chemical sprays had the power to destroy the weed, some of these chemical materials were examined by the Water Hyacinth Committee, which notably included Griffiths, a South African scientist, and another Bengali chemist; but none of the claims of effectiveness of the sprays could be substantiated. At the same time, an institutional incapacity also surfaced. At the conference of the Union Boards of Dhaka in July 1933, the Governor of Bengal, Sir John Anderson, conceded that it was 'abundantly clear' that eradication could only be achieved by 'simultaneous attack over the whole field of operations'. But he noted that the Department of Agriculture and Industries, under whose purview the issue of the water hyacinth lay, had not the machinery, even if a method could be agreed upon, to carry out a local campaign against the hyacinth throughout the province.[42]

After 1936, with the introduction of Water Hyacinth Act, an opportunity arose for legal efforts in getting rid of the weed. However, twenty long years lapsed between the first initiation of the debate of destruction/utilisation and the formal legislation to combat the hyacinth in Bengal. There were instances of legislation in Cochin China (1908), in Burma (Water Hyacinth Act of 1917), in Madras (Agricultural Pests and Diseases Act of 1919), and in Assam (Water-Hyacinth Act of 1926). The question, therefore, arises as to why did it take such a long time to undertake a legislative course of action in order to fight the water hyacinth and how the legislation, when introduced, impacted on agrarian Bengal Delta. The following sections focus on these issues.

TOWARDS LEGISLATION

In 1919 the Government of Bengal made queries about the legislation on the water hyacinth that had been introduced in Burma, with a view to adopting a similar legislative measures in Bengal. After analyzing the reply from Burma, McAlpin, Secretary to the Department of Agriculture in Bengal, found that the Burmese government had dropped measures for total eradication and had confined their action to keeping open the main water-ways. In private circles McAlpin termed the letter from Burma a 'blow', felt that the Burma Water Hyacinth Act was a failure and suggested that they 'had, therefore, better say nothing about it'. McAlpin in this connection doubted that whereas an Act for total eradication had been a failure in a province where the government had greater executive powers than in Bengal, such an Act would 'most probably be quite useless' in Bengal. He, therefore, suggested dropping the question of legislation. The file was then sent to the Governor for cancellation of the programme, when the Personal Secretary to the Governor, referring to probable consequence of the development, noted: 'I am afraid this is going to be worse even than the rabbits in Australia!'[43]

While the first attempt to introduce legislation on the water hyacinth was thus dropped, a by-law was framed and was approved at a conference held in Dhaka in January 1921. The Dhaka conference resolved that legislation was the only way to contain the water hyacinth. It was nevertheless found that a similar by-law was not introduced in other districts, except sparingly in a few sub-districts; nor was the government ready to legislate the issue of eradication of the water hyacinth on a comprehensive scale all over the province. It was reported that the government was awaiting the result of the working of the Dhaka by-law before committing itself to any form of legislation.[44] But the Dhaka by-law itself was far from being operationally perfect. Apart from being localised in nature, the by-law was weak as it did not provide for notices for clearing to be issued more than once a year. The Water Hyacinth Committee itself reported that the Dhaka by-law failed in that it only stipulated clearance of the weed once a year though experiments had shown at least two clearings were necessary within a short interval as there were generally a number of plants missed in the first clearing. It appeared, however, that even if there were clearing operations more than once a year or even once a month, the situation probably would not have improved as reflected in the statement of some of the delegates of the Dhaka conference who were against the very idea of local legislation. They argued that each district was affected differently by the hyacinth, and it was difficult to impose penalties on individuals who claimed that the land was invaded by the hyacinth from upstream in another district. It was agreed by the delegates that District Boards were powerless unless an Act was introduced and applied all over India.[45]

The Water Hyacinth Committee prescribed that 'some form of legislation should be adopted which will ensure that concerted action is taken when applying methods designed to destroy the weed'. While these recommendations were placed, it became apparent, from the minutes of the meetings of the Committee, that it was not easy to translate them into reality. The wording of the recommendations was such that legislation would follow the invention of scientific methods of eradication. There was also the question of political correctness in that, as argued by Sir Jagadish Bose himself, any kind of legislation could be misunderstood and antagonise the people and create trouble, while owing to the poor state of funding, the government would not be able to aid the people. Another member of the Committee, S.N. Sufi, remarked that they could not penalise people unless they [the Committee on the Hyacinth] could tell the sufferers the best way of eliminating the weed. He warned that their best intention might be thwarted by the fear that they were simply going to introduce a new mode of taxation without doing any appreciable good.[46] Though the committee members felt legislation would be politically incorrect, they nevertheless recommended 'some form of legislation', not a legislation of a comprehensive kind. This of course was a wrong line of action since, given the pattern of spreading of the hyacinth, no agenda could have been successful in eradicating the weed without a comprehensive inter-district and inter-provincial effort. At the same time, the Committee, though aware of its practicality, did not recommend frequent and regular cycle of destruction of the weed. For instance, in the case of French Cochin China it was made obligatory for the landlords and tenants to clear the weed during the first three days of every month. Though authorities in French Cochin China failed to apply the regulations rigorously, it was nevertheless found that the very idea of monthly clearings was never taken up in the by-laws and regulations in Bengal. The question of legislation was further held up in the wake of the economic depression of early 1930s.[47]

The debate about the ways and means of dealing with the hyacinth continued anyway, particularly in relation to the recommendation of the Royal Commission on Agriculture in India. In their report, the Commission recommended that the problem of the water hyacinth in Bengal should be dealt with by legislation similar to that which had been enacted in Assam, Burma and Madras. It doubted, however, whether legislation prescribing the destruction of the hyacinth, or measures to prevent its spread such as the construction of storage pounds or floating fences, would prove more than palliative. The Commission, therefore, recommended that the formulation of a programme for research on this weed should be one of the first questions to be taken up by the proposed Council of Agricultural Research. The Government of India favoured the second of these recommendations.[48]

While the question of legislation was shelved as a matter of secondary importance, the prioritised scheme of research on the destruction of the weed surprisingly failed to include Bengal whereas Bihar and Orissa, where the problem was much less acute than in Bengal, was given more attention. After examining the papers sent from the above three provinces, the Council felt deeply about the situation in Bihar and Orissa, but with respect to Bengal it came to the conclusion that 'no action was required on the part of the Council'.[49] The Bengal Waterways Act which was passed a few years later, in 1934, made only a passing reference to the problem of the hyacinth. The Act suggested the formation of a Waterways Board which could clear or destroy the weed in any district where there were 'navigable channels under the control and administration of the Board'. This meant that the water hyacinth of only the large 'navigable channels' came under the jurisdiction of the Board.[50]

At last, the first all-Bengal legislation was passed in 1936. The Act provided for some tough measures in the case of failure to eradicate the weed. In some ways, the legislation appeared to be too tough and difficult to sustain for ordinary people. By this Act, the collector of a district was empowered, if he failed to recover the cost of eradication, to enter on and take possession of any land or water at his discretion. He could do so when costs were due and he had the power to retain possession of the land and 'turn the same to profitable account until the said costs together with interest thereon' could be realised from the profits or paid by the occupier. The ceiling of the interest rate was fixed at 6.25 per cent.[51] The Act of 1936 also stipulated that the amount so spent by the Collector in the course of eradication of the weed would be 'recovered from the persons benefited with interest'. Beside the vexed question of interest this legislation made one thing clear: the Government took no responsibility which now rested entirely on the occupiers of land affected by the weed,[52] although the Water Hyacinth Committee of 1921 had warned against such a measure, i.e., legislating without instructing how to eradicate the weed. The Act of 1936 neither specifically stated when and how many times a year/month clearing operations had to be undertaken. Then there was the problem of infringement on private areas. By this Act, the Collector of a district gained the power to use land for the destruction of the water hyacinth for six months. For compensation, it was provided that if any material damage or injury was caused thereby to the occupier of such land, the Collector shall 'pay to him such compensation as shall be agreed upon in writing between the Collector and such occupier; provided that in assessing such compensation the manurial value of water hyacinth destroyed thereon shall be taken into account'. In addition, the very idea of eradication, as envisioned in the legislation, was defeated in that the provision of the possibility of commercial uses of the weed were left intact. In Clause 18, it was stated that notwithstanding anything contained elsewhere in this Act, any person or class of persons, authorised by the Local Government, might 'sell, remove or keep water hyacinth for a prescribed purpose'.[53]

LEGISLATION AND BEYOND

It seems that even if the 1936 Act had been better crafted, drives for eradication of the water hyacinth could probably not have been successful, particularly because the government failed to prioritise the issue of containing the weed within its general schema of governance. For instance, before launching an inside-out drive against the hyacinth following the legislation, the government decided to wait until the results of the research on the weed, which was being carried out in Orissa under the auspices of the newly formed Council of Agricultural Research, had been received. The Government hoped that the research in the Council would produce sufficient new materials to justify a re-examination of the whole water hyacinth problem.[54] In June 1938, the Minister in Charge of the Agriculture Department, Tamizuddin Khan, informed the Legislative Council that an accurate estimate of the area covered by the hyacinth throughout the province of Bengal would require considerable time and expenditure and a comprehensive drive for eradication was not considered necessary.[55]

In the last week of April in 1939 a 'Water Hyacinth Week' was launched by the government to start a 'concerted and simultaneous drive' all over the Province in order to eradicate the weed. This appeared to be the best possible effort on the part of the Muslim League-Krishak Praja coalition government to meet its election pledges, which had included an assurance of eradication of the water hyacinth. The Week brought a mood of enlightened festivity: civil servants were mobilised, ministers moved into every corner in the countryside, and people in general joined hands – all in the name of eradicating the water hyacinth. Students were advised to form boat racing clubs in the hope that once established, members of the club would have the 'double enjoyment' in not only participating in boat races but clearing the weed wherever they appeared. In some areas, boys were encouraged to kill as many snakes as possible since these snakes often hid in the thick mat of the water hyacinth. In Dhaka, a 17-year old boy was promised a gold medal for bagging most of the 64 snakes killed during Water Hyacinth Week. The girls did not lag behind the race and the Chief Minister of Bengal, H.S. Suhrawardy, himself acknowledged that the work done by some of the school girls in Bogra District was 'even better than the results achieved by the boys'.[56] Observing the enthusiasm of the Scouts, school boys, pundits, maulovis, peasants, landlords and lawyers in Kishorganj, Suhrawardy hoped that in 'fighting common enemies like water hyacinth, there should be no difference between the different communities' and that the 'healthy teamwork was bound to destroy all Hindu Muslim quarrels'.[57]

At the end of the Week, however, it was found that apart from one English civil servant having 'sun-stroke' and another being 'stuck in the mud',[58] no long-lasting solutions to the problem beyond political show-downs were in the sight. No doubt considerable areas were cleared of the weed, but as the Week ended, the orchestrated enthusiasm also faded away: the ministers returned to Kolkata, the officials to their sub-divisional headquarters and the school-goers to the classrooms. Those peasants and villagers who had been in the actual field of agrarian activities before the Hyacinth Week continued to face the same water hyacinth, which apparently survived the Week. To celebrate a Water Hyacinth Week might have been a politically correct move from a ruling party, but its failure was equally inevitable precisely because the problem was also biological and environmental in nature, which demanded an examination of the changes in the ecological system that encouraged the growth of the plant. These issues were indeed raised. Two weeks before the Water Hyacinth Week was launched, Sudhir Chandar Sur opposed the idea of such a Week which he thought was intended to remove the water hyacinth without treating the causes of its growth. Sur attributed the growth of the weed to the obstacles to the current of rivers and other water courses posed by cross roadways, railway embankments and the feet of pillars of railway bridges. Sur argued that due to obstacles, different waterways failed to perform their natural function of clearing away large amounts of organic matter to the sea via bigger rivers. This resulted in the deposition of this organic matter in the beds of the watercourses and the water hyacinth found a congenial environment there. But Sur felt that compared to the long-term implications of the blockage of water currents, the effect of the water hyacinth was minimal. Sur even suggested that the water hyacinth was better for the time being since it consumed organic matter, preventing many parts of the Delta being transformed into marshes charged with animal organic matter. In this context, Sur thought that he would welcome the water hyacinth for some time until the weed itself threatened to choke up the already dying water courses of Bengal. He suggested that the water hyacinth itself should not be tackled unless the artificial agencies which had reduced the water currents in big rivers had been tackled first, since development in this direction would automatically lead to the clearance of the weed.[59]

There is no denying that Water Hyacinth Act of 1936 reflected a growing consensus on the importance of getting rid of the weed and concern for the agro-ecological future of East Bengal. What seems important in this context is to examine how this consensus was informed and articulated by different agencies in the society and the state. In many cases local efforts were frustrated by lack of cooperation and coordination between the government and common people as well as between different government departments. For instance, it was alleged that in the *Arial beel* areas in Munshiganj of Dhaka, about fifty thousand flood-stricken cultivators had cultivated their lands having invested substantial borrowed capital with the encouragement of a certain local government officer.

But the cultivators were at the brink of disaster as no initiatives to implement a promised Water Control Scheme had taken place. When this was referred to in the Legislative Assembly, the Minister for Agriculture noted that it was not a government scheme but was 'suggested, worked and paid for by the local people with the assistance of a Special Officer'. The scheme was specifically aimed at constructing a barricade across the waterways surrounding the low lands of the *beel* in order to check the spread of the hyacinth, but the Speaker of the Assembly categorically denied any government responsibility regarding this and remarked that the construction of a barricade rested entirely on the local people. However, the Speaker did not elaborate why in such circumstance the peasants would resort to agitation.[60] In another instance, while it was claimed by the provincial government of Bengal that the Act of 1936 was introduced to empower the district authorities, land belonging to railway authorities were not covered by the Act as this was under the control of the Government of India.[61] Since railway and roadside ditches and waterways blocked by railway embankments were places of regeneration and growth of the hyacinth, the exclusion of these lands from the jurisdiction covered by the Act of 1936 amounted to a technical farce as far as the programme of eradication of the water hyacinth was concerned.

An amended Bengal Water Hyacinth (Amendment) Act, 1940, empowered an authorised officer to prepare a scheme of any work relating to the water hyacinth and to realise the cost for such scheme proportionately from the persons benefitting from this scheme. There was, however, no provision empowering the authorised officer to realise the cost of the removal and destruction of the water hyacinth which could be intercepted in any common flowing channel as a result of the execution of such a scheme. Therefore, instructions were given to the authorised officer to be 'so good as to take every care in the execution of schemes under section 3 of the Amendment Act so that no water hyacinth is intercepted in any flowing channel'.[62] Then there was the problem of co-ordination in the whole project of combating the water hyacinth. A special officer, who was appointed to deal with the water haycinth, noted that work against the weed, including local clearance and the setting up of barriers in key positions, could not be implemented properly because of differential administrative arrangements. For instance, the officer observed that government works relating to water supply or setting up of dispensaries were done more or less by respective decentralised departments, but this was not the case with the water hyacinth. This meant that, in terms of dealing with the water hyacinth problem, there was no contractor to take over the work and carry this out in anticipation of payment and that there was no organised agency to help.[63]

Given the varied and often self-seeking response to the problem of the water hyacinth by different agencies within the society and the government, the legislation and apparent consensus to destroy the weed was found to be ineffective in many ways. The lack of genuine efforts to tackle the problem was amply matched by the lack of focus on the problem of the hyacinth within the policies and programmes of local political groups. Referring to the fact that there was an unthinkable *hahakar* [widespread hopelessness] and tremendous poverty in Bengal due to the growth of the 'bloody plant', a Bengali newspaper commented:

> The rural inhabitants of Bengal have gradually become sick and idle. There is no enthusiasm, nor encouragement or initiative among them. They don't try to destroy this enemy [hyacinth]. They are sitting idle thinking that this is a curse from God. If some day God himself withdraws the weed, only then their lands would be free and the mouths of the rivers be opened. This class of fatalist cowards even dreams of *swaraj* [self-rule, as opposed to British colonial rule]! [64]

Thus, the water hyacinth survived the wrath of the Bengal Chamber of Commerce in the 1910s, the scientist's chemical spray in the 1920s, and electoral commitment, legislation and above all a historic 'water hyacinth week' in the 1930s – all aiming toward its destruction. Ultimately, it also survived in two consecutive post-colonial states, Pakistan and Bangladesh. Indeed, it still occupies a major portion of the water bodies in Bangladesh. For a tiny, relatively weak aquatic weed, ninety per cent of which comprised harmless water with a tinge of 'feminine' beauty, this has been no mean achievement.

CONCLUSION

In the wake of the weakening struggle against the water hyacinth in late colonial Bengal, one commentator noted, as quoted above, that if the nationalists who wanted independence from British colonial rule were not even successful in fighting a water weed, then how would they be able to run a nation? But, as we see today, the problem of invasive species as well as other environmental issues cannot be simply tagged with post-colonial promises. Perhaps the strongest threads that connect the colonial state to post-colonial state are the varied ways in which the forces, agencies and ideas shape the unstable parameters of governance. The dilemma of pursuing simultaneous programmes in development and conservation persists today in an even more complex form. For the specific case of the water hyacinth, in Bangladesh as well as in other developing countries, the debate continues whether to completely eradicate the weed or utilise it for profit and development. Those who are in favour of complete eradication of the hyacinth refer to its link with cholera, malaria, dengue, depletion of fish resources and even climatic change. Considering the predicament of the water hyacinth in developing countries, S. Gopal, an authority on this plant, has cautioned against its utilisation. He notes: 'Developing countries should not encourage the propagation of this weed for utilisation. The interests of humanity can only be safeguarded by seeking effective long-term control of water hyacinth, rather than by its utilisation.'[65] But there are others who enthusiastically favour the utilisation of the weed, for example, in the form of making paper or toys, using it in the biogas plants and removing arsenic from water. The hyacinth has even been used to explain cultural politics of feminism in Bangladesh by a feminist group which think that the water hyacinth is a beautiful plant with attractive flowers, but as a weed it represents the peripheral condition of women in the male-dominated society and, therefore, it 'challenges this concept as the women's movement does to the partriarchal notions'![66]

What can the state do? There is hardly any doubt that the water hyacinth is a serious invasive species that has settled in at least 50 countries in the southern hemisphere; but it is also true the state has gained some power with its significant control over science and technology.[67] Researchers have identified and developed many useful biological and chemical means of fighting invasive species, but the water hyacinth, in particular, remains a problem because there persists lack of political will as well as consensus among private business concerns and the people at large in a given multitude of interests, ideas and forces. Without finding a solution to the myriad of social and economic problems, scientific feats alone may not be helpful in finding a working solution to the problem of invasive species in general.[68] Therefore, unless the state is able to sponsor a balanced relationship between science and human psychological and material orientations, the water hyacinth is going to stay with us.

FIGURE 5. A tank choked with hyacinth in Comilla town in central Bangladesh.
Photo taken by the author in Autumn 2003.

NOTES

An earlier version of the essay was read by Professors Christopher Bayly, David Arnold and Alfred Crosby whose comments were greatly helpful and much appreciated. I am indebted to anonymous reviewers whose critical interventions made it possible to put my arguments into proper perspective.

[1] Some representative works include Richard Tucker, 'Dimensions of Deforestation in Himalaya: The Historical Setting', *Mountain Research and Development* VII, 3 (1987): 328–31; M. Rangarajan, 'Production, Desiccation and Forest Management in the Central Provinces, 1850–1930', *Indian Economic and Social History Review* 31 (1994): 147–67; Richard Grove, *Green Imperialism: Colonial Expansion, Tropical Island Edens, and the Origins of Environmentalism, 1600–1800* (Cambridge: Cambridge University Press, 1995); *Environment and History* 2, 2 (1996: Special issue on South Asia).

[2] For studies on water, see Ian Stone, *Canal Irrigation in British India: Perspectives on Technological Change in a Peasant Society* (Cambridge: Cambridge University Press, 1984); Rohan D'Souza, *Drowned and Dammed* (Delhi: Oxford University Press, 2006). An assessment of water-related works in colonial India can be found in Rohan D'Souza, 'Water in British India: The Making of a "Colonial Hydrology"', *History Compass* 4, 4 (2006): 621–28; For a collection of useful essays on both forest and water history in India, see David Arnold and Ramachandra Guha (eds.), *Nature, Culture, Imperialism: Essays on the Environmental History of South Asia* (Delhi: Oxford University Press, 1995).

[3] Ramachandra Guha, *The Unquiet Woods: Ecological Change and Peasant Resistance in the Himalaya* (Berkeley: University of California Press, 1990); Ramachandra Guha and Madhav Gadgil, 'State Forestry and Social Conflict in British India', *Past and Present*, 123 (May, 1989): 141–77; Arun Agrawal, *Environmentality: Technologies of Government and the Making of Subjects* (Durham, N.C.: Duke University Press. 2005); David Hardiman, 'Power in the Forest: the Dang 1820–1920', in *Subaltern Studies* VIII, (New Delhi, 1994); Ajay Skaria, *Hybrid Histories. Forests, Frontiers and Wilderness in Western India* (New Delhi, 1999).

[4] The presence of the plant was first considerably felt in Florida in the 1890s, in Queensland of Australia in 1895, in South Africa in 1900, in Cochin China in 1908, and in Myanmar in about 1913. By this time, it had invaded most of Southern and northern Africa.

[5] Kabita Ray, *History of Public Health. Colonial Bengal 1921–1947* (Calcutta: K. P. Bagchi and Company, 1998), 284; See also Seith Drucquer, 'On the Rivers of East Bengal', *The Geographical Magazine* XII (March 1941): 150–51.

[6] Drucquer, 'On the Rivers of East Bengal', 350; This theory seems quite plausible since there is evidence that towards the end of the nineteenth century the number of visitors to Calcutta Botanic Garden increased to such an extent that the authorities found it difficult to deal with cases of violation of the garden rules. This had made it necessary to request the government to sanction certain additional rules. See *Annual Report of the Royal Botanic Garden* (Calcutta: Government of Bengal [hereafter, GoB], *1897–8*), 1.

[7] 'Council Question', March 1921, Agriculture and Industries Department [hereafter, AID] (Agriculture Branch), bundle 34, list 14, file 6, National Archives of Bangladesh, Dhaka [hereafter, NAB].

[8] About the German 'conspiracy', see Kabita Ray, *History of Public Health*, 284–5.

⁹ For a note on plant research and plant migration at the hands of private companies, see William Neinary and Karen Middleton, 'Plant Transfers in Historical Perspective: A Review Article', *Environment and History* 10 (2004): 3–29, p. 13.

¹⁰ AID (Agriculture Branch), 1921, 'A' Proceedings, bundle 34, list 14, file 32, NAB.

¹¹ *Amrita Bazar Patrika (*Hereafter *ABP)*, 26 March 1926, 4.

¹² J. Chaudhuri, 'Agrarian Problems of Bengal–1', *The Bengal Cooperative Journal* [hereafter, *BCJ*] XXI (January–March 1936): 117.

¹³ Radhakamal Mukerjee noted in the early 1930s that a 'few prickly pears introduced into Eastern Australia and water hyacinth into the delta of Eastern Bengal – both as botanic curiosities – have now covered thousands of miles and become a serious menace to agriculture, and communications'. See Radhakamal Mukerjee, 'An Ecological Approach to Sociology', in Ramachandra Guha (ed.), *Social Ecology* (Delhi: Oxford University Press, 1994), 25.

¹⁴ *Bengal Legislative Assembly Proceedings (Hereafter BLAP)* LIII (1938): 224–5.

¹⁵ *BLAP* LIV (1939): 93; also see *BLAP* LV (1940): 273–4.

¹⁶ *BLAP* LIV (1939): 32–3

¹⁷ 'Lilac Devil in Bengal', *ABP*, 21 August 1928, 12.

¹⁸ Benoyendranath Banerjee, 'Some Economic Problems of Bengal — 1: The water hyacinth', *BCJ* XIX (1933): 32, 35.

¹⁹ J. Chaudhuri, 'Agrarian Problems of Bengal–1'.

²⁰ Mostopha Kamal Pasha, 'Water Hyacinth', *Banglapedia. National Encyclopaedia of Bangladesh* (Dhaka: Asiatic Society of Bangladesh, 2002).

²¹ 'A Note on the Water Hyacinth', by Kenneth McLean, Secretary to Water Hyacinth Committee, in *Report of Water Hyacinth Committee* (Calcutta, 1922), (hereafter, *RWHC*), XVI; See also M.C. McAlpin's note of 16 April 1919, in Revenue Department (Agriculture), 'A' Proceedings, nos. 24–27, July 1919, NAB.

²² *BLAP* LIV (1939): 458–60; *BLAP* LIII (1938): 378–80.

²³ 'Geographical Records', *Geographical Review* 36, 2 (1946): 329.

²⁴ Babu Nibaran Chandra Das Gupta, *Bengal Legislative Council Proceedings* (hereafter, *BLCP)* I, 3 (1921): 76–7.

²⁵ Recent researches, however, have proved that *V. cholerae* are found to concentrate on the surface of the water packed with the water hyacinth. See W.M. Spira et al., 'Uptake of *V. cholerae* Biotype El Tor from Contaminated Water by Water Hyacinth (*Eichornia crassipes)*', *Applied Environmental Microbiology* 42 (1981): 550–3.

²⁶ C.A. Bentley's note on 15 February 1921, AID (Agriculture Branch), bundle 34, list 14, file 10, NAB.

²⁷ Report by S.N. Sur, Assistant Director of Public Health, Malaria Research Unit, Bengal, 24 September 1926, NAB; The debates whether mosquitoes could thrive with the water hyacinth was going on also in the US about this time. In response to the suggestion by a biologist that the growth of water hyacinth over the surface of a body of water was immediately followed by the destruction of mosquito larvae in that water, another biologist, Alfred Weed, referring to the result of his research, noted that the growth of water hyacinth over the water was 'followed by a great increase in the mosquito population'. See Alfred C. Weed, 'Another Factor in Mosquito Control', *Ecology* 5 (January 1924): 110–11.

[28] Benoyendranath Banerjee, 'Some Economic Problems of Bengal—1'.

[29] 'Tour diaries of the Collector of Bakarganj', J.T. Donovan Papers, file I: Bengal 1927–1931, Centre of South Asian Studies, Cambridge, UK (Hereafter, CSAS).

[30] Babu Nibaran Chandra Das Gupta, in *BLCP*, 1, 3 (1921): 76–7; for other references to the devastation caused by the water hyacinth in Bengal see *BLAP*, LIX, 4: 159; LIV, 2: 138; XXXIV, 3: 632. See also M. Azizul Huque, *The Man Behind the Plough* (Calcutta, 1939), 16; L.S.S. O'Malley, *Bengal District Gazetteers: Faridpur* (Calcutta, 1925), 8.

[31] *RWHC*, 2, xv–xvii.

[32] J.R. Blackwood, Director of Agriculture, Bengal to Secretary to GoB, Revenue Department, 2 September 1915, bundle 34, list 14, file 202, NAB.

[33] 'Water Hyacinth', Communiqué of the Government of India, Revenue Department (Agriculture Branch), Proceedings nos. 24–27, July 1919, file, 9-M-1, NAB (hereafter 'Communique')

[34] Robert S. Finlow, 'Water Hyacinth (kachuri, Tagoi, or Bilati Pana)', 9 November 1917, in 'Communiqué'.

[35] Since its birth in 1886, the Shaw Wallace Company dealt in different businesses including tea, Bengal silk, oil, tinplates, shipping of jute and gunnies, flour mills, coal mining, Swiss dyes and chemicals, and from 1944 to 1947 as one of the Bengal Government's chief rice and paddy procurement agencies. In 1914, the Company started operations in the business of fertiliser 'specializing in organic and inorganic mixtures for plantation and ryot crops'. It is not clear though whether the Shaw Wallace had a hand in introducing the water hyacinth in East Bengal or whether the water hyacinth dragged Shaw Wallace into East Bengal. But it is probable that the Company's turning to the Bengal water hyacinth may have been informed by the introduction, in 1917, of the Water Hyacinth Act in Burma, where the Company had business concern. For a profile of the Shaw Wallace Company see 'The Varied Activities of Shaw Wallace', in the Bengal Chambers of Commerce Centenary Supplement, *ABP*, 24 March 1946, 26.

[36] Messrs Shaw Wallace & Co., Calcutta to Fibre Expert to GoB, 12 August 1916, Revenue Department (Agriculture Branch), in 'Communiqué'.

[37] Notice no. 2, in 'Communiqué'.

[38] M.C. McAlpin, Secretary to GoB, Revenue Department, to All Commissioners of Divisions, 3 July 1919, AID (Agriculture Branch), 'A' Proceedings nos. 26–27, bundle 34, list 14, file 9-M-11 (5), NAB.

[39] *RWHC*, 2.

[40] 'Agrarian problems of Bengal', *BCJ* XXI (1936): 118; See also Benoyendranath Banerjee, 'Some economic problems of Bengal—1': 34.

[41] B.K. Banerjee, 'Water Hyacinth', *ABP*, 25 September 1935, 8. It may be noted that this argument was taken up in spite of the fact that Sir Jagadish Chandra Bose himself objected to any chemical option as he feared that it could lead to water pollution affecting both humans and fish.

[42] Banerjee, 'Some Economic Problems of Bengal—1': 34–5.

[43] 'Extracts from notes and orders in Agriculture', Revenue Department (Agriculture Branch), 'A' Proceedings for July 1919, nos. 24–27, file 9-M–11, NAB; The metaphor of the 'Rabbits of Australia' appears pertinent from the following fact: 'Sometime in the 1850's a man was charged at the Colac (Victoria) Police Court with having shot a rabbit,

the property of John Robertson of Glen Alvie. He was fined 10 pounds. A few years later, Robertson's son spent 5000 pounds a year in an attempt to control rabbits.' By 1869 it was estimated that 2,033,000 rabbits had been destroyed on his property and that they were as thick as ever. http://rubens.anu.edu.au/student.projects/rabbits/history.html , last accessed 2 April 2005.

[44] AID (Agriculture Branch), bundle 34, list 14, file 6, 1921, NAB; See also G.P. Hogg, Secretary to GoB, to the Secretary to Government of India, Department of Education, Health and Lands, 3 August 1929, AID (Agriculture Branch), bundle 34, list 14, file b155, NAB.

[45] *RWHC*, XXIX–XXX

[46] *RWHC*, III, VI.

[47] G.P. Hogg, Secretary to GoB, to the Secretary to Government of India, Department of Education, Health and Lands, 3 August 1929, AID (Agriculture Branch), bundle 34, list 14, file b155, NAB.

[48] A.B. Reid, Joint Secretary to Government of India, Department of Education, Health and Lands, to Secretary to GoB, AID, 22 May 1929, AID (Agriculture Branch), bundle 34, list 14, file 155, NAB.

[49] (Second) Report showing the progress made in giving effect to the recommendations of the Royal Commission on Agriculture in India. Part I—Central Government, for the period 1st November 1929 to 31st December 1930', Public Health Department, 'B' Proceedings, nos. 110–115, list 14, bundle 15, file P.H. 2C-2, NAB.

[50] Bengal Act XII of 1934: The Bengal Waterways Act, 1934, section 41 (5); 'navigable channel' meant 'any channel which is navigable during the whole or a part of the year by a vessel of two-foot draught or over'; this approach to selective means to tackle the weed came at a time when all discussions of getting rid of the plant seemed to end in 'nothing but a tacit admission that it was too costly and altogether too vast an undertaking'. See 'Personal Reminiscence', E.W. Holland Papers, p. 32, CSAS.

[51] Bengal Act XIII of 1936: The Bengal Water Hyacinth Act 1936 and the Rules Thereunder, Clause 12.

[52] Kabita Ray, *History of Public Health*, 295.

[53] Bengal Act XIII of 1936.

[54] Answer by Nawab K.G.M Faroqui to the question by Maharaja Giris Chandra Nandi, *BLCP* XLV, 342

[55] *Bengal Legislative Debates* (1939): 970–2.

[56] *ABP*, 5 May 1939, 8.

[57] *ABP*, 4 May 1939, 4.

[58] Most of the English civil servants apparently enjoyed the occasional drives for dealing with the water hyacinth as these provided a break from routine office work. O.M. Martin recollected that 'in order to encourage this movement, my wife and I would don bathing costumes and do manual labour along with the villagers. Some of the villagers took up the work with great enthusiasm, and I could easily have made every villager join in the work, if I had allowed the vigorous minority to coerce the lazy majority. Sometimes the volunteers begged me for permission to take sticks in their hands, and drive the lazy ones to the work. I did not dare to give this permission, without any legal authority to do so; but at times I was sorely tempted to let the enthusiasts have their way. It was not a job

that everybody liked, as the water-hyacinth was full of curious repulsive-looking creatures like snakes and crabs. But it was a healthy change from scribbling notes on office files.' See 'Memoirs of O.M. Martin, part II', O.M. Martin Papers, p, 308, CSAS.

[59] Sudhir Chundar Sur, *ABP*, 14 April 1939, 16.

[60] *BLAP* LIV (1939): 87–8.

[61] *BLAP* LII (1938): 378–80.

[62] K.C. Basak, Secretary to GoB, AID, to Collector, Faridpur, 7 June 1941, Faridpur Files, General Department (Revenue), Collection no. 3A, File 20, NAB.

[63] Special Officer, Water-Hyacinth, to District Magistrate, Faridpur, 17 February 1941, Faridpur Files, General Department (Revenue), Collection no. 3A, File 20, NAB.

[64] 'Attempts to Destroy the Water Hyacinth', *Dacca Prakash*, 3 March 1935, 5.

[65] Quoted in http://www.fao.org/docrep/006/y5031e/y5031e0c.htm#bm12 , last accessed 8 October 2007.

[66] See http://membres.lycos.fr/ubinig/eventboimela.htm, last accessed 8 October 2007.

[67] Raymond L. Bryant and Sinead Bailey, *Third World Political Ecology* (London: Routledge, 1997), 53.

[68] Philip E. Hulme, 'Biological Invasions: Winning the Science Battles but Losing the Conservation War', *Oryx* 37, 2 (2003): 178–93.

'An Enemy of the Rabbit': The Social Context of Acclimatisation of an Immigrant Killer

Philippa K. Wells

INTRODUCTION

There is little doubt that Victorian Britons were enthusiastic practitioners of the art of acclimatisation in colonised lands. New Zealand was one of those lands colonised not only by British immigrants but also by a veritable army of plants, birds, fish, insects, and mammals. Although some of those introductions have proved benevolent and at times beneficial, there have also been those for which we in the present can find few or no redeeming features, such as gorse, broom and the Australian brush-tailed possum. However, in judging those dedicated individuals, Acclimatisation Societies and Governments who were directly or indirectly responsible for introductions now considered undesirable, it is important to appreciate the historical context in which such introductions were made. Frequently it would not have occurred to advocates that there might be serious negative consequences for native flora and fauna. After all, the new species did not threaten the existence of target species at their point of origin and there was little or no evidence that might suggest that things would be different in New Zealand. Even where there were warnings of negative impacts, advocates were prepared to accept that (perhaps regrettable) possibility in the interests of the greater good achieved thereby.

The history of the family Mustelidae (mustelids, specifically stoats, weasels and ferrets) in New Zealand, serves as a salutary tale in this respect. Their introduction as predators on the rabbit population has been described by King as 'a simple matter of survival ... farmers were struggling for their lives'.[1] Nevertheless, the history is arguably unusual for the period in that it was by no means uncontroversial either at the outset or by the conclusion. In addition, it is significant in signalling shifts in a broader discourse of acclimatisation as a means of effecting change.

By way of justifying this claim, this paper is organised as follows. First, it briefly traces the historical and philosophical background against which these predators were identified as 'a simple matter of survival'. Secondly, it plots and contextualises the political debate that finally led to their sanction and support. Thirdly, an all-important epilogue to the story traces and rationalises shifts in the political status of mustelids in New Zealand between 1888 and 1903. Finally, this history is placed in its wider context of acclimatisation as a historically-specific manifestation of a discourse of change.

HISTORICAL BACKGROUND

Mid-nineteenth-century New Zealand was not new to acclimatised species. The Maori, on their arrival in previous centuries, had brought with them such species as the gourd (hue), sweet potato (kumara), dog (kuri) and rat (kiore). European species made their first appearance with Captain Cook's visit in 1773, when he landed the pig that came to be known as the Captain Cooker in Ship Cove in the Bay of Islands, and planted cabbages on Long Island. In the fifty years following the onset of widespread British settlement in 1840, over 180 species of exotic fauna and a large range of exotic flora were to arrive in the colony. Many of these new-species introductions were neither accidental nor incidental but were in large part a reflection of a popular and official conceptualisation of the colony as the 'Britain of the South'. Two distinct but overlapping meanings can be associated with this term, both of which were instrumental in shaping contemporary acclimatisation practice.

BRITAIN OF THE SOUTH AND ACCLIMATISATION

First, New Zealand offered a romantically- envisaged, even Utopian, 'Britain of the South'. Although R. Grove identifies the powerful symbolism of the tropics (garden and island) as offering those seeking escape from the decadence and corruption of Europe – 'a possibility of redemption, a realism in which paradise might be recreated or realised on earth, thereby implying a structure for a moral world'[2] – such symbolism can equally, or perhaps even more validly,[3] be located in temperate locations such as New Zealand. Settlers, who through duty, necessity or desire were compelled to leave a land corrupt, urbanised, overcrowded and polluted, had the 'British plough' to convert the New Zealand 'desert'[4] into 'its original garden-like condition';[5] and the things of 'home'[6] to fill it – including game birds and songsters (for example, pheasants, quail, larks and thrush), shade trees (oak and elm) and small animals (including rabbits and hares).

However, a distinctly pragmatic undertone can often be detected to such romantically-inspired acclimatisation: rabbits and hares would be a source of meat and skins; goats would be useful for clearing scrub; and shade trees would provide shelter and timber. Even 'fellow passenger', when waxing lyrical over the delightful habits and appeal of small birds, also drew specific attention to their usefulness: 'the value of [thrush and starling] to the agriculturalist cannot be overstated'.[7]

'AN ENEMY OF THE RABBIT'

A second meaning frequently attributed to the 'Britain of the South' is that of economic pragmatism, echoed in moves by Britain to pursue colonisation as a means of keeping New Zealand's putative resources out of the hands of France, and in contemporary writings, speeches and attitudes.[8] In the immediate case of acclimatisation, P. Star argues that utility served as an important impetus, citing the Otago Acclimatization Society in support: 'no country requires ... acclimatization to add to its resources more than New Zealand'.[9] The country had no large protein sources (being populated mainly by small birds and carrying no indigenous land mammals), only a small range of edible root vegetables and virtually no fruit. In accordance with such a purpose, early examples of introductions include sheep, poultry, cattle, pigs, various fodder and vegetable plants, bumble (or humble) bees (to fertilise red clover) and birds such as sparrows to 'kill pests (caterpillars) for farmers'.[10]

However, it can be argued that such pragmatism had a romantic aspect. The allotment scheme devised by the New Zealand Company in the case of the Wellington settlement – one urban to 100 rural acres – and the celebration of 'the soil-based family as the fundamental foundation of the social order'[11] were to help shape an enduring truth of rural virtue. 'Numerous politicians' speeches, newspaper editorials and even doggerel reiterated the view of British critics of industrialisation that the transition from a rural to an urban society constituted some kind of fall'.[12] New Zealand's destiny as the 'Britain of the South' therefore lay in agriculture, 'with predominantly European people growing European crops and raising European sheep and cattle on European grass',[13] a destiny requiring acclimatisation of those species.

Regardless of underlying motivation for particular instances of acclimatisation, New Zealand practitioners in the nineteenth century looked to the local scientific community for support and advice in its realisation,[14] just as they did for other changes to the landscape. In justifying such assistance, scientists could look to a particular theoretical construct – the Displacement Theory or displacement.

JUSTIFICATION – DISPLACEMENT

Briefly, this theory – an extension of the Darwinian concept of 'survival of the fittest' – has been described as a 'nineteenth century blind alley'[15] that nevertheless had influential supporters, including contemporary scientists and writers,[16] who referred to its concepts in explaining and predicting the decline of species in New Zealand after the commencement of colonisation. As Charles Darwin explained: 'if all the animals and plants of Great Britain were set free in New Zealand, a multitude of British forms would in the course of time become thoroughly naturalized there, and would exterminate many of the natives'.[17]

The theory was also instrumental in shaping attitudes with respect to the management and use of the forest resource.[18] Indicatively, in criticising Premier Sir Julius Vogel's[19] forest conservation proposals in 1874, John Sheehan, in the House of Representatives, alluded to a 'mysterious law' that meant that 'the moment civilization and the native forest come into contact, that moment the forest begins to go to the wall'.[20] Roche in his study of forest policy concludes that the implications of such faith were long-term and fundamental. As he puts it: 'importantly in the longer term was the way in which [the Popular and Official views, influenced by the displacement theory] ... shaped a limited view of forestry ... which emphasised tree planting and not the sustained harvesting of natural forest'.[21]

There is persuasive evidence that for nineteenth-century New Zealand settlers the displacement theory was not only predictive but also normative.[22] Darwin theorised that because 'hardly a single inhabitant of the southern hemisphere has become wild in any part of Europe...the productions of Great Britain stand much higher in the scale than those of New Zealand'.[23] By 1859, settlers had assumed a status as 'the dominant people of the land'.[24] As part of the normal process of scientific and social advancement of this dominant race, it was both appropriate and necessary that decadent natives be replaced by superior Europeans, or in some cases their numbers controlled. Only those natives that met European standards would be granted commensurate legal status (notable examples being the paradise duck (pari), swamp hen (pukeko), and pigeon (kereru) that all enjoyed the dubious prestige of being classed as game).

By way of contrast, the shag (kawau) could be shot at any time because of its predation on imported trout. The kea (a native parrot) was similarly targeted for its liking for sheep. As one contemporary writer explained in the latter case, 'so severe did the nuisance become that the aid of the Legislature had to be invoked for the purpose of extirpating the bird'.[25] The Otago Acclimatization Society offered bounties for the destruction of hawks and kingfishers for their effect on introduced species,[26] while the native trout (kokopu) faced competition from the aggressive imported varieties (both Rainbow and Brown).

It was against this historical background of enthusiastic and widespread acclimatisation that various attempts were made to introduce the rabbit, both as a source of food and fur and as game. The first attempts proved to be failures or achieved only limited success; the animal could not survive the different climatic and vegetation conditions. However, the introduction in Southland in 1864 of wild rabbits that behaved 'in the proverbial way'[27] was to prove successful beyond the wildest dreams or nightmares of those involved or affected. By the 1870s a population explosion of these animals threatened the viability of pastoral farming in New Zealand (the wool industry then providing the 'backbone' of the economy). A hunt was on for a solution.

'AN ENEMY OF THE RABBIT'

THE RABBIT NUISANCE – A CHOICE OF SOLUTION

In 1875, the Provincial Superintendent appointed a Commission of Inquiry 'into the extent to which the rabbit nuisance prevails in Southland'.[28] Words employed in the Commission's report (tabled in May, 1876) to describe the rabbit and its depredations conveyed urgency and desperation – 'nuisance', 'evil', 'infested' and 'calamities'. This impression was reiterated in the conclusion: 'if the public estate is to be rescued from serious depreciation, and private interests from calamities and losses, in no small measure the results of an outside visitation ... this can only be obtained by the application of a remedy which shall be immediate, compulsory and universal'.[29]

In hindsight it seems almost inevitable that this 'remedy' should have been identified as biological, an inevitability reflected in the rapid identification of mustelids as the best chance of controlling the pest and restoring 'the balance of nature'. However, their advocacy was to quickly prove controversial. Although there were various individuals involved in this debate in a range of official and popular contexts, its focus and significance can best be introduced by way of two of the original parties, Professor Alfred Newton, Professor of Zoology at Cambridge University, and the man he described as both 'thoughtless'[30] and 'a fool',[31] Frank Buckland.

THE ZOOLOGIST AND THE 'FOOL'

Shortly after the Commission reported back, Macrorie and Cuthbertson, an Otago-based firm of stock and station agents, wrote to Frank Buckland, an English acclimatisation enthusiast[32] asking for weasels to be sent to New Zealand, where pastoralists were willing to offer £5 a pair.[33] In his column, Buckland expressed the opinion that 'no doubt the weasels would kill a great many rabbits, but I believe they are more enemies to rats, mice and small birds'.[34] He went on to suggest that, given the difficulties in keeping weasels alive in captivity, ferrets would be a better option.

Despite having little time for Buckland, Newton sent him a letter of protest, warning of the devastating consequences of importing weasels or like species to New Zealand. 'No person ... can for a moment doubt that what remains of this [native] fauna will absolutely and almost instantaneously disappear ... Even if it be doomed why should we hasten its end?' Newton also wrote to such leading New Zealand scientists as Sir James Hector,[35] Walter Buller and Frederick W. Hutton,[36] urging prevention of this 'disastrous importation'. Buckland responded to Newton's concern by including the script of his letter in his column and commenting on it as follows: 'I should be exceedingly sorry to do anything to injure the natural history of our friends in New Zealand, and shall therefore take the admonition of Professor Newton and pause a while before sending out the ferrets to New Zealand'.[37]

However, he also referred to a 'friend...who has lived a good many years in New Zealand' as a 'practical sheep farmer', who was in favour of introducing ferrets to 'let the sheep have their proper share'. In another place, he asked that if not advisable to send ferrets to New Zealand, 'would [Professor Newton] and the naturalist whose opinions he represents, be kind enough to suggest some practical remedies by which the rabbits may be kept under?'[38]

Newton's and other expressions of opposition to the proposal (reproduced by Buckland in his Land and Water column the following week) suggest a growing awareness on the part of the British scientific community of the fragility of the New Zealand ecosystem and of the importance of its preservation. For example, noted ornithologist and naturalist Mr James E. Harting framed his opposition thus: 'I tremble to think of the fate of the pheasants .... But ... I plead not so much on behalf of acclimatised game birds as on behalf of the native avifauna'.[39]

'XYZ' blamed 'gamekeepers, [who] killed hawks to conserve pheasants',[40] for the rabbit problem and went on to accuse the owners of game preserves of destroying 'the weeka [sic] rails by hunting them with greyhounds, in order to make room for the pheasants'. George D. Rowley went further in describing 'such a mistake (introducing polecats) as much I should look upon a proposition to run a railway through Westminster Abbey on Utilitarian principles'.[41]

The two opposing positions were thus revealed: for Buckland and his New Zealand correspondents (for whom the views and economic needs of 'practical' farmers were of primary importance) sheep outclassed birds. For British-based academics and naturalists, New Zealand represented a unique ecosystem, worthy of preservation and protection. The only question that remained to be decided was: who would win on a rabbit-sick New Zealand pasture? Despite a ubiquitous discourse of change, it was not quite a forgone conclusion. Instead, opposition to the proposal to introduce these predators sparked a parliamentary initiative to prevent it.

Newton had directed his initial plea to Hector (then Director of the New Zealand Geological Survey and Colonial Museum, and the Manager and Editor of the New Zealand Institute). In his absence, Hon.Walter B.D. Mantell, a member of both the Philosophical Society and Legislative Council and with a 'passion for natural history',[42] took prompt action in both Houses of Parliament. Action was taken in the House of Representatives through Sir George Grey,[43] then a member of a disparate opposition.

Mantell's and Grey's original intention was to push through an amendment to s29 of the Protection of Animals Act 1867 so as to add polecats, stoats and weasels to the list of prohibited imports. In moving the second reading of this amendment, Grey focused on the hazard posed by mustelids to birds, particularly insectivorous ones. According to 'eminent naturalists', he explained, the most undesirable of the family were weasels, given they 'would materially interfere with the agriculture of the country' because they would kill the birds which destroyed the grain-eating insects.[44]

This was clearly a strategy appropriate to a House with a majority of small farmers, who valued birds of any stripe for their role in controlling crop-damaging insects.[45] However, Arthur P. Seymour (Wairau) argued in the present case that 'rather than being a Protection of Animals Act it was a Noxious Animals Prohibition bill'.[46] This initiative (to have such animals subject to a prohibition-focused new statute rather than within existing 'protectionist' legislation) had the implication that species could and should be exempted if deemed on balance to be useful rather than injurious. Accordingly for Seymour, stoats and weasels should not be considered noxious because 'it had been suggested in many places that the true mode, and perhaps the only mode open to them [the pastoral farmers] to prevent the increase in rabbits was by the introduction of these animals'[47] (albeit with a possibility of harm to other fauna protected under the Protection of Animals legislation).

Similarly, during the committee stage, those opposing its coverage proposed a series of amendments to exempt foxes (Edward Wakefield), polecats, stoats and weasels (John C. Wason) and weasels (John C. Andrew) on the basis that their economic value exceeded their noxiousness. It is perhaps indicative of the strength of feeling in the House against these importations that the amendments were all defeated and an overwhelming majority (38 to 9) agreed that the clause banning the importation of noxious animals should remain unchanged. The bill passed its second and third readings on the same day and was referred to the Legislative Council.

During his introductory speech in the Council, Mantell took some care to contextualise it as a measure that 'merely provided for an increase in the protection of our native and imported birds and other animals by the extension of the prohibition of the importation of noxious animals' (to include specifically polecats, stoats and weasels).[48] No doubt mindful of the domination of the Council by the pastoralists (of the 35 members, 19 are identified as farmers[49] – mostly pastoral), he sought to garner support for the amendment by drawing support from 'good authority' that mustelids would be of no avail in solving 'what might be called a rabbit scare amongst gentlemen of the pastoral persuasion'.[50] Hon. George S. Whitmore from the Hawkes Bay endorsed Mantell, warning that 'in a short time [mustelids] would be a much greater nuisance than the rabbits themselves',[51] as did Hon. William H. Nurse (from Southland) who described himself as 'a practical farmer'[52] and Hon. William Robinson from Nelson.[53] However, those speaking in opposition to the measure sought to disarm its proponents by discounting the predictions of disaster. For example, Hon. Mathew Holmes from Otago[54] asked whether there were 'any birds worth preserving in this country?' They only had a few parrots and the kiwi. Anyway, surely these messages of doom were excessive – 'birds had not been destroyed in England [where these predators were common], why should they here?'[55] Hon. Captain Thomas Fraser, also from Otago, clearly ranked fauna in order of relative value with his comment that he was 'very fond of birds, but if it came to a question of whether he would have birds or sheep he would certainly vote in favour of the sheep. He would be delighted to see a shipload of stoats'.[56] Finally, and somewhat ironically in view of his sponsorship in the House nine years previously for protection of 'useful' indigenous species, for the now Hon. John Hall, native fauna was not even worth a mention. Instead, mustelids 'would do more good than harm [because] the only harm which he understood...was that they would attack some of the introduced game' (thereby 'interfering a little with the pursuits of sporting men').[57]

Mantell was probably prepared for such opposition from those Councillors from areas most affected by the rabbit plague, but may well have listened to two other speeches with a sinking heart, realising that, even if a majority were willing to take steps to control the importation of mustelids for the future, it may be too late. Firstly, Hon. George M. Waterhouse, a pastoralist from Wellington, after claiming 'that they were all agreed that it was desirable... to facilitate the acclimatization of animals that might be useful to man' (including weasels), revealed that 'he had, within the last three or four months, turned loose a considerable number of ferrets',[58] while the Hon. Dr Daniel Pollen of Auckland confessed to having 'some weasels in his possession'.[59]

Nevertheless, the bill went to Committee, where a proposal to amend the measure to exempt weasels from its coverage was defeated, but only by virtue of the Chairman exercising a casting vote. The bill then passed its second reading by the smallest of margins (14-12). At this point, however, its advance came to an abrupt halt. Clearly, its passage was not considered urgent given that it was committed for its third reading in six months.

It is important that this political initiative was unlikely to have emerged in a vacuum. King makes the point that Mantell's attempt to ban these species must have been spurred at least in part by strong expressions of opposition from local ornithologists as well as from Newton. This is of interest in itself as it appears to run counter to the facilitation of change. One of the few published examples of such opposition is a paper presented by Buller two months after the bill had been committed. This paper is of note for two reasons. One is that Buller refers to the Legislature 'having rejected' the proposal to ban the importation – a reference that suggests that although theoretically it was not due back to the Council for several months, it was by this time clear the bill would advance no further. Secondly, Buller describes the proposed introductions as 'one of the worst predaceous vermin', quoting from Newton's letter to him in support.[60] He then went on to challenge the merits of the case that would 'no doubt' be argued by the other side: 'that sheep are of more practical account to the colony than kiwis and wekas' [woodhens].[61] Despite such eloquence there is little indication that this paper attracted attention in either scientific or lay circles; it did not apparently spark any sustained protest against possible importations over the rest of the 1870s and in the end it certainly did not deter the advocates of such importations seeking state approval, participation and support..

However, opposition to the proposal to import mustelids was not limited to the scientific community but also emerged in the major Otago newspapers (*Otago Daily Times* and *Otago Witness*). The day after reprinting Buckland's earlier pieces from *Land and Water*, the *Times* described the acclimatisation as a 'remedy worse than the disease' and expressed the opinion that 'the evil is best settled by such remedial measures as the wisdom of the Assembly has already suggested' (these being manual and direct methods such as trapping and poisoning).[62] In the same week the *Witness* carried an editorial roundly condemning the proposal to import 'polecats'. Maybe settlers would not 'regard the extinction of the woodhen with the sentimental regret that a BUCKLAND (sic) would feel for it, but that they would be better off with the rabbit than with the weasel or polecat'. If this importation were allowed, 'it is likely that someone will take a fancy to keep snakes... or alligators.... If not, why not?' In words reminiscent of the old lady and her fly, the *Witness* called for 'some stop to be put to the endless chain of animals that imagination may suggest might be poured into New Zealand as a cure for some other evil'.[63]

Nevertheless, the opposition of the *Witness* must be viewed with caution, not necessarily as an attack on acclimatisation of mustelids *per se* but on another issue that had a high political and social profile: that of land ownership and occupation. By way of clarification, the theme of both this editorial and that of the previous week was the idle absentee land owner, who embodied the most undesirable characteristics of British tradition. In the first of these editorials, the focus was on the pejoratively-termed 'squatter' deeply indebted to the British-owned banks and other financial institutions. Squatters, argued the editorial, were those:

> who buy with money borrowed outside the Colony. It *always* pays to sell land to men who buy with money saved or brought into the colony by themselves.... In the first case, which is usually the case of the squatter, every shilling wrung from the grudging soil by the toil of the shepherd or the ploughman goes home to feed Lombard St and Kent. In the latter case it... refreshes a whole community.[64]

Perhaps the 'squatters' who sent all profits extracted by the labour of hirelings 'home' [to England], would be the most likely to be tempted to import snakes and alligators purely as rarities and curiosities. These 'idle rich' were also most vocal in demanding assistance from the toilers of the community in solving the rabbit problem. The problem, the *Witness* maintained, could be solved easily, not by introducing stoats and weasels, but by carving up the estates into smaller farms.[65] These farms would then provide a good living, not only for the working owner, but also for the community in which they resided – clearly in tune with the 'honest rural toiler as the foundation of the ideal society' thinking of many of the settlers.[66] The *Witness* went on to pronounce that 'we may carry our argument even to the length of deprecating the introduction of gamekeepers beyond a certain point. It would be a sad pity to have our old friend of the velveteens' (a derogatory reference to gamekeepers) 'introduced here'.

Despite this (somewhat limited) evidence of support for a ban on mustelids, the Noxious Animals bill that would have realised it never re-surfaced, a fate that may have had several origins. Perhaps, even with the support for the measure in the House, the grudging and ambivalent reception in the Legislative Council was enough to persuade its supporters that the bill would not pass its third reading. Its opponents would have a chance to marshal their forces before it reappeared. Alternatively, or in addition, it is at least possible that the revelations made by Pollen and Waterhouse suggested that the argument against them was now academic at best. Prevention was no longer possible to achieve. It is also possible that political issues of greater moment (most specifically the pending abolition of provincial government) distracted attention from the relatively trivial matter of native species protection.

Whatever the immediate reason for its failure, it remained legal for private individuals to import mustelids on their own behalf, although Government did not as yet take an active part. In addition, the door was left open, once pastoralists regained sufficient power, for changes in policy to be sanctioned.

By 1881, when the importation and liberation of mustelids was given specific political sanction rather than merely implicit approval, several developments had helped strengthen the power base of the pastoral sector. First, the onset of an extended economic depression – sometimes called the 'hungry eighties' – led to political pressure for measures to increase employment and national income through exports. As an indication of the degree to which this depression claimed the attention of legislative decision-makers, in 1880 Parliament was called in May (three months early) to hear a financial statement that 'reinforced the gloomy mood and antagonised many MPs'.[67] With a continued emphasis on rural commerce (particularly wool), it is inevitable that much attention would be paid to farming. Secondly, the pending introduction of refrigerated shipping[68] offered some hope to livestock farming, principally that of sheep (as now the meat as well as wool could be offered to the European market), provided productivity could be maintained or improved.

A new report into the rabbit problem, tabled during the 1881 recess by a joint House and Council Select Committee, chaired by Holmes, reflected a heightened degree of political concern with the problems faced by this sector and the need to improve its outlook. Consequently, the report recommended a raft of measures that would, *inter alia*, shift most legal responsibility (and cost) for management of the rabbit problem from the pastoral sector and locally elected Rabbit Boards to central Government, and, most pertinently, provide 'for the protection of natural enemies of the Rabbit at present in the colony'.[69]

Witnesses and others who made written submissions to the committee generally supported such a recommendation. For example, two pastoral run-holders (a Mr Fraser, and a Mr Rees) supported any natural enemy provided that enemy did not attack sheep or lambs, while Mr W.C. Buchanan from Carterton (Chairman of the local Rabbit District) poured scorn on any suggestion that they would cause damage, including to lambs. Mr R.F. Cuthbertson suggested that the Indian mongoose be added to the list of possibilities, while Mr G.F. Bullen from Kaikoura believed 'that ferrets will be the salvation of the country'.[70] Bullen's unconditional support seems odd at first glance, given his recognition of woodhen (weka) as a useful weapon against rabbits, yet one readily and frequently destroyed by the 'hundreds' of ferrets he had personally liberated over the previous eight years. However, it can be rationalised by his connection of solution (ferrets) to the problem (rabbits). Wekas ran a poor second in his estimation to ferrets as obviously superior predators.

A lone voice of opposition was that of Mr Jackson of Featherston. In his view, although tame ferrets were useful in the battle against the rabbit, they should not be liberated because 'when they become wild they are very dangerous'.[71] Stoats, weasels and polecats should not be introduced at all.[72] As a measure of his concern, he would sooner have a hundred rabbits than a dozen weasels. However, when pressed for an explanation, he could only say that they 'do a great deal of mischief in the old country'. Although that explanation is of passing interest because it contradicts a more generally-held opinion that they would on balance be useful, it proved in the end to be of little importance to the Committee's recommendations.

The legislative measure that emerged from this report (the Rabbit Nuisance Act 1881), of most moment in this context for its provision of legal protection for 'enemies' of the rabbit, sparked neither division nor debate in the House of Representatives and virtually no debate in the Council (and that was largely to do with the licensing of dogs for rabbit hunting). Offering further evidence of the level of support is its rapid passage: in the House the bill was introduced on 6 September, went through its committee stage and third reading on the 9th and passed in the Legislative Council on the 15th.[73]

This support in the House in particular may at first glance seem surprising; after all, electoral reform in 1879 extended voting rights to all adult males rather than just those who held land. Surely, newly represented interests would be more likely to resist rather than support a measure that would benefit pastoralists more than most. Perhaps some rationale for this support can be found not only in the gloomy outlook affecting all aspects of the economy, but also in two immediate occurrences.[74]

The first of these was the pending implementation of socially and politically significant land reform that involved the break-up of the large pastoral estates. No longer would rabbits be a problem only for pastoral farmers; a Government intent on land reform measures would have to become more deeply and directly involved. Indicatively, Holmes (who had chaired the committee), when moving the second reading of the Rabbit Nuisance bill in the Council, emphasised that the Government had both a vested interest in clearing the land, because 'it would be impossible for small settlers to live there unless the rabbit-pest was dealt with',[75] and a statutory obligation to do so in relation to unoccupied land.

A second immediate factor was the Representation bill, a measure that altered the basis of defining electorates from numbers and communities of interest to population (which meant that a significant proportion of sitting members were likely to lose their seats), and introduced a 25 per cent 'country quota' (which meant rural electorates had a smaller population base than did the urban). Debate on that bill had occupied the House in a virtually continuous sitting from Tuesday, 23 August to Monday, 6 September, a sitting that involved a large number of divisions, numerous stonewalling speeches and obstructive strategies. It finally passed its third reading in the early morning hours. The House then adjourned at 4.15 am. The Rabbit Nuisance bill came up for its second reading at 7.00 the following evening when the House reconvened (and sat until 1 am). Less than a day's respite from an exhausting marathon scarcely afforded time for any intending opponent to marshal his forces.

The Act empowered the Governor-in-Council to 'declare any animals, the importation whereof is not prohibited ... to be natural enemies of the rabbit, and... prescribe that any such animals shall be deemed to be protected under this Act' (s24). The members of the Legislature and the country as a whole were to be left in little doubt as to the identity of such an enemy – s25 referred specifically to ferrets, weasels or other such animal in providing a penalty for their destruction or capture without the consent of the landowner or Rabbit Inspector (in the case of Crown lands).

It was from that point that the economic benefits that must flow from the presence of mustelids were deemed to be sufficiently great as to demand their official protection, albeit with some acknowledgement that exceptions may be made to that protection. Even those limited exceptions were not to last – a mere one year later, pursuant to the Rabbit Nuisance Act 1882, no longer were individual landowners able to give consent to the destruction of the predators. Only the Rabbit Inspector, empowered under s29, was able to grant such permission, hardly likely to be forthcoming where rabbits maintained an on-going presence.[76]

Of more general moment perhaps, it was from then that the importation of mustelids and their breeding for release was adopted as official taxpayer-funded Government policy,[77] a policy that resulted in thousands being imported and/or bred for release over the following decade. Between 1884 and 1886 alone, 4000 ferrets, 3099 weasels and 137 stoats were liberated.[78] Ironically perhaps, the positive effect on the rabbit population in Britain due to this mass emigration led to suggestions that they be returned. Even if there was a chance that the native fauna would therefore be put in peril, it was considered a chance that should be taken in the interests of the country as a whole. However, this is not quite the end of the story. An epilogue offers some hint of the shifting sands on which acclimatisation of these predators was built.

EPILOGUE

Despite the Superintending Rabbit Inspector reporting mustelids as 'rendering good service' in 1888,[79] the seeds of concern were by that time already sown. Within a few years, those seeds had produced disquiet, as to the presence of these predators, and opposition to their protection. Carrying the analogy further, it is also evident that advocacy in their favour persisted despite efforts at eradication.

The original articulations of disquiet and opposition, although not the only ones to appear in print, came from members of the scientific community. Early examples of statements to that effect that appear in the *Transactions, inter alia*, predicted that mustelids would spread 'as the rabbit has done'.[80] In addition, they described the difficulty of protecting the birds against an animal that in Austria 'we destroy ... at every opportunity'[81] (a warning at odds with Holmes' and others' dismissal in the Legislative Council of messages of doom), and railed against the 'incredible folly of the Government in turning out ferrets on the western shore of Lake Manapouri'[82] (this being a lake in Fiordland, an area covered by dense native bush, exhibiting no rabbit problem but home to thousands of native birds).

Over the following decade such disquiet became louder and more widespread, although even by that time opinions were not consistent. Buller must be considered a prominent figure in this context, although opinions differ on the extent to which he expressed such disquiet and the motivation that drove it. King claims that Buller was 'tireless in his opposition, ... and continued to denounce the idea for years after it was too late'.[83] By way of contrast, Galbreath claims that after Buller's critique in 1876 he barely mentioned the issue again in his published papers, at least until it suited his purposes.[84] I have located seven negative references after 1876 in his addresses in the *Transactions* (1891 being the earliest of these and 1898 the last), a passing mention in the second edition of the *Book on New Zealand Birds* (published in 1888), as well as some reference to concerns expressed by his correspondents.

However, these negative references are intrinsically inconsistent. Buller seemed reluctant, at least at first, to single out mustelids from other predators to make a special case. One of the first references (in 1891) was to the effect on thrush of 'diggers' dogs ... wild cats, stoats and weasels',[85] and in the same year, while discussing the reasons for extinction of birds on the West Coast, Buller was inclined to blame 'the Norway rat ... for much of the mischief'.[86] In June 1894 he railed against the depredations of 'bloodthirsty animals like stoats, weasels and ferrets',[87] but moderated his comments with an allusion to the 'inscrutable law of nature' – displacement – that caused species to die out 'long before our drastic colonization'.

After 1894, a change to his tone can be detected.[88] In a paper delivered later in that year, he branded the decision by 'our wise Government' to buy up and import hundreds of these predators as an 'act in the light of a crime', and as 'shipment after shipment of these vermin arrived ... had raised my voice in protest ... but all to no purpose'.[89] The following year, he again condemned the 'insane policy of introducing predatory animals ... in the vain hope of suppressing the rabbit nuisance'.[90] He contended that this policy was initially adopted in response to the 'clamour of a few faddists whose idea was to exterminate the rabbits at any cost',[91] and in 1896 extended to the effect on kiwi and woodhen [weka] of the 'ravages' of stoats and weasels.[92] Finally, he made two references in a single address to 'predatory animals'[93] ... thoughtlessly introduced by a too impulsive Government'.[94]

In a footnote to this address, Buller claimed that 'my ... views as to the absolute wickedness of [the introductions] are too well known to need repetition',[95] perhaps implying that after long and loud protest he was now ready to lay the issue to rest (somewhat at odds with Galbreath's comment). In the same location, he quoted at some length Newton's disgust and anger at the 'extraordinary atrocity' wreaked by mustelids on New Zealand's avifauna.[96]

Whatever motives and dedication can be attributed to Buller, he was not alone amongst members of the Philosophical Societies in denouncing these predators and those responsible for their presence. For example, in 1891 Travers referred to mustelids as having 'to be killed as vermin',[97] while Rev Peter Walsh exposed an irony in the landowners' advocacy for their importation. Not only had they proved both 'an intolerable nuisance'[98] and an abject failure in controlling rabbits, the arrival of those rabbits had reportedly been celebrated by the landowners 'with a champagne lunch'. Similarly, Thomas Kirk (in his presidential address in 1895) talked of the accelerated rate of extinction faced by birds 'of exceptional interest' since the introduction of the stoat, weasel and ferret';[99] and Guthrie Smith described the introduction as a 'crime'.[100] Finally, Bathgate positioned his criticism of this 'grave error' in the wider context of the acclimatisers, whose 'zeal was greater than their knowledge' and whose mistakes were 'fraught with evil results'.[101]

Nevertheless, not every member of these societies was singing from the same hymn book. In 1890, Thomas White expressed his disappointment in the *Transactions* that the Hawkes Bay Rabbit Board had decided against importing weasels. 'The balance of nature', he explained, 'is presently upset...so man is *required* (italics added) to place the weasel in the opposite scale',[102] (the implication being that it was not only desirable but a duty owed to Nature for man to import the predator). Another notable example is one Coleman Phillips, entrepreneur, member of the Wellington Philosophical Society and a loyal supporter of acclimatisation of 'useful' species.[103] In 1888 Phillips kept the minutes of a meeting of settlers of Wairarapa,[104] where the desirability of introducing ferrets as a control on rabbits was vigorously debated. As he later noted, 'there was such an outcry by the small farmers to the proposal...that I thought it expedient to bend to the storm and oppose the introduction of other ground vermin.'[105] The resultant resolution, moved by Phillips, was 'that the introduction of stoats, weasels, mingeese or fox ... is unnecessary'.[106] This motion for Phillips had the desired effect as 'objection to the ferret practically ceased – it also had the effect of preventing any person thinking of introducing the fox or mongoose'.[107]

Such variance of opinion and position was reflected elsewhere in society over this same period. On the one hand were those pastoral landowners in the 1870s and early 1880s who *knew* that predators were the only effective weapons against the ravages of the rabbit. For them, the benefits flowing from their introduction drowned out any expressions of concern or reservation that might be expressed. Ensuring their on-going 'power and ... influence'[108] depended on their making immediate and necessary changes to maintain productivity of the land, and allowing 'insufficient time...for earnest consideration'[109] of potentially negative consequences further down the line.

By the end of the decade, however, political and economic power had shifted. The pastoral farmer was again facing falling economic fortunes and rising pressures: 'many large holdings ... were mortgaged up to the hilt .... In many cases... the land itself, overrun by rabbits with which half-submerged runholders were powerless to cope, was deteriorating ...'.[110] Their saviour had failed to live up to expectations. By way of contrast, the proven success of refrigerated shipping (that first began in 1882) had improved viability for smaller agricultural units, while the 'political revolution'[111] of 1890 contributed to the power of those employed in the service industries. This trend continued until 'from 1895 onwards ... the change-over from wool to mixed farming for frozen meat, butter and cheese, resulted in closer settlement and the rise of new industries such as freezing works, butter and cheese factories and other processing plants'.[112]

These sectors of society, who now held economic power, possibly had little first-hand knowledge of the rabbit problem experienced by the pastoralists. It is also possible they did not really care much about it. With the basis of their prosperity in industries other than wool, they were still expected to contribute to the costs of rabbit control. It would hardly be surprising should they be prepared to accommodate values beyond that of grassland productivity and expect their elected representatives to promote them.

Amongst such representatives were those scientist-politicians who featured prominently in native species protection efforts from the early 1890s onwards. Examples of such individuals in the House included Harry Ell, who pushed for the creation and protection of scenic reserves, George Thomson, an erstwhile acclimatisation supporter who became a vocal critic of particular instances, and Alfred Newman who helped lead the campaign to establish Tongariro National Park. Most particularly in this context, Thomas MacKenzie (who a year later advocated the reservation of Fiordland as a National Park) was to declare bluntly his condemnation of mustelids in 1893, when a member for Clutha and opponent and vocal critic of the ruling Liberal Government: 'Past Governments and the present Government had liberated throughout the length and breadth of the country weasels and ferrets, which were doing no good in the way of the destruction of rabbits, but were ... destroying every bird they came into contact with'.[113]

Despite this increasingly vocal condemnation and emergent hostility to their presence both inside and outside Parliament, it would be for a further decade before the first steps would to be taken against mustelids, with a particular focus on their protected status as enemies of the rabbit. These first moves were ultimately followed by the removal of all protection, although that process was to prove both glacial in pace and torturous in contrivance, involving four separate steps over a fifty-year period.

The first hint that the time was ripe for consideration of the issue can be found in a question put to the Minister of Lands (Hon Thomas H. Young) by Francis Mander, Member for Marsden, in July 1903. He asked 'whether the Government will consider the necessity of removing fines for destroying [devastating] stoats and weasels in the North of Auckland?'[114] While Young deemed it unnecessary to change the law in this respect, as there had 'not been a single prosecution' for their destruction (revealing a somewhat flexible official attitude towards the enforcement of the Rabbit Nuisance Act 1882), Thomas Duncan (member for Waitaki) was of the opinion that the effect of removing the fine for their destruction would be to leave the country 'desolate'.[115] Nothing further was said on the question at this point but the issue was certainly not laid to rest: a mere two months later an amendment was moved to the Animals Protection Act 1867. This amendment would authorise local authorities or acclimatisation societies to petition the Governor for an Order-in-Council declaring that 'natural enemies' 'which have since proved to be enemies of game and poultry, may be killed within the district defined by the order'.[116] It should, perhaps, be noted that the focus of the amendment, and consequently the theme of speeches for the bill, was narrow; limited to specific areas, requiring overt action on the part of the bodies concerned and on the protection of game, rather than native fauna in general. William F. Massey pointed to the rapid disappearance of the pheasant,[117] and Archibald D. Willis to the 'insufferable nuisance' posed by the stoats and weasels to the native game.[118] Ell from Christchurch also spoke of the destruction of ground game by stoats and weasels that he described as 'brutes'.[119]

By way of contrast, those opposed to this aspect of the amendment spoke in wide terms, holding fast to the virtue historically granted mustelids as economic necessities, and correspondingly anxious to remind the House of the 'enormous benefits conferred by the introduction'[120] and their 'importance to the settler'.[121]

'AN ENEMY OF THE RABBIT'

Of particular note in this context, Bennett dismissed Ell's negative remarks on mustelids as those of a purported 'authority on things he knows nothing about' and hoped that the Minister would 'never consent to do away with these "vermin" ...until the rabbits are entirely exterminated'.[122] As what was proposed fell far short of 'doing away' with the mustelids, it is easy to dismiss this statement as mere political hyperbole.

At the same time however, his statement suggests an undercurrent of concern amongst advocates of the 'vermin', and of heightened negative sentiment, most particularly disillusionment and antipathy. That such concern was not unfounded is evidenced by the move by Government away from active involvement in Mustelidae breeding, distribution and use for rabbit control (a move that more than merely hints at disillusionment with their suitability and effectiveness). A degree of antipathy is suggested not only by the successful passage of this amendment through both houses, but also by the somewhat acerbic classification, by Hon. John Rigg, of parliamentarians 'along with the stoats and weasels and the polecats and other pests of that kind',[123] when speaking to the Industrial Conciliation and Arbitration bill (the debate having followed the third reading of the Animals Protection Amendment Act).

As a conclusion to this historical saga, this 1903 measure was to prove symbolic in terms of the political status of mustelids in New Zealand. It also marked the beginning of an inexorable, albeit painfully drawn-out, slide in their status as the pastoral farmers' champions in the battle against rabbits.[124] They were no longer a solution but a problem: sparking an enduring (and continuing) search for means of defending the indigenous 'aristocrats of the Animal Kingdom' from the 'shrewd, vulgar,...cunning,...greedy and ferocious invaders',[125],[126] and for strategies whereby their numbers might be controlled.[127]

Finally, how does the fall from grace of mustelids fit within the wider discourse that shaped acclimatisation practice and theory as New Zealand moved into the twentieth century? Some indication can be obtained through an examination of the rationale and extent of shifts in that discourse.

REFLECTION – SHIFTS IN A DISCOURSE OF ACCLIMATISATION

Perhaps more than merely by chance, the redefinition of mustelids in the discourse of the 1890s and beyond coincided with two developments. First, from late in the nineteenth century, both professional scientists and amateur practitioners began to doubt the value of displacement as a theoretical construct. Secondly, protectionist sentiments gained acceptance in the broader New Zealand society.

Insofar as the Displacement Theory is concerned, although it would appear that Buller and others drew on the predictive aspect of the theory in formulating arguments for conservation by way of island reserves during the 1890s,[128] by the beginning of the twentieth century observers were challenging its inherent logic. Thomson (1900) concluded that 'some native species appear to be holding their own, and even to benefit by those attendant circumstances',[129] while Leonard Cockayne (1901), Kirk (1895) and James Drummond (1907) were ready to brand such theorising as 'spurious'.[130] Other field observers also highlighted the divergence between reality and the theory, with one of them speaking of Nature's display of 'a marvellous power of resistance and recuperation', despite the damage caused by fire and cattle.[131]

It is important to emphasise that many of the reservations now expressed with the theory were not concerned with species decline; on the contrary, it was clear that many species, previously endemic, were now scarce or extinct. However, both professional and amateur naturalists were now challenging the old explanations offered for their decline. Potts is notable in being one of the first to change his view on the inevitability of decline of indigenous species; he later posited human (European) influences as a direct cause,[132] although support from others was not immediately forthcoming.[133] Guthrie Smith, with no formal qualifications but with his years of careful observation behind him, also ascribed to the view that such displacement was a consequence of the loss of habitat brought about by settlers. As he was to write, 'woodland species cannot live without woodland, jungle and swamp-hunting birds cannot survive without jungle and swamp'.[134]

More specific to the matter of acclimatisation, by the later 1890s, members of the same scientific community that earlier facilitated change through this process had shifted their position dramatically, now denouncing specific introductions as destructive and wrong. They placed the blame for that destruction squarely on the European (British) settler. At the same time and as part of the same logic, many of these members both contributed and lent support to a heightened popular perception of native species as worthy of protection, rather than weak, decadent and without value.

The emergence of such protectionist sentiments have been attributed to a range of factors, including the emergence of a New Zealand-born generation, who perceived the country as a separate and distinct place, with its own worthy characteristics, that should not be threatened by ill-considered importations.[135] Indicatively, the anonymous writer of a piece published in the *Otago Witness* in 1894 lamented the failure of colonists to 'be content with what they found here, without importing creatures that exterminate the natives'.[136] Similarly, in a letter to the *Otago Daily Times* in 1900, 'Disgusted' branded the barn owl as an example of 'rubbish and vermin' that should therefore never be introduced.[137]. Bathgate's suggestions that the antelope, eland, shrew and toad would have been better imports than were mustelids were not taken further, while the escape of a pair of racoons, imported for their curiosity value to the Government Gardens in Rotorua, caused much official consternation in 1903. This consternation only subsided on the discovery of their dead bodies several weeks later.

Despite this heightened awareness of the potential implications of acclimatisation for the protection of the native flora and fauna, however, it continued to be pursued deliberately through the twentieth century. But it followed a somewhat narrower mandate of refinement or enrichment rather than change, and pursued a pace more reminiscent of trickle than flood. Attention was increasingly turned on species deemed 'useful', a few prominent examples being the possum (for fur), hawks and magpies (to control rodents and insects), game (including pheasants, Canadian geese, deer, chamois, thar and trout that could be used to attract tourists to reserve areas that were otherwise considered waste) and, at least for Sir James Hector, the American kit fox which, he considered, would have been very useful in spreading tapeworm, a rabbit parasite.[138] As a final indication of its enduring enthusiasm, with the financial and official encouragement of Prime Minister William F. Massey and Hon. Robert Heaton Rhodes (Minister of Tourist and Health Resorts), a heather-planting programme was undertaken in the Tongariro National Park between 1912 and 1919 by the man who would be appointed as the first ranger in 1916: John Cullen. He aspired to create an antipodean Scottish shooting moor. Although game birds never became established, problems with the heather persist into the present.

CONCLUSION

Although the proposal to import 'shiploads' of predators to control the rabbit population generated a surprising level of concern about the potential effect on the avifauna of New Zealand, the political, economic and social characteristics of the time provided overwhelming support for introduction. Even though those seeking to prevent the importation came close to achieving a political ban in October 1876, victory may well have proved pyrrhic and short-lived: mustelids were already in the country (albeit not in great numbers) and the opinion in favour of their introduction would prove unstoppable. It is tempting to speculate on the possibility of a different outcome had the issue arisen twenty years later. On one side of the scale, public and political support for conservation and concern over ill-considered introductions had increased, while the economic power base had shifted and the scientific rationale for acclimatisation had been deconstructed and found wanting. That may have provided sufficient cause for careful and considered thought on the question. On the other side, however, must be placed the continued enthusiasm for the introduction of 'useful' species, the inadequacy of mechanical means of controlling the rabbit problem, and an enduring focus on farming as the backbone of the New Zealand economy. These latter factors may well have tipped the balance.

NOTES

[1] C. King, *Immigrant Killers – Introduced Predators and the Conservation of Birds in New Zealand* (Auckland: OUP, 1984): 90.

[2] R.H. Grove, *Green Imperialism: Colonial Expansion, Tropical Islands, Edens and the Origins of Environmentalism 1600–1860* (Cambridge: CUP, 1995): 13.

[3] E. Dieffenbach, *Travels in New Zealand with contributions to the geography, geology, botany, and natural history of that country*, 2 vols, (London: John Murray, 1843) I, 2, judged that colonists in the tropics had become 'decrepit, and degenerated'.

[4] W. Yate, *An Account of New Zealand and of the Church Missionary Society's Mission in the Northern Island*, (London: R.B. Seeley, 1835): 194

[5] H. Sewell, NZPD (HR), 4 (first series), 1862: 690 when speaking on the Native Lands Bill (No 2).

[6] D. Thom, *Heritage, the Parks of the People* (Auckland: Lansdown Press, 1987): 72.

[7] A Fellow Passenger, 'To New Zealand with British Birds', *Otago Witness*, 11 March, (1871): 5.

[8] For example, a Mr Holloway from the English Labourers' Union (reported in the *Otago Witness* (1874) 18 April: 10) specified the need for manufactories, trade, commerce and the development of minerals as preconditions for New Zealand to become the Britain of the South, while Captain Cook's reports and species introduction foreshadowed "the way in which New Zealand would service the expanding British and American maritime fleets" (J. McAloon, 'Resource Frontiers, Environment and Settler Capitalism', in *Environmental Histories of New Zealand*, ed. E. Pawson and T. Brooking (Melbourne: OUP, 2002): 52, 66.

[9] Otago Acclimatization Society, *First Annual Report of the Otago Acclimatization Society* (1865), quoted in P. Star, 'From Acclimatization to Preservation: Colonists and the Natural World in Southern New Zealand 1860–1894', (PhD Thesis, University of Otago, 1997): 80.

[10] M. Turnbull and I. McLaren, *The Land of New Zealand, being a Companion Volume to the Changing Land: a Short History of New Zealand*, ed. M. Turnbull, (London: Longmans, 1964): 81.

[11] M. Fairburn, 'The Rural Myth and the New Urban Frontier. An Approach to New Zealand Social History 1870–1940', *New Zealand Journal of History* 9(1), (1973): 2, 8.

[12] T. Brooking, 'Use It or Lose It, Unravelling the Land Debate in Nineteenth Century New Zealand', *New Zealand Journal of History* 30(2), (1996): 141, 146.

[13] A.W. Crosby, as quoted in R. Galbreath, 'Displacement, Conservation and Customary Use of Native Plants and Animals in New Zealand', *New Zealand Journal of History* 36(1), (2002): 36, 38

[14] Star, 'From Acclimatization to Preservation: Colonists and the Natural World in Southern New Zealand 1860–1894': 126.

[15] N. Clayton, 'Weeds, People and Contested Places', *Environment and History* 9 (2003): 301, 314.

[16] Sir Joseph D. Hooker (G.C.S.I., C.B., F.R.S), Ernst Dieffenbach (Professor of Geology and writer), Ferdinand R. von Hochstetter (writer and explorer), William T. L. Travers

(lawyer, politician and naturalist), Thomas H. Potts (politician and naturalist) and Sir Walter Buller (ornithologist).

[17] C. Darwin, *The Origin of Species by Means of Natural Selection*, 6th edn. (London, John Murray, 1899): 152.

[18] It should be noted that indigenous forest or bush was one of the few 'native' resources to be identified, even then of lesser use or value than planted exotic timber. By comparison, most of the other native flora and fauna was considered of little or no value.

[19] Sir Julius Vogel was Premier of New Zealand from 8 April 1873 to 6 July 1875 and 15 February 1876 to 1 September 1876. He is most known for a nationwide public works programme, achieving the abolition of the provinces in 1876 and for instigating the first conservation strategy, albeit short-lived, for forest resources.

[20] NZPD (HR), 16, 1874: 351.

[21] M. Roche, 'The State as Conservationist, 1920–60. "Wise Use" of Forests, Lands and Water' in *Environmental Histories of New Zealand*, ed. E. Pawson and T. Brooking (Melbourne: OUP, 2002): 183, 184. This philosophy was reflected in a report in the *New Zealand Herald* (23 May 1876: 3), 'It will be a specific duty, we believe, to gather information as to the renewal of forests when exhausted.... It is to be hoped that the whole subject of tree planting will be considered.' Evidence suggests that this view persisted in both official and popular circles into the twentieth century.

[22] G. Wynn, 'Conservation and Society in Late Nineteenth Century New Zealand', *New Zealand Journal of History* 11(2) (1977): 136 and 'Pioneers, Politics and the Conservation of Forests in Early New Zealand', *Journal of Historical Geography* 15(2) (1979): 171, 179; G.H. Scholefield, *New Zealand in Evolution: Industrial, Economic and Political* (London: Fisher Unwin, 1909).

[23] Darwin, *The Origin of Species by Means of Natural Selection*: 152.

[24] R. Galbreath, 'Displacement, Conservation and Customary Use of Native Plants and Animals on New Zealand', *New Zealand Journal of History* 36(1) (2002): 36, 42.

[25] W. Gisborne, *Colony of New Zealand, its History, Vicissitudes and Progress*, London: E.A. Petherick and Co, 1888): 11.

[26] Star, 'From Acclimatization to Preservation: Colonists and the Natural World in Southern New Zealand 1860–1894': 90–1.

[27] C. King, *Immigrant Killers – Introduced Predators and the Conservation of Birds in New Zealand* (Auckland: OUP, 1984): 82.

[28] Commission to Inquire into the Extent of the Rabbit Nuisance in the District of Southland, *The Rabbit Nuisance in Southland, Report on*, by the Hon. Sir J.L.C. Richardson and W.H. Pearson, (1876) AJHR, H-10: 3, 4.

[29] Commission to Inquire into the Extent of the Rabbit Nuisance in the District of Southland, *The Rabbit Nuisance in Southland, Report on*: 9.

[30] Newton to Hutton, reprinted in *Otago Witness*, 28 October 1876: 18.

[31] Newton to Buller, 23 July 1876, quoted in Buller, 'On the Ornithology of New Zealand' a Paper Read before the Wellington Philosophical Society, 22 November 1898, *Transactions and Proceedings of the New Zealand Institute* 31 (1898): 1, 26.

[32] In an earlier column ('Trout Farming in Otago, New Zealand', *Land and Water*, 22 January 1876: 70), Buckland had described himself as an 'enthusiast [for trout fishing] at home' and as a member of the Fisheries Preservation Society. In his thesis, Star also

notes his erstwhile position as secretary of the by then defunct London Acclimatization Society (129). G. Wynn, 'Remapping Tutira: Contours in the Environmental History of New Zealand', *Journal of Historical Geography* (1997): 418, 420, mentions that Buckland's acclimatization organisation was founded in 1860. He also refers to the 'mania for acclimatization in the UK' (441, n. 11).

[33] F. Buckland, 'Weazels for New Zealand' (sic), *Land and Water*, 8 July 1876: 10, reproduced in *Otago Witness*, 9 December 1876: 21.

[34] Buckland, 'Weazels for New Zealand': 21.

[35] Director of the Colonial Museum and Geological Survey, founder and Manager of the New Zealand Institute, advisor to the New Zealand Government on scientific matters.

[36] The letter he wrote to Hutton was reprinted in the *Otago Witness*, 28 October 1876, 18.

[37] Buckland, *Land and Water*, 15 July 1876, 22. This letter along with Buckland's rejoinder and other correspondence on the issue is included in the reprint in the *Otago Witness* 9 December:21, after the failed political attempt at prohibition (see also further discussion, infra).

[38] Buckland, *Land and Water*, 15 July 1876: 22.

[39] *Land and Water*, 15 July 1876: 22–3.

[40] *Land and Water*, 15 July 1876:39. The *Otago Daily Times*, 14 Nov. 1876: 2, while clearly opposing the importation (see reference infra) albeit somewhat scornfully described this correspondent as 'rather ignorant ... of the state of things out here ... indeed, he seems to know remarkably little about New Zealand'.

[41] G. D. Rowley, *Land and Water*, 15 July 1876:22.

[42] Ministry for Culture and Heritage, *The Dictionary of New Zealand Biography VI*, ed. C. Orange, (Wellington: Department of Internal Affairs, 1990): 267.

[43] An ironic note must be sounded here. Grey was an enthusiastic advocate and sponsor of acclimatization. Kawau Island in the Hauraki Gulf (that he bought in 1862) became a repository for a range of exotic animals, a range that included possums and brushtailed rock wallabies (both now considered pests), zebras, emus, monkeys and antelopes.

[44] NZPD (HR), 23, 1876: 273.

[45] As an interesting aside, the sentiment expressed by Grey was clearly reminiscent of that displayed by John Hall (as member for Heathcote, Canterbury) nine years previously. As Hall had explained, the Protection of Animals bill then under discussion: 'consisted mainly of a consolidation of the present Acts... which had been passed for protecting animals that had been imported into the country at considerable cost and trouble; it was also thought desirable that indigenous animals which were of advantage to the country should be protected'. NZPD (HR), 16, 1867, Part II: 1231.

[46] NZPD (HR), 23, 1876: 274. It was reported back from Committee under that name.

[47] NZPD (HR), 23, 1876: 274.

[48] According to J. Druett, *Exotic Intruders, the Introduction of Plants and Animals into New Zealand*, (Auckland: Heinmann, 1983): 170–1, the first ferrets arrived in New Zealand in 1867, imported by a Mr Morton and kept on his behalf by the Canterbury Acclimatization Society in the Domain Gardens. Stoats and weasels were first officially introduced in 1885.

[49] W.K. Jackson, *The New Zealand Legislative Chamber*, (Dunedin: UOP, 1972): App IV, 234-5.

[50] NZPD (LC), 23, 1876: 609.

[51] NZPD (LC), 23, 1876: 610. Interestingly, Whitmore had been the part-owner of a large sheep-run near Napier since 1861.

[52] NZPD (LC), 23, 1876: 612.

[53] Robinson was also a pastoral runholder.

[54] One of those areas most affected by rabbits.

[55] NZPD (LC), 23, 1876: 612.

[56] NZPD (LC), 23, 1876: 609.

[57] NZPD (LC), 23, 1876: 610.

[58] NZPD (LC), 23, 1876: 612. It is worth noting that although specific bans (mainly of diseased animals) were in place at this time, it was not until much later that recognition was given to the necessity of controlling the species introduced into New Zealand.

[59] NZPD (LC), 23, 1876: 609. Pollen did not apparently have any direct connection with farming. 'One of the earliest Auckland settlers', he became a Government agent in Auckland. (W. Gisborne, *New Zealand Rulers and Statesmen* (London: Sampson Low, Marston and Company, 1897: 263.)

[60] W.L.A. Buller 'On the Proposed Introduction of the Polecat into New Zealand' *Transactions and Proceedings of the New Zealand Institute* 9 (1877): 634, 635

[61] Buller 'On the Proposed Introduction of the Polecat into New Zealand' *Transactions and Proceedings of the New Zealand Institute*: 634, 635.

[62] *Otago Daily Times*, 14 November 1876: 2.

[63] *Otago Witness*, 18 November 1876: 13.

[64] *Otago Witness*, 11 November 1876: 13. I could find very little coverage in any other of the major papers in either 1876 or 1881 on the question of the importation of these predators into New Zealand. Even the *Christchurch Press* (despite being published in Canterbury, an area affected by rabbits) apparently did not see the issue as sufficiently important to warrant their attention.

[65] It is of passing interest that this mooted solution to the problem of rabbits is at odds with the conclusion of the commissioners in their report. They believed that the problem of rabbits would be worse under such a scenario because the occupiers would have fewer resources for the battle than did the pastoral holders.

[66] M. Fairburn, 'The Rural Myth and the New Urban Frontier. An Approach to New Zealand Social History 1870–1940', *New Zealand Journal of History* 9(1) (1973): 3; T. Brooking, 'Use It or Lose It, Unravelling the Land Debate in Nineteenth Century New Zealand', *New Zealand Journal of History* 30(2) (1996): 141.

[67] J.E. Martin, *The House, New Zealand's House of Representatives 1854–2004*, (Palmerston North: Dunmore Publishing in association with the Clerk of the House and the History Group, Ministry for Culture and Heritage, 2004): 82.

[68] The first freezer-ship (S.S. Dunedin) left New Zealand for England in 1882. Of the entire cargo of frozen sheep carcasses, only one was rejected on landing.

[69] Rabbit Nuisance Committee, *Rabbit Nuisance Committee, Report of the*, (1881) AJHR, I-6.

[70] AJHR: 18.

[71] AJHR: App C, 9.

[72] AJHR: App C, 10.

[73] NZLC Journals and Appendices, 1881–2: 279.

[74] Interestingly, based on Jackson's data (*The New Zealand Legislative Chamber*, 234–5), the proportion (although not the number) of farmers in the Chamber fell between 1876 and 1881 – from 19 out of 35 to 19 out of 43. However, this shift did not have any negative effect on the level of support for the measure as sufficient of the recently appointed members had connections to pastoral farming (at least two) or political reasons for favouring the measure (at least two).

[75] NZPD (LC), 40, 1881: 514.

[76] Of passing interest are the words used by Hon. Richard Oliver when moving the second reading of this bill in the Legislative Council. The new Act, he explained 'would protect [ferrets] from being molested by strangers'. (NZPD (LC), 43. 1882: 598.

[77] By 31 July 1883 the Superintending Inspector was able to report on the setting up of breeding establishments at three locations (B.P. Bayly *The Rabbit Nuisance, Annual Report on,* (1883) AJHR, H-18: 1 and by July 1884 on the release of nearly 4,000 ferrets that 'in some places are said to be doing good work' (AJHR, H-2: 2).

[78] Rabbit Biocontrol Advisory Group, *A Hundred Years of Rabbit Impacts, and Future Control Options* (Wellington: Ministry of Agriculture and Fisheries, n.d.), first retrieved from http://www.maf.govt.nz/mafnet/publications/rabbit-biocontrol-advisory-group/rbag0010.htm#E10E60, 16 May 2006)

[79] A. J. P. Thomas, *Report on the Rabbit Nuisance,* (1888) AJHR, H-18: 2.

[80] H.B. Martin, 'Objections to the Introduction of Birds of Prey to Destroy the Rabbit', *Transactions and Proceedings of the New Zealand Institute* 17 (1884): 179, 182.

[81] A. Reischeck, 'Observations on the Habits of New Zealand Birds, their Usefulness or Destructiveness to the Country', *Transactions and Proceedings of the New Zealand Institute* 18 (1885): 96, 103.

[82] E. Melland, 'Notes on a Paper entitled "the Takahe in Western Otago" by Mr James Park F.G.S.', *Transactions and Proceedings of the New Zealand Institute* 22 (1889): 295, 299.

[83] King, *Immigrant Killers*: 85.

[84] Galbreath, 'Colonization, Science and Conservation: the Development of Colonial Attitudes toward the Native Life of New Zealand, with Particular Reference to the Career of the Colonial Scientist Walter Lawry Buller (1838–1906)': 134. Galbreath remarks that Buller really only referred to the matter again when involved in the campaign to establish off-shore reserves, and, given his enthusiastic involvement in the collection of (dead) specimens for Rothschild, questions his motive in doing so.

[85] W.L.A. Buller, 'Further Notes and Observations on Certain Species of New Zealand Birds (with Exhibits)', *Transactions and Proceedings of the New Zealand Institute* 24 (1891):75, 75.

[86] Proceedings of Otago Institute, 'Paper Read by J. Richardson on the Extinction of Native Birds on the West Coast' 11 August, *Transactions and Proceedings of the New Zealand Institute* 24 (1891): 713.

[87] W.L.A. Buller, 'Illustrations of Darwinism or the Avifauna of New Zealand Considered in Relation to the Fundamental Law of Descent with Modification', Read before the Wellington Philosophical Society, 27 June 1894, *Transactions and Proceedings of the New Zealand Institute*, 27 (1894): 75, 96.

[88] Perhaps more than coincidentally, around the time of increasing scientific scepticism as to the theoretical basis of displacement, see discussion infra, and around the time Buller got involved in pressing for the establishment of off-shore reserves (n86).

[89] W.L.A. Buller, 'Some Curiosities of Bird-life', *Transactions and Proceedings of the New Zealand Institute*, 27 (1894): 134, 137.

[90] W.L.A. Buller, 'Notes on New Zealand Ornithology, with an Exhibition of Specimens', *Transactions and Proceedings of the New Zealand Institute* 28 (1895): 326, 327.

[91] Buller, 'Notes on New Zealand Ornithology, with an Exhibition of Specimens', (1895): 329.

[92] W.L.A. Buller, 'On the Ornithology of New Zealand', *Transactions and Proceedings of the New Zealand Institute* 29 (1896): 179, 193 and 203.

[93] W.L.A. Buller, 'On the Ornithology of New Zealand', *Transactions and Proceedings of the New Zealand Institute* 31 (1898): 1, 26.

[94] Buller, 'On the Ornithology of New Zealand', (1898): 1, 4.

[95] Buller, 'On the Ornithology of New Zealand', (1898): 26.

[96] A. Newton, assisted by H. Gadow, *A Dictionary of Birds* (London: Adam and Charles Black, 1896): 224–5.

[97] W.T.L. Travers, 'Comment on W.L. Buller, Further Notes and Observations on Certain Species of New Zealand Birds' (Transactions 72), *Transactions and Proceedings of the New Zealand* 27 (1891): 699.

[98] P. White, 'The Effect of Deer on the New Zealand Bush; a Plea for the Protection of our Forest Reserves', *Transactions and Proceedings of the New Zealand Institute* 25 (1892): 435, 435.

[99] T. Kirk, 'The Displacement of Species in New Zealand, Presidential Address to Wellington Philosophical Society, 3rd July 1895', *Transactions and Proceedings of the New Zealand Institute* 28 (1895): 1, 7.

[100] H. Guthrie Smith *Tutira, the Story of a New Zealand Sheep Station*, 3rd edn. (Edinburgh and London, 1953): 354.

[101] A. Bathgate, 'Notes on Acclimatization', *Transactions and Proceedings of the New Zealand Institute* 30 (1894): 266, 270.

[102] T. White, 'On Rabbits, Weasels and Sparrows', *Transactions and Proceedings of the New Zealand Institute* 23 (1890): 201, 204.

[103] Indicatively, some years later and in a different context, Phillips was to write: 'I am utterly sick and tired of reading the lamentable effusions of a few extremists who wish to stop all progress for the sake of unattractive Native scenery or a few useless Native birds. I have been over sixty years in New Zealand and never found any practical advantage in either...' (From C. Phillips to the Editor, *Otago Daily Times*, 16 April 1925).

[104] Held on 28 June 1888.

[105] Written as an Annotation to the Minutes, 1890.

[106] Resolution 16.

[107] Written as an Annotation to the Minutes, 1908.

[108] King, *Immigrant Killers*: 85–6.

[109] Ibid.

[110] Morell, *Britain and New Zealand*: 28.

[111] J.E. Le Rossignol and W.D. Stewart, *State Socialism in New Zealand* (London: Harrap): 19, describe the 'legislation of the past twenty years' as socialistic 'in that it has been brought about by a political uprising of the middle and lower classes against the rich'. However, R.H. Hutchinson, *The 'Socialism' of New Zealand* (New York: New Review Publishing Association, 1916): 9 describes it as being 'in another sense... no revolution, for though the seat of power may have been shifted, the economic and political structure... remained the same. Dominance had merely been transferred from the shipping companies back to the farmers; but this time it was to the smaller farmers who had enlisted the city labourers in their cause.'

[112] According to B.B.M. Pickering, 'State Policy and Hydro Electricity in New Zealand' (M.A. Thesis University of New Zealand, 1949): 85–6 (citing J.B. Condliffe, *New Zealand in the Making* (London: G.Allen and Unwin, 1930). W.P. Morell *Britain and New Zealand* (London: Longmans, Green and Company, 1944): 31–2 explains it thus: 'closer settlement was achieved not so much by the taxation or repurchase of large estates as by a new extension of small farms', a development made feasible by the introduction of refrigeration in 1882.

[113] He was pleading for rangers to police areas of native bush against wanton destruction through fire. His motion included native birds but 'he acknowledged that very little could be done', (NZPD (HR), LXXIX, 1893: 262).

[114] NZPD (HR), 124, (1903): 71.

[115] NZPD: 71.

[116] NZPD (HR), 125 (1903): 693.

[117] NZPD (HR), 126, (1903): 71.

[118] NZPD: 71.

[119] NZPD: 72.

[120] NZPD: 71 per Walter C. Buchanan (Wairarapa).

[121] NZPD: 72, per James Bennett (Tuapeka).

[122] NZPD: 72.

[123] NZPD: 393–4.

[124] Although outside the scope of this paper, this story is interesting in itself.

[125] J. Drummond, *Our Feathered Immigrants; Evidence for and against Introduced Birds in New Zealand* (Wellington: Government Printer, 1907): 1.

[126] Approximately 100 years after Resolution Island was abandoned as an off-shore reserve on its invasion by stoats, the Department of Conservation is taking steps towards its re-establishment.

[127] The submissions received on a Department of Conservation report, 'What Can we do About Ferrets?' (Wellington: Department of Conservation, 1999) resulted in a change to the Biosecurity Act whereby the ferret – the only domesticated member of the family – became classified as an unwanted organism, unable to be bred or sold.

[128] Potts had floated the idea in 1872 (T.H. Potts, 'Help Save our Birds', *Nature* 2 May, (1872): 5–6), and in 1877 Buller had concluded that 'expiring races of animals and plants linger longest and find their last refuge on sea-girt islands of limited extent' (W.L.A. Buller, 'On the Ornithology of New Zealand', a paper read before the Wellington Philosophical Society, 22 September 1877, *Transactions and Proceedings of the New Zealand Institute* 10 (1877): 211). However, it was not until 1892 that any moves in that direction were made (with Governor Lord Onslow commissioning Buller in 1891 to compose his Memorandum that resulted in the establishment of such island sanctuaries as Little Barrier Island and Resolution Island).

[129] G. M. Thomson, 'Plant Acclimatization in New Zealand', *Transactions and Proceedings of the New Zealand Institute* 33 (1900): 313, 321.

[130] P. Star, 'Native Bird Protection, National Identity and the Rise of Preservation in New Zealand to 1914', *New Zealand Journal of History* 36(2) (2002): 123, 127.

[131] Rev. P. Walsh, 'On the Future of the New Zealand Bush', *Transactions and Proceedings of the New Zealand Institute* 31 (1896): 490, 493.

[132] T.H. Potts, 'On Recent Changes in the Fauna of New Zealand', a paper read before the Philosophical Institute of Canterbury, 12 December, reprinted in *Out in the Open: a Budget of Scraps of Natural History, gathered in New Zealand* (Christchurch: Lyttelton Times, 1882): 221, 223.

[133] This list included W.T.L. Travers, botanist and member of the Linnean Society; T. Kirk, appointed Chief Conservator of Forests in 1885; T.F. Cheeseman, appointed Secretary of the Auckland Institute and Curator of the Auckland Museum in 1874; and J. Buchanan, long-time contributor to the TNZI in the area of botany.

[134] H. Guthrie Smith, *Tutira: The Story of a New Zealand Sheep Station*, 4th ed. (Wellington: A.H. and A.W. Reed, 1969): 202–3.

[135] This has been identified by various authors – for example see P. Star and L. Lochhead, 'Children of the Burnt Bush, New Zealanders and the Indigenous Remnant, 1880–1930 Water' in *Environmental Histories of New Zealand*, ed. E. Pawson and T. Brooking (Melbourne: OUP, 2002): 119, 122 and 131–2, P. Gibbon, '"Going Native": a Case Study of Cultural Appropriation in a Settler Society, with Particular Reference to the Activities of Johannes Anderson in New Zealand during the First Half of the Twentieth Century' (Unpublished PhD Thesis, University of Waikato, 1992): 31 and Galbreath: 193.

[136] Otago Witness, 'Our Native Birds', *Otago Witness* 26 April (1894): 5.

[137] 'Disgusted', Letter to the Editor, *Otago Daily Times* 18 April (1900): 6.

[138] Sir J. Hector, Address to Meeting of the Wellington Acclimatization Society, as reported in *Otago Daily Times*, 19 May 1897: 2.

Motives for Introducing Species: Palestine's Carp as a Case Study

Dan Tamir

In loving memory of Christine Beatrice Müller, 1961–2008

INTRODUCTION

On 11 July 1934, a sixty-nine year old man of Scottish origin arrived at Jerusalem, the centre of British colonial administration in Palestine. 'Late Director of Fisheries with the Government of Madras, and Fishery Adviser to the governments of Sierra Leone, Mauritius, the Seychelles, Malta and Baroda', James Hornell was directed by His Majesty's High Commissioner for Palestine 'to carry out a survey of the fishery resources of the country, with a view to propose measures for their improvement'.[1]

Those improvements included modernising the marine fishing fleet, renovating harbour facilities, regulating fishing work, building curing and canning plants and, last but not least, building fish ponds and stocking them with newly introduced fish species. The introduction of one of those fish species, the common carp (*Cyprinus carpio*), was so successful that eleven years later Palestine became a carp exporter, as Palestinian fish hatcheries supplied fingerlings for the introduction of this species to Cyprus.[2] At that time, neither Hornell nor the other people who worked on implementing his recommendations suspected that some of the fish they were introducing carried a potential hazard to ecological systems; namely, that those species might become alien invasives.

Biological invasions create both direct and indirect problems for humans. Invasive species not only affect individual species, but can also change drastically entire ecosystems. Such biological invasions pose a serious threat to global biodiversity, second only to habitat destruction, in bringing species to their extinction.[3] Furthermore, invasive species cause damages whose costs are estimated in billions of $US.[4] As commonly understood, biological invasions are the result of humans introducing species into habitats where they are non-native. Such an introduction might take one of two basic forms, differing not in their possible outcomes but rather in their primary causes: the first form is an unintended, accidental delivery (such as rats boarding a ship, or ants burrowed inside raw wood logs), where humans are nothing more than blind – even if somewhat careless – bearers of the invasive species.[5] The second is a planned, deliberate introduction of a species, which then goes out of control, and spreads beyond the limits designated for it by its human introducers. Although most introduced species do not survive in their new habitat, some of them do, and become invasive.[6]

There is now a vast and deep body of research about the ecological and physiological aspects of biologic invasions caused by intended introduction.[7] Thorough comprehension of the problem of species invasions requires understanding the phenomenon not only on the causational level, but on the functional and intentional level as well.[8] Various works examined the human perception of introduced, 'alien' or 'exotic' species. Among other things, such works showed the ways new species intertwine in political and economic systems, or demonstrated how people tend to project human phenomena on other species and vice versa.[9]

Kennedy and Lucks have drawn the outlines of the modern global web of commerce and exchange, so complex and omnipresent that it created a system in which one should actually expect the unexpected. The shrinking of our world, they write, 'provides one lesson after another about the Law of Unforeseen Consequences'.[10] Until now, however, outside a selected set of agricultural pests, there has been relatively little research into the socio-cultural and economic causes of specific introductions per se.[11] Furthermore, while considerable research has been done on introduction to regions such as North America and Australia, introductions to areas such as the Middle East are relatively unexamined.[12]

While the modern accepted model for invasion – sometimes summarised as 'Right Plant [or Animal], Right Place, Right Time'[13] – seems to deal with the physical and biological conditions required for a species to succeed in its invasion, the question still remains as to the incentives for humans to bring it there in the first place. Evaluating those processes and finding possible motives for the introduction of species may help us identify, understand and – should the need arise – avoid and prevent such undesired introductions in the future.

Two common assumptions are that the incentives for deliberate species introductions are either economic or socio-cultural. Some scholars[14] emphasise introductions' varied socio-cultural components, namely traditional aesthetic preferences. Other researchers put more weight on the economic aspects of the invasion process,[15] seeing physical needs and expectations for material revenues as an explanatory factor for introductions. And indeed, both assumptions are simple and logical, far from surprising, and supported by clear evidence. This article, however, tries to explore such socio-cultural and economic motives and the interactions between them, while also suggesting a third motive for species' introductions – an ideological one – using the introduction of the common carp to Palestine as a case study.

There were two main reasons for focusing on this specific species and this exact place. First, some forecasts claim that the development of aquaculture is bound to replace fisheries just as animal husbandry replaced hunting on land thousands of years ago.[16] Even if these predictions are a bit exaggerated, it is already clear today that the environmental effects of aquaculture are considerable. The carp, specifically, is a global invasive: it inhabits not only hundreds of freshwater bodies worldwide, but also tops the IUCN's list of 100 worst invasive species.[17] Carp is also considered an invasive in Israel,[18] where invasive species are considered not only a threat to wild biodiversity, but as damaging crucial natural services such as keeping genetic banks of wild forms, pollination and food sources. As awareness of the problem increases, a recent Israeli governmental report recommended exterminating invasives and banning the import of new species.[19] The second reason for choosing carp as a case study is the historical sources. Unlike plants, migratory birds or terrestrial animals, freshwater fish do not often migrate between watersheds without conscious human assistance; they therefore make good case studies for human intervention.[20] Carp's introduction to Palestine is no exception, and detailed records are available from the archives of 'The Jewish Agency', the main driving force behind the introduction process.

The first part of this article, therefore, surveys the *cultural* background and the cultural elements which encouraged the importation of the carp to Palestine during the 1930s. The second part investigates the *economic* calculations and decision making regarding this introduction endeavour. The third part suggests a third, more theoretical motive, namely aspects of the 'Spirit of the Time': general *ideological* currents which promoted such introduction experiments. The article then concludes with an assessment of these three groups of explanatory factors, and an attempt to estimate their cumulative influence.

SOCIO-CULTURAL MOTIVES

Although his appointment as an advisor to the High Commissioner was due to his merit as an expert in zoology, one may assume that Hornell, who made a large part of his academic career as an anthropologist,[21] was also well acquainted with the cultural aspects of human life. Like languages and tools, the use of animals and relations with them are an inherent part of every human culture.[22] As groups of humans migrate from one place to another, they tend to carry their cultural habits and heritage; thus, human migrations were the driving force behind the introduction of species for millennia. When immigrants from overseas colonise a new homeland, the way of life that they establish usually incorporates habits they had practised in their land of origin – a 'cultural capital of knowledge, beliefs, subsistence methods and social organisation accumulated in their homeland', writes Jared Diamond.[23] Sheep in Iceland, cows in Minnesota, pigs on the most remote Polynesian islands – all were brought by human immigrants from their respective homelands. When successfully absorbed and propagated in the new place, such groupings of common plants and animals carried by immigrants – which Crosby calls 'portmanteau' biota – helped immigrants to create some version of their homeland where they too could prosper.[24]

The common carp was no exception to this pattern. Debate persists about the exact time and place in which humans first domesticated and began to raise it, but there is clear evidence of its being held by the ancient Romans.[25] Carp farming expanded during the middle ages, and from the thirteenth century there are records of wealthy men managing carp ponds in England.[26]

While the carp's nutritional value increased after generations of cultivation and breeding in Europe, its glamour dimmed a bit during the centuries to come: from the mid-seventeenth century the carp began to lose prestige in Western Europe, in favour of other species, especially the trout. In central and Eastern Europe, however, it remained greatly appreciated. This cultural pattern later reproduced itself in places where European immigrants settled overseas: in North America, for instance, although the common carp was farmed in places as far inland as Nebraska in the second half of the nineteenth century, its main markets were located in New York, Boston and Philadelphia, where east European immigrant population was centred.[27]

The same pattern could also be detected in Palestine. Later and smaller in numbers than the immigration wave from central and eastern Europe to North America, the stream of immigrants who left those regions and travelled to Palestine at the beginning of the twentieth century likewise carried with it some of its cultural and culinary habits. The introduction of the carp to Palestine was therefore also propelled by the cultural habits of those immigrants, which included some traditional dishes.[28]

As lovers of home-made food know, traditional dishes require traditional ingredients. And so, in 1926, Mordechaj Schwarz, a young student at the Miqve Jisrael agricultural school near Jaffa, asked his schoolmaster for permission to raise some fish at the irrigation pond of the school's citrus orchard. Gaining permission, Schwarz brought some carp from Vienna, where his family was in the fish marketing business. Schwarz held the fish in the irrigation pool for a while, but when he wanted to dig a new pool where the fish could also lay eggs and reproduce, the head of the regional health department, afraid that a new pool might increase the danger of malaria in the region, forbade him to do so. Those fish had no descendants, and were probably consumed by young Schwarz and his fellow students.[29]

About a year later, a committee of seven experts was called by Meir Dizengoff, director of the Urban Colonisation Department of the Palestine Zionist Executive. Dizengoff, best known as the charismatic and popular mayor of Tel Abib during its formative years (1911 to 1925), summoned the committee with the mission to find out about the possibilities of developing fisheries in Palestine.[30] To judge by his title and his former position, one may presume that Dizengoff's main concern was the supply of food for the growing urban population of his beloved city.[31] While their concerns were about local fish supply, the committee members' professional experience was gained in other places: Pevsner had been working for twelve years on the Aral sea, the Caspian sea and the Volga; Ratner and Kudrianski were fish merchants near the Volga, while Wolodarski made his business around the Caspian sea; Soloweiczick worked for twenty years in the area of the Visla in Poland; Wolkowski ran a fish farm near Kobna, in Lithuania; and Karatkov had already made a career as a fisherman in Ukraine. Although most of their attention in the first meeting was given to marine fisheries, and despite the wide agreement that there were still enough fish in the country, the concern was expressed that 'if the exploitation of fish from the Sea of Galilee will continue at its current rate for a few more years, we shall undoubtedly be witnessing the dreary vision of a sea void of fish'. A possible preventive measure was suggested by Soloweiczick: new kinds of fish should be brought to Palestine.[32]

At the committee's next meeting, about three weeks later, a sub-committee was appointed, with the task of suggesting practical means for bringing over new kinds of fish.[33] Diligent and devoted to their mission, the sub-committee members returned a month later, with a recommendation to introduce three new fish species. Unsurprisingly, the first species on the list was the common carp.[34]

Meanwhile, Dizengoff wrote to the directors of PICA (Palestine Jewish Colonization Association; a charity fund established by Edmond James de Rothschild with the aim of encouraging industrialisation and agricultural development in Palestine), asking for their help in finding an adequate place for 'raising fish, as is widely common in Russia and in other countries'.[35] A month later, he sent another letter to the Director of Lands at the Mandate's government in Jerusalem, in which he wrote that 'settling the matter of fisheries in our country might provide cheap food to all its residents; by doing that we shall be able also to reduce the price of meat and other necessities'. He then added that 'in the countries of Europe it's common to use natural lakes or to create artificial ones' for aquaculture, and expressed his department's interest in leasing governmental lands in the area of Tul-Karm for building fish ponds.[36]

Due to either technical or administrative problems, Dizengoff's initiative did not gain momentum. It was not until 1934 that Branco Sitzer, an immigrant from Croatia, established the first fish farm in Palestine, at Kurdani, near Acre. Although it was ultimately used primarily to store regular fish deliveries from Europe before their marketing to local retailers (who were mostly concentrated in Tel Abib and Haifa), Sitzer's fish farm produced and delivered significant commercial quantities of fish before going bankrupt about a decade later.[37]

The members of Dizengoff's committee, Schwarz and Siltzer all shared a Central and East European background; a clear East European influence is evident also in the aforementioned letters. Dizengoff was not the only one who connected East European immigrants and freshwater fish: at the beginning of the 1930s, at about the same time of Sitzer's arrival, the initiative for building new fish farms in Palestine shifted to the Department of Trade and Commerce within the Zionist executive. In 1933 Nahum Tischby, head of the department (himself an immigrant from Germany), asked the 'Jewish Agency' in Poland to find some fish experts and send them to Palestine. Next to the economic justifications, Tischby pointed out that 'the Jew likes fish by his nature, and especially the carp'.[38]

This explanation resonates from other sources as well. In a book published in 1939 surveying the development of fisheries in Israel to date, Naphtali Wydra wrote about the introduction of the carp that 'Jews are used to it, and they tend to prefer it to other kinds of fish'.[39] Such reflections on the direct connection between immigration from Eastern Europe and the introduction of the carp were common among those who brought it from Europe physically. Šmu'el Ṣarig, one of the founders of the fish farm in Tel Yamal, also believed that carp were brought because they were eaten in eastern Europe. The other founders of Tel Yamal came from Galicia, and he recalls that before the establishment of the fish farm there, carp were directly imported from Vienna to Tel Abib before the holiday seasons.[40]

The cultural preference for carp becomes even more evident if one remembers that Palestine never lacked fish. While the introduction of terrestrial mammals to Iceland or to some Pacific islands was due to their total absence before human colonisation, Palestine did have an abundant ichthyofauna: not only does the country have a coastline, but it also had many species of freshwater fish, mainly in the Sea of Galilee and the Hula lake, and even in the streams running

FIGURE 1. A map of Palestine

down to the Mediterranean.[41] It seems that one can summarise the motive for the introduction of the carp in one sentence: 'They just liked to eat *Gefülte Fisch*!'[42]

These aforementioned cultural reasons and motives, deriving from traditional habits and aesthetic preferences of immigrants, indubitably encouraged the introduction of the carp into Palestinian waters during the 1930s. But immigration and culinary heritage alone cannot explain such introductions, largely because of two additional reasons.

One of these reasons is that there were other widespread introductions, which took place without any migration context. At the same time that the carp was doing its first fin-strokes in Palestine, the rainbow trout was transported from the north-western United States to many other parts of the world (including Palestine), although human immigration from these regions was marginal to non-existent. Other non-immigration-related introductions abound: Chinese palms decorate gardens (and lately also invade forests) in southern Switzerland, grey squirrels jump between trees in Italy, and fluffy mink swim in British rivers. Closer to this article's geographic focus are the eucalyptus (*Eucalyptus globules*, *E. leucoxylon*), imported to Palestine from Australia long before Australian battalions took part in conquering it,[43] or the Common Mynah (*Acridotheres tristis*) brought from India to Tel Abib during the late 1980s, without any immigration wave from the subcontinent.[44] All these examples can prove that human immigration is not a *necessary condition* for species introduction.

Nor does every immigration wave bring its entire biotic entourage with it either. There were species that European immigrants to Palestine in the 1930s did not bring with them. Those aforementioned Australian soldiers brought neither kangaroos nor dingos nor Koala bears. Human immigration itself is not a *sufficient condition* for species introduction.

Why, then, were certain animals brought to Palestine by immigrants, while other species were left behind? And what made people in Palestine – as in many other places – introduce species of which they had no previous experience from faraway lands? Part of the answer lies in the economic realm.

ECONOMIC MOTIVES

We clearly cannot explain the interest of the Tel Abibian fishing committee in freshwater aquaculture solely by its members' east European background. More material factors influenced the carp's introduction to Palestine as well. These economic considerations can be divided into three complementary and mutually supportive categories. On the most immediate level it was the need to *supply food* to Palestine's growing population; on the macro-economic level it was the *economic independence* of the Palestinian mandate territory from neighbouring countries; and on the micro-economic level, it was the *direct profit* anticipated by fish farmers.

MOTIVES FOR INTRODUCING SPECIES

255

The concerns expressed by Dizengoff in the mid-1920s about possible *food shortages* did not disappear. Between 1926 and 1936 Palestinian farmers experienced a decade of poor harvests brought on by an unfortunate accumulation of droughts, animal diseases and plagues of locusts.[45] Except on the coast and in the vicinity of the Sea of Galilee, edible fish were rare. Hornell's verdict was clear, claiming that 'there is no dearth of good quality food fishes either in the sea off the Mediterranean coast, or in the Gulf of Aqaba in the south'.[46] More alarming than the poor fish harvest at sea was the fact that 'regarding lacustrine fisheries, there is definite evidence of most serious depletion'. No wonder, therefore, that the import of fresh fish from neighbouring countries was steadily mounting.[47] In a letter of July 1935 to the head of Haifa custom office, Tischby pointed out that 'Palestine depends very considerably upon most of its essential food stuffs upon foreign countries'.[48]

Food shortages were not a new threat for British colonialism. Confronted with the need to supply food to the growing population in their colonies and mandated territories, British officials resorted to the husbandry of freshwater fish. It had been regarded as an adequate remedy to the shortage in locally produced protein not only in Palestine, but in many other parts of the British Empire as well.[49] Attempts to introduce freshwater fisheries were a part of a policy whose declared aim was improving grim living conditions in the colonies. As this policy's major manifestation one may consider The Colonial Development Bill of 1929, which was supposed to provide direct aid to the colonies.[50]

The growing population of Palestine[51] demanded ever greater food supplies, and these were partially brought from other countries. The fish were no exception: while cured and canned fish were imported from countries as far away as Norway,[52] fresh fish were imported mainly from Egypt and Iraq, and some from Syria. Egyptian fish came mainly from the sea and from estuaries and were imported by train; Iraqi and Syrian fish originated from the freshwater fisheries of the Tigris and Euphrates, and maybe some other lakes as well, and were transported by trucks packed with ice.[53] Although their desert journey from their place of origin to the market in Tel Aviv lasted between two and a half to three and a half days,[54] Hornell found that fish from Iraq arrive 'in excellent condition, firm and red-gilled'.[55]

The quantities imported from those neighbouring countries were considerable: Hornell calculated that in the first six months of 1934, this import summed up in more than 690,600 kilograms, which meant an annual import of about 1,300 tons of fish – quite a lot for a maritime country with a population of a little more than 1 million people at that time. The bulk was imported from Egypt, while Iraq was the second exporter and Syria only the third.[56] Those countries, however, were not an integral part of the British mandate regime of Palestine, and had independent economies: Syria had been under French mandate rule since 1920, Iraq got its independence from British mandate in October 1932, and Egypt, although still deep in the British sphere of influence, had also its own customs, duties (and visa) system.[57]

The 'Jewish Agency', which was the main implementer of Hornell's advice, was clearly aware of the imbalance in trade between Palestine and its neighbours. According to governmental statistics quoted by one of the Agency's economic researchers,[58] in 1935, Palestine imported goods from Iraq to the value of £219,776, while Palestinian export to Iraq was only worth £7,070, what the researcher described as 'an extremely adverse trade balance between the countries'. The great difference in production costs made Palestinian farmers call for the institutionalising of a protective tariff, in order to help them compete with cheap Iraqi farm products.[59]

Trade relations with Egypt were not much different, and the 'Jewish Agency' was well aware of it. With a much larger population and lower per capita foreign investments, wages in Egypt were much lower than in Palestine; combined with the availability of freshwater along the Nile, this helped in reducing production costs to levels lower than those in Palestine.[60] The trade rate between Palestine and Egypt in the mid-1930s was 7.3 to 1 in favour of the Egyptians, and was partially due to a protectionist policy of the Egyptian government, which apparently hindered Palestinian industrialists and traders from entering it by delaying their entrance visas.[61]

Last but not least among the economic motives for the introduction of the carp was the expected profitability of fish breeding for farmers in Palestine of that time. This *profitability* was not self evident, especially considering the regional competition mentioned above.

Profitability considerations were taken into account from the very beginning of the attempts to introduce fish farming. The basic report submitted to the Fishing Committee of the Urban Colonization Dept., which was titled 'The Possibilities of Growing Pond Fish in Palestine',[62] contained – along with geographical, zoological and nutritional chapters – an estimate of the costs of such an enterprise. Those estimates were quite crude and very optimistic (as proved later by Branko Sitzer's financial difficulties), but nonetheless, financial aspects were seriously considered.

A few months after his first fish fry arrived from Zagreb, Sitzer could proudly report to Tischby that due to the relatively warm water temperatures in Kurdani, the fish were about to reach within one year the same weight they reach in Europe after three years. This was very good news, and Tischby easily calculated that with such outcomes and considering the needed input, the ponds were about to bring revenues of 'not less than 10 Palestinian £ per year per dunum'.[63] A week later, in another letter, Tischby already presented a general plan to introduce carp to Jesud ha-Mayala in the Hula valley, the Fešxa springs on the shore of the Dead Sea and to the Sea of Galilee.[64]

A few months later, in his report, Hornell was less excited but still showed cautious optimism in this aspect, as he wrote that 'no extensive pond-culture

MOTIVES FOR INTRODUCING SPECIES

seems now to be possible in Palestine, but there are many large ponds, irrigation reservoirs and small marshes in private hands which can be utilised to considerable profit, if stocked with carp fry in limited numbers'.[65] He concluded his observation about the future prospects of freshwater fish farming in writing that he

> ...found no streams in Palestine sufficiently cool to induce trout to breed; neither are these waters suitable for the gourami, for this is a fish that flourishes only if it lives in water of continuously high temperature; a fall to 15°C would render its culture economically a failure even if the fishes survived. Of all fishes, the various varieties of Carp as bred in Central Europe are the most suitable for pond culture in this country, and all effort should be concentrated upon these.[66]

Hornell showed no cultural preference or traditional tendencies; in his eyes the carp was simply the species most likely to acclimatise successfully. His sharp observations and rich experience were right: within less than seven years, fish farming became Palestine's most profitable branch of agriculture per unit of land,[67] and reached a production rate 5 to 6 times the production rate of carp in central European fish farms. The success of carp led to the introduction of more species: after the first attempts of British officers to develop their angling opportunities failed a few years before, Sklower reported that in May 1946 he received the first eggs of the Rainbow Trout from North America.[68] Moreover: the success of freshwater fish ponds was so great, that a few years later experiments began in breeding sea fish in saltwater ponds built in a similar way.[69]

However, easy as it might be to relate the introduction of the carp directly to economic motives, there is some evidence which shows that economic considerations were not always supportive of the introduction. For example, in February 1937, three years after releasing the first carp in the Kurdani ponds and about four years after the beginning of the work there, Branko Sitzer still had to apply for loans from the 'Jewish Agency' in order to keep his fish farm running. This is in spite of the fact that 'the fish acclimatized very well, spawned offsprings in April 1934, and already had 4 generations', as Sitzer proudly wrote. The expenses were huge: building the basic infrastructure cost him £6,300, and the expected wage costs for his workers amounted to more than £530 for 7 months (October 1937 to April 1938) – a serious sum in those days.[70]

A few months later, two fish experts – Jakob Katz and Gerhard David – were asked by the secretariat of Tel Yamal to examine and evaluate the status and future prospects of the fisheries there.[71] Beside a detailed examination of the water, the ground and the food given to the fish, they also included in their report two detailed appendixes calculating the expected costs both of building larger infrastructure and of maintaining and feeding the fish. Their detailed calculations served Dr. Wydra once again in the report he compiled and sent to one of the professionals at the 'Jewish Agency', checking the possibility of breeding fish in Tel Yamal.[72] Wydra's idea was not to build new ponds (an enterprise which would have cost large sums of money, as proven by Sitzer's farm), but – 'with a small investment in improvements and enhancements' – to block a part of an existing stream, the Saxne near Bejt Š'an. The estimated costs here for the first year – £430 – were far lower than those required in Kurdani, not only because of the fact that there was no need to build new ponds, but also because of two more reasons: the land was already leased to the 'Jewish Agency', and there were no wages for workers and guards, Tel Yamal being a commune village. A few years later, Tel Yamal became the largest fishery in Palestine, and began exporting fish to other fisheries, both at home and abroad.[73]

Sitzer was a pioneer, and as such he was probably more prone than his followers to all kinds of mishaps – biological, technical, bureaucratic and financial. But the uncertainty about the possible profitability of carp farming did not cease when other fish farms were constructed by better-organised entrepreneurs. In a letter sent to a group of people in Berlin who considered the possibility of immigrating to Palestine dated April 1938, Wydra clearly stated that 'although we think that with a right investment, proper terrain and a professional manager there is a nice way to make a living [from fisheries, DT], one still cannot say for sure how much profit one could make, and one cannot give any guarantees for it'.[75]

And indeed, there was little basis for predicting a profit in this field: lack of professional experience in breeding fish in Palestine's climate on the one hand together with competition from good quality fish from neighbouring countries did not guarantee economic sustainability of fish farms in Palestine.

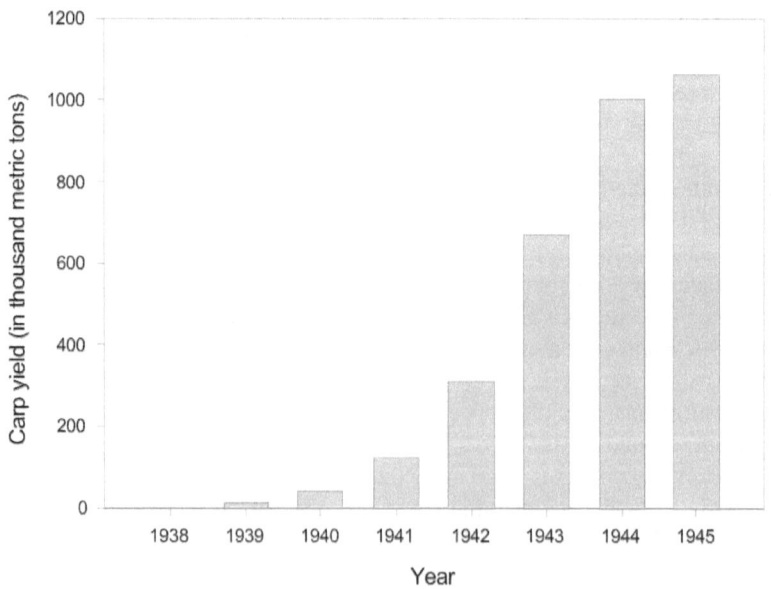

FIGURE 2. Carp production in Palestine, 1938–1945[74]

MOTIVES FOR INTRODUCING SPECIES

But there was yet another motive which contributed to the introduction of carp to Palestine. This third motive was based on the introducers' ideological milieu; to a certain degree, it reflected the spirit of the time.

IDEOLOGICAL MOTIVES

Estimating and analysing the possible intellectual factors which influenced past human actions is somewhat more complicated than estimating and analysing more material factors such as economic considerations or even cultural traditions. As cultural customs and traditions usually leave material traces behind them and economic considerations can usually be detected through financial accounting and inventory lists, these give us more direct evidence about people's actions than about the thoughts which motivated them in the first place.

There are two clues, however, that help us reveal ideological tendencies. The first is explicit statements. Such testimonials beginning with 'I think that…' – often self-biased and lacking self-reflection – might serve, under proper scholarly criticism, as evidence of one's thoughts and ideas. The second means is analysis and interpretation of implicit expressions. The accumulation of such explicit and implicit expressions, put into a historical context, might provide us with the basic notion of ideas, feelings and ways of thought which dominated the life of a certain generation.

Therefore, this final part of the article takes both implicit and explicit expressions from the documentation cited above and examines it in the light of the historical literature surveying the discussed era, to show how the carp's introducers' thinking was anchored in the common intellectual paradigms of that time. The intellectual climate in which the carp was introduced combined two components. The first component is the modern desire to *control the environment* and subject it to rational rules. This desire was characteristic of European colonial regimes in general.[76] The second component is the modernist desire to do things *'because they are there'*: regarding new experiments and enterprises as a basic feature of human behaviour.

Institutions and individuals can work separately on introductions, oppose each other, or collaborate in the pursuit of the shared aim, working as complementary agents.[77] It seems that in the case of carp's introduction to Palestine, the latter was the case.

Control over the Environment

Human attempts to gain control over natural powers and exploit natural resources are as old as humanity itself. Agriculture, by definition, is a human endeavour aimed at manipulating other organisms to extract more goods from them. As Zygmunt Bauman posed it, 'the legibility and transparency of space, declared in modern times to be the distinctive mark of rational order, were not, as such, modern inventions; after all, in all times and places they were indispensable conditions of human cohabitation'. But modernity did bring something new to this ancient human action. The modern novelty was 'the positing of transparency and legibility as a goal to be systematically pursued – a *task*; something which still needs to be enforced on recalcitrant reality, having first been carefully designed with the help of specialists' expertise'.[78]

Bauman uses this interpretation of modernity mostly to analyse modern ruling methods and global economic systems. His observations, however, may also be valid for modern aquaculture (and agriculture in general). The engineering of large water bodies – rectifying rivers, deepening lakes, drying swamps and fortifying banks – was a common phenomenon in European environmental thinking of the late nineteenth and early twentieth centuries. It was a project clearly identified with progress and modernity, and in most cases viewed positively: changes in the aquatic landscape were regarded as valuable 'improvements'.[79]

Defining what part of the environment needs to be 'improved' is clearly a subjective matter, as the definition of 'improvement' is always in the eye of the beholder. In this case, 'improving' meant bringing water bodies under control, to increase the productivity of a certain resident species. The main aim was to increase efficiency: the production of more fish, more food, and hence more protein per unit of water. This endeavour demanded the reduction of uncertainty while increasing transparency and legibility. This transparency was pursued literally: the recalcitrant reality of the turbid, uncontrolled lakes and rivers was to be replaced by systematically designed ponds. Specialists' expertise meant that fishery experts replaced fishermen. The carp met these requirements fully and combined very well in this scheme. Not only did its high reproduction rate and durability make it 'efficient', but its life cycle was also well known and familiar to those specialists.

This modern fashion of 'improving' water bodies did not skip the modernisation process in Palestine. Such 'small improvements' were needed to turn the free-running, shallow brook in Tel Yamal into an industrial carp cultivation plant in 1937.[80] In a similar vein, C. Craig Bennet, the chief officer of fisheries at the government's department of agriculture and fisheries, assumed the same year that 'there are no great difficulties in the way of improving the production' of fish in the Xula lake; this will only require 'more intensive fishing'.[81] The same intention of 'increasing and improving' the fishery in the lake (through the introduction of new carp species) is mentioned again in a letter written by Meerovitch the following year.[82]

Such 'state projects of legibility and simplification' were a must for many modern states in their quest for control. Disposing an unusual degree of power, colonial regimes have been active agents of such simplification and standardisation; this standardisation of new terrains – both metaphorically, referring to societies and social structures, and literally, with the conquest of new areas

MOTIVES FOR INTRODUCING SPECIES

261

– were an integral part of twentieth century colonial rule.[83] Due to the vast scope of rule of colonial superpowers, this state project made a considerable contribution to homogenisation: in this manner, the same methods and species for 'improving' lakes and rivers were used by the British government in India, Central Africa and Palestine.

This modernist approach was by no means the practice of the British government alone; it was also common among the leaders and managers of the Zionist organisations, who came mostly from central Europe, and to a large extent shared the same modernist ideas about re-shaping the landscape in an efficient, scientific way.[84] These motives, however, address only the institutional, state-organised side of the story. The other side of it was the opposite desire: not to dominate and control, but to break boundaries and stretch human achievements as far as possible.

'Because it's there'

The first documentation of an intention to introduce new species of fish to Palestine is from Jerusalem, in January 1923.[85] At the end of that winter, in March 1923, near the end of a lecture tour to North America, the mountaineer George Mallory was briefly interviewed by a *New York Times* reporter who wanted to know why Mallory wanted to climb Mount Everest. 'Because it's there,' said Mallory, in an answer that soon became myth.[86] Despite (and actually, maybe even *because of*) the fact that the most famous statement in mountaineering history was probably not more than a remark thrown towards an obstinate reporter, it might reflect some deeper way of thought of that time: the willingness to dare and challenge existing borders and limits.

This somehow deterministic pattern of doing things just because they are possible can also be traced to the introduction of the carp. In a letter sent to Fredrick Kisch in May 1934, Naxum Tischby refers to his 'plan to develop the cultivation of carp and other fish species', stating that he knows that

> ... your Excellency might see my plan as something imaginary, but I have the proof that very imaginary things about which I wrote 15 years ago have indeed come true.[87]

Imaginary or not, he declares with certainty that 'there are no technical difficulties in implementing this plan', and goes further to suggest adding geese and ducks, eucalypts, poplar trees, bananas, oranges, potatoes and 'hundreds of species of early vegetables and fruits'.[88] While being quite practical about carrying out the plans once they arrived to the implementation phase, Tischby's grand tendency was to try whatever was possible, and see what would evolve.[89]

As a matter of fact, it seems that professionalism was not always the leading line in the work of the Jewish Agency's Sea and Fisheries department. Lack of scientific order and organisation, false research methods, bad facilities, inefficient working systems and turbid work relations – all these are evident from a letter of July 1945, about 8 years after the beginning of the first introduction attempts.[90] To a certain extent, the Jewish Agency's agricultural and industrial development in Palestine at the time took the shape of random experimentation: to try what comes, with the hope it will succeed. Naturally, after a while only the successful survived.

At a first glance, the tendency to break boundaries and challenge existing patterns might be seen as standing in contrast to the modernist imperative to control and standardise environment and society. But these two components have also been complementary, providing another example of the duality inherent in modern human development, termed by Horkheimer and Adorno as the 'Janus face of Modernity'.[91] In an inherently dialectic fashion, the innovativeness of a certain stage becomes a limiting factor in the next; breaking these limitations requires further innovation and so it goes on. Many times, these 'stages' coexist and work simultaneously rather then independently of each other.

In the case of Israeli carp, more technical (and soon technocratic) innovative ideas resulted in a more constructed, controlled and constrained environment. In our case, the dual face of Janus were incarnated by two players: a group of British government officials wearing the mask of standardisation and efficiency, and a group of Zionist activists, wearing the mask of challenging and daring. While their drives might have been different and even opposite in a way, the re-shaping of the landscape was the joint outcome of their work.

CONCLUSION

As proven many times before in the histories of biological exchanges, successful domestication is likely to lead towards the introduction of the domesticated species far beyond their original environment. Considering the potential environmental threats that introduction entails, it is important to understand the human mechanisms underlying such introduction processes.

Tracing the introduction (and hence the possibility of invasion) of species into Palestine is usually not an easy task. Sitting on a crossroads between Asia, Africa and Europe and settled by humans for millennia, the environment of the whole Fertile Crescent has been subject to long and deep processes which altered it thoroughly. One of the cradles of human civilisation – agriculture, animal domestication and trade – it is hard to think of a place in the world more influenced and shaped by human activity than this area. However, the introduction history of some species is well documented, and the common carp is one of them.

Two common assumptions are that the motives for deliberate species introductions are either economic (physical needs and expectations for material revenues) or socio-cultural (namely, traditional customs, habits and preferences). In the case of the introduction of the common carp to Palestine in the 1930s,

MOTIVES FOR INTRODUCING SPECIES

both motives were intertwined and played a crucial role. The carp's introduction would not have been possible without them.

The dream of 'remaking the land' was the leitmotif of nineteenth-century European settlement.[92] There is no reason to believe it ceased to be such a leitmotif with the unfolding of the twentieth century, especially in regions which fell under European rule only then. The former provinces of the Ottoman Empire provide an example for such twentieth-century acquired regions.

The cultural motive for the carp's introduction was provided by the considerable number of immigrants from central Europe who were used to the carp and enjoyed eating it. The main local forces who pushed towards this introduction were local leaders and office holders who came to Palestine some years previously from central Europe. In this aspect, they were not different from central European immigrants in other parts of the world at the time, who also carried with them parts of Europe's 'portmanteau biota'.

The economic incentive for introduction was mostly due to the growing local demand for food, and an economic policy aimed at reducing the country's dependency on imports. It was equally propagated by the local British administration and private investors who saw a possibility for making their living out of fish cultivation.

The third motive accelerated the first two. The intellectual climate and ideological tendencies prevalent in that era were represented by modernisation-oriented elites, which were eager for innovation and novelties on the one hand, while seeking 'efficiency' and standardisation on the other. As the world's biggest colonial force at the time, the British administration took similar agricultural measures all around the globe: the main British professional advisor who initiated this introduction had previously been doing much the same thing in half a dozen other colonies. No wonder there was widespread biotic homogenisation in these areas. The introduction of species is a quintessential process of globalisation, and the story of the Common Carp is just one more example of it. Globalisation breaks down borders between places, while controlling and standardising them: 'Global law, local orders', as Bauman describes it.[93]

Introductions of exotic species into one's own environment are aimed at improving and ameliorating the human condition. Whether consciously or not, they are accompanied by a certain level of optimism and belief that these deeds are positive and beneficial.[94] With the increasing knowledge of the ways and mechanisms by which ecosystems function, scientists tend to become more pessimistic – or at least cautious – about introducing new species into them. Such a shift from optimism to pessimism might reflect a move from modernism to another ideology. Learning from past experiences, however, is still up to us.

NOTES

This article is based on a Master thesis written at the Institute of Environmental Sciences of the University of Zürich. I would like to thank Marc Hall and Bernhard Schmid from the University of Zürich, Tamar Dayan and Menachem Goren from Tel Aviv University, Dani Golani from the Hebrew University and Amnon Loja from Haifa University for their help and assistance.

[1] James Hornell, *Report on the Fisheries of Palestine* (Jerusalem, 21 Nov. 1934. Central Zionist Archives: S8/1978).

[2] William A. Dill, *Inland Fisheries of Europe* (FAO, Rome, 1990), p. 53.

[3] Daniel Simberloff, 'Biological Invasions: How are they affecting us, and what can we do about them?', *Western North American Naturalist* **61** (2001): 308–315.

[4] D. Pimental, L. Lach, R. Zuniga and D. Morrison, 'Environmental and Economic Costs of Nonindigenous Species in the United States', *BioScience* **50** (2000): 53–65.

[5] R.N. Mack, D. Simberloff, W.M. Lonsdale et al., 'Biotic Invasions: Causes, Epidemiology, Global Consequences, and Control', *Ecological Applications* **10** (2000): 689–710.

[6] Marc Hall, 'The Native, Naturalized and Exotic: Plants and Animals in Human History', *Landscape Research* **28** (2003): 5–9.

[7] For a general introduction to the subject and a basic list of books and articles for further reading, see Christopher Bright, 'Invasive Species: Pathogens of Globalization', *Foreign Policy* **116** (1999): 50–64. For a detailed model of invasions specifically by freshwater fish, see Peter B. Moyle and Theo Light, 'Biological Invasions of Fresh Water: Empirical Rules and Assembly Theory', *Biological Conservation* **78** (1996): 149–161.

[8] Timo Myllyntaus, 'Environment in Explaining History: Restoring Humans as Part of Nature', in: Timo Myllyntaus and Mikko Saikku (eds.), *Encountering the Past in Nature: Essays in Environmental History* (Athens: Ohio University Press, 2000), p. 157.

[9] See Philip J. Pauly, 'The Beauty and Menace of Japanese Cherry Trees: Conflicting Visions of American Ecological Independence', *Isis* **87** (1996): 51–73 and Pauly, 'Fighting the Hessian Fly: American and British Responses to Insect Invasion, 1776–1789', *Environmental History* **7** (2002): 485–505.

[10] Donald Kennedy and Marjorie Lucks, 'Rubber, Blight and Mosquitoes: Biogeography Meets the Global Economy', *Environmental History* **4** (1999): 369–383.

[11] Charles Perrings et al., 'Biological Invasion Risks and the Public Good: an Economic Perspective', *Conservation Ecology* **6** (2002): 1.

[12] For a comprehensive analysis of introduction mechanisms and the forces driving them in Australia and North America, see Thomas R. Dunlap, *Nature and the English Diaspora: Environment and History in the United States, Canada, Australia and New Zealand* (Cambridge: Cambridge University Press, 1999), chapter 2: 'Remaking Worlds: European Models in the New Lands' (pp. 46–70).

[13] Paul Robbins, 'Comparing Invasive Networks: Cultural and Political Biographies of Species Invasion', *The Geographical Review* **94** (2004): 139–156.

[14] Robbins, Ibid.

[15] Perrings, Ibid.

[16] C.M. Duarte, N. Marbá and M. Holmer, 'Rapid Domestication of Marine Species', *Science* **316** (20 April 2007): 382–383.

[17] See ISSG list of 'World's Worst Invasive Alien Species', available online at http://www.issg.org/database/species/search.asp?st=100ss&fr=1&sts. For a recent evaluation of the influence of common carp (together with other introduced species) on aquatic habitats around the Mediterranean, see I.D. Leonardos, I. Kagalou, M. Tsoumani and P.S. Economidis, 'Fish Fauna in a Protected Greek Lake: Biodiversity, Introduced Fish Species over a 80-year Period and their Impacts on the Ecosystem', *Ecology of Freshwater Fish* **17** (2008),: 165–173.

[18] Daniel Golani and Dan Mires, 'Introduction of Fishes to the Freshwater System in Israel', *Bamidgeh – The Israeli Journal of Aquaculture* **52** (2000): 47–60.

[19] Uriel Safriel (ed.), *Migvan Biologi v-Pitux Bar-Qajma': Sikummej Ybodat Cevet 'Migvan Biologi' b-Misgeret "Estrategja l-Pitux Bar-Qajma' b-Jiṣra'el'* [Biological Diversity and Sustainable Development: Proceedings of the Biological Diversity Team within the Frame of 'Strategy for a Sustainable Development in Israel'], (Jerusalem: Ministry of the Environment, 2002), pp. 26–28.

[20] Jerry Towle, 'Authored Ecosystems: Livingston Stone and the Transformation of California Fisheries', *Environmental History* **5** (2000): 54–74. Towle emphasises that not every introduction is destructive or even harmful. However, this does not influence the relevance of the act of human introduction.

[21] H.S. Harrison, 'James Hornell, 1865–1949', *Man* **49** (1949): 66–67.

[22] See, for instance: George Perkins Marsh, *Man and Nature* (New York: C. Scribner & Co., 1869); Richard Lee and Irven de Vore (eds.), *Man the Hunter* (Chicago: Aldine, 1968); Edward O. Wilson, *Biophilia* (Cambridge: Harvard University Press, 1986); Stephen R. Kellert and Edward O. Wilson (eds.), *The Biophilia Hypothesis* (Washington, DC: Island Press, 1993).

[23] Jared Diamond, *Collapse: How Societies Choose to Fail or Succeed* (New York: Penguin Books, 2005), p. 187.

[24] Alfred W. Crosby, *Ecological Imperialism: The Biological Expansion of Europe, 900–1900* (Cambridge: Cambridge University Press, 1986), p. 89. Crosby refers in his book specifically to European immigrants – as was the case in the introduction of the carp to Palestine. His observation, however, is relevant to all immigrations.

[25] Despite the common belief that the Romans brought carp to Europe from China, it is more likely that they were swimming around the Danube delta much earlier. See Eugene K. Balon, 'About the Oldest Domesticates among Fishes', *Journal of Fish Biology* **65** (2004): 1–27.

[26] Christopher K. Currie, 'The Early History of the Carp and its Economic Significance in England', *Agricultural Historical Review* **39** (1991): 97–107.

[27] Darin Kinsey, '"Seeding the Water as the Earth": The Epicenter and Peripheries of a Western Aquacultural Revolution', *Environmental History* **11** (2006): 527–566.

[28] Anat Helman, 'European Jews in the Levant Heat: Climate and Culture in 1920's and 1930's Tel Aviv', *Journal of Israeli History* **22** (2003): 71–90.

[29] Amnon Loja, 'Branqo Zicer ve-mifyalej ha-daggim be-Kurdani, 1934–1947' [Branco Sitzer and Pisciculture in Kurdani, 1934–1947], *Qatedra* **111** (April 2004): 76–94.

[30] Dizengoff was the first chief of Tel Abib, since 1911. In 1922, when the little town was declared a city, he became its first mayor. He resigned in 1925 in order to become director of the said colonisation department, a position he held for three years. In 1928 he returned to be the mayor of Tel Abib. He was the Mayor for eight more years, until his death in 1936.

[31] At the census of October 1922 the total population of Palestine was 763,600; in the census of November 1931 it was already 1,033,300: a growth of 35% within 9 years. See Arnon Golan, 'Jewish Nationalism, European Colonialism and Modernity: The Origins of the Israeli Public Housing System', *Housing Studies* **13** (1998): 487–505. The actual numbers might have been even higher, as many immigrants – especially from neighbouring countries – were not registered and lacked proper if any documentation. The growth of population in the city of Tel Abib was even more rapid: there were 3,600 residents in Tel Abib in 1921; their number reached 42,000 by 1930. At least a very large part of the newcomers were immigrants from Central and Eastern Europe. See Anat Helman, 'Taking the Bus in 1920s and 1930s Tel Aviv', *Middle Eastern Studies* **42** (2006): 625–640. With some fluctuations, this growth tendency continued during the 1930s and 1940s.

[32] All details about the members of the committee and about their discussions are taken from the protocol of the first meeting of the Fishing Committee, held on 29 Dec. 1926 (CZA, S8/1329/4). A seventh member of the committee, Mr. Jaffe, was originally from Palestine.

[33] Protocol of the second meeting of the Fishing Committee, 17 Jan. 1927 (CZA, S8/1329/4)

[34] Protocol of the third meeting of the Fishing Committee, 17. Feb. 1927 (CZA, S8/1329/4). The other fish species suggested were *Osphronemus olfax* (also known as *Osphronemus gorami*) and pikes (*Esocidae* spp.). Soloweiczick had the idea of bringing all these fish from Egypt. All these fish species are alien to Egypt as well: the *Esocidae* originate from northern Europe and north America, while the *Osphronemus olfax* comes from SE Asia.

[35] A letter from Dizengoff to the directory board of PICA, 9 Jan. 1927 (CZA, J15). It is interesting to notice that next to the Hebrew words 'giddul daggim', which literally mean 'raising of fish', Dizengoff added in his handwriting the German term, *Fischzucht*. Since there were no fish farms in Israel at the time, he apparently had to coin the Hebrew term himself, and wanted to make sure it was well understood by the readers of his letter.

[36] A letter from Dizengoff to the Director of Lands, 1 Feb. 1927 (CZA, S8/1329/1). Dizengoff also pointed at the economic interest in his request, adding that building such ponds will need a lot of work, and thus allow many people to earn their living from it.

[37] Loja, 'Branqo Zicer'.

[38] Letter from Tischby to the polish office of the 'Jewish Agency', 22 Jan. 1933 (CZA S8/1329/1), cited by Loja, ibid. The term 'Jew' in the Zionist jargon of those days designated mostly people from Central or Eastern Europe.

[39] Naphtali Wydra, *Ha-Dajig be-'Erec Jiṣrael* [Fishery in the Land of Israel] (Tel Aviv: The Israeli Marine Sector, 1939), p. 38. Wydra was the head of the Marine Department of the 'Jewish Agency' during the 1930s and 1940s, and was in charge of the technical and professional aspects of developing freshwater fisheries as well.

[40] Interview with Šmu'el Şarig, Nir David, 28 Sep. 2006. Founders of Nir David (in its old name 'Tel Yamal') began breeding carp in 1938. The fish from Vienna referred to are probably those imported by Sitzer.

[41] Menachem Goren and Reuven Ortal. 'Biogeography, Diversity and Conservation of the Inland Water Fish Communities in Israel', *Biological Conservation* **89** (1999): 1–9.

[42] 'Gefülte Fisch' (German for 'Stuffed Fish') is a traditional Central- and Eastern-European delicacy, consisting of a combination of whole freshwater fish, together with ground fishmeat, spices and vegetables. While Christian families usually eat it at Christmas, Jewish families usually eat it at Jewish Easter (Passover) and New Year (in September–October).

[43] The first attempts to introduce Eucalyptus took place in the 1860s and 1880s, and successful afforestation of Eucalypts between the years 1895–1899. See Gideon Biger and Nili Liphschitz, 'Australian Trees in the Land of Israel, 1865–1950', *Journal of Israeli History* **16** (1995): 235–244.

[44] See C. Holzapfel et al., 'Colonisation of the Middle East by the Invasive Common Myna *Acridotheres tristis* L. with Special Reference to Israel', *Sandgrouse* **28** (2006): 44–51. The mynah, an intelligent and friendly bird, was brought as a pet.

[45] Roza I. M. El-Eini, 'The Implementation of British Agricultural Policy in Palestine in the 1930s', *Middle Eastern Studies* **32** (1996): 211–250. In the political context, El-Eini makes a link between the stress put upon the farmers and the public unrest and ethnic clashes in August 1929.

[46] Hornell, *Report on the Fisheries*, p. 3.

[47] Ibid., pp. 5, 94.

[48] Letter from Tischby to Kingsley William Stead, head of the customs department in Haifa harbour, 23 Jul. 1935 (CZA 1329/1). The aim of the letter was to assure a custom-exemption for a new delivery of Yugoslavian breeding fish ordered by Sitzer. Tischby argued that the Mandate's Custom Ordinance guaranteed exemption from duties for 'animals of all classes', fish included.

[49] Bernard H. Bourdillon, 'Colonial Development and Welfare', *International Affairs* **20** (1944): 369–380. In this short and critical account of the Empire's colonial policy in the 1930s, Bourdillon, who was then the Governor of Nigeria, sharply criticises the British colonial policy; some of his sharp observations can be read today as prophecies about the current failures of 'development' policies in the third world.

[50] There are reasonable doubts, however, regarding the Bill's efficacy. See David Meredith, 'The British Government and Colonial Economic Policy, 1919–1939', *Economic History Review* **28** (1975): 484–499.

[51] See note 21 above.

[52] Giddul ha-Daggim b-Brejkot [The Husbandry of Fish in Ponds], *Ha-'Arec*, 1 Jul. 1947.

[53] Hornell, *Report on the Fisheries*, p. 96.

[54] B-Šuq ha-Daggim šel Tel Abib [In the Fish Market of Tel Abib], *Ha-'Arec*, 22 Jul. 1936, p. 3. The original weights are 2000–2200 Rotl; one Rotl is approx. 2.56 Kgs.

[55] Hornell, *Report on the Fisheries*.

[56] Ibid., p. 95.

[57] For a detailed account of the British Mandate Government's protection ploicy, see R.I.M. El-Eini, 'Trade Agreements and the Continuation of Tariff Protection Policy in Mandate Palestine in the 1930s', *Middle Eastern Studies* **34** (1998): 164–191.

[58] Memorandum on the Palestine-Iraq Trade written by D. Horowitz to the Economic Research Institute of the 'Jewish Agency', February 1937 (CZA S54/201).

[59] Ibid. The memorandum refers specifically to farmers raising poultry and eggs, but we may assume that the situation was similar in other agricultural branches as well.

[60] Letter from Tischby to Rotenstreich, titled 'My Voyage to Egypt', 27 Mar. 1936 (S54/207).

[61] Letter from Tischby to Schartok, 2 Dec. 1937 (CZA S54/207).

[62] Report from the archive of the Urban Colonization Department, no exact date. (CZA S8/2153)

[63] Letter from Tischby to F. H. Kisch, Jerusalem, 8 May 1934 (CZA S8/1329/1)

[64] Letter from Tischby to F. H. Kisch, Jerusalem, 16 May 1934 (CZA S8/1329/1). The letter was probably written after Kisch, another Zionist official at the time, showed willingness to give Sitzer's farm some financial aid.

[65] Hornell, *Report on the Fisheries*, p. 8.

[66] Ibid., p. 9. Gourami (*Osphronemus gorami*) was one of the species suggested by Soloweiczick back in 1927 (see note 24 above). Rainbow trout (*Oncorhynchus mykiss*, another member of the ISSG's 100-list) were actually introduced to some streams in upper Galilee in the mid-1930s and again in 1946; they established an invasive population. See Golani and Mires, 'Introduction of Fishes'.

[67] 'Hitqadmut ha-Dajjig ha-Jehuddi' [Advance of the Jewish Fishery], *Ha-'Arec*, 5 Feb. 1941 (Copy in CZA/1329/2).

[68] Dr. Alfred Sklower, 'Fischzucht in Palästina in den Jahren 1938 bis 1946' [Fish Farming in Palestine in the Years 1938 to 1946] (CZA S74/103). In another paragraph in his report, Sklower, who was the director of the JA's Fisheries Research Station in Şde Naxum (near Tel Yamal), wrote that the annual production was as much as 10 times higher. Some of the descendants of these rainbow trout also became invasive (Golani and Mires, 'Introduction of Fishes'), while others are regularly grilled and fried in Israel to this very day.

[69] 'Brejkot l-Giddul Dag Jam' [Ponds for Breeding Sea Fish], *Ha-'Arec*, 23 Aug. 1944. (Copy in CZA/1329/2).

[70] A letter from Sitzer to the Jewish Agency (Probably to Wydra), 10 Feb. 1937 (CZA S4/214).

[71] Jakob Katz and Gerhard David, 'Fischerei in Tel Yamal' [Fishery in Tel Yamal], Haifa, 7 Nov. 1937 (CZA S9/1564). Their visit to the fisheries took place one week before.

[72] Letter from Wydra to B. K. Meerovitch, 18 Nov. 1937 (CZA S9/1564/3).

[73] See note 1.

[74] Source: Sklower, 'Fischzucht in Palästina', footnote 62. The yield in 1938 was only 800 kg; the data of 1945 refers only to the first 11 months of the season.

[75] Letter from Wydra to the 'Xaluc Association' in Berlin, 18 Apr. 1938 (CZA S54/Y).

[76] Not only the British, but also the French colonial rule became centres of organised acclimatisation. For more about the similarities and differences between those two sys-

tems see Michael A. Osborne, 'Acclimatizing the World: A History of the Paradigmatic Colonial Science', *Osiris* **15** (2000): 135–151.

[77] Towle, 'Authored Ecosystems'.

[78] Zygmunt Bauman, *Globalization: The Human Consequences* (Cambridge: Polity Press, 1998), p. 33.

[79] Marc Cioc, *The Rhine: an Eco-Biography, 1815–2000* (Seattle: University of Washington Press, 2002), p. 12 onwards.

[80] Letter from Wydra to B.K. Merowitch, 18 Nov. 1937 (CZA, S9/1564/3).

[81] Letter from Craig Bennet to Meerovitch, [exact date unclear, second half of 1937] (CZA, S25/7430).

[82] Letter from Meerovitch to The 'Hakšarat ha-Ješub' Company, 9 May 1938 (CZA, S25/7430)

[83] James C. Scott, *Seeing Like a State: How Certain Schemes to Improve the Human Condition Have Failed* (New Haven: Yale University Press, 1998), pp. 9, 97. Scott uses the term 'High Modernism' to describe this 'improvisation' approach.

[84] See Gideon Biger, 'Ideology and Landscape of British Palestine, 1918–1929', in Alan Baker and Gideon Biger (eds.), *Ideology and Landscape in Historical Perspective* (Cambridge: Cambridge University Press, 1992).

[85] Letter from Prober to Tischby, Jerusalem, 6 Jan. 1923 (CZA, S8/1326), quoted by Loja, 'Branqo Zicer'. The idea was to introduce fish to ponds and reservoirs around Jerusalem; the initiative remained on the paper only. Although the large waves of immigration were still yet to come, this incentive was probably rooted in the memory of partial food shortages which characterised the last years of WWI in Palestine.

[86] Like every good myth, this story about Mallory's phrase has no concrete and documented source. A relatively detailed version of the story is quoted by Mark Jenkins, *In the Good Company of the Dead,* http://www.thehardway.com/stories/mallory.htm. Mallory, alas, died in his attempt.

[87] Letter from Tischby to Kisch, Jerusalem, 16 May 1934 (CZA, S8/1329/1)

[88] For a detailed review of government lead agricultural improvements in Palestine at the time see El-Eini, 'The Implementation of British Agricultural Policy'.

[89] This 'scattergun experimentation' approach was not an innovation here. Livingston Stone, the living spirit behind the introduction of many freshwater species to California who actually became the 'author' of many Californian ecosystems, did the same (see Towle, 'Authored Ecosystems'). What might have been new here was only the extent and the width of the varieties tried and considered.

[90] Letter from Sklower to Wydra, 07 Jul. 1945 (CZA, S74/7). The list of failures begins with stating that 'since one and a half years the Agency was not able to find me a desk and a chair'. According to Sklower, conditions were so miserable that he had to do his work at home.

[91] Max Horkheimer and Theodor Adorno, *Dialektik der Aufklärung* (Frankfurt am Main: Fischer, 1990).

[92] Dunlap, *Nature and the English Diaspora*, p. 46.

[93] Bauman, *Globalization*, p. 103.

[94] Towle, 'Authored Ecosystems'.

Index

— A —

Acacia 'Wattle' 73, 144, 147, 148, 151, 153, 154, 157–8, 159
Adaptation. *See* Naturalisation
Alder 146
Animals, introduced
 –as exotics 2–4, 12
 –how to deal with 7, 17–18, 20, 22, 221–39
 –legislation regarding 221–39
Aquaculture 248–63
Armadillo, nine-banded (*Dasypus novemcinctus*) 1, 4, 5
Asian long-horned beetle (*Anoplophora glabripennis*) 40
Ash (*Fraxinus* spp.) 146
Aspen (*Populus tremuloides*) 6
Australia 7, 8, 49, 68, 70, 71, 72, 73, 80, 87, 88, 104, 106, 109, 124–143, 147, 150, 157, 158, 198, 249, 254

— B —

Banks, Joseph 75, 76
Basutoland (Lesotho) 147, 152, 153, 154, 156
Bengal, East 197–215
Biodiversity 2, 17, 18, 19, 21, 22, 28, 31, 57–62, 83, 97, 105, 114, 185, 248, 250
Biota 30, 31, 33, 37, 60, 62, 73, 741, 131, 133, 134
 –'Portmanteau' 250, 263

Bison (*Bison bison*) 42
Britain 73
 –invasive species in 171–196
 –weeds in 97
 –trade 154, 158
Brown, John Croumbie 149, 150, 153, 155, 158
Brown tree snake (*Boiga irregularis*) 7, 12, 21, 48, 50
Buckland, Frank 225–6, 229
Buller, Walter 106, 225, 228, 233–4, 237

— C —

California 6, 8, 20, 49, 71, 76, 87, 88
Carp (*Cyprinus carpio*) 248–63
Cape Colony 144–61
Cattle egret (*Bubulcus ibis*) 42–3
Cluster concept 10–16
Cockayne, Leonard 94, 108, 110, 113, 114
Colonialism 30, 68, 70, 75–7, 81, 83–4, 97, 95, 104, 108, 129, 144, 149, 152, 197, 259, 260–1, 263
 –British 76–77, 84, 129, 144, 147–9, 151–2, 156, 158, 197–8, 214, 221–47, 248, 255
 –Dutch 75, 76, 144–61
 –French 77, 78, 81, 146–7, 209, 255
Community (of species) 4, 12, 15–16, 21, 31, 35, 40, 41, 48, 50, 51, 56, 74, 134, 136–7

Community membership criterion 8–10, 13–14, 15–16
Continental drift 133–5, 140,
Conflicting views of introduced species 17–18, 235
Cook, James 107, 222
Costs and benefits of introduced species and their control 8, 20–1, 48–9, 50, 104, 172, 181, 203–6, 232, 235–6, 248
Crops
  –as introduced species 49, 51, 68, 72–3, 75, 76, 78, 79, 80–87, 223
  –as opposed to weeds 88, 101, 104
  –cash 84–7
  –problems due to invaders 48, 199–203
  –trees as 145, 150, 152, 153, 161
Crosby, Alfred 68–72, 74, 76, 78, 79, 82, 83, 87, 197, 250

— D —

Darwin, Charles 70, 106, 107, 110, 125, 139, 173, 223–224
Desiccation, discourse of 145, 150, 159, 160
Displacement theory 76, 106, 108, 223–4, 234, 237, 238
Domin, Karel 129–30, 133

— E —

East India Company, Dutch 75, 144–7, 160
Ecological assemblage 9, 10, 34, 38–62
Ell, Gordon 105, 113–114
Empire/imperialism 68–72, 74–9, 88, 144, 197–8, 255, 263

Eucalyptus 8, 20, 49, 72, 76, 131, 135, 145, 147, 151, 153–4, 155–7, 159, 254
Exotic species, defining 4–16, 38–42

— F —

Fish 16, 44–7, 201, 214, 248–63
Forestry 76–7, 86, 144–170, 185, 224
  –scientific 145, 153
Florida 1, 5, 50
Fruit trees 78, 144, 145–8, 150–5, 261

— G —

Galapagos finches 4–5, 8–9, 13, 16, 42–3
Game shooting,
  –vegetation cover for 181, 239
  –introduced 222, 226, 230, 239
  –effects of introduced species on 226, 236
Gardens
  –botanical 69, 73, 75–77, 78, 103, 124, 145, 147, 149–52, 151–8, 160, 198
  –escapes from 171–88, 254
  –private 28, 32–3, 48, 57, 59, 73, 78, 80, 101–3, 107, 114, 147, 171–88, 254
Glacken, Clarence 95
Globalisation 31, 59, 60–62, 263
Gondwanaland 105, 135–7
Grafting stock 176, 179, 182
Grassland 42, 109, 111, 144, 145–50, 160, 235
Great Lakes 16, 47
Guam 7, 12, 48

Index

— H —

Hawaii 7, 17, 42, 52, 72
  –feral pigs in 17, 18, 19, 22, 37–8, 54–6
Herbert, Desmond 130–3, 135, 138–139
Hooker, Joseph 75, 106, 107, 110, 124–7, 129–33, 177
Hooker, William 75
Hornell, James 248, 250, 255–7
Horse, Mustang (*Equus caballus*) 10, 40, 54, 56
Human
  –activities in prehistoric times 55, 97–8, 262
  –beings as alien species 13–14, 39, 132–4
  –influence in introductions, 'washing away' of 38, 51, 54–5, 62
  –restoration/reintroduction of species 28, 43–4, 56–7
Hybridisation 73, 173, 176, 187
Hydrological change, caused by trees 159–61

— I —

Improvement, ideology of 76, 100–01, 103–5, 112, 114, 159, 248, 260–1, 263
Informality, of plant transfers 69, 78–9, 88, 145

— J —

Jekyll, Gertrude 176
'Jewish Agency' 250, 252, 256–8, 261–2

— K —

Kew Gardens 75–77, 96, 124, 157, 175
Knapweeds (*Centuria* spp.) 21–2
Kudzu (*Pueraria lobata*) 38, 49, 54, 56, 57, 61

— L —

Lesotho 144, 147, 151, 155, 161
Livestock 68, 78–9, 86, 110, 223, 224, 226, 230, 250
  –pastoralism 80, 86, 224, 227–37
  –and plant transfers 80

— M —

Madagascar 70, 71, 78, 80–82, 85–87
Maize 68, 72, 73, 75, 78, 79, 83, 84, 86, 87, 206
Maori 106, 107, 222
Marsh, George Perkins 103–4, 106
Missionaries 107, 146–8, 154, 160–1
'Mixoecology' 34–5
Modernity 260–1, 262
Monarch butterfly (*Danaus plexippus*) 8, 49
Mustelids 221–47

— N —

Natal 144–5, 148, 150–2, 154–61
Native Americans 30, 83
Nativism 28–36, 37–67
Naturalisation 3, 13–15, 37–65, 70, 107, 136–7, 171, 183–7, 238–9
Nazism 32–3, 57
New Guinea 124, 129, 131, 133
Newton, Alfred 225–6, 228

New Zealand 68, 80, 94-115, 124, 126, 185, 221–247
'Noxiousness'. *See* 'Perniciousness'

— O —

Oak 8, 146, 147, 185, 222

— P —

Palestine 248–63
Pastoralism 80, 86, 224, 227–37
'Perniciousness'/'noxiousness' 28, 70, 96, 97, 104, 107, 109–11, 140, 227, 230
Pine 72, 76, 109, 111, 145, 146–7, 154
Prickly Pear (*Opuntia* spp.) 69–70 72, 78, 80–2, 84, 86–8
Propagule pressure 171

— Q —

Queensland 129, 130–2
 –northern rainforests 126–7, 129, 136, 138–140

— R —

Rabbit 181, 184, 208, 221–47
Rackham, Oliver 97–8
Restoration/reintroduction of species 28, 43–4, 56–7
Rhododendron ponticum 73, 171–88
 –control of 185–7

— S —

Salisbury, Sir Edward 96–8
Skertchly, Sydney Barber Josiah 127–30, 133

Smith, Herbert Guthrie 106, 234, 238
South Africa 29, 33, 34, 68, 70–74, 77, 80–1, 84, 86, 87, 133, 144–70
Spruce, Norway 146

— T —

Tamarisk, 'saltcedar' (*Tamarix chinensis* and *Tamarix ramossisima*) 3, 4, 12, 14, 39
Thomson, G.M. 107, 108, 113
Trout 239, 251, 257
 –in Yellowstone 46
 –in New Zealand 224
 –in Palestine 254, 257
 –westslope cutthroat (*Oncorhynchus clarki lewisi*) 45

— U —

United States National Park Service 2, 19, 37, 38, 40, 43–4, 45, 47

— V —

Van Riebeeck, Jan 145–7
Von Humboldt, Alexander 126

— W —

Wallace, Alfred Russell 106–7, 125, 131, 139
Water hyacinth 197–215
'Washout' of human influence in introductions 38, 51, 54–5, 62
Water pollution 50, 201
Webb, Len 134–40
Weeds 37, 48, 61, 70, 71, 79, 94–115, 197–215

–problems of defining 68, 48, 80–3, 95–8, 186–7
–in literature and ideas 99–103
–in medicine 101
–management and legislation 21–2, 105–110, 111–12, 197–215

Wolf, Grey (*Canis lupis*) 2, 5
–in Yellowstone 43, 44, 56–7

— X —

Xenophobia towards introduced species 33–5, 57–8, 61–2

— Y —

Yellowstone Park 30, 42, 46–7, 59–60, 61
–bison in 42
–wolves in 43, 44, 56–7
–mountain goats in 37, 55
–elk and moose in 43
–lake trout (*Salvelinus namaycush*) in 46

— Z —

Zebra mussel (*Dreissena polymorpha*) 47–8, 50

www.ingramcontent.com/pod-product-compliance
Lightning Source LLC
Chambersburg PA
CBHW021137230426
43667CB00005B/156